For Abby,
    The only thing better than your
past is your future !
    Our warmest good wishes go with
you as you walk into that future !
                    Much love,
                    Cousin Sylvia Lubliner

The 29th of May, 1999
The 14th of Sivan 5759

GREAT
MOMENTS
in
JEWISH
HISTORY

GREAT MOMENTS
in
JEWISH HISTORY

Elinor Slater & Robert Slater

JONATHAN DAVID PUBLISHERS, INC.
Middle Village, New York 11379

GREAT MOMENTS IN JEWISH HISTORY

Copyright © 1998
by
Elinor Slater & Robert Slater

No part of this book may be reproduced
in any form without the prior written consent
of the publisher. Address all inquiries to:

Jonathan David Publishers, Inc.
68-22 Eliot Avenue
Middle Village, New York 11379
www.JonathanDavidOnline.com

2 4 6 8 10 9 7 5 3 1

Library of Congress Cataloging in Publication Data
Slater, Elinor, and Slater, Robert
    Great moments in jewish history/ by Elinor Slater & Robert Slater.
        p. cm.
    Includes index.
    ISBN 0-8246-0408-3
    1. Jews—History—Micellanea.   I. Slater, Robert,   II. Title.
DS118.S53   1998
909' .04924—dc21   98-7528
                                                              CIP

Book design by John Reinhardt Book Design

Printed in the United States of America

IN MEMORY OF OUR GRANDPARENTS

Flora and Harry Nachman
Ethel and Louis Resnik
Jack and Minnie Slater
Sam Israel
Molly and Isadore ("J.L.") Levy

Acknowledgments

The authors wish to thank the following people and institutions for their help with this book: Kevin Proffitt, of the Jacob Rader Marcus Center of the American Jewish Archives, Cincinnati, Ohio; Reuven Milon, Dina Mendelson of the Bet Ya'acov Institute archives at Rabbi Levine Square, Jerusalem; the State of Israel Government Press Office Photography Department, Jerusalem; the Yad Vashem photo archives, Jerusalem; Amalia Keshet and Tania Zhilinsky of the Visual Resources Department of the Israel Museum Photo Archives, Jerusalem; Reuven Kopler of the Central Zionist Archives, Jerusalem; David Harris; Mordechai Liebling; Jack Cohen, Jerusalem; Harriet F. Polonsky, Brandeis University, Office of Public Affairs; and Robert Kaplan.

Special thanks to Professor Lee Levine of the Hebrew University for taking time to read portions of the manuscript and giving the authors advice on various topics in the book.

We are grateful beyond words for the efforts of our editor, Judy Sandman, and Jonathan David production coordinator, Fiorella deLima. Judy exhibited an extraordinary amount of knowledge and editing skills as she labored to craft our own efforts into the best possible end-result. Fiorella did a wonderful job in making sure that the thousands of little details that went into the production of this book are all in place. We thank both Judy and Fiorella for their hard work and wisdom.

It has been our good fortune to have worked with our friends at Jonathan David Publishers, especially Alfred Kolatch, David Kolatch, and Marvin Sekler, on a number of previous books. Starting with *Great Jews in Sports* (1983) written by Robert Slater on his own, and followed by *Great Jewish Women* (1994), *Great Jewish Men* (1996) and now *Great Moments in Jewish History*, written jointly by Robert and Elinor Slater, we have enjoyed a long and fruitful relationship with Jonathan David Publishers, and we deeply appreciate the years we have spent together. Many thanks.

ROBERT SLATER
ELINOR SLATER
Jerusalem

Contents

MOMENTS OF DESPAIR

MOMENTS OF CREATIVITY

Foreword

The turning points in Jewish history that have been selected for inclusion in this work are presented chronologically in four distinct categories: Moments of Courage, Moments of Joy, Moments of Despair, and Moments of Creativity. In each moment, we have endeavored to isolate an example of a larger trend in Jewish history. Louis Brandeis, for instance—the first Jewish Supreme Court Justice—typifies all Jews who have achieved high national office in the United States.

Careful consideration has been given to the title of this book. How, one might ask, can Moments of Despair—such as the building of the death camp at Auschwitz (June 1940); the Wannsee Conference (January 20, 1942), at which Nazi officials decided to carry out the Holocaust; the Arab terrorist attack against Israeli athletes at the Munich Olympics (September 5, 1972); and the assassination of Israeli Prime Minister Yitzhak Rabin (November 4, 1995)—be considered "great"? As used in the title *Great Moments in Jewish History*, the word "great" carries the meaning "more than of ordinary size or meaning; of unusual significance, whether positive or negative." Familiar examples of the latter usage are "Great Train Robbery" and "Great Earthquake of 1906."

To the extent that it was possible, in each piece we have tried to pinpoint the exact moment at which an event occurred. We know, for instance, *when* on May 14, 1948, David Ben-Gurion read Israel's Declaration of Independence and then proclaimed the establishment of the new state of Israel (4:32 P.M.); and we know *when* on May 11, 1960, the Israelis captured the architect of the Holocaust, Adolf Eichmann (8:00 P.M.). In instances when it was impossible to ascertain the exact moment when an event occurred, we have tried to determine the hour or day. Of course, as one goes farther back into Jewish history, pinpointing time is impossible. Nevertheless, momentous events such as Abraham's passing a test of faith; the mass suicide at Masada, and the writing of the Babylonian Talmud have not been excluded on this basis.

We recognize that there will be legitimate differences of opinion over our selection of great Jewish moments. Indeed, we invite our readers to discuss with us and among themselves which moments ought to be considered "great" and which are undeserving of that characterization. Yet be assured that the moments were selected after extensive research and consultation with Jewish scholars. Our goal has been to assemble a list that not only captures the key moments of Jewish history but also reflects the diversity and breadth of Jewish life through the ages.

ELINOR SLATER
ROBERT SLATER
Jerusalem

MOMENTS
of
COURAGE

Moses Leads Children of Israel Out of Egypt

THIRTEENTH CENTURY B.C.E.

The Exodus is the pivotal event in Jewish history. Departing from Egypt, throwing off the yoke of slavery, the children of Israel became a distinct people with a purpose and with a message to the world. Most important, the Exodus provided evidence of God's power, delivering the Jews from the Egyptians and providing them with their own land.

The Bible tells us about many great men and women who helped shape Jewish history and culture. None was as great as Moses, a leader who, following God's guidance, led the children of Israel out of Egypt and shaped them into a people ready to become a nation. The departure of the children of Israel from Egypt, known as the Exodus, occurred during the thirteenth century B.C.E. and is the crucial event in early Jewish history. Because he led the people at that time, Moses is renowned as the main figure in the emergence of Judaism. His magnificent achievement was the transformation of a group of slaves into a people with the potential to become God's "treasured possession," "a kingdom of priests and a holy nation."

Moses was, unquestionably, the most significant prophet in the Bible. Through Moses, God gave the Jewish people the Torah, with its laws governing justice and holiness and ethical relations among humankind. Moses established God's word as the basis for all Jewish beliefs, worship, and moral behavior for future generations.

Moses was born in Egypt at a time when the Israelites were slaves there and Egyptian persecution of his people had reached its height. His mother was Yocheved, his father Amram, both were of the tribe of Levi. Moses had an older brother, Aaron, and a sister, Miriam.

Pharaoh had ordered the children of Israel to perform forced labor. In order to reduce their numbers he also ordered the Hebrew midwives, Shiphrah and Puah, to kill Israelite boys at birth. When the midwives refused, Pharaoh instructed his entire people to throw every newborn Hebrew boy into the Nile. When Moses was born, Yocheved managed to hide him for three months. Then, to save his life when he had grown too big to hide, she placed him in a wicker basket and hid him in the bulrushes along the banks of the Nile. Miriam kept watch to find out what happened to him.

Pharaoh's daughter found the child when she went to the Nile to bathe. She adopted him as her son and called him Moses, which means in Hebrew "drawn out" of the water. Moses was raised in the Egyptian court, but he was forced to flee after he killed an Egyptian taskmaster who had been persecuting Israelite slaves. Finding refuge in the land of Midian, Moses was welcomed into the household of Jethro, the Midianite priest. Moses married Jethro's daughter Zipporah. He tended her sheep and remained there for many years.

One day, in the wilderness, Moses had an encounter with God. From within a bush that burned but was not consumed by the fire, God spoke to Moses, ordering him to return to Egypt to lead his people to freedom. Moses was reluctant to become a spokesman for his people because he stammered. When God made Moses' brother Aaron the public spokesman of God's instructions to Moses, Moses agreed to take on the mission. Moses was then eighty years old.

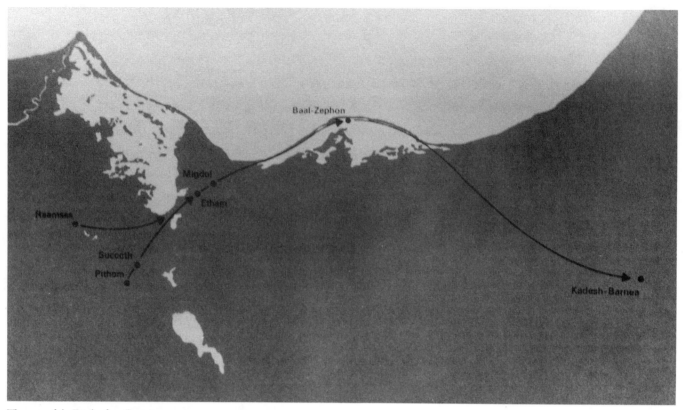

The route of the Exodus from Egypt.

Returning to Egypt with his brother, Moses confronted the Pharaoh and insisted that the Israelites be freed. Pharaoh refused. He would not permit them even to enter the desert briefly to worship their God. Indeed, he threatened to treat them even more harshly.

God then afflicted the Egyptians with ten plagues, announced beforehand to Pharaoh by Moses and Aaron, who also performed miracles in the hope of persuading Pharaoh to release the Israelites. With the announcement of the tenth and most brutal plague, the killing of all the firstborn Egyptian males, Pharaoh relented and ordered the children of Israel to leave Egypt.

The Egyptians were so frightened by the plagues that, in order to hasten the departure of the Israelites, they provided them with gold and silver, jewels and fine clothes; they drove before the Israelites herds of cattle and flocks of sheep and goats. The Israelites left Egypt with such urgency that they baked their dough before it had time to rise; their unleavened bread is the origin of the matzah used at Passover even today.

However, Pharaoh changed his mind and ordered his army to pursue the children of Israel, who were heading for the Sea of Reeds (often incorrectly called the Red Sea) on their march to the Sinai Desert. Pharaoh's horsemen and chariots overtook the Israelites as they were encamped on the western shore of the Sea of Reeds. Noticing the Egyptian army approaching, the Israelites panicked and cried out to God.

Instructed by God, "Moses held out his arm over the sea and the Lord drove back the sea with a strong east wind all that night, and turned the sea into dry ground." The splitting of the sea permitted the children of Israel to cross safely over to the eastern shore. But when Pharaoh and his horsemen and chariots tried to pursue the children of Israel through the dry floor of the Sea of Reeds, the sea closed suddenly, and the Egyptians were drowned. Realizing what had happened, Moses and Miriam burst forth in a song of thanks: "I will sing to the Lord, for he has triumphed gloriously; horse and driver he has hurled into the sea" (*Exodus* 15:1).

At the time of their departure, the Israelites had lived in Egypt four hundred thirty years. While the patriarch Jacob had arrived in Egypt with a household of just seventy people, by the time his descendants left they numbered six hundred thousand men (this figure does not include boys and women); a "mixed multitude" of non-

Israelites, apparently slaves themselves, went out with them, supporters of the Israelite uprising.

At first, as they began their journey, the Israelites were in good spirits. They soon realized, however, that their survival was at stake. To avoid clashes with the powerful Philistine army, Moses decided that the Israelites would not proceed to Canaan by the direct route northward but, rather, would take a circuitous route from one wilderness into another, from one oasis to another—a journey that would take forty years—in preparation for their arrival in the Promised Land.

The events of the Exodus—the persecution in Egypt, the plagues, the parting of the sea—have become crucial elements in building the consciousness of Jewish peoplehood. The escape of this enslaved people acquired great importance in the memory of those Israel-ites who took part in it, and to those who came later, those who learned of it through word-of-mouth, the Exodus became the central, defining event in Jewish history. God's direct, decisive intervention, there at the frontiers of Egypt, convinced future generations of Jews of divine support for their cause.

It was Moses himself who singled out the Exodus as the most incredible event in human history. He suggests that the Jews ask themselves whether, from the first day of human history, "anything as grand as this ever happened, or has its like ever been known . . . has any god ventured to go and take for himself one nation from the midst of another nation by prodigious acts, by signs and portents, by war, by a mighty and outstretched arm and awesome power, as the Lord your God did for you in Egypt before your very eyes?"

Israelites Receive the Ten Commandments

1230 B.C.E.

This defining moment in the emergence of the Jewish people and Judaism occurred almost three thousand years ago on a mountain in the Sinai Desert. It was there that God delivered to Moses, who had led the Israelites out of Egypt, tablets containing the set of utterances known as the Ten Commandments. According to Jewish tradition, God also transmitted the rest of the Torah to Moses as the children of Israel journeyed from Egypt to the Promised Land.

A mountain in the Sinai Desert was the site of the Jewish people's second defining moment—the Exodus from Egypt being the first. This was the giving of the Ten Commandments at Mount Sinai, the event commemorated on the fiftieth day after the beginning of Passover by the festival of Shavuot. It may be said that there were three main actors in this event: God, who uttered the Ten Commandments; Moses, who transmitted God's words to the people; and the people themselves, who accepted the Covenant with God and gathered to experience God's presence and receive the Torah.

The giving of the Torah was preceded by three days of preparation during which the people purified themselves. On the third day, they assembled at the foot of the mountain, on which "there was thunder, and lightning, and a dense cloud . . . and a very loud blast of the horn; and all the people who were in the camp trembled" (*Exodus* 19:16). God then uttered the Ten Commandments. Awed by the manifestations that accompanied the divine utterance, the people drew back and designated Moses as their intermediary: "You speak to us,"

Moses brings the Ten Commandments, the tablets of the law, to the children of Israel. From the Sarejevo Haggadah, which originated in thirteenth-century Spain.

they said to Moses, "and we will obey; but let not God speak to us, lest we die.' " After reassuring them, Moses climbed the mountain and remained at the top for forty days. During that time, God presented him with two stone tablets inscribed with the Ten Commandments. According to the tradition accepted by Orthodox Jews, Moses also received the Oral Torah on Mount Sinai, that is, the supplementary laws, handed down orally, that were compiled in written form in the Talmud.

There are several ways of dividing the utterances into ten. The generally accepted Jewish division is:

1. "I the Lord am your God who brought you out of the land of Egypt." (Though not worded as an imperative, this statement is traditionally considered to imply the commandment to believe in God.)
2. "You shall have no other gods beside Me. You shall not make for yourself a sculptured image. . . ."
3. "You shall not swear falsely by the name of the Lord your God."
4. "Remember the Sabbath day and keep it holy."
5. "Honor your father and your mother."
6. "You shall not murder."
7. "You shall not commit adultery."
8. "You shall not steal."
9. "You shall not bear false witness."
10. "You shall not covet."

Philo and Josephus, however, regarded "I the Lord am your God" as merely a preamble. They identify "You shall have no other gods beside Me" as the first commandment and "You shall not make for yourself a sculptured image" as the second. Their division was followed by the Greek Church Fathers and is accepted by most Protestant churches.

The Ten Commandments fall into three categories. The first four deal with the relationship between human beings and God; the last five deal with relations among human beings, and the fifth acts as a bridge between the two, since it deals with children's obligations toward their parents, who are traditionally considered to stand in the place of God in relation to their children.

Jewish tradition offers many interpretations of what the people heard at Mount Sinai. According to some, they heard the entire Written and Oral Torah. According to others, they heard the Ten Commandments. According to still others, they heard only the first two commandments. There is a tradition that they heard only the first word: anokhi, "I" or "I am." And according to some Jewish mystics, they heard only the first letter

of the first word—the letter alef, which, in the Hebrew alphabet, is silent.

The Ten Commandments are the basis of the covenant between the Jewish people and God, first made by Abraham, then renewed by Jacob, and renewed again by Moses in a solemn, public forum before the entire Jewish people.

Unfortunately, the children of Israel were unable to sustain the high level of commitment they had demonstrated in accepting the Covenant. By Moses' fortieth day on the mountain, the people below began to de-

Moses holding the tablets of the law. Sculpture by Michelangelo.

spair of his return. They asked Aaron to make them a visible "god" to replace Moses. Aaron melted down the people's gold and made a golden calf, which they began to worship. When Moses came down and saw the people dancing around an idol, he smashed the two tablets of the commandments in his fury.

Moses asked God not to punish the Israelites, who repented and refrained from wearing ornaments as a sign of mourning. Moses then asked to see God's presence, a request God denied, but God ordered Moses to "carve two tablets of stone like the first" and to carry them up the mountain so that God could inscribe on the new tablets the words that had been inscribed on the broken ones. Moses obeyed and again climbed the mountain. There, God revealed to Moses God's "back"—the Thirteen Attributes of mercy still recited on the major festivals. Again, Moses remained on the mountain for forty days. He then returned to the people, radiant, carrying the new tablets inscribed with the Covenant.

Upon his return, Moses also transmitted God's instructions for the building of a Tabernacle, a portable sanctuary to house the tablets. The people poured all their wealth and energy into the work. According to the Midrash, "The gold Israel contributed for the sanctuary was a means of reconciliation for the Golden Calf." The second set of tablets, a collaboration between God and Moses, lasted longer than the first, which had been entirely God's work. The second set of tablets, in the Ark of the Covenant, was eventually housed in the Holy of Holies in the Temple in Jerusalem and remained there until the destruction of the First Temple in 587 B.C.E.

Moses led the Children of Israel for the remainder of their stay in the desert—another forty years, for God had decreed that none of the Israelites who left Egypt would be able to enter the Promised Land except Caleb and Joshua, the two spies who, unlike the other ten, had urged immediate entry into the land. Even Moses was not allowed to enter, but God granted him a panoramic view of the Promised Land from the top of Mount Nebo in Moab. Moses died in Moab at the age of one hundred twenty; the *Book of Deuteronomy* relates that "his eyes were undimmed and his vigor unabated." The leadership of the people passed to Joshua, whom Moses had appointed. Moses died alone, and God buried him. According to the Midrash, the burial place remained a secret so that it would not become a shrine.

The *Book of Deuteronomy* states in its final sentences, "Never again did there arise in Israel a prophet like Moses, whom the Lord knew face to face." Yet Judaism is careful not to ascribe to Moses divine or even semidivine traits. It was God, not Moses, who gave the Torah to the Jewish people. Moses had human faults and failings. Accordingly, Judaism is not called "Mosaism." Jewish tradition considers Moses the greatest of all Jewish teachers, the man with whom God spoke "face to face," the intermediary between God and humanity who received God's law for the Jewish people and humankind.

Esther Saves Jews of Persia

465 B.C.E.

The biblical heroine Esther is one of the most loved women in Jewish history. It was she who saved the Jews of Persia when they faced extinction at the hand of King Ahasuerus and his wicked prime minister Haman. The main character of the biblical book that bears her name, Esther has been described as one of the most beautiful women who ever lived.

Esther was a descendant of the tribe of Benjamin. An orphan, she was brought up in the Persian capital, Shushan, by her cousin Mordecai, who adopted her as his daughter. Her Hebrew name was Hadassah, which means "myrtle"; the rabbis explain that, just as the myrtle spreads fragrance, so Esther spread good deeds throughout the land.

Her beauty soon attracted notice. (According to a midrashic source, Mordecai may have married her.) Mordecai, who is described in the *Book of Esther* as sitting in the palace gate, may have been an official in the household of Ahasuerus, the king of Persia (identified by some with Xerxes I, who ruled from 486 to 465 B.C.E.)

The *Book of Esther* relates that Ahasuerus gave a banquet for the nobles of his one hundred twenty-seven provinces. His queen, Vashti, gave a separate banquet for the women. After seven days of drinking, the king summoned Vashti to the men's feast. She refused to come. The king, therefore, sent her away and issued a decree that all wives should obey their husbands. Later, in a calmer state of mind, Ahasuerus decided to take a new queen. He sent for all the beautiful maidens of the kingdom so that he could choose from among them. He chose Esther, Mordecai's adopted daughter. She became queen but, following Mordecai's instructions, told no one that she was Jewish.

About the same time Mordecai learned of a conspiracy against the king and informed the king through Esther. Mordecai's deed was recorded in the annals but not rewarded.

Some time later, Haman the Agagite was appointed prime minister. Mordecai refused to bow down to Haman because Haman was a descendant of the Amalekite king Agag, and Mordecai remembered that the Jews had been commanded to "blot out the memory of Amalek from under heaven." Haman was enraged. When he learned from other courtiers that Mordecai was Jewish, he decided to kill not only Mordecai but all the Jews.

Haman cast lots (*purim*) to decide which month was favorable for his plan. The lot fell on the month of Adar. He then disclosed to the king that there was a people (he did not mention the Jews by name) who were "scattered and dispersed" in the kingdom, who had laws of their own, and who did not obey the king's laws. He made clear that he thought these people should not be permitted to live in the kingdom but should be destroyed. The king supported him, and letters were sent to every province decreeing that the Jews should be slain on the thirteenth of Adar.

Upon learning of the decree, the Jews began to mourn and fast. Mordecai sent a messenger to Esther, urging her to appeal to the king. She was afraid that if she went to the king uninvited, he would have her killed because, according to Persian law, anyone who entered the king's presence uninvited was to be put to death unless the king extended his golden scepter to that person; moreover, the king had not summoned Esther for thirty days. Mordecai pressed Esther further, and she relented, deciding that trying to save the Jews was worth the risk of being found out as a Jew and punished for being Jewish.

Esther. From the Rothschild Miscellany, illuminated manuscripts. Italy, 1470-1480.

She told Mordecai she would fast for three days and then go to the king, and she asked him to instruct the Jews of Shushan, as well, to fast for three days on her behalf.

On the third day, she put on her finest clothes and went to the king. Pleased to see her, he extended the golden scepter and asked her what she wanted. She invited him and Haman to a banquet. During the feast, he again asked what she wanted and promised to grant her wish. She asked the king and Haman to a second banquet the following night. Haman was delighted, but when he met Mordecai, who again did not bow to him, he was more furious than ever. At his wife's suggestion,

Haman built a gallows fifty cubits high and decided to ask the king to have Mordecai hanged on it.

That night, unable to sleep, the king asked that the royal records be read to him. He learned that Mordecai had uncovered a conspiracy against him and was told by his servants that Mordecai had not been rewarded. Just then, Haman entered the courtyard, intending to ask the king to have Mordecai hanged. The king sent for Haman and asked him, "What should be done for a man whom the king desires to honor?" Flattering himself that the king wished to honor *him*, Haman suggested that such a man be dressed in royal garments, set on the king's horse, and led through the streets by a courtier of high rank. The king ordered him to honor Mordecai in this way.

At the second banquet, the king again asked Esther what she wished. This time, she revealed that both she and her people faced the threat of destruction. Angered, the king asked who was to blame. Esther pointed to Haman. Furious, Ahasuerus left the feast, and "Haman remained to plead with Queen Esther for his life." When the king returned, he found Haman collapsed on Esther's couch and immediately accused him of trying to rape the queen. One of the servants at the banquet then told the king about the gallows Haman had made for Mordecai—"the man whose words saved the king"— and the king immediately ordered Haman to be executed on the gallows Haman had prepared for Mordecai.

Though Haman was dead, the Jews still feared destruction, for the decree against them was still in effect. Esther again appealed to the king. Though, like all royal decrees, the original decree could not be revoked, Ahasuerus issued new decrees allowing the Jews to defend themselves against attack. On the thirteenth of Adar, they successfully defended themselves; they celebrated on the fourteenth. (The Jews of Shushan were still fighting on the fourteenth and celebrated on the fifteenth.)

Esther and Mordecai declared that the anniversary of this deliverance should be observed every year with feasting, gift-giving, and charity to the poor. Jews still commemorate this deliverance in the yearly festival of Purim, on the fourteenth and fifteenth of Adar, with the reading of the *Book of Esther* in the synagogue. Noise-makers are used to drown out the name of Haman. Children (and some adults) wear costumes, and many girls dress as Queen Esther. The previous day is observed as the Fast of Esther in Jewish tradition. Though it is observed to commemorate Esther's own fast and her request that the Jews of Shushan observe a fast while she made preparations for her appearance before Ahasuerus to plead for her people, this fast was a much later institution.

Though the author of the *Book of Esther* is unknown, he was probably a Jew living in a Persian city who wanted to leave a record of the annual festival of Purim for later generations of Jews. The book exists in two versions—the Hebrew version, one hundred sixty-seven verses in length, which is read in synagogues, and the longer Septuagint version, in Greek, which is two hundred seventy verses long.

Evaluating Esther's character, Adin Steinsaltz, the noted Jewish scholar, wrote:

> There is the danger she underwent for the sake of the nation, and her declaration that a day of celebration and feasting be initiated to commemorate the events. This was the act of a woman who had carried out a dangerous mission and felt a need to perpetuate that mission, not only in the deepest social and national sense but also as something of profound significance in her own life. She felt her deed had value as a sacrifice and epitomized the many tasks fulfilled for national or ideological reasons.

Steinsaltz argued that Esther was not a totally pure soul:

> The moment when Esther was required to go to Ahasuerus, and use every means of seduction and temptation at her disposal in order to lift the sentence of death that had fallen on the Jews, was not just a moment of personal danger. She was required to pass from a passive state to an active one, to become the temptress. Previously Esther could claim that, to some extent, she was in a situation in which she was held under duress. From the moment when she took the initiative in approaching the king to seduce him, she lost her last shreds of innocence.
>
> Where previously she could feel pure, at least in spirit, she was now, to some extent, sullied . . . consciously she now decided to endanger not only her life but her soul; and from this moment onward, she becomes the savior of the Jewish people (*Biblical Images*, 1984).

Ahasuerus and Esther enthroned. Wall painting from the synagogue of Dura-Europos. Third century A.D.

THE JERUSALEM PUBLISHING HOUSE

Judah Maccabee Rededicates the Temple

25 KISLEV, 164 B.C.E.

> In the second century, when the Seleucid ruler Antiochus IV Epiphanes sought to Hellenize all Jews and, thereby, to wipe out Judaism, Hasmonean fighters from Modi'in led the resistance. At first, Mattathiah the priest led the revolt, and then his son Judah, known as Maccabee (the Hammer). He liberated Jerusalem and purified the Temple of idolatry, an event Jews celebrate with the winter holiday of Hanukkah.

After the break-up of Alexander the Great's empire, one of his generals, Seleucus, founded a dynasty in the eastern part of the old empire. Its capital was the city of Antioch in Syria. In the second century B.C.E., Palestine gradually fell under Syrian control. Because the Syrians had adopted the Greek way of life—that is, became Hellenized—the process of Hellenization was hastened in all the areas under their control. Many Jews, especially in the cities, voluntarily became Hellenized and attained positions of power under the Seleucids.

One of the Seleucid rulers, Antiochus IV Epiphanes, sought to Hellenize Jews by force. He banned circumcision and observance of the dietary laws and the Sabbath, with the punishment of death for disobedience. He also erected a statue of Zeus in the Temple in Jerusalem and ordered that pigs be sacrificed on the altar; similar, smaller shrines were set up in all Jewish cities.

Not surprisingly, observant Jews were horrified. In 168 B.C.E., when the imperial Syrian commissioner Apelles arrived in the town of Modi'in in the district of Lydda to see that the decrees of Antiochus were carried out, Mattathiah, a member of the clan of Hasmon and

Judah Maccabee, eighteenth century.

THE ISRAEL MUSEUM/DAVID HARRIS

12

Judah Maccabee pursuing the enemy.

the priest of the town, refused to obey him. Apelles had an altar built to Zeus and summoned all the inhabitants before it. "Come forth and do the command of the King," he ordered the aged priest, Mattathiah the Hasmonean. Mattathiah not only refused but killed the Hellenized Jew who stepped forward to obey.

Mattathiah and his five sons fled into the mountains. There, they were joined by many others—plain folk, poor farmers, and sheep herders. They waged guerrilla warfare from their hiding place and helped the people continue their observance of Jewish law; they broke heathen altars; and when parents showed fear, they even circumcised infant boys by force.

In 167 B.C.E., when Mattathiah felt it time to relinquish leadership, he called his five sons together; John, Simon, Judah, Eleazar, and Jonathan. Judah, known as the Hammer because of his great skills as a fighter, was appointed military leader. Simon was entrusted with all the political affairs. "And now, my children," said the old priest, "be zealous of the Torah, and give your lives for the Covenant of your fathers!"

The band of fighters Judah led was small. At first, they were untrained as soldiers and fought with primitive weapons, but they captured arms from the enemy and soon became formidable warriors. Judah Maccabee was a brilliant tactician who confused the enemy by launching surprise attacks. Before each battle, Judah and his men fasted and prayed. Eventually, the Maccabees won four decisive victories over the Syrian armies and finally liberated Jerusalem, except for the Acra fortress, in Kislev164 B.C.E. Judah found the Temple profaned and partly in ruins. Its great gates had been burned and the chambers for the priests torn down. Angrily, the Maccabees and their followers smashed the statue of Zeus. The Jewish adherents of the Hellenistic party in the capital fled to Syria to escape the vengeance of the people they had betrayed.

Judah and his men cleared the Temple of debris. They swept its courts clean and purified the sanctuary. They had new Temple vessels made, for Antiochus had taken the old ones to Antioch. The Temple's sacred service was entrusted to priests and Levites from among the ranks of the rebels.

On the twenty-fifth day of the month of Kislev in 164 B.C.E., Judah Maccabee rededicated the Temple during a solemn convocation of the people. The newly appointed priests lit the menorah and offered incense on the golden altar and burnt offerings on the altar of sacrifices. Judah Maccabee decreed that, to commemorate the occasion, beginning on that same day every year the Jews should celebrate Hanukkah, the Festival of Dedication, for eight days every year, beginning on the twenty-fifth of Kislev. The eight-day festival was modeled after Sukkot, which Judah and his men had been unable to observe during their guerrilla campaign.

Aided by internal rivalries in Syria, Judah Maccabee obtained new religious freedom for the Jews. In what proved, in the long run, to be his most questionable decision, Judah sent messengers to Rome to negotiate an alliance against the Syrians. He was declared a friend of Rome, but the Romans sent no help: Judah was killed in battle in 160 B.C.E. His brother Jonathan took over command, but the Jewish resistance movement was weak. It took another eighteen years before the Syrian hold over the Jews was broken—under a third brother, Simon, who was proclaimed leader and high priest. Simon's descendants also took the title of king, and the Hasmonean dynasty, though not descended from King David, regained control over much of the territory of King David's empire on both sides of the Jordan. Their autonomy was short-lived, however. In 63 B.C.E., the Roman general Pompey conquered Jerusalem for Rome.

The Talmud offers a supernatural explanation for the lighting of candles during the eight days of Hanukkah: When the priests were preparing for the service of re-dedication, they found only a single cruse of oil that had not been profaned by pagan rites. This cruse contained only enough oil for one day; yet it burned for eight days. According to the Talmud, the festival commemorates this miracle, which is not mentioned in earlier sources.

Though work is permitted on Hanukkah, the holiday is marked by special passages in the liturgy, and the ceremony of lighting the Hanukkah lamp is performed nightly in the home for eight days. One candle is lit on the first night, and the number increases by one each night until eight are lit on the eighth night. Many Jews place the Hanukkah lamp in the window to demonstrate that no force in the world can crush the Jewish spirit.

An Academy Is Founded at Yavneh

70 C.E.

> With the fall of the Second Temple, the center of Jewish life collapsed. Instead of sacrifice, rabbinic study, and prayer, synagogue and home observance became the main elements of the Jewish religion. The impetus for this change of direction came from Yohanan ben Zakkai's establishment of a center of scholarly learning at Yavneh, in Palestine, where he and his disciples made critical decisions that have affected the development of Judaism to this day.

The fall of Jerusalem and the destruction of the Second Temple in 70 C.E. forced the remaining Jews to adjust to a new reality. All the outward symbols of the religion had been destroyed, especially the sanctuary with its system of sacrifices. The leading scholars and teachers realized that Judaism could no longer depend on public, physical institutions for its survival and that a new direction was needed.

The Jews had always made the Torah and the traditions that grew out of obeying its laws the driving force of their religion. At no time in Jewish history was the importance of the Torah more apparent than at the time of the Temple's destruction. Most of the hereditary priestly families and the upper classes of Judaism had been wiped out. Though many considered the Zealots, with their desperate armed resistance against Rome, to be the staunchest defenders of the Jewish faith, the successful defenders, ultimately, were the scribes and scholars.

As Jerusalem collapsed, the Jews looked to their teachers for leadership. The leading Jewish teacher was Yohanan ben Zakkai, the most respected of the Phari-

sees. He believed that Jews should live by the spirit, not by the sword, and that the war against Rome had, therefore, been a mistake. He felt that Judaism would survive, despite Jerusalem's defeat, through the transmission and development of its tradition of learning.

To advance his cause, Yohanan ben Zakkai decided to put his case in person before the Roman general, Vespasian. The city was under siege, and no one was allowed to leave. It was against Jewish law, however, for a dead body to remain in Jerusalem overnight. Rabbi Yohanan, therefore, decided to be smuggled out of the city in a coffin. Reporting that their master had died, some of his pupils sought permission of the Romans to carry his body outside Jerusalem for burial. Though the mission was dangerous, the pupils brought the "body" outside the walls, past the Roman guards, and into Vespasian's camp. Yohanan then rose out of his coffin and made his way to Vespasian. Aware of Yohanan's opposition to the Zealots and influence in the Jewish community, Vespasian was probably prepared to grant almost any request Yohanan made. He must have been surprised when Yohanan asked only for permission to open a school in a little seacoast town that the Jews called Yavneh and the Romans, Jammia. From the Roman camp, Yohanan went straight to Yavneh, which was crowded with refugees from Galilee and Judea. He gathered around him scholars who, like himself, believed that the Jews had been mistaken in resisting the Romans through violence, and they began meeting regularly in the courtyard of Rabbi Yohanan's home to study.

Yavneh soon became known as "the great city, the city of scholars and rabbis." Pilgrims from Asia visited the city three times a year. Most of the *tannaim* (religious scholars) of the period were teachers there, and a synod of rabbis, which replaced the Sanhedrin, functioned as a *bet din*, or court, and made crucial decisions affecting Jewish life and observance.

Among the most important were rituals that allowed Jews to express their grief for the loss of the Temple and yet continue their ordinary life. A sequence of daily prayers was established that followed the structure of the sacrifices and included descriptions of them and petitions for their restoration. These prayers constitute the basis of the daily prayer book, or *siddur*, still used today. Ceremonies such as the eating of the Passover meal were to continue, but on a new basis, in the home, where the table was to represent the altar even at ordinary meals. Rituals of mourning were also incorporated into ordinary activities such as weddings and the building of houses. The new prayers and rituals were supported ideologically by Rabbi Yohanan's teaching that God accepted prayer and deeds of lovingkindness as the equivalent of sacrifice.

Other significant decisions made at Yavneh included the arranging of the definitive canon of the Bible, between 70 and 132 C.E. The annual calculations of the Jewish calendar were made at Yavneh as well.

The relationship between Rome and Yavneh was mixed. Though Rome sometimes harassed, and even persecuted, the rabbis of the academy, the Romans understood that the rabbis of Yavneh were opposed to violence. "Do not hurry to tear down the altars of the gentiles," one rabbi suggested, "lest you be forced to rebuild them with your own hands." Rome, therefore, allowed the rabbis wide judicial powers.

Though the academy developed a procedure for ordaining new rabbis according to merit, the power at Yavneh was vested in those families who had distinguished themselves in scholarship for several generations. By 90 C.E., Rabbi Gamaliel II, grandson of the man who had taught Saint Paul, had succeeded Yohanan ben Zakkai and was recognized as the *nasi*, or patriarch, by the Romans.

With the outbreak of the Bar Kokhba Revolt in 132 C.E., Yavneh ceased to be the center of Jewish life in the Land of Israel and the diaspora. After the revolt was crushed the rabbinical authorities, led by the disciples of Rabbi Akiba, moved to the town of Usha in western Galilee. Attempts were made—all unsuccessful—to transfer the synod of rabbis from Galilee back to Yavneh. The rabbis of Usha, however, continued the work begun at Yavneh, especially by articulating the concept of the Oral Torah—the chain of transmission extending from Moses to the rabbis—and, thereby, established the foundation of Rabbinic Judaism as it is known today.

Anan ben David Leads the Karaites

760 C.E.

The Karaites were religious purists who believed that the laws written in the Bible were the only ones Jews were obligated to follow. They did not accept rabbinic tradition—the Talmud in particular—as valid or binding. They saw themselves as the only true Jews. Their founder was Anan ben David. Though the Karaites challenged the geonim—the leaders of the Babylonian talmudic academies—the followers of the Talmud dominated, and talmudic Judaism prevailed over the Karaite view.

The most serious challenge to early Rabbinic Judaism was posed by the Karaites, who rejected the concept of the Oral Torah developed by the rabbis of the Mishnah and in the talmudic academies of Babylonia and accepted the Written Torah as the sole authority for the proper conduct of Jewish life. The sect derived its name from *mikra*—"that which is read," or Scripture; hence the name *Karaim*—Scripturalists. They called their opponents Rabbanites. The Karaites themselves claimed that their sect originated before the destruction of the First Temple. However, the first historical evidence of their existence appeared only in the ninth century C.E. within the Babylonian Jewish community. The Karaites were always a minority within the Jewish community, but they were fanatical and zealous.

According to their opponent's story, which appears in many Jewish histories, they owe their origin to a dispute over the successor to a certain childless exilarch—the head of the Babylonian Jewish community—around 760 C.E. The exilarch's closest relatives were his two nephews, Anan and Hananiah. Anan, the older brother, was clearly the more competent and learned of the two. But the geonim distrusted Anan, who had spent time among Jewish sectarians in Persia, and they were afraid Anan would use his authority to oppose their interpretations of talmudic law. They therefore appointed the younger, weaker brother, Hananiah, and asked the caliph, who ordinarily would not have intervened, to ratify their choice.

Anan then spoke out against the geonim, the Talmud, and Jewish tradition. When his followers declared him a counterexilarch, Anan was imprisoned for rebellion. On the advice of a fellow prisoner who was well versed in Islamic law, he appealed to the caliph. He represented himself as the founder and leader of a new religious movement and won his freedom by using arguments with which the Muslim ruler would sympathize.

Talmudic Judaism had promulgated many laws and customs that had no basis in the Bible. Many of those laws and customs seemed complicated and burdensome. The Karaites believed that the Bible is the only valid authority for Jewish life and that the rabbis had misinterpreted it and obscured its true meaning. The Karaites held that each Jew has a right to interpret the Bible without having to rely on the "official" explanations of the talmudic academies. Consequently, the obligation of the true Jew was to study the Bible with great care in order to discover the meaning of its laws and commands. Each person's interpretation was considered authoritative. Nevertheless, the final authority was the Torah. The Karaites' main principle was Anan ben David's personal dictum: "I will search diligently in the Torah and will

Karaite merchants of the Crimea, 1862.

eaten with dairy products), and forbade consultation with physicians, since, in the Torah, only God is called a healer.

The teachers who followed Anan ben David, especially Benjamin of Nahawendi (about 830 C.E.) and Daniel al-Kumisi (about 900 C.E.), solidified the movement and produced commentaries of their own. It was under the former that the movement acquired its name. Karaism was accessible to the common people, who read the Bible but did not understand talmudic disputation and who had come to perceive Babylonian Jewish leaders as an aristocracy. Because of its sophisticated commentaries, it also attracted many educated Jews.

Gradually, the movement expanded beyond Babylonia into Persia, Egypt, Palestine, and some sections of the nearby Byzantine Empire. In the ninth century C.E., many Karaites settled in Jerusalem, which became an important center of Karaism.

The Karaites had their own liturgy and their own body of religious scholarship written in Hebrew. Like the Samaritans, they considered themselves not only Jews but "the only true Jews" and denied all evidence of continuity with the talmudic tradition, which they unconsciously demonstrated even while rejecting it. Therefore, the Rabbanite majority perceived the Karaite movement as a schismatic tendency that would lead to the dissolution of Judaism.

The first effective refutation of the Karaites was that of Sa'adia Gaon (882-942), the most renowned scholar of his time. In 928, the exilarch appointed him head of the Sura talmudic academy in Babylonia to arrest its decline; a native of Egypt, Sa'adia Gaon was the first non-Babylonian to be appointed to such an office. Sa'adia enjoyed controversy and wrote polemics against the Karaites throughout his life. He used the Karaites'

not rely on my own opinion."

Though the Karaites considered talmudic law burdensome, the Karaite version of Jewish law was far more stringent and harsh. The rabbis made many compromises for the sake of health and safety that the Karaites would not allow. On the Sabbath, for example, the Talmud permitted the enjoyment of light and fire kindled before the Sabbath; the Karaites, however, insisted that all fires be extinguished before nightfall on Friday and that only cold food could be eaten on the Sabbath. The Karaites also increased the number of fast days, placed additional restrictions on the eating of meat (though they allowed the few permissible types of meat to be own methods against them; reasoning on the basis of Scripture, he traced talmudic laws to their biblical sources. In his *Beliefs and Opinions* (*Emunot ve-Deot*), he provided a philosophical basis for Rabbinic Judaism.

After Sa'adia, Karaism lost most of its influence, but it persisted in parts of Europe. During the Middle Ages, the Karaites produced important biblical commentators and writers on law and philosophy. As late as the seventeenth century, the Karaite Isaac of Troki, in Lithuania, refuted the claims of Christianity in a work that was translated into Latin, and the well-known Italian rabbi-scientist Joseph del-Medigo found, when he lived in Vilna and was court physician to Prince Radziwill, that he was able to share his intellectual interests only with Karaites. Traditional Jews in Russia and Poland thought little of the Karaites, however, because some of the Karaite customs and rites were derived from Islam and especially because the Karaites were opposed to the Talmud, in which the Russian and Polish Jews excelled. Accordingly, the Karaites had to live in tiny ghettos of their own in the midst of the large ghettos of Jewry as a whole. Rabbinic authorities barred contact with them so that mainstream Jews would not become infected by their thinking.

Rabbinic Judaism, despite the Karaites' challenge, eventually emerged triumphant. But the effort of combating them led to new directions in rabbinic scholarship. The Karaite insistence on the primacy of the Bible stimulated interest in biblical studies and a more systematic approach to the Hebrew language. Karaism's main antagonist, Sa'adia Gaon, translated the Bible into Arabic and wrote biblical commentaries; he also wrote a treatise on unique and rare Hebrew words, as well as a systematic Hebrew grammar. Thus, Anan ben David's courage in opposing Rabbinic Judaism influenced the new developments within it.

Rothschilds Found a Banking Dynasty

1792

The name Rothschild has become synonymous with international banking. The family's success began in the eighteenth century, when the founder of the house of Rothschild, Mayer Amschel Rothschild of Frankfurt am Main, in what is now Germany, created a powerful banking domain, which his sons expanded into London, Paris, Naples, and Vienna. The Rothschilds financed the building of the Suez Canal, France's reparations to Germany after the Franco-Prussian War of 1870-1871, and Italy's independence.

The family name Rothschild comes from *roth schild,* or "red shield," that is, the sign of the red shield that hung in front of the house of Isaac Elhanan Rothschild, who acquired a house on Judengasse, the main Jewish street in Frankfurt, in the 1560s; Isaac died in Frankfurt in 1585. In the eighteenth century the Rothschilds and Schiffs shared a double house in the Frankfurt Judengasse: they hung house signs, Zum Roten Schild and Zum Schiff alongside each other. Mayer Amschel Rothschild, the first wealthy member of the family, bought the Schiffs' half of the house when one of the Schiffs decided to move to London.

Until the birth of Mayer Amschel Rothschild, the son of Amschel Moses Rothschild, on February 23, 1743, the Rothschilds had been undistinguished merchants and communal servants, but the birth of Mayer Amschel began a new era for the family.

According to Egan Corti, author of a 1928 book on the Rothschilds, Mayer Amschel was "a tall, impressive-looking man of pronounced Hebraic type; his expression, if rather sly, was good-natured." Like most

Mayer Amschel Rothschild.

eighteenth-century gentlemen, Mayer Amschel wore a wig, though as a Jew he was not permitted to have it powdered. He also had a small, pointed, black beard.

In his youth Mayer Amschel attended a rabbinical school in Fürth; after his father's death, however, he was sent to Hanover, where he trained to become a banker and also became an expert in coins, medals, sculptures, and paintings. He then returned to Frankfurt and became a trader, specializing in antiques and old coins; he was a money-changer as well. In 1764, at the age of twenty, Mayer Amschel started to engage in business with the future landgrave of Hesse-Cassel, William IX. (A landgrave was a German nobleman of that period—the equivalent of a count.) William IX, an avid coin collector, was heir to the largest fortune in Europe. In 1769, Mayer Amschel was appointed supplier to the principality of Hesse-Hanua and, that same year, was given the title of court agent; as the court agent, he supplied William with rare coins and printed his own coin catalogs.

In 1770, Mayer Amschel Rothschild married Gudule Schnapper, who bore him nineteen children; five sons and five daughters survived.

When William became landgrave in 1785, Mayer Amschel was one of only a dozen Jewish court agents who competed to do business with him and who were able to lend large amounts of money to him and other rulers. Gradually, Mayer Amschel increased his financial dealings with William, aided by his close connection to the landgrave's confidential financial adviser, C. F. Buderus, who later became Mayer Amschel's silent partner. Mayer Amschel offered his merchandise to the imperial court.

By the early 1790s, Mayer Amschel had become one of Frankfurt's wealthiest citizens. When Frankfurt was invaded by France in 1792 the landgrave's finances were in disarray. With the liberation of Frankfurt, it was left to Mayer Amschel to put Landgrave William's finances back in order. As William's intermediary, the house of Rothschild won great respect. Honors were bestowed on Mayer Amschel, among them the German Order of Saint John for his successful handling of William's financial affairs.

In 1792 Mayer Amschel brought his two older sons, Amschel Mayer and Salomon Mayer, into partnership with him. The other sons, Nathan Mayer, Karl Mayer, and James Mayer, were brought in as partners upon reaching their maturity. The five brothers were dubbed the "Frankfurt Five" and were sent to the capitals of Europe. For the next twenty years they built up the most important international banking syndicate of the era. Amschel Mayer took over running the parent bank in Frankfurt. Salomon Mayer opened the Rothschild bank in Vienna. Karl Mayer set up a bank in Naples. James settled in Paris in 1812 and acted as agent for Nathan in London.

In 1800, Mayer Amschel was appointed imperial crown agent, a post that entitled him to carry arms and to benefit from certain tax exemptions. He was also allowed to move freely throughout the imperial domain. When Napoleon rose to power, however, the landgrave went into exile, and the Rothschilds began providing the French leader with loans.

Mayer Amschel's greatest stroke of luck came after the Battle of Jena in 1806. It was then that William IX, exiled from his country, entrusted Nathan Mayer, who was headquartered in London, with the purchase of sizeable amounts of British securities. Through remarkably astute speculation, Nathan Rothschild managed to create a fortune for the landgrave.

Mayer Amschel and his sons played a critically important function for those who wished to do business in Europe discreetly. They became go-betweens, sending coded messages to different parts of Europe, conveying money in secret sections of coaches, concealing documents and bullion at their home in Frankfurt.

On September 16, 1812, on Yom Kippur, the holiest day of the Jewish calendar, Mayer Amschel had been fasting. He had spent hours in the synagogue and that evening felt severe pains. Writing a new will, Rothschild sold to his five sons all his shares in the business, his securities, and other possessions, as well as his large stocks of wine, for the sum of one hundred ninety thousand gulden, far below their true value. His sons became the exclusive owners of the business. Three days later, Mayer Amschel, the founding father of the House of Rothschild, died at the age of sixty-seven.

Mayer Amschel's testament contained this statement:

> I will and ordain that my daughters and sons-in-law and their heirs have no share in the trading business existing under the firm of Mayer Amschel Rothschild & Sons. . . [which] belongs to my sons exclusively. None of my daughters, sons-in-law and their heirs is therefore entitled to demand sight of business transactions. . . . I would never be able to forgive any of my children if contrary to these, my paternal wishes, it

should be allowed to happen that my sons were upset in the peaceful possession and prosecution of their business interests.

These words showed how little confidence Rothschild had in his daughters' choices of spouses. (It would have been out of the question for unmarried women to inherit the business in that era.)

Between World War I and World War II, the growth of other major banking concerns and the effects of high taxation limited the relative significance of the House of Rothschild. Before and during World War II the Nazis were eager to expropriate the Rothschilds' assets. By that time, however, the Rothschilds had transferred their properties to holding companies in neutral or noncombatant countries.

After World War II, the Rothschilds exploited new opportunities created in the field of merchant banking. They constructed modern offices and acquired major interests in Canada, investing in films and television.

In January 1994, descendants of the Rothschild family marked the two hundred fiftieth birthday of the founder of the Rothschild banking empire. Nathaniel Charles Jacob Rothschild, whose title is the fourth Baron Rothschild, and other descendants of Mayer Amschel Rothschild, gathered at his grave at an old Jewish cemetery in Frankfurt.

Brandeis Becomes First Jewish Supreme Court Justice

JANUARY 28, 1916

> *The American jurist Louis Brandeis was the first Jew appointed to the United States Supreme Court. He served on the high court for twenty-three years and was one of the few justices to support the social legislation President Franklin Delano Roosevelt had initiated, which came to be called the New Deal. Brandeis's emergence as a leader of American Zionism encouraged many American Jews to embrace the establishment of a Jewish homeland in Palestine without feeling that they had diminished their loyalty to the United States.*

Louis Brandeis was born on November 13, 1856, in Louisville, Kentucky; he was the youngest of the four children born to Adolph and Frederika Brandeis, immigrants from Prague to the United States. His mother, whose family name was Dembitz, was a descendant of followers of the pseudo-messiah Jacob Frank. Louis Brandeis's parents appreciated intellectual achievement but showed little interest in Judaism.

Brandeis was especially fond of one of his uncles, Lewis Dembitz, a scholarly attorney, author, and Zionist who was known as "the Jewish scholar of the South." In honor of his favorite uncle, Louis changed his middle name from David to Dembitz.

Louis grew up in Louisville and graduated from high school at age fifteen. About that time, the family business was dissolved because of financial setbacks, and the Brandeises made an extended visit to Europe in 1872. Between 1873 and 1875, Louis attended the Annen Realschule in Dresden. He disliked German academic discipline, noting, "In Kentucky you could whistle." Encouraged by his Uncle Lewis to return to the United States, Louis entered Harvard Law School. To pay the tuition, he borrowed money from his older brother and also tutored other students. Louis Brandeis graduated first in his class before his twenty-first birthday.

He practiced law in Boston, defending the rights of consumers and labor unions, interests that until then had not enjoyed much advocacy. He was called the "people's attorney" because he defended those with little representation—namely, the poor. He was described as ascetic, compassionate, and commanding. To some, he seemed reminiscent of Abraham Lincoln. By the mid-1890s, Louis Brandeis had acquired a reputation as one of America's best lawyers.

In 1908, Brandeis submitted a brief to the United States Supreme Court in which he defended an Oregon statute that regulated working hours for women. That document, containing over one hundred pages of supporting facts, became known as the "Brandeis Brief." It helped pave the way for the introduction of sociological data in the defense of public policy before the judiciary system.

Brandeis was considered one of the leading progressive reformers in the country. In 1912, when Woodrow Wilson was elected President, he turned to Brandeis for advice on political and social reform. Brandeis's 1914 book, *Other People's Money*, exerted a strong influence on Wilson, and his ideal of a highly competitive economy served as the basis for Wilson's New Freedom, which aimed at establishing more economic opportunities in the United States by restricting monopolies and reducing protective tariffs.

In his early life, Brandeis felt little interest in Juda-

A portrait of Louis Brandeis.

ism, but he was favorably impressed by his religion's emphasis on justice and ethical values. In 1911, Brandeis encountered the Jewish working class for the first time when he arbitrated a garment workers' strike in New York. The workers' intelligence and their ability to see issues from the point of view of the other side impressed him.

That same year, 1911, Brandeis's fateful meeting with Jacob De Haas, editor of the Boston-based newspaper the *Jewish Advocate*, heightened his Jewish consciousness. De Haas, secretary to Theodor Herzl in London, aroused Brandeis's interest in Jewish history, and especially the burgeoning Zionist movement. Brandeis devoured every word of the reading material De Haas provided him. Brandeis explained: "My sympathy with the Zionist movement rests primarily upon the noble idealism which underlines it and the conviction that a great people, stirred by enthusiasm for such an ideal, must bear an important part in the betterment of the world." Just before World War I, Brandeis became chairman of the Provisional Committee for General Zionist

Affairs in the United States, a post that essentially made him the leader of American Zionism. He favored, as every Zionist did, the reestablishment of a Jewish homeland in Palestine, a homeland that would be based on American democratic ideals.

On January 28, 1916, President Wilson nominated Brandeis to the Supreme Court, a political bombshell that set off a controversial four-month-long Senate debate over his confirmation. Wilson knew that the Senate's conservatives would oppose the nomination as soon as they learned of it and, therefore, avoided telling any of the senators before his official announcement. "A ghastly joke," said the New York *Tribune*. The New York *Sun* called Brandeis "utterly and even ridiculously unfit." *The New York Times* was more restrained but complained that Brandeis was "essentially a. . . striver after changes and reforms." To the Boston *Morning Globe*, Brandeis was "a radical, a theorist, impractical with strong socialistic tendencies." And former President Taft called the appointment "a fearful shock. . . one of the deepest wounds that I have had as an American. . . . He is a muckracker, an emotionalist for his own purpose, a socialist." Taft, the president and former presidents of the American Bar Association, urged the Senate to reject Brandeis, as did fifty-five leading Bostonians, including A. Lawrence Lowell, president of Harvard University. The Democratic and liberal press came to Brandeis's defense. At Harvard Law School, nine of the eleven faculty members endorsed Wilson's choice. Though the opponents of the nomination seemed to outnumber its supporters, Wilson held firm, and the anti-Brandeis group could not block the nomination. Hence, Brandeis became the first Jew to serve on the high court.

Brandeis's closeness to President Wilson has been credited with securing American support for the Balfour Declaration, the 1917 declaration of British policy favoring the establishment of a Jewish national home in Palestine.

After World War I, Brandeis became the honorary President of the World Zionist Organization, but a rift occurred between Brandeis and American Zionists, on the one hand, and Chaim Weizmann and the Eastern European Zionists, on the other. Assailing the way Zionist funds were being handled, Brandeis sought to place the Zionist movement on a sounder, more efficient economic footing, but was rebuffed by Chaim Weizmann. So contentious was the controversy that Brandeis and his allies withdrew from the World Zionist Organization, though they continued to support Zionist ideals.

Supreme Court portrait. Brandeis is seated bottom left.

On the Supreme Court, Brandeis was one of the few justices to support President Roosevelt's New Deal. At a time when a majority on the Court was striking down new social legislation, Brandeis voted for accepting minimum-wage laws, price-control laws, and legislation that protected trade unions against injunctions in labor disputes. Franklin Roosevelt hailed Brandeis as "Isaiah" because he was a great teacher and reflected that prophet's passion for social justice.

During the twenty-three years he served as a justice, Louis Brandeis was known as one of the most gifted legal craftsmen in the Court's history. Some believed that had Louis Brandeis not been Jewish he might well have become Chief Justice of the Supreme Court. He supported judicial restraint, the view that courts should not usurp the role of the legislative branch on the wis-

dom of public policy. He also believed that the courts had a special role to play in the field of civil liberties. He once said: "Order cannot be secured merely through fear of punishment; it is hazardous to discourage thought, hope and imagination; fear breeds repression; repression breeds hate; hate menaces stable government." He was a strong believer in dispersing power among the states rather than allowing too much power to be concentrated at the federal level.

Brandeis died on October 5, 1941, just before his eighty-fifth birthday; he did not live to see the founding of the state of Israel in 1948. But a kibbutz there, *Ein Hashofet* (Spring of the Judge) was named for him. And in Waltham, Massachusetts, near Boston, where he began his career, a university established by Jewish sponsors bears his name.

Sarah Schenirer Founds Beth Jacob School

1918

The founding of the first Beth Jacob school for Orthodox young women in 1918 was a turning point for Jewish women. Sarah Schenirer, the founder, was born in Cracow, Poland, in 1883 and was a pioneer in religious education for Orthodox Jewish girls, who, she believed, should receive not only a secular education but a religious education as well. The original school expanded into a network of schools—initially in Poland and eventually throughout Europe. The Beth Jacob movement was revived after World War II. Its center, in Jerusalem, administers schools throughout the world.

Sarah Schenirer came from a Hasidic family; her father, a merchant, was a follower of the *rebbe* of Belz. Like many Polish Jewish girls of her time, she attended Polish elementary schools and acquired her only religious instruction from a rabbi who visited her school once or twice a week and distributed popular ethical works in Yiddish, written for women.

Even as a child, Sarah was attracted to religious learning. She thought it absurd that, while Orthodox boys and young men received a full religious education in yeshivas, Orthodox girls received a secular education in Polish elementary schools but were denied a religious education. She was convinced that, without a solid Jewish religious background, young Jewish women like herself would eventually leave Orthodox Judaism and be unable to transmit its values to their children.

During her teens, she became a seamstress and studied the Bible and rabbinic texts at night, a rare activity for girls of that era. After a while, she established her own small, but flourishing, dressmaking business. Sa-

rah thought it odd that her customers knew precisely what they wanted when it came to choosing a dress but had no idea how to meet their spiritual needs, and she saw it as her mission to help them meet those needs. "I felt," she said afterwards, "I must help them to see that they were ready to give up, not a shell but the very substance without which they and their dear ones would perish. But I was without education. I lacked the gift of speech to convey my convictions."

Sarah was sympathetic to the plight of these young women, for she had seen them often at synagogue. "When the father comes home from the *Rebbe*," she wrote, he is too dazzled to see what will come out one day into the glaring light, revealing a breach that has gone beyond repair. While the men bend and sway in the rhythm that tradition has created, and their heads are held aloft into almost visionary heights, the girls go dancing, skipping, dreaming on in their own way, along the path of a world which is wide open, unfenced, and pitiless. Their paths and the parents' paths may never meet."

She sensed that Jewish fathers and daughters were strangers, living in different worlds, and she wanted to set the daughters on a proper path. Education was the answer, Sarah decided—first for herself and then for them.

With the outbreak of World War I, Sarah and her family fled to Vienna. There, she attended the religious services and lectures of Rabbi Dr. Moshe Flesch, a follower of the Neo-Orthodox movement founded in Germany by Rabbi Samson Raphael Hirsch. Though Rabbi Flesch's lectures were in fact traditionalist, Sarah found them modern and progressive in relation to her

Hasidic background. Moreover, her interest in religious education for women was supported by the fact that the Neo-Orthodox movement in Germany had established schools for girls. In 1917, Sarah returned to Cracow with some basic ideas for the religious education of women and sought the approval of the *rebbe* of Belz. Sarah and her brother sent him a note, when he was at Marienbad, asking whether she might educate Jewish women in the Torah. "May the Lord bless your work with success," was his answer. That was sufficient encouragement for her.

Sarah began working toward her goal. Abandoning her dressmaking business to teach full time, Sarah gave talks to groups of young women. She brought a blackboard and some benches into the small room at home that she had used as a dressmaker and gave classes for women her age. Attendance was poor, however, and Schenirer decided to concentrate her efforts on young girls who had not yet been influenced by secular education.

In 1918, she opened a school for young girls. The school began with twenty-five students, all under seventeen years of age; by the end of the year, it had eighty students, and Schenirer moved it into a three-room apartment. The language of instruction was Yiddish rather than Polish. Sarah sent two of her assistants to open schools in other places. That same year, the Cracow branch of the ultra-Orthodox movement Agudat Israel adopted her program of schools for girls. Thus began the network of Beth Jacob schools in Poland.

The school was called Beth Jacob (House of Jacob)—more popularly, in Ashkenazi pronunciation, *Bais Ya'akov*. The name, suggested by a man on the original committee that supported the school, was chosen because Jews familiar with traditional interpretations of the Bible immediately associate the phrase with women. *Exodus* 19:3 reads "Thus shall you say to the house of Jacob and declare to the children of Israel"; Rashi, citing a *midrash*, associates the "children of Israel"—or more literally, "sons of Israel"—with the Israelite men and the "house of Jacob" with the women. This verse is further associated with a verse in *Isaiah* (2:5) that became the school's motto: "O House of Jacob!/ Come, let us walk/By the light of the Lord."

Though the *rebbe* of Belz had given Sarah his blessing, he refused to give his Hasidim permission to send their daughters to her school. Soon, however, she received full support from the *rebbe* of Ger, whose adherents' daughters constituted the majority of her early

Portrait of Sarah Schenirer.

COURTESY OF BET YA'ACOV INSTITUTE, RABBI LEVINE SQUARE, JERUSALEM

students. A major *responsum* of Rabbi Israel Meir ha-Kohen, known as the *Hafetz Hayyim* from the title of his most famous work, gave systematic, ideological support for women's education. Sarah now had the support of the spiritual leader of eastern European Jewry, and several other Lithuanian rabbis expressed agreement. They argued that women who were born Jewish should be permitted to learn what was taught to non-Jewish women who planned to convert to Judaism. They also took into consideration the less isolated position of the traditional Jewish community in relation to the changes introduced by modern life.

In 1923, at her own initiative and from her own small funds, Sarah began to train teachers for the Beth Jacob schools. By 1925, there were twenty Beth Jacob schools, some at the high-school level. Sarah occasionally addressed large groups of women in other towns and encouraged them to found Beth Jacob schools for their daughters. During the summers Sarah organized courses outside Cracow, in the country, to train former students as teachers. By 1937, two hundred forty-eight Beth Jacob institutions existed in Poland, with an enrollment of thirty-five thousand, and even more schools had been established in Poland by the beginning of World War II, two years later. Sarah also started the Bnos (Daughters) Youth Organization for religious girls, since she realized that graduates of the Beth Jacob elementary schools needed support from their peers.

Sarah's educational movement grew not only because of the perceived need for schools like those she founded, but also because of her personality. Sarah's pupils were moved by her piety, sincerity, and integrity. Cheerful, charismatic, possessing a sense of humor, she was loved and revered by her students.

Not much is known about her personal life. It appears, from her obituary, that Sarah was married to a man who was less observant and from whom she eventually was divorced, and that she married a second time in her later years. After a brief illness, she died in 1935 in a Vienna hospital at age fifty-two.

Beth Jacob schools were founded in other countries, including Palestine, before World War II; there, teachers' training colleges were begun in Tel Aviv and Jerusalem. During World War II, the Nazis destroyed many of the Beth Jacob schools in Europe. After the war, however, the network was resurrected, particularly in the United States, but the emphasis of the schools had shifted from adapting Jewish tradition to modern circumstances to defending Jewish tradition from modernity.

Sarah's collected writings, translated into Hebrew from the original Yiddish, were published in Tel Aviv in the late 1950s. Schenirer's last testament read in part:

> My dear girls, you are going out into the great world. Your task is to plant the holy seed in the souls of pure children. In a sense, the destiny of Israel of old is in your hands.
>
> Be strong and of good courage. Don't tire. Don't slacken your efforts. You have heard of the Hasid who came to his rabbi and said joyfully, "Rabbi, I have finished the whole Talmud." "What has the Talmud taught you?" asked the rabbi. "Your learning is fine but your practical task is the main thing."

The Haganah Is Organized

1920

The Haganah, the Jewish armed forces in Palestine, was founded in response to the unprovoked Arab attack on Tel Hai in March 1920 and the assault on Jewish Jerusalem in April of that year. These events made clear that the Jews in Palestine required a new, better-organized system of self-defense controlled by a central Jewish authority. The Haganah eventually developed into the defense force of the state of Israel.

As early as 1907, the Jews in Palestine organized a small defense organization, initially known as Bar Giora and later called Ha-Shomer (the Guard). Ha-Shomer's defense efforts marked the first time in the twentieth century that the Jews in Palestine organized themselves systematically against Arab violence. The members of this early Jewish militia were both soldiers and farmers. They stood watch over remote, isolated outposts situated dangerously close to hostile Arab populations. The members of the militia viewed their defense tasks as a personal mission undertaken for the benefit of an entire nation. With the outbreak of World War I, Ha-Shomer went underground and supported the Jewish Legion, organized within the British army, as the best means of defense for the Yishuv—the Jewish community in Palestine. At the end of World War I, however, when Palestine became a British Mandate under the League of Nations, the British Mandatory government prevented Palestinian Jews from bearing arms and thus made organized Jewish self-defense all but impossible. Ha-Shomer was in a state of fatigue and near collapse, and its leaders urged the British Military Occupation Force to help in Ha-Shomer's revival.

During the years after World War I, Arab attacks against the Yishuv increased in intensity. In 1920, Captain Joseph Trumpeldor, a Jewish immigrant who had been an officer in the Russian army, fell, with his followers, defending Tel Hai in Upper Galilee against Arab marauders, and anti-Jewish Arab riots occurred throughout the Yishuv.

During the 1920 Arab riots, Vladimir (Ze'ev) Jabotinsky, founder of the Revisionist movement in Zionism, organized an abortive self-defense effort in the hope of reviving Ha-Shomer, but it was suppressed by the British.

The Jews of the Yishuv felt that the British had been far too lenient toward the instigators of the 1920 riots and had little confidence that the British Mandatory government would provide them with sufficient protection against Arab attacks. They realized that they needed to look to their own defense and that they had to find a way to train and to acquire arms. They also realized that it was no longer sufficient for the Jews simply to guard the agricultural settlements; the cities, too—indeed, the entire Yishuv—required defense.

The Haganah (defense) was formed in 1920 at a conference of the Achdut ha-Avodah (Workers' Unity) party, which accepted Ha-Shomer's resolution to disband and appointed a special committee to establish a more broadly based self-defense organization. Defense now became a responsibility of the Yishuv as a whole, along with its other tasks in the economic, political, and cultural fields. From the start, it was understood that the Haganah was subordinate to the political arm of the Yishuv, the Jewish Agency.

The Haganah was forced to operate in total secrecy.

A Haganah cavalry patrol defending the Jewish settlements during the 1938–1939 riots.

According to a 1936 Haganah memo, the Jews "came to realize that it was impossible to depend upon the British authorities. . . and that the Yishuv must create an independent force, completely free of foreign authority," in short, an underground.

After the earliest months of Achdut ha-Avodah sponsorship, the Haganah came under the supervision of Histadrut. At first, it operated out of a single room in Histadrut House in Tel Aviv; later, it had two additional administrative centers, in Jerusalem and Haifa. Most of its leaders were Histadrut officials, and its membership came largely from Socialist ranks. Nor was this Socialist orientation to be changed, especially after 1936, when the Zionist Congresses, like the Yishuv as a whole, had a majority of Labor Zionists. Nevertheless, the ideo-

logical persuasion of the Haganah rarely influenced its efficiency or the loyalty it claimed from most of the Yishuv.

The riots of 1929 were the critical turning point for Jewish self-defense in Palestine. It became clear that what was required was to train not merely a small cadre of Jewish defenders but all the able-bodied Jewish youth of Palestine. Newer, more modern weapons were also needed. David Ben-Gurion and Chaim Arlosoroff, both leaders of the Yishuv, were determined, therefore, to give increased priority to Haganah activities and to strengthen the Haganah in both numbers and arms. When they first asked the Zionist Congress for more funds in 1931, their appeal failed, largely because the General Zionists in the Congress objected to giving Socialists a monopoly over the Yishuv's defense. By 1936, however, the Haganah was receiving more funding from the Jewish Agency. Officers' training courses were organized, weapons purchased illegally from Europe were smuggled in, and secret armories were constructed to produce lightweight weapons. In 1936, Haganah membership numbered twenty-five thousand.

The Haganah participated actively in the establishment of every new Jewish settlement. Its task was especially challenging between 1936 and 1939, when it followed a policy of self-restraint in response to Arab attacks. Settlements were put up quickly,

Haganah members in training during February 1948.

sometimes in the course of a day. The night before Jews took possession of land for a new settlement, a watchtower was assembled nearby. The outer wall of the settlement, protected by barbed wire, went up first, and by early afternoon, the entire settlement would be functioning, often with chickens and cows in the midst of the settlers.

The Haganah supported clandestine Jewish immigration to Palestine up to the outbreak of World War II in Europe. During World War II, it played a dual role. On the one hand, it supported Jewish units in the British army—and developed networks within them for the secret acquisition of arms. On the other, it built up its own defense forces in Palestine, where it faced hostility from British authorities.

With the founding of the state of Israel, the Haganah abandoned its underground character. Prime Minister David Ben-Gurion's Order of the Day of May 13, 1948, transformed the Haganah into the defense force of the new state.

Anielewicz Leads Warsaw Ghetto Uprising

MAY 8, 1943

One of the great Jewish heroes of the Holocaust, Mordecai Anielewicz became a powerful symbol of Jewish resistance because of his stand against the Nazis in the Warsaw Ghetto. As commander of the Warsaw Ghetto uprising, he represented Jewish opposition not only to the Nazis but to tyranny in general.

Mordecai Anielewicz was born to a Jewish working-class family in Wyszków, Poland, in 1919, and grew up in Warsaw. While still very young, Anielewicz joined the Socialist Zionist movement, Ha-Shomer Ha-Tsa'ir, and eventually became one of its leaders. On September 7, 1939, a few days after the Germans invaded Poland, he fled Warsaw, as did many other leaders of the Zionist youth movement. Anielewicz found his way to the Soviet-occupied part of Poland and tried to reach Romania, from where he intended to travel to Palestine. He was captured by the Soviet authorities, however, and was imprisoned.

Upon his release from jail toward the end of 1939, he returned to Warsaw, stopping en route at several Jewish communities to determine how they were faring under the mounting Nazi threat. He stayed in Warsaw only briefly and went on to Vilna, where a number of Zionist-oriented youth lived. Some of these Zionists, like Anielewicz, were determined to reach German-occupied Poland to organize and lead a resistance movement. Anielewicz conducted seminars, established an underground press, and attempted to obtain weapons.

The Nazis had virtually imprisoned hundreds of thousands of Jews behind the walls of ghettos in many Pol-

A portrait of Mordecai Anielewicz.

ish cities, including Warsaw. In the summer of 1942, Anielewicz persuaded the Jewish political leaders of the Warsaw Ghetto that military resistance, however irra-

Nazis round up Jewish survivors of the Warsaw Ghetto for the journey to the concentration camps as the ghetto burns behind them.

tional it seemed, provided the best chance of survival. Speed counted, since the Nazi "resettlement" of the Jews had reached a new height. Reports filtered into the ghetto that Jews in the German-held parts of the Soviet Union were being murdered.

That news spurred Anielewicz to establish an armed Jewish underground. His Jewish allies employed strong-arm tactics to raise funds among the few well-off Jews in the Warsaw Ghetto. With the money, the resistance purchased a few revolvers and hand grenades from Italian army deserters and from members of the Polish Communist Party. The weapons were then smuggled into the Ghetto.

The first underground resistance group, known as the Antifascist Bloc, was prevented from taking action when some of its Communist members were arrested. The Bloc was quickly dissolved, to be succeeded by the Jewish Fighting Organization (JFO). Learning that only sixty

thousand Jews remained in Warsaw and that the JFO was in a weakened condition, Anielewicz became the JFO commander early in 1943 and vowed to strengthen the group of Jewish fighters. He recruited seven hundred fifty fighters and was able to obtain nine rifles, fifty-nine pistols, and a few hand grenades. On January 18, during the Nazi deportation drive, the initial armed clashes between Germans and Jews took place. In one brief battle, during which many Jewish fighters were killed, some of Anielewicz's own fighters saved his life. For a while, the Jewish fighters operated under a pleasant illusion: The German deportation of Jews ceased temporarily, and the Jews attributed the halt to the achievements of Anielewicz's army. That reputation reinforced the twenty-four-year-old Anielewicz's military leadership inside the Ghetto. Pretending to build air-raid shelters, Anielewicz and his Jewish fighters constructed dugouts that were connected to the Warsaw sewer system. They built bunkers as well, urgently preparing for full-scale armed resistance.

On Passover eve, April 19, 1943, the Germans began their final deportation effort in Warsaw. Relying upon the Waffen-SS, they were determined to destroy the Ghetto. To ward off the Nazis, the armed Jewish underground, under Anielewicz's command, used all available weapons. The fighting began in the streets, then shifted to the bunkers. On April 23, Anielewicz wrote what turned out to be his final letter:

> What happened is beyond our wildest dreams. Twice the Germans fled from our ghetto. One of our companies held out for forty minutes and the other, for over six hours. . . . I have no words to describe to you the conditions in which the Jews are living. Only a few chosen ones will hold out; all the rest will perish sooner or later. The die is cast. In the bunkers in which our comrades are hiding, no candle can be lit for lack of air. . . . The main thing is: My life's dream has come true; I have lived to see Jewish resistance in the ghetto in all its greatness and glory.

Inspired by Anielewicz's example, a courageous Jewish resistance, however weak and ineffective in the long run, managed to make the battle far more difficult for the Germans than the resistance fighters had hoped. The Jews managed to kill sixteen Germans and wound eighty-five others.

On May 8, one hundred twenty Jewish resistance fighters, the last major group of Jewish fighters in the Ghetto, were holed up at 18 Mila Street. The Nazis mounted a heavy offensive. Though the building entrance was bombed, the Jews were unharmed and took shelter in a bunker. When the Nazis learned that the Jews were unharmed, they began drilling into the bunker overhead in order to shoot at the Jews from closer range. Anielewicz ordered guards to establish themselves at the five entrances of the bunker. The drilling went on for another two hours. The Jews waited. Someone called out in Yiddish to the Jewish fighters that they should come out and surrender. The Germans fired shots and threw hand grenades into a tunnel leading to the bunker. A Nazi soldier entered the tunnel. He was shot and killed by the Jewish defenders. The Nazis retreated.

Drilling resumed. Surprised to be still alive, Mordecai Anielewicz made a solemn promise: He would die in this bunker, fighting the Nazis. The Nazis reiterated their demand for surrender. It was rejected. The Nazis fired gas through a hole that had been drilled into the bunkers, forcing a few Jewish fighters to crawl toward the exits. They sought to surrender. Anielewicz would not. He remained behind to talk to the remaining fighters about their options, none of them good.

One of the Jews, Aryeh Wilner, proposed suicide for no other reason than to prevent the Nazis from taking them alive. Another Jewish fighter, Michael Rozenfeld, suggested that they should die killing Nazis. Escaping and fighting were no longer realistic options, however. They could either die by suicide or die by gas. Anielewicz was against suicide. He wanted to believe that somehow the Jews might survive the gas. He ordered his "soldiers" to wet pieces of cloth in a puddle under the water tap and to cover their faces but his attempt did not work.

Anielewicz died, along with one hundred of his fighters. The remaining Jewish fighters held out for another eight days. Altogether, several thousand Jews died in the Warsaw Ghetto resistance.

Kibbutz Yad Mordekhai, near the Gaza Strip along the Mediterranean coast, is named after Mordecai Anielewicz.

"Sonneborn Institute" Is Founded

June 1945

With great secrecy, American Jews went to work to obtain all kinds of military equipment for the fight that Palestinian Jews planned to wage in defense of their national homeland. The work was dangerous, and sometimes those who were involved were arrested, but fortunately, American officials behaved leniently when confronted with the American Jewish arms effort. While the American aid helped turn the tide in favor of the new state of Israel in its war for independence against the Arabs, the paucity of Jewish arms made the war touch and go throughout.

In June of 1945, a few weeks after Germany had surrendered, ending the European phase of World War II, David Ben-Gurion arrived without fanfare in New York. Ben-Gurion, chairman of the Jewish Agency Executive, anticipated that the Palestine question would be resolved now that the war was over—and that it would be resolved in Palestine itself. He intended to make his military preparations well in advance.

With the help of Henry Montor, executive vice-president of the United Jewish Appeal, Ben-Gurion was put in touch with Rudolf Sonneborn, a wealthy industrialist and scion of an affluent German-Jewish family. He had become committed to Zionism in 1919, when Louis Brandeis first interested him in the movement. In ensuing years, Montor had become a generous contributor to Zionist causes.

The destiny of Palestinian Jewry would depend on the outcome of an armed struggle, the future Israeli prime minister told Sonneborn, and Ben-Gurion asked Sonneborn to harness the brainpower, energy, and skills of American Jewry to assure a Jewish victory in Palestine.

Sonneborn reacted enthusiastically to the opportunity to be of service. Without delay he summoned sixteen of his most trusted confidants, all wealthy fellow Zionists, to a secret meeting with Ben-Gurion in Sonneborn's luxurious New York duplex.

The meeting lasted eleven hours. A confrontation with the Arabs was inevitable if the Jews were to establish a national home in Palestine. The Jews in Palestine had only two years to prepare their defenses. Once Japan surrendered, immense quantities of surplus military equipment would become available in the United States at bargain prices. Ben-Gurion's military and intelligence advisors, at his side, then sketched the methods by which equipment could be obtained and smuggled into Palestine.

Ben-Gurion invited his listeners to organize themselves into an American arm of the Haganah—the Yishuv's clandestine defense arm—and discreetly to enlist others in the secret fund-raising and weapons-purchasing effort. Everyone present agreed to help.

Soon afterward, the "Sonneborn Institute" opened its headquarters in a suite of unmarked offices on West Fifty-seventh Street. Branches were opened in other major North American cities. Each of the original group recruited new members on his own. Soon a network of volunteer committees throughout the United States and Canada was linked with the Sonneborn Institute. All functioned outside normal Zionist channels and United Jewish Appeal activities and without their knowledge.

As a result of the Sonneborn Institute, military equipment was secretly acquired, dismantled, and its parts

Teddy Kollek headed a special unit that handled the purchase of ships and equipment.

no lack of illegalities, from petty to international. And every second the dream of a Jewish state was in jeopardy."

Among Kollek's activities was a special unit that handled purchasing ships and equipment and recruiting personnel to transport the ships to Europe, where Jewish immigrants (mostly in southern France and southern Italy), were gathered up and taken to Palestine. The Americans could have construed these efforts as illegal in light of their embargo against exporting war material and recruiting soldiers for a foreign country.

Running shipping operations from Los Angeles was Hank Greenspun, a New York-born newspaper publisher who had fought in World War II, who organized the loading of boats with war material from California, sending the ships through Mexico, Hawaii, and the Philippines. South American governments bought tanks and innumerable other items and shipped them to Palestine. Army surplus, including blankets, tents, and canteens, were purchased through American dealers.

Within the first half year of the operation, eight million dollars was raised for the purchase of machinery and blueprints for Palestinian Jewry's underground munitions industry.

Based in their own inconspicuous office at the Hotel Empire on Broadway and Sixty-third Street, a group of Palestinian Jews fanned out across the United States, scouring scrap-metal yards and used-machinery lots, purchasing whatever they could.

The Sonneborn Institute arranged for the goods to be put into storage, usually in "safe" warehouses in Brooklyn and elsewhere. Much of the equipment was dismantled and its parts shipped separately to Palestine as "industrial machinery."

The Institute recruited young people, often college students who normally would not arouse suspicion, to conceal arms in buildings, factories, even private homes. Every once in a while they were discovered and arrested. J. Edgar Hoover, director of the Federal Bureau of Investigation, was approached and informed of the

shipped to Palestine as "textile machinery." Yet, hidden as they were in underground kibbutz warehouses, the parts could not be assembled until the British left Palestine.

Teddy Kollek, who repesented the Haganah in America between 1947 and 1948, described his work in his memoir *For Jerusalem: A Life* (1978). It touched on experiments in weapon production, chemistry, and physics; . . . dealings with factories and junkyards, liaisons with spies, mobsters, movie moguls, statesmen, bankers, professors, industrialists, and newspaper men; and

Institute's activities. Fortunately for the Jewish cause, he proved surprisingly sympathetic. He agreed to be "flexible" so long as violations of federal weapons export laws were not flagrant.

The scope of the secret arms project expanded dramatically in the autumn of 1947. Full-scale war loomed in Palestine. An air-transport service was urgently required. The key American recruit was Adolf Schwimmer, a wartime Ferry Command pilot and more recently a Trans World Airlines flight engineer. He organized the "Schwimmer Air Freight Company" and through dummy corporations began to buy and overhaul mothballed military transport planes.

The headquarters of the operation was a private airport in Burbank, near Los Angeles. In ensuing months, ten transport planes and three heavy bombers would be flown directly to Palestine from the airstrip. The bulk of their cargo was munitions secured in different parts of the world by Schwimmer and his contacts. One of those contacts, Hank Greenspun, organized staging areas in Nicaragua, Panama, and the Dominican Republic. By the end of 1948, seven months after the state of Israel had been established, some fifty military planes—transports, trainers, bombers, and fighters—had been flown directly, or crated and shipped, from these countries to Israel. As a rule, the transports and bombers were loaded with extra equipment and flight crews, and their first stop was Zatec, Czechoslovakia. Here the sympathetic Czech government had placed an entire airstrip at the disposal of the Zionists.

Planes arrived in Palestine from other countries as well, including bombers and fighters often flown illegally by veterans of the Allied air forces from Britain and the United States. For each plane that crashed or was detained en route, two others landed safely. The American Jewish effort to secure arms for the Jews of the Yishuv played a key role in the War of Independence and in making sure that once the new state of Israel was established it would have the military might to guarantee its survival.

King David Hotel Is Bombed

JULY 22, 1946 • 12:37 P.M.

> *Just after midday on July 22, 1946, members of the Irgun, the Jewish underground military organization in Palestine under the leadership of future Israeli prime minister Menachem Begin, set the fuses for the bombs that were planted in the basement of the King David Hotel in Jerusalem—the city's most famous hotel and site of British administration headquarters. At 12:37 P.M. the bombs went off in one of the most spectacular military actions of the period as the Irgun aimed at ending British control over Palestine and speeding the day when a Jewish state would be created on Palestinian soil.*

The southern wing of the six-story luxury King David Hotel served as headquarters for the British administration in Palestine. To the Irgun, the Jewish underground military organization, the headquarters, as the nerve center of the hated "foreign regime," was a worthy target.

Menachem Begin, head of the Irgun, believed that the Haganah, the Jewish defense organization of the Yishuv, would approve his plan to blow up the King David Hotel. Since the British had a large number of intelligence documents belonging to the Haganah, there was every reason to assume that the Haganah would approve of the target.

Begin raised the idea with Haganah leaders Moshe Sneh and Israel Galili, describing the planned attack as possibly the largest against the British to this date. Moshe Sneh replied affirmatively in a note: "You are to carry out as soon as possible the hotel . . . Inform us of timing." Begin was ecstatic.

He instructed Yisrael Levi, the eighteen-year-old

The southern wing of the King David Hotel is totally destroyed by the 1946 bombing.

commander of the Irgun's operations in Jerusalem, to prepare for the attack. Levi took his deputy and two young women to the La Regence Cafe at the hotel for surveillance work. Levi assigned others to learn the routines of employees in and out of the hotel.

Irgun operations officer Amichai Paglin met with his Haganah counterparts. Yitzhak Sadeh, commander of the Palmach, the Haganah's striking force, insisted there be no loss of life. Paglin minimized the problem, knowing that the British normally evacuated a building in plenty of time once notified that explosives had been planted. When Paglin said he would plan on forty-five minutes between notification and the explosion, Sadeh said that was too much time—the British would be able to remove documents along with its people. They settled on a half-hour.

Begin ordered his men to carry out the action on July 22nd. That morning, the Irgun forces who were planning the attack gathered at a Jerusalem synagogue for a briefing. Nobody knew the target. Paglin's presence suggested that the target was very important. The plan was for the Irgun's assault force to gain entry to the ground-floor cafe through the service entrance; the men would disguise themselves as Arabs who were bringing the daily delivery of milk.

Once inside, the force would overcome the kitchen staff, place them under guard, then open the door to let colleagues in. Anyone in the cafe would be forced to join the kitchen staff. In the meantime milk churns, carrying the explosives, would be rolled one hundred fifty feet into the hotel basement and placed next to the main pillars supporting the hotel's upper stories. Each churn had a detonation mechanism. Paglin, who had designed the mechanisms, insisted that warning signs be placed alongside the churns to prevent anyone from mistakenly trying to dismantle them.

Levi, as mission commander, conducted the briefing unaware that his deputy—German-born Heinrich Rheinhold—was in fact a British plant. The briefing over, Reinhold asked permission to leave for a few moments. Though he did not suspect Rheinhold, Paglin refused the request. By now nervous and irritated, Rheinhold asked if he could at least phone a girlfriend. Again, Paglin told him that no one could leave. The other men assumed that Rheinhold was nervous in advance of the operation.

Near the middle of the day the assault force, dressed in Arab garb and appearing to be part of the hotel staff, brought the milk churns to the service entrance of the La Regence Cafe. Knocking on the outer door, they announced the delivery of the milk and were quickly let in.

Seconds later, fifteen Arab waiters, cooks, and cleaners were isolated in a side room and placed under guard. Meanwhile the demolition team moved the churns into place. Hearing a suspicious noise, a pair of armed British guards investigated, eventually realizing that something was amiss. One was killed with a machine-gun burst; the other was seriously wounded.

The Irgun commander set the detonators for thirty minutes and ordered his men to withdraw from the hotel. Arab employees were allowed to leave and told to depart quickly. Meanwhile, the backup team detonated a charge that made noise and smoke on the roadway outside the hotel, a ploy to deflect attention from the Irgun's route of retreat.

By 12:10 P.M. the assault force had left the hotel. One Irgun member, wounded by an Arab soldier during the escape, was taken by waiting taxi to a first-aid post in the Old City; he died there before the police could reach him.

The main entrance to the King David Hotel.

At a prearranged point, Levi waved to three women who then went to public phones. One called the King David Hotel to warn of the impending blast, one the nearby French consulate, and one the editorial office of the *Palestine Post*.

The *Palestine Post* and the French consulate phoned the British administration with the warning. Because the women did not identify themselves as members of the Irgun, no one knew who was behind the operation.

Though they had taken such warnings seriously in the past, the British chose to ignore this one. Sir John Shaw, secretary to the Palestine government, had

The King David Hotel as it stands today.

received the message and had plenty of time to order an evacuation of the premises, but he cockily pronounced to a police officer, "I don't accept orders from these Jews. I give the orders here."

At 12:37 P.M. the explosion went off. Everyone in Jerusalem heard the blast. Those near the hotel scurried for cover as the southern wing of the hotel collapsed into a pile of debris. Two hundred people were injured, half of them fatally. Of the one hundred dead British officials, fifteen were Jewish.

Immediately, a massive man-hunt for the perpetrators was begun. But the Irgun force had vanished. Paglin was on his way to Tel Aviv to report to Begin. When Begin opened his door to Paglin, the Irgun chief already knew how much damage had been caused, how many people had died. Begin knew something had gone wrong, but he had no way of knowing that the British secretary simply had refused to carry out an evacuation. Begin promised Paglin that the Irgun would stand behind him and his men.

When Paglin's men convened for a debriefing, Reinhold failed to show up, arousing suspicion that he had been caught and had begun talking about the operation to the British. Reinhold inflicted much damage on the Irgun. Within twelve hours of the attack on the King David Hotel, all of the Irgun's meeting places and members' homes were known to the Jerusalem police. When it was discovered that Rheinhold had left the country, the Irgun tried to track him down, by now convinced that he had been an inside man. After Israel attained statehood, Begin no longer had the appetite to find him and have him killed.

On the day after the attack, the Jewish Agency Executive, which, according to some sources, had no advance warning of the attack, issued a sharply worded condemnation that shocked Begin and his men. After all, the Haganah, which was associated with the Jewish Agency, had sanctioned the assault on the hotel, and the Irgun had not been responsible for the British failure to heed the warning.

British Capture Exodus 1947

> The story of the Exodus 1947, sailing from France for Palestine, forced away from the Promised Land by the British, is a sad and tragic symbol of the traumas and difficulties Jews faced after World War II in finding a safe shelter—specifically, in reaching what would become the new state of Israel. No other event was more poignant and disturbing than the plight of these forty-five hundred refugees who were turned away from port after port, forced to journey without a home in sight. The Exodus incident had a profound effect on international public opinion, reinforcing the British decision to leave Palestine.

Nothing so dramatized the plight of Jewish immigrants, desperately trying to reach Palestine after World War II, than the *Exodus 1947*.

The British retained a strong interest in limiting Jewish immigration to Palestine in order to demonstrate evenhandedness in policies toward Arabs and Jews; to have allowed unrestricted Jewish immigration would have angered the Arabs, clearly something the British did not want to do.

After the end of World War II and particularly in the six months preceding the events surrounding the *Exodus 1947*, the British had managed to keep the illegal traffic of European Jewish refugees trying to reach Palestine to a minimum.

Despite British efforts, eleven thousand "illegals" entered Palestine during the winter and spring of 1947. Under British and United Nations pressure, ships were not permitted to depart from European ports for Palestine. Yet several broke through the blockade, among them the *Exodus 1947*.

Israel Government Press Office

Small children disembark before the Exodus is deported from Haifa.

ISRAEL GOVERNMENT PRESS OFFICE

The Israeli flag waves above the Exodus.

The eighteeen-hundred-ton four-decker ship began its life as a small American Chesapeake Bay ferry. Although the British embassy tried to prevent its sailing, on July 18, 1947, the *President Garfield* slipped cable and set out from the French port of Setè. Once on the high seas, the crew hoisted the ship's blue and white flag with the Star of David and its true name: *Exodus 47*. Nothing more than leaking tubs, some ships like the *Exodus 47* broke up or foundered in severe storms.

Six British destroyers and one cruiser were waiting offshore of Setè. A British warship escorted the *Exodus* and its 4,550 passengers into Haifa harbor.

On the journey to Palestine, the immigrants were forced to endure much suffering: extreme overcrowding, hunger, thirst, and illness. Some refugees died. But the harshest ordeal was the frustration that so many of the immigrants were to confront at journey's end. Twelve miles outside Palestinian territorial waters, a British armada consisting of six destroyers and one cruiser, which had escorted the *Exodus* since it sailed from Setè, closed in on the ship for boarding.

A wild hand-to-hand struggle ensued—and suc-

ceeded for several hours—as the displaced persons tried to fight off the British boarding party. Eventually the British began using machine guns and tear gas bombs, killing three Jews and wounding one hundred others. Throughout the battle, a blow-by-blow account of events was being radioed to the headquarters of the Jewish forces in Tel Aviv; it was later rebroadcast throughout the world. It was only when the British started to ram the ship and threatened to sink it that the crew surrendered. To the immigrants' great sorrow and frustration, they were able to see the Promised Land but unable to set foot upon it.

Listing badly, the ferry was towed into Haifa Harbor. The ship's passengers were removed to three prison boats for deportation to Cyprus, an unpleasant prospect for the Jews since in the last year, twenty-six thousand Jews already had been packed onto that island, causing terrible overcrowding in its two internment camps. The Mossad, Israel's intelligence service, purposely planned to fill the camps to overflowing in order to call attention to the Jews' plight.

Instead of heading toward Cyprus, however, the three

ships headed for the French coast. British foreign secretary Ernest Bevin had decided to take revenge on the *Exodus* survivors for their insolent defiance by returning them to their port of origin, France. He was annoyed that the French had allowed the immigrants to leave France in the first place.

Shortly thereafter, on British transports that were essentially prison ships, the refugees were carried off to Marseilles. Once there, the Jews refused to disembark, save for a handful, the ill and pregnant among them.

Offering hospitality to the refugees, the French government also was prepared to provide medical care. Though the heat was suffocating and there was much illness including a contagion of rashes and boils, the Jews turned down the French proffer of help. Journalist Ruth Gruber gave an eyewitness account of their plight:

> Squeezed between a green toilet shed and some steel plates were hundreds and hundreds of half-naked people who looked as though they had been thrown together into a dog pound . . . Trapped and lost, they were shouting at us in all languages, shattering each other's words . . . The hot sun filtered through the grillwork, throwing sharp lines of light and darkness across the refugees' faces and their hot, sweaty half-naked bodies. Women were nursing their babies, old women and men sat weeping unashamed, realizing what lay ahead.

For three weeks the unfortunate passengers clung to their prison bars in the stifling August heat, refusing to disembark. Finally, the French government, concerned by the possibility of epidemics, ordered the vessel to depart. At this point the British Cabinet, during an emergency meeting, decided that all it could do was ship the Jews back to Germany, their original point of departure.

Two months after the start of their ill-fated journey, the refugees arrived in Hamburg. Some fifteen hundred of them refused to disembark. As the local German inhabitants watched in disbelief, the Jews were carried off the ship by British troops wielding clubs and hoses. On September 10, 1947 the displaced persons were transported on trains to British internment camps at Poppendorf and AmSatu. It was an ironic and dismal end to their journey. To every question the refugees gave the same response: *"Eretz Yisrael"* (the Land of Israel).

The plight of the refugees aboard the *Exodus* was widely reported throughout the world. Members of the United Nations Special Committee on Palestine (UNSCOP), an eleven-nation investigative board set up on May 13, 1947 to study the Palestine issue, were moved by the *Exodus 1947* episode as it developed. UNSCOP delegates had watched the ship's arrival at Haifa Harbor and had seen the wounded being brought ashore.

The group departed for Beirut on July 20. A week later, arriving in Geneva, the members voted to dispatch a subcommittee to refugee centers in Germany and Austria. There the visitors encountered a community of refugee Jews, some two hundred fifty thousand of them, who thought of little else but departing for Palestine.

The fate of the thwarted passengers of the *Exodus* weighed heavily on the UNSCOP members. The commission called for the withdrawal of the mandate granted to Great Britain by the former League of Nations in 1920 and for dividing the territory into two sovereign states: one Jewish, one Arab, with an internationalized Jerusalem. Once a sovereign Jewish state existed, Jewish immigrants could flock to its shores without being hindered by external parties such as the British.

The terrible moments of the *Exodus 1947* on the high seas were a crucial turning point in the Zionist struggle to achieve a Jewish homeland. For out of the UNSCOP report, which called for the creation of a Jewish state, came the partition agreement of November 29, 1947. This accord gave the Jews of Palestine the incentive to estabish their own state in May of 1948.

Arabs Invade New Jewish State

MAY 14–15, 1948 • 12 A.M.

Israeli Prime Minister David Ben-Gurion proclaimed the birth of the Jewish state at 4:30 P.M. on May 14, 1948, at a special session of the Jewish National Council in the Tel Aviv Museum. The council normally would have met in Jerusalem, but, because the Holy City was under siege, most of its leaders were in Tel Aviv. Egyptian air raids started that evening. The Arab invasion of Israel—armies from six Arab states—had begun.

At midnight on May 14–15 the British left Palestine, having decided that they had lost cotrol over a situation in which Jews and Arabs were in constant and increasingly violent conflict over possession of the Holy Land. Only eight hours after the historic announcement of Jewish statehood, expeditionary armies of six Arab states invaded Israel and attacked the new state.

From the north, Lebanese forces moved across the border; from the east came the Syrian army and Transjordan and Iraqi soldiers. The Egyptian air force attacked Tel Aviv, while Egyptian soldiers marched twenty-two miles south of Tel Aviv. Saudi Arabian soldiers fought under Egyptian command.

Sir John Bagot Glubb, the British commander of the Transjordanian Arab Legion, described his men as they moved through Amman on their way to the battle:

> It was a sultry May day, with a haze of dust hanging over the roads. In the city of Amman and in every village along the road the people were gathered, cheering and clapping wildly as each

Evacuating the wounded after the air attack.

ISRAELI GOVERNMENT PRESS OFFICE

unit drove past. The flat roofs and the windows were crowded with women and children, whose shrill cries and wavering trebles could be heard above the roar and rattle of the vehicles, and the cheering of the crowds of men beside the road. The troops themselves were jubilant, applauding and cheering in their trucks, and waving to the crowds. The vehicles were decorated with green branches and bunches of pink oleander flowers. "The procession," noted Glubb, "seemed more like a carnival than an army going to war."

Indisputably, the Arabs had a serious military advantage. As of May 12, the Haganah, the underground Jewish force that had been compelled to operate in extreme secrecy, had recruited only thirty thousand men and women. Though the Arab forces were not considerably larger, the Arabs had far greater firepower than the Jews. As sovereign states, they had no trouble acquiring arms. The Haganah possessed only small arms, a number of homemade armored cars, and several light training planes. With a striking strength of some twenty thousand soldiers, including a considerable number of women, the Haganah forces also had roughly the same number of militia assigned to defending Jewish settlements and villages.

In the earliest stages of the war, the greatest strength of the Jewish state was the reality that they were fighting for their homes, for their homeland.

When the last British soldier left on May 15, the naval blockade against Palestinian shores was lifted, and the Israeli fighting forces were free to import badly needed arms and ammunition from abroad. That is precisely what they did as quickly as possible. Israel's biggest supplier of all was Czechoslovakia. The Israelis managed to airlift seventy five-millimeter field guns, small tanks, Bren guns, and machine guns from the Czechs.

Still, the situation for the Israelis was bleak. As Abba Eban wrote in *My People: The Story of the Jews* (1968):

> Whoever surveyed the military position on May 14, 1948, was bound to look to the future with

This apartment building was damaged in the Egyptian air attack.

ISRAEL GOVERNMENT PRESS OFFICE

very grave concern. The question was whether the Jewish forces could withstand the four regular Arab armies—the Egyptian, Jordanian, Syrian, and Lebanese—now joining the battles. These were fresh, well-organized according to the pattern of regular armies, and were also well-equipped. Two of them possessed tank units. All of them had field artillery regiments. Three had air forces with fighter squadrons, and Egypt had a squadron of bombers. The Haganah was unable to match this impressive superiority of Arab arms. It had exactly four field guns, a single tank, and a single fighter plane plus a few private planes.

So perilous was the Jewish military position in those opening days of battle that on May 21, 1948, Yigael Yadin, operations officer of the Haganah, surveyed the military situation and the prospect of further Arab penetrations across Israel's border by grimly noting that Israel's plans to deal with the Arab invasion were simply that. "All our forces and all our arms—all of them—will have to be concentrated in those places which are likely to be battlefields in the first phase of the battle."

Yadin acknowledged that the other side enjoyed superiority in arms at the time, but Israel's prospects simply could not be judged on military considerations, arms against arms, units versus units, since the Israelis did not have sufficient quantities of arms or soldiers. "The problem," he suggested, "is to what extent our men will be able to overcome enemy forces by virtue of their fighting spirit, of our planning and our tactics. It has been found in certain cases that it is not the numbers and the formations which determine the outcome of battle, but something else. However, objectively speaking, there is no doubt that the enemy enjoyed a great superiority at this time."

Israel's air force, for example, could not compare with the Arab air forces, for as Yadin acknowledged, "We have no air force. The planes have not arrived yet . . . Their air force is a hundred and fifty times the size of ours . . . No other pilots would dare to take off in planes like ours." Summing up, he believed that his country's prospects of military success seemed "delicately balanced. Or—to be more honest—I would say that Arab superiority is considerable, if indeed their entire forces enter battle against us."

As it turned out, the Arab invasion failed to achieve its objective of defeating the Jews and the Israeli forces were able to hold off the Arabs. A truce was called in June 1948, but the fighting was renewed and continued, however sporadically, until early 1949, when negotiated cease-fires with most of the Arab countries effectively brought the fighting to a halt. On May 28, 1948, the Haganah had become the Israel Defense Forces.

Knesset Stormed Over Reparations Issue

January 7, 1952

One of the most burning debates in the early days of Israeli statehood was whether to accept German reparations for the Holocaust. There were many, especially Holocaust victims, who thought no amount of money could ever compensate for the crimes perpetrated by the Nazis. Yet other, more pragmatic, voices thought justice would be served, even if only in part by accepting the reparations and using the money to help build the Jewish state. The controversy boiled over on the day the Knesset was to decide the issue.

In 1945, on behalf of the Jewish Agency, Chaim Weizmann submitted a claim for financial reparations from Germany to the United States, the Soviet Union, Great Britain and France. The Allied Powers urged Israel to approach Germany directly with its demands. Despite their misgivings, and feeling there was no other choice, the Israeli government sent the request for reparations to West German chancellor Konrad Adenauer. On September 27, 1951 Adenauer told the Bundestag, the federal assembly of Germany, that he clearly recognized Germany's obligation to the Jewish people and the state of Israel.

Israel's opposition leader, Menachem Begin, who had lost his parents and brother in the Holocaust, did not want Israel to deal with the German people or government, even on the issue of reparations.

Prime Minister David Ben-Gurion, however, believed that Israel must be pragmatic. The considerable funds that German reparations could provide would be a significant contribution to Israel's economy. At the time Israel's economic situation was severely strained by massive immigration, a shortage of natural resources, and its underdeveloped industry. The aid it had received from the United States thus far was too little. Ben-Gurion was determined to pursue reparations. He said: "We must take care of our people, and what is more just than that we should be able to rehabilitate them and erect for them a home with the monies of those who bear moral responsibility for the loss of their property in Europe?" The debate over reparations reached its height in the early 1950s.

Menachem Begin and his Herut party sought to defeat the move to approve reparations from Germany. "If negotiation with Germany can happen, then anything is permissible in the state of Israel," Begin cried, speaking at a meeting held in Tel Aviv two days before the Knesset was to convene to ratify the agreement. Though tensions were high, the crowd was quiet.

On January 7, 1952, the Knesset was ringed with barbed wire and cordoned off by hundreds of policemen armed with nightsticks and tear gas grenades.

The Knesset convened in the knowledge that West Germany had already allocated one billion dollars to Israel, apart from personal compensation to be paid directly to the survivors of the Holocaust. Feelings were high enough to cause the recall of Knesset members from trips abroad for the controversial vote. On Begin's orders one member of Herut who had suffered a heart attack was brought into the parliament building on a stretcher.

Thousands of Herut members and various opponents to any agreement with Germany rallied near the Knesset building. As Ben-Gurion rose to tell the Knesset, "We will not allow the murderers of our nation also to be its

The Jerusalem Post *headline tells of the drama surrounding the Knesset storming.*

heirs," Begin addressed the crowd outside. In a voice that broke with emotion he told them:

> There is no sacrifice we will not make. We will be killed rather than let this come about. This will be a war for life or death. A Jewish government that negotiates with Germany can no longer be a Jewish government.
>
> When you fired a cannon at us, I gave an order—no! Today I gave an order—yes! . . . There is no German who did not kill our fathers. Every German is a Nazi. Every German is a murderer. Adenauer is a murderer.
>
> This will not be a short or cold war. Maybe we will go hungry for want of bread. Maybe we will again part from our families. Maybe we will go to the gallows. No matter."

Begin was close to tears as he stepped down and walked toward the Knesset to take part in the debate inside. The crowd menacingly followed.

As they approached the building, the police tried to stop them but were forced to give way to the angry stream of people. Police barricades were thrown to the ground, and the mob pelted the Knesset building with stones. The open space in front of the main doorway became a battleground. The wounded groaned. Protesters shouted. Police cursed. The sounds of police and ambulance sirens could be heard in the background.

Meanwhile, inside the debate continued in an atmosphere made even more tense by the bedlam outside. Knesset member Yochanan Bader of Begin's party ran in and screamed: "Gas against Jews! That's how you welcome reparations!" Indeed, some tear gas used by the guards at the door to try to keep the crowds at bay was seeping into the Knesset chamber.

Some protestors threw stones and broke windows high up in the walls of the chamber. Pieces of glass flew everywhere. Dust, smoke, and gas brought tears to the eyes of Knesset members.

The storm died down toward evening. The police had arrested hundreds of rioters, and scores of police and demonstrators were hospitalized. Begin ascended the Knesset podium and said: "I appeal to you at the last moment as a Jew to Jews, as the son of an orphaned nation, of a mourning nation. Stop! Don't do this thing—it's obscene! There has been nothing like this ever since we became a nation, and I'm trying to give you a way out . . . As a Jew I will resist! Go to the nation. Hold a referendum!"

When Begin spoke of the police behavior, Ben-Gurion retorted, "You are hooligans."

"You are a hooligan," Begin responded. There was an uproar. Begin was told that he would have to apologize to the Prime Minister before he would be allowed to continue, but Begin demanded a similar apology. "If I don't speak here, then no one will," he shouted.

The Knesset speaker declared the session closed, to be reconvened that evening, but Begin resumed speaking. "There are some things dearer than life—and this is a matter for which people are prepared to leave their families and go to war. There will be no negotiation with Germany! Nations have gone to the barricades on lesser issues. We are ready to do anything to prevent this."

Prime Minister Ben-Gurion, preparing for the worst—an insurrection against the government by Begin and those who opposed German reparations—then spoke. "A democracy knows how to defend itself against that; and if there is a need for defense, then it will be undertaken by the army and the police."

By a majority vote the Knesset decided to enter into negotiations to receive restitutions payments from Germany. The actual negotiations began at the end of March 1952.

Begin and other members of his party tried to prevent the start of the negotiations by asking for a mass meeting to take place in Tel Aviv. The demonstration was held on the eve of negotiations in late March and was the largest rally Israel had ever known, about 70,000 people gathered in one of the central squares of Tel Aviv. When talk of physical violence arose, Ben-Gurion had thousands of members of the professional unions and kibbutzim bussed into Tel Aviv rather than call out the police and army.

The two "warring" sides met face to face on the streets of Tel Aviv. Begin again called on the Prime Minister to stop all contact with Germany regarding reparations. Begin implored the crowd not to allow itself to be incited to violence.

Nonetheless, Knesset members assailed Begin for inciting people to violence.

He was suspended from taking part in Knesset activities for two weeks. Begin called the suspension an act of "moral and political cowardice." Begin never forgave the Germans. He and his party members continued to urge the public not to buy German goods.

The Israeli government continued to adapt to the policy of dealing with the new Germany. In 1965, it established diplomatic relations with West Germany.

Israelis Capture Adolf Eichmann

MAY 11, 1960 • 8 P.M.

On May 11, 1960 Israeli intelligence agents tracked down Adolf Eichmann, the architect of the Nazi Holocaust, in Buenos Aires, Argentina, where he was hiding with his family. He was smuggled out of the country and flown to Israel. There he stood trial and was executed for masterminding the killing of six million Jews during World War II.

The name Eichmann is the personification of evil. As the Nazi SS officer who conceived and carried out the program to exterminate European Jewry during World War II, Eichmann was known as "the great transport officer of death." In 1950 he managed to escape to Argentina, settling into a secret existence under the assumed name of Ricardo Klement, along with his wife Vera and his three sons. Israeli political and intelligence leaders considered the capture of Eichmann a top priority—if only they could discover his whereabouts.

The first solid information about Eichmann's hiding place came from a senior West German official, Dr. Fritz Bauer, chief prosecutor of Hesse province, himself a Jew; he had obtained the information from the West German secret service, which had learned of Eichmann's location during the interrogation of two agents of a Nazi escape organization.

Argentina had long protected Nazis, so asking for the extradition of Eichmann was not an option. Israeli Prime Minister David Ben-Gurion authorized the mission to capture Eichmann and bring him to Israel to stand trial.

After trailing the son of the man they suspected to

Adolf Eichmann in 1960.

be Eichmann, Israeli agents tracked the son to a house on Garibaldi Street in Buenos Aires. For some time they observed the habits of the family, seeking positive proof that the father was Adolf Eichmann. The final proof came on March 21, 1960 when they watched the Klements celebrating their silver wedding anniversary on the same day as Eichmann's wedding anniversary.

Isser Harel, head of Israel's intelligence services, arrived in Buenos Aires and developed the plan to capture Eichmann and fly him out of Argentina with forged papers. Thirty Israeli operatives rented "safe" houses as bases for the operation and a fleet of cars, which was exchanged constantly to avoid suspicion. If the plot failed, the political repercussions would be vast. The agents arranged for documents, plane tickets, visas, and health certificates.

The plan was for Eichmann to be flown out of Argentina on an El Al plane that would be going to Buenos Aires to drop off a delegation of Israelis attending celebrations in honor of Argentina's one hundred fiftieth year of independence.

On May 11 the Israelis were ready. At 7:34 P.M. two cars were parked on Garibaldi Street, one with its hood raised, as two men studied what seemed to be a breakdown. Another man hid on the floor of the back seat, ready to sprint out. About thirty yards away, near the other car, another man tried to figure out why his motor would not start. Eichmann's bus usually dropped him off at 7:40 P.M. The 7:40 bus pulled up, on time, but Adolf Eichmann was not on board. The agents worried that the presence of their cars might begin to arouse suspicion from the residents of Garibaldi Street.

At precisely 8:00 P.M. the next bus came; this time Eichmann was on it. He alighted from the bus, and began walking toward his house. Suddenly he was blinded by bright headlights. Two men tackled him. Panic-stricken, Eichmann let out a single scream. He was thrown into the back seat of the car, his head jammed between the knees of one of the Mossad men. Eichmann was bound and gagged. Dark goggles were placed over his eyes so he would not recognize his captors and so he would have no idea where he was being taken. He was covered with a blanket.

"If you make one move, you will be shot," a Mossad agent told him in German. An hour later, Eichmann lay blindfolded, dressed in pajamas, on a bed in a "safe" house elsewhere in the city, one leg shackled to the bed frame.

The Israelis took their time interrogating Eichmann. They wanted to be absolutely certain they had the right man.

Searching for his SS number tattooed in the usual place, just under the armpit, the agents found only a scar. Eichmann, obsequiously cooperating with his captors, explained that when he briefly was in American hands after the war he had tried to remove the number with a razor blade. All other identifying features matched Israeli records. The man admitted he was Eichmann. He told his captors his National Socialist Party membership number (889895) and his SS numbers (45326 and 63752), and in perfect Hebrew perversely he recited the Shema. He had learned Hebrew from a rabbi, Eichmann noted. Under guard, Eichmann remained in that room for a week. The agents were prepared to leave at once had they been discovered, but they were not. Isser Harel looked at Adolf Eichmann, surprised at how ordinary he seemed.

Eichmann was in a panic that his captors would shoot him. At one stage he refused to eat, fearing that the food had been poisoned. He insisted that someone else taste the food first. The agent whose job it was to cook Eichmann's daily diet of soup, eggs, and boiled chicken with mashed potatoes admitted that she was tempted to poison the prisoner's food.

The El Al plane was due to leave Buenos Aires on May 20. Harel was confident that Eichmann's family would avoid the police even after the kidnapping. To ask the police for help meant explaining why Ricardo Klement was someone in whom kidnappers might be interested. (Eichmann's family contacted hospitals, but, as Harel correctly predicted, not the police.) When the Eichmann family contacted other ex-Nazis, those families departed Argentina at once, fearing that they too would be captured. Most fled to Uruguay.

To make sure that Eichmann would be able to get on the El Al plane without causing suspicion, the Mossad team planted an agent supposedly suffering from brain damage after a fake accident, in a local hospital. The plan was for the Israeli "patient" to make slow, steady progress. When, on the morning of May 20th, he had recovered enough for doctors to release him, he was given proper medical papers and told he could fly home to Israel. Upon being released, the "patient" was replaced by Eichmann, dressed in an El Al airline uniform, and equipped with all the proper medical papers and photographs. Eichmann signed a document revealing his true identity and declaring that he was prepared to travel to Israel to stand trial there.

Drugged so that he would not know what was going on, Eichmann was kept conscious enough so that, as he

ISRAEL GOVERNMENT PRESS OFFICE

Eichmann stands trial in Jerusalem in 1961.

walked, he could be supported on either side by two men. Seated in the second car of a convoy of vehicles for the "air crew," Eichmann was driven to the staff entrance of the airport and was taken on board the plane without incident. Twenty-four hours after leaving Buenos Aires, the plane touched down at Lod Airport near Tel Aviv.

Isser Harel drove directly to the prime minister's office. "I have brought you a little present." Ben-Gurion was speechless. He had known that Harel was on Eichmann's trail but none of the details.

The next day Ben-Gurion addressed the Knesset: "I have to announce that a short time ago one of the greatest Nazi criminals was found by the Israeli secret service. Adolf Eichmann was responsible, together with other Nazi leaders, for what they called the 'Final Solution of the Jewish Problem—the extermination of six million European Jews. Adolf Eichmann is already under arrest in Israel, and shortly he will be brought to trial in Israel . . . "

Argentina lodged a complaint against Israel with the United Nations Security Council. The Israeli govern-

ment expressed regret for having violated Argentine law, resolving the diplomatic crisis that had arisen between the two countries when Eichmann's capture was announced. Western jurists and journalists questioned the legality of the kidnapping until Eichmann's trial began in April 1961.

Eichmann was defended by Dr. Robert Servatius, a German lawyer from Cologne who had represented some of the Nazi war criminals at the Nuremberg Trials. Attorney General Gideon Hausner was the chief prosecutor. During the five-month trial, the court heard over one hundred witnesses and studied more than sixteen hundred documents. Eichmann argued that he had only been following orders.

Found guilty of crimes against humanity, he was sentenced to death—the first and only death sentence to be passed in Israel. He appealed to the Israel Supreme Court, which dismissed his appeal in May 1962, and he was executed that month. The trial provided a dramatic opportunity for the Jewish state to remind a new generation of Israelis—and the world—about the horrors of the Holocaust.

World Learns of Israel's Nuclear Capability

December 19, 1960

For as long as Israel has possessed nuclear capability, it has denied having it. Nonetheless, numerous articles in the foreign press about Israel's acquisition of those capabilities have given Israel the reputation of being a nuclear power. That reputation has served Israel well since the 1950s and may be one reason why a number of Arab leaders, starting with Egyptian President Anwar Sadat in 1977, eventually sought peace agreements with the Israelis.

David Ben-Gurion, Israel's first prime minister, was a realist. He knew that the burgeoning state of Israel faced tremendous odds against survival: after all, neighboring Arabs states—Lebanon, Syria, Jordan, and Egypt—all wished to bring an end to the Jewish state.

To win the 1948 War of Independence, Israel required a whole array of armaments—from pistols to planes—and, in large measure, it was the acquisition of those armaments that turned the tide in favor of the Jewish state.

Yet, in the aftermath of that war, Ben-Gurion worried that a second Holocaust might befall the Jews. He knew that the Jews' military situation remained perilous. The Arabs had lost one war; but they could rearm and try again to defeat the state of Israel.

With the development of nuclear-weapons technology, Ben-Gurion thought it essential that Israel acquire a doomsday device—never to use, only to deter. And so he put his trusted political confidant, Shimon Peres, to the task. In late 1953, Peres, thirty years old, became director general of the Ministry of Defense. Peres teamed up with a scientist named Ernst David Bergmann, who became the scientific father of Israel's nuclear weapons program. Bergmann, a brilliant, German-born organic chemist, the son of a rabbi, served as chairman of Israel's Atomic Energy Commission, starting in 1953. Prior to that he was scientific director of the Weizmann Institute of Science.

Ben-Gurion, Peres, and Bergmann had a great deal of trouble convincing other Israeli officials that the Jewish state needed nuclear weapons. These officials considered the bomb too expensive, too reminiscent of the gassing of Jews in the Holocaust. Was it not immoral, these critics argued, for Israel, whose citizens had been the victims of mass slaughter, to build a weapon of mass destruction? Then, too, how would Israel ever keep the device a secret? Finally, given the fact that Israel was trying to cultivate warm relations with the United States, would an Israeli bomb not imperil that association?

Answering these questions was not easy. Yet, during the early 1950s Israel went ahead in secret to develop the best nuclear program it could. Israeli scientists already had gone abroad to study the new fields of nuclear energy and nuclear chemistry. Israel engaged in a joint research program with the new French Atomic Energy Commission.

By 1953, researchers at the Weizmann Institute had pioneered a new process for creating heavy water, essential to modulate a nuclear chain reaction; they also devised a more efficient means of extracting uranium from phosphate fields. Two years later, Washington helped finance and fuel a small nuclear reactor for research, located at Soreq, south of Tel Aviv. Ernst Bergmann's dream of building Israeli nuclear power plants was sincere, but it also provided a solid cover for his plan to develop the atomic bomb.

The major turning point for Israel came just before the 1956 Sinai Campaign. Egypt had been receiving military aid from the Soviets, and Israel feared that once again it was in mortal danger. Just six weeks before the war broke out, Israel sought help from the French in trying to build a bomb.

When the war occurred, Israel hoped that it would be permitted to minimize the Egyptian military threat as much as possible by occupying newly conquered Egyptian territory—until Egypt was sincere about making peace with the Israelis. But America intervened, forcing Israel to retreat from the Sinai Peninsula and the Gaza Strip. There was extreme disappointment in Israel, but the highly select number of Israelis who were part of Israel's secret effort to build a bomb were encouraged, for it was increasingly clear that Israel needed it.

Israel planned to build a nuclear reactor in Dimona, a town in the heart of the Negev. Peres had no difficulty convincing Ben-Gurion, who had a passion for the Negev, that the reactor should be located there. The Israelis planted large trees to block the view of would-be photographers and had perimeter patrols stationed around the site.

Hundreds of French engineers and technicians began pouring into the Negev in 1957. Requiring numerous workers, the Dimona plant hired many of the most skilled Israeli scientists and technicians. None of them were permitted to say what kind of work they did. No one ever mentioned the bomb in written messages. The presence of twenty-five hundred French citizens and special French schools in Beersheba, the largest town in the vicinity of Dimona, aroused some attention. By early 1960 the reactor at Dimona was taking shape.

Military attachés of the various foreign embassies in Tel Aviv reported the French presence in Beersheba to their superiors, and there were a number of rumors that they were building a nuclear weapon, but no one could prove what the French engineers were actually doing. To protect their work, it was said that the French simply were involved in seawater desalinization or agricultural research. Some described the factory in Dimona as a manganese processing plant. The Americans were told that it was an agricultural research facility, at other times that it was a chemical plant.

The stories were never challenged. No one had sufficient proof. The Israelis engaged in secret fund-raising abroad. The Committee of Thirty—wealthy Jews who were asked to quietly raise money for the "special weapons" program—was formed in 1960. Some forty million dollars was raised. The overall cost, however, was hundreds of millions of dollars annually. The Israeli government underwrote the rest.

Reporter John Finney broke the story on December 19, 1960 on page one of *The New York Times*, to wit that Israel, with the aid of the French, was building a nuclear reactor to produce plutonium. The story indicated that American officials were annoyed, having been kept in the dark by both France and Israel.

By December the dome of the reactor had become visible from nearby roads in the Negev and could be photographed by military attachés. On December 21, Ben-Gurion publicly described to the full membership of the Knesset what was being built: a twenty-four-megawatt reactor "dedicated entirely to peaceful purposes."

The reactor went critical—that is, began a sustained chain reaction—sometime in 1962 with no significant problems. It could operate at more than seventy megawatts, far greater than the twenty-four megawatts publicly acknowledged by the Israeli government.

By mid-1964, the reactor had been functioning for nearly two years, and the reprocessing plant, with its remote-controlled laboratories and computer-driven machinery, was now ready to start producing weapons-grade plutonium from the reactor's spent uranium fuel rods. Meanwhile, Israeli leaders, including Ben-Gurion and Moshe Dayan, were dropping hints that Israel might be developing nuclear weapons but would never confirm the reality.

According to Seymour M. Hersh, writing in his 1991 book *The Samson Option: Israel's Nuclear Arsenal and American Foreign Policy*, sometime early in 1968, Dimona finally was ordered into full-scale production and began turning out four or five warheads a year—there were more than twenty-five bombs in the arsenal by the 1973 Yom Kippur War.

There is no evidence that the Israeli cabinet ever made a formal decision to build nuclear weapons at Dimona. Myths surrounded the program. One had it that the first warhead had a phrase in English and Hebrew welded to it: "Never again."

Israel's secrecy surrounding its nuclear-weapons program alienated a number of American leaders, especially President John F. Kennedy. Yet, the Israelis decided to swallow American concerns. Whatever criticism was thrown their way was worth enduring so long as Israel could keep the bomb.

(All information in this chapter is derived from non-Israeli sources.)

Brother Daniel Denied Israeli Citizenship

NOVEMBER 19, 1962

> With the founding of the state of Israel in 1948, the question of who is a Jew turned into one of the most perplexing and controversial ones to resolve. Even after the state's founding, for the first ten years, religious and secular authorities avoided a confrontation over the definition of who is a Jew. It was only on March 13, 1962, when a Carmelite friar named Brother Daniel petitioned the Israeli Supreme Court to let him settle in the country under the Israeli Law of Return, that the battle began in earnest over who could—and could not—be considered Jewish. While the Israeli Supreme Court's decision, rejecting Brother Daniel's claim, did more to resolve the question of who was not a Jew than who was, it did spark the debate in Israel that would become largely political and that would last to the present day.

Oswald Rufeisen, who would later become Brother Daniel, had been born to Jewish parents in Poland in 1922. He was an ardent Zionist as a youngster. During the German occupation of Poland in World War II, he became separated from his parents and posed as a Silesian Christian, helping hundreds of Jews, before escaping and hiding, disguised as a nun, in a convent. He converted to Christianity in 1942 and three years later joined the Carmelite order of monks in Poland, becoming Brother Daniel. He hoped to serve the order in the new state of Israel, but it was only after he waived his Polish citizenship in 1958 that he was permitted to settle in Israel, entering the country on an Israeli travel document. He sought Israeli citizenship under the Law of Return, declaring that he was of "Christian religion and Jewish nationality."

The Ministry of Interior declined his request, saying it did not recognize such a dichotomy.

On March 16, 1962, Brother Daniel petitioned the Israeli Supreme Court, hoping to reverse the Interior Ministry's decision.

Both secular and orthodox Jewish forces in Israel hoped that the high court would try to resolve the question of whether Jewish nationality and religion are the same. It was a sticky issue raised in modern times by the creation of the state of Israel, which was being forced to resolve definitions of Jewish identity that had in the past been avoided.

Indeed, for the first ten years of statehood, Israel dealt with issues of Jewish identity through administrative directives, holding that no one who subscribes to a different religion may be registered as a Jew either in nationality or religion. That of course was the basis for the Interior Ministry's rejection of Brother Daniel's claim. Such a view had yet to be codified in Israeli civil law, however. That vacuum led inevitably to the Israeli Supreme Court's decision to wrestle with and try to resolve the Jewish identity issue once and for all.

Brother Daniel, a short, bearded man, appeared before the Supreme Court in brown habit and sandals, arguing, "My religion is Catholic, but my ethnic origin is and always will be Jewish. I have no other nationality. If I am not a Jew what am I? I did not accept Christianity to leave my people. It added to my Judaism. I feel as a Jew."

Brother Daniel's plea was decided on November 19, 1962, when the Supreme Court handed down its decision.

It ruled four to one against him, insisting that a Jew

who had voluntarily converted to Christianity could not be considered a Jew under the Law of Return, effectively dismissing his claim that someone could remain a Jew in nationality even after freely choosing to convert to Catholicism.

Justice Moshe Silberg, delivering the majority opinion, posed the problem this way: "Once more the question must be asked, what is the ordinary Jewish meaning of the term 'Jew,' and does it include a Jew who has become a Christian?" His reply? "The answer to this question is, in my opinion, sharp and clear—a Jew who has become a Christian is not deemed a 'Jew.'"

Supporting Silberg's view was Justice Moshe Landau, who emphasized the strong link between the religious and national components: "The meaning of this law cannot be severed from the source of the past from which its content is derived, and in these sources nationalism and religion are inseparably interwoven." A Jew who changes his religion "ceases to be a Jew in the national sense . . . He has denied his national past, and can no longer be fully integrated into the organized body of the Jewish community as such. By changing his religion, he has erected a barrier between himself and his brother Jews."

As for Brother Daniel's suggestion that nonrecognition of his Jewish nationality would mean turning Israel into a theocratic state, Justice Silberg noted: "Israel is not a theocratic state, because, as the present case demonstrates, the life of the citizens is regulated by the law and not by religion. If the religious categories of Jewish law applied, the petitioner would indeed be regarded as a Jew." What Silberg meant was that Brother Daniel met the religious definition of a Jew, which was to be born to a Jewish mother.

But the court chose not to decide Brother Daniel's case on religious grounds. It did not try to determine whether it agreed with the definition of a Jew as prescribed in Jewish law. Instead, the court preferred to deal with the more narrow issue of how a Jew should be defined (or in Brother Daniel's case, how a Jew should not be defined) for the purposes of allowing someone to take advantage of the Israeli Law of Return, a law passed by Israel's Knesset and—most importantly for the purposes of this case—not based on Jewish law.

The Supreme Court was not saying that civilian law should take precedence over Jewish law on questions of Jewish identity—or any other questions for that matter. The court did not try to make such a sweeping decree.

The case received much public attention. The secular community, which had grudgingly supported Brother Daniel's case only because it was contemptuous of the Orthodox Jewish hold over a whole variety of issues of personal status, was not displeased with the court decision for even it recognized that, when all was said and done, the man had chosen freely to become and remain a Catholic friar! For its part, the religious community also took satisfaction with the court's decree, agreeing that a man who had abandoned his religion willingly could not expect to be welcomed back happily into the Jewish fold.

As for Brother Daniel, he received half a loaf, certainly not the whole one. In August 1963, he was granted Israeli citizenship, not under the Law of Return, but rather after fulfilling the requirements for naturalization under Israel's Nationality Law.

The Israeli Supreme Court showed courage in trying to come to grips with one of the stickiest issues of Israeli society. That it did not resolve the issue once and for all was hardly surprising. In later years, the court would display more forbearance for those who sought to become Israeli citizens even though their Jewish identity was in question. But, even this did little to still the debate. The one constant through the years is the Israeli Supreme Court's continuing centrality in the effort to resolve the thorny question of *who* is a Jew.

Six-Day War Erupts

JUNE 5, 1967 • 7:45 A.M.

In the early hours of June 5, 1967, Israeli fighter planes bombed military airports in Egypt and Syria, effectively eliminating Arab air power and securing an Israeli victory in the Six-Day War. Israel's triumph changed the Arab-Israeli conflict—assuring Israel's survival but creating the controversy over whether Israel should control the lives of hundreds of thousands of Arabs indefinitely.

At 7:45 A.M. on Monday, June 5, 1967, Israeli fighter planes launched a preemptive attack destroying the air forces of Egypt, Jordan, Syria, and Iraq, marking the start of the Six-Day War. The aircraft had taken off at precise intervals in order for them to arrive on target at the same instant and achieve total surprise.

The Israeli fighter planes came in two waves. In the first wave, from 7:45 to 8:55 A.M., one hundred three Israeli planes devastated six Egyptian airfields, sixteen radar stations, and one hundred ninety-seven aircraft. In the second wave, starting at 9:34 A.M., one hundred sixty-four Israeli planes attacked fourteen bases, destroying one hundred seven Egyptian planes. The Egyptians lost seventy-five percent of their air strength—three hundred four out of four hundred nineteen aircraft—before they could absorb the size of the disaster and get their planes in the air. Israel's decision to devote so much energy to building up a powerful air force had paid off. As surprising as the success of the Israeli air attacks, Israel's overall triumph in the Six-Day War proved even more startling to some Western analysts, who had, on the war's eve, predicted

that the Jewish state would suffer military defeat at Arab hands.

For Israel, the eleven years since the 1956 Sinai Campaign had been remarkably peaceful and productive. The country's 2.7 million Jews had grown used to feeling secure, and Israel's frontiers in early 1967 were reasonably quiet, with good prospects that they would remain so. Yet, the "peace" that the 1956 Israeli victory had brought had been as tense as it was illusory. Egypt's Gamal Abdel Nasser, though mauled badly by the 1956 defeat, had shown great resilience, gaining new popularity by portraying himself as the Arab David facing the Israeli Goliath.

In mid-May of 1967, the Middle East had begun sliding into a war that seemed to catch Israel unprepared. Nasser began moving thousands of troops across the Suez Canal into the Sinai, within striking distance of Israel. On May 17, the Egyptian president demanded that those United Nations troops stationed for a decade along the Israeli-Egyptian frontier from below the Gaza Strip to Eilat, leave. Five days later, Nasser announced that he was closing the Straits of Tiran to all ships bound to and from Israel. By then the Egyptians had amassed one hundred thousand troops and one thousand tanks in the Sinai, compared to Israel's sixty thousand soldiers and four hundred tanks. War seemed inevitable.

The Israeli Government oscillated between uncertainty and confusion, its leaders unable to decide what to do. Nothing symbolized the government's difficulties more than the speech given on May 28 by Levi Eshkol, who served both as prime minister and defense minister. His rambling, stammering radio talk created

ISRAEL GOVERNMENT PRESS OFFICE

Israeli soldiers at Government House.

fresh frustration and increased sentiment within Israel in favor of selecting Moshe Dayan, the hero of the 1956 Sinai Campaign, as defense minister. Dayan's appointment to that post on June 1 electrified the country, giving soldiers and civilians alike new self-confidence.

To create the illusion in Egyptian minds that Israel had no intention of launching a military attack, Defense Minister Dayan embarked upon a clever campaign of disinformation. On Saturday, June 3, the Jewish Sabbath, the army was ordered to relax. Soldiers were allowed to have their children visit them at their bases. News photographers were permitted, even encouraged, to take shots of Israeli soldiers on leave.

On the morning of June 5, a piece by American columnist Joseph Alsop appeared called "The Meaning of Moshe Dayan," comparing his appointment to the defense ministry to the return of Winston Churchill to the British Cabinet in 1939, suggesting that the Dayan appointment was Israel's acknowledgment that the Jewish state wanted to preempt any Arab attack.

When Israel's air force thundered over Egyptian skies early on June 5, swooping down and smashing the Egyp-

tian air force on the ground, the Egyptians realized how wrong they had been in thinking that Israel had put off plans for a military attack. Syrian planes managed to bomb the Israeli towns of Tiberias and Megiddo in the north. Israeli planes destroyed the entire Jordanian air force of twenty-eight planes and fifty-three of Syria's one hundred twelve planes. Israel also destroyed nine Iraqi planes at Iraq's Habbaniyah air force base.

At 10:30 A.M. on June 5 Moshe Dayan announced over Israel Radio that the war had begun. "At this time we do not have precise situation reports of the battles on the southern front," he said. This was only partly true. "Our planes are locked in bitter combat with enemy aircraft . . . " Again, only partly true. The combat had hardly been bitter, and most of it was over. "They are greater in numbers but we will overcome them," Dayan said of the enemy's armed forces. "They are more numerous than we. But we shall beat them. We are a small people, but a brave one." Those last few sentences were entirely true.

In the opening hours of the war Israel's air force had set the stage for one of the most spectacular military defeats of the modern era. Six days later, a new Israel

Israel Government Press Office

Israeli armor goes into battle.

had been created, one that many had dreamed about but had doubted would ever occur. The Israel Defense Forces had won a victory of huge dimensions. It now stood on cease-fire lines encompassing twenty-seven thousand square miles of territory, three and one-half times its prewar size. The Old City of Jerusalem had been captured. Egyptian forces were no longer in Gaza, less than fifty miles from Tel Aviv. Instead, Israel's army was within striking distance of Cairo. One million Arab inhabitants had come under Israeli occupation. Israeli troops controlled the eastern bank of the Suez Canal and the western bank of the Jordan River, seemingly ideal boundaries.

The price Israel had paid had been high: eight hundred three dead and another three thousand six wounded, yet far lower than what had been predicted. Israel's air force, having performed so amazingly, lost

fifty of its two hundred planes. Egypt suffered fifteen thousand dead and twenty thousand wounded; Jordan another one thousand dead and two thousand wounded. Some one hundred thousand Arabs fled from the West Bank to the eastern side of the Jordan River.

For Israel, the Six-Day War victory held out the hope that, in the wake of their humiliating defeat, the Arabs would sue for peace, bringing an end once and for all to the Arab-Israeli conflict. It was a genuine if naive dream, and events soon proved that the Arabs had no desire to turn their swords into plowshares.

Israel's remarkable military triumph thrilled Jews around the world. Now that this tiny country had achieved such a spectacular deed and appeared likely to survive, the eyes of the Jewish world—indeed the whole world—focused on the Jewish state.

Entebbe Hostages Rescued in Daring Mission

JULY 3, 1976 • 11:01 P.M.

The story of Air France flight 139 began at 8:59 A.M. on June 27, 1976, when Captain Michel Bacos took off from Ben-Gurion Airport near Tel Aviv on a routine flight to Paris via Athens. After the plane was hijacked and flown to Entebbe, Uganda, Israeli soldiers carried out one of the most daring rescue missions in modern history.

As Air France flight 139 made its final approach over Athens Airport, four terrorists were passing through the lax security at Athens International Airport, about to board the plane. At 12:20 P.M. the plane took off for Paris with two hundred forty-six passengers, including seventy-seven Israelis. Eight minutes later, the four terrorists from the Popular Front for the Liberation of Palestine, waving guns and grenades, hijacked the plane.

Israel's Prime Minister Yitzhak Rabin, presiding over a weekly Cabinet session, learned that the plane had been hijacked and that radio contact with Captain Bacos had been lost. Israeli security authorities feared that the plane was heading for Ben-Gurion Airport. Shortly before 3:00 P.M., the Air France plane landed at Benghazi, Libya. A pregnant woman was permitted to deplane.

Taking on forty-two tons of fuel, the airliner, with a range of twenty-five hundred miles, took off at 9:50 P.M. heading south—away from the Middle East. Five and one-half hours later, the plane landed at Entebbe, Uganda. The leader of Uganda, Idi Amin, was no friend of the Jewish state.

At midday on Monday, June 28, the hostages were driven through a cordon of Ugandan soldiers, who

Yonatan Netanyahu.

pointed their weapons ominously at the terrified passengers, to a terminal building. Idi Amin arrived soon thereafter to express his support for the terrorists. All the Israeli government could do was ask the press not to publish the names of Israeli hostages in the hope that they might be mistaken for citizens of other countries.

On Tuesday afternoon, June 29, the hijackers separated Israelis and Jews from the other passengers, and, responding to Amin's request, permitted forty-seven non-Jews to be released. The act was eerily reminiscent of the way the Nazis had separated able-bodied Jews from the weak upon their arrival at concentration camps during the Holocaust, sending the weaker ones to their immediate deaths.

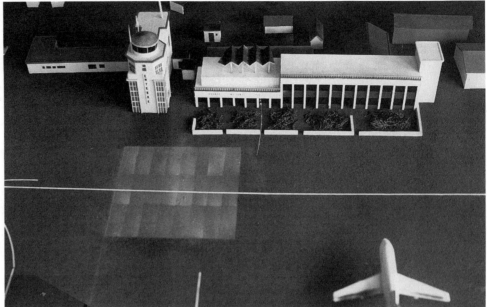

A model of Entebbe Airport control tower.

Israeli officials assumed at first that a military rescue mission was unthinkable: it would be impossible to maintain the element of surprise over a distance of more than twenty-five-hundred miles. On Wednesday, June 30, the forty-seven freed hostages who arrived in Paris, supplied Israeli intelligence with vital information about the number of hijackers, the location of the passengers, and the size of the Ugandan forces at the airport.

The hijackers had demanded the release of fifty-three Palestinian "freedom fighters" who were in jails in Israel, France, Switzerland, Kenya, and West Germany. If Israel did not release the prisoners by 2:00 P.M. Israeli time, Thursday, July 1, the hijackers planned to blow up the plane and its passengers.

With only ninety minutes to go before the ultimatum expired, the Israeli government voted to negotiate with the hijackers, putting aside a long-standing Israeli policy against bargaining with terrorists in hostage situations. Rabin explained why: "As long as we had no military option, we had no right to tell the hostages that for reasons of principle we could do nothing for them, and that they were at the mercy of the murderers. Life is more precious than a political stand." Planning for a military rescue was underway.

Israel's decision to negotiate encouraged the hijackers to extend their deadline to 2:00 P.M. Sunday, July 4 . Meanwhile, another one hundred hostages, all non-Jews, were freed.

Early Saturday morning, July 3, Israel's chief of staff, Mordecai Gur, informed Rabin that the rescue operation was set to go. Rabin faced a tough decision. He feared that up to twenty hostages would die during a rescue mission. Yet he was persuaded that the operation had to be attempted. At 1:45 P.M. the rescue planes took off. Fifteen minutes later, the Israeli Cabinet approved the mission, to be carried out by the Israel Defense Forces (IDF). Rabin told his wife Leah that evening: "Tomorrow morning—either Israel's shares will be sky-high, or I will be hanged in [Tel Aviv's] Kikar Medina."

Flying low to avoid radar surveillance, the four Israeli planes plowed through stormy weather, their cockpit windows turning blue from flashes of static electricity.

Rabin and his colleagues gathered in the Tel Aviv office of Shimon Peres, minister of defense. Shortly before 11:00 P.M., Rabin and Peres heard a terse "over Jordan" crackle through the radio transmission, the first indication that the troops had reached Lake Victoria near Entebbe.

As the lead plane prepared to land, Lieutenant Colonel Yonatan Netanyahu, commander of the strike force, and his troops piled into a Mercedes and two Land Rovers, engines running, aboard the plane. In the Mercedes was an Israeli soldier disguised as Idi Amin. At 11:01 P.M., only thirty seconds behind schedule, the first Israeli plane touched down. The rear ramp of the plane already open, the vehicles reached the ground and moved away before the giant Hercules rolled to a stop. Paratroopers placed emergency beacons next to the runway lights in case the control tower shut them down. "I am on Shoshana," an Israeli lieutenant colonel barked over his radio to his Israeli superiors back home. "Shoshana" was the Israeli code word for the Entebbe airport.

The Mercedes approached several Ugandan soldiers, who saluted at the presumed sight of their leader; a second later, as the car doors opened, the Israeli soldiers inside the vehicle, using pistols fitted with silencers, killed the Ugandans. A hijacker peeked out the front door to check on the noise, but, when shots were fired at him, he quickly retreated. Inside the terminal, a second terrorist, aware of the attack, fired at the hostages sprawled around him, many of whom were sleeping. An Israeli soldier felled the terrorist with two bullets. A voice boomed over a bullhorn in Hebrew and English: "This is the IDF. Stay down." A bewildered young hostage leaped from his mattress and launched himself at the soldiers in the doorway. He was cut down by a carbine burst.

Another hijacker fired at the intruders, but his bullets went high, hitting windows and showering glass into the room. A second Israeli assault team raced through another doorway. One of the terrorists threw a grenade at them, which landed harmlessly. A machine gun burst from an Israeli soldier killed the remaining terrorists. The entire Israeli assault lasted three minutes. Netanyahu, waiting outside to supervise the assault

Rescued hostages leaving the Hercules.

teams, was fatally hit in the back by a bullet from a Ugandan soldier atop the control tower.

Near midnight Rabin and his staff learned that all but three of the hostages had been rescued and were on their way home. Three hostages lost their lives, two at Entebbe. Another hostage, Mrs. Dora Bloch, who earlier had been taken to a hospital in Kampala, was murdered on Amin's orders. Three hostages and five Israeli soldiers were wounded; all the terrorists were killed. One of the first to congratulate Rabin was Menachem Begin, leader of the Likud opposition bloc in the Knesset.

Though Rabin and Peres quarreled privately over who deserved the credit for the success of the mission, even their bickering did not diminish the excitement that many felt at Israel's derring-do. Israeli morale had suffered following the 1973 Yom Kippur War. But on July 4, 1976, Israelis had a reason to feel good again. And around the world the Jewish state's reputation soared.

Israel Bombs Iraqi Nuclear Reactor

JUNE 7, 1981 • 5:30 P.M.

> *In 1981, Iraq was within two years of being able to build nuclear weapons. Despite pressure to stop the Iraqis by diplomatic means, Prime Minister Menachem Begin ordered Israeli planes to bomb the French-built Tammuz I nuclear reactor at El-Tuwaitha, ten and one-half miles southwest of Baghdad, five hundred fifteen miles from Israel. It was one of the most controversial moves ever made by an Israeli prime minister, and, as it proved, one of the most important and courageous.*

Shortly before the Jewish holiday of Shavuot, the Feast of Weeks, was to begin on June 7, 1981, the first of the F-15 fighter planes that had been stored in underground bunkers took off from Israel's Etzion air base in the eastern Sinai; they were joined by F-16 bombers. Flying low to avoid Arab radar, the jets headed east across the Gulf of Aqaba toward Jordan. When Jordanian radar picked up one of the planes, an Israeli pilot replied to the Jordanian air controller in perfect Arabic, apparently convincing the spotters that the sighting was either a Jordanian or Saudi aircraft.

At 5:10 P.M. the lead fighter plane penetrated Iraqi airspace. Twenty minutes later, the warplanes sighted their target, the distinctive cupola housing the Iraqi nuclear reactor at El-Tuwaitha. The F-16s began their bombing runs. The lead bomber fired a pair of video-guided smart bombs, which hit predetermined spots in the domed concrete. Other planes dropped bombs weighing over a ton each that went through the jagged holes of the reactor's cupola.

The roof of the reactor collapsed, burying the reactor's radioactive core under hundreds of tons of concrete and steel debris. Fire engulfed the building. Iraqi antiaircraft guns were ineffective. The Israeli planes raced home after destroying Iraq's hope of becoming a nuclear power, hopefully for good.

Iraq's Tammuz I nuclear installation had been in the planning stages since 1978, when France provided Saddam Hussein's government with small quantities of enriched uranium fuel. Jerusalem and Washington protested to the French, but President Giscard d'Estaing was not moved to change his mind. In 1981 François Mitterrand became France's new president, and his government was more sympathetic to Israel. It tried—unsuccessfully—to renegotiate the terms of the contract with Iraq.

Israeli Prime Minister Menachem Begin could have delayed the planned attack until Iraq was closer to possessing the bomb. Begin's critics believed that he had enough time to pursue a diplomatic solution, but Begin was adamant that the reactor should be wiped out at once. His memories of the Holocaust had led him to vow that "never again" would Jews be made vulnerable.

On Sunday afternoon, June 7, Prime Minister Begin's military attaché, Brigadier General Ephraim Poran, called all fourteen members of the Israeli Cabinet and asked each to come to a special session with Begin at his Jerusalem home. A few Orthodox Cabinet members complained that the meeting was too close to the start—at sundown—of Shavuot. As each minister drove up to Begin's residence in Jerusalem's Rechavia district, a security man whisked away his car. At 5:15 P.M. Begin walked from his book-lined office to the reception area where the ministers had gathered. His face portrayed little emotion.

Prime Minister Menachem Begin and F-16s used in the raid.

"Well," he began matter-of-factly, "six of our planes are now on their way to their target in Iraq. I hope our boys will be able to complete their mission successfully and return to base." Begin had called the ministers together to discuss how they should react if the attack was not a success.

The ministers were shocked and speechless. Begin was not required to consult them—and he was confident that everyone in his cabinet would support the operation, once each became aware of its objective. One minister thought that Begin had misstated the target of the mission and meant Syria. The minister was thinking of Israel's continuing military confrontation in Lebanon over Syrian SA-6 missiles.

Thirty minutes later, a telephone call interrupted the Cabinet meeting. General Rafael Eitan, chief of staff, told Begin tersely that the attack had been a total success. Israel had taken Iraq thoroughly by surprise and destroyed the two hundred sixty-million dollar nuclear research center.

Just before 7:00 P.M., there was yet another telephone call, this one announcing the safe return of all the Israeli aircraft. The Cabinet was jubilant as the meeting ended. Begin had only one other task to perform. He called Samuel Lewis, the American ambassador to Israel and told him of the successful raid. "You don't say," was Lewis's laconic reply.

The world was shocked when it learned the news. Critics of the raid argued that Israel had taken international law into its own hands. In the words of a *Time* magazine story on the raid, "[Israel] had dismayed their friends, increased their isolation and vastly compounded the difficulties of procuring a peaceful settlement of the confrontations in the Middle East . . . "

The raid jolted the administration of Ronald Reagan, who condemned the attack and suspended delivery of four more F-16s to Israel; only on August 17 was the suspension lifted and the planes delivered.

Egyptian president Anwar Sadat was thoroughly astonished by the raid. He had held a highly-publicized

ISRAEL GOVERNMENT PRESS OFFICE

Menachem Begin and Cabinet members meet with air force unit that carried out the raid.

summit meeting with Begin in the Sinai just three days earlier but had not been advised of the plan. Cynics in Israel thought Begin had timed the raid close to the Israeli election on June 30th.

To Begin, however, the deed was totally understandable in the context of the Holocaust. "The Iraqis were preparing atomic bombs to drop on the children of Israel. Haven't you heard of 1.5 million little Jewish children who were thrown into the gas chambers? . . . Another Holocaust would have happened in the history of the Jewish people, never again, never again. Tell

your friends, tell anybody you meet, we shall defend our people with all the means at our disposal."

Nearly a decade after the attack some of those critics changed their minds. When Saddam Hussein invaded Kuwait in the summer of 1990 and threatened Israel with chemical and biological weapons, those critics understood that, had Saddam had nuclear weapons, he might have been prepared to threaten or even to use them against Israel. Saddam's behavior during the Gulf War vindicated Menachem Begin's decision to attack the nuclear reactor near Baghdad.

MOMENTS
of
JOY

Abraham Passes Test of Faith

EIGHTEENTH CENTURY B.C.E.

Abraham's faith in God began developing from the moment God told him to leave his native land and journey to a land that God would show him. The final test of Abraham's faith was God's request that he sacrifice his son Isaac. Abraham obeyed and took the boy to a mountain in the land of Moriah, where he bound him. Just as Abraham held the knife above his son, an angel prevented the sacrifice. Abraham had passed the ultimate test of faith. No incident in the Bible has stirred Jewish emotion more than the binding of Isaac.

Gabriel Metsh, Sacrifice of Isaac—oil on canvas, 17th century.

Few moments in Jewish history are as dramatic as the binding of Isaac, Abraham's most difficult act of obedience to God. Abraham's entire life and relationship with God determined his choice at that moment. The story began when Abraham, who probably lived in the nineteenth century B.C.E. in Ur of the Chaldees in Mesopotamia, left his native country at the command of God, who guided him to Canaan. According to a *midrash*, Abraham had rejected the idolatry of his upbringing even as a child; he is generally regarded as the first monotheist. God entered into a covenant, or pact, with Abraham and offered him protection as long as Abraham, for his part, obeyed God's commandments. It is by keeping this covenant with God, symbolized by male circumcision, which Abraham performed on himself and the men of his household at God's command, that Abraham's descendants, the Jewish people, retain their uniqueness.

God promised Abraham that his offspring would become a great nation. Nevertheless, ten years after the first divine promise of many offspring, Abraham and his wife, Sarah, remained childless. She, therefore, gave her maidservant Hagar to Abraham, and when Abraham was eighty-six years old, Hagar bore him a son, who was called Ishmael. Thirteen years later three tired travelers visited Abraham, who welcomed them with warm hospitality. They told Abraham that he and

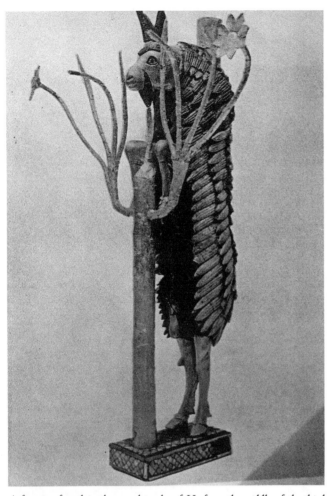

A figurine found in the royal tombs of Ur from the middle of the third millennium B.C.E. represents a ram caught in a thicket,

This relief discovered in the Sinai Peninsula illustrates the way it was assumed Abraham rode on his ass, while his son and his servants walked beside him.

Sarah would have a son, though they were both advanced in age. Sarah was standing behind them at the entrance of the tent, listening. She laughed. "Now that I am withered, am I to have enjoyment—with my husband so old?" she said to herself (*Genesis* 18:12). The angels, for the three men were angels whose nature Abraham had not recognized, then told Abraham that God had decided to destroy the nearby cities of Sodom and Gomorrah because of the wickedness of their inhabitants. Abraham argued with God. "Will you sweep away the innocent along with the guilty?" he asked. "Far be it from you! Shall not the Judge of all the earth deal justly?" (*Genesis* 18:23–25). God finally agreed that if ten righteous people could be found in the cities, God would not destroy them. Because there were not even ten, however, God, through the "men" who had visited Abraham, rescued only Abraham's nephew, Lot,

and his family, and the cities were destroyed by fire and brimstone.

Abraham then traveled to the Negev and settled between Shur and Kadesh. The following year, Sarah, at age ninety, bore Abraham a son who, because of Sarah's laughter, was named Isaac, from the Hebrew verb "to laugh."

Isaac's birth led Sarah to fear that her son's inheritance was threatened by Hagar's son Ishmael. She demanded that Hagar and Ishmael be expelled from their home. Abraham agreed, but only after God's intervention in favor of Sarah.

Later, God tested Abraham by asking him to sacrifice his son Isaac: "Take your son, your favored one, Isaac, whom you love, and go to the land of Moriah, and offer him there as a burnt offering on one of the heights that I will point out to you" (*Genesis* 22:2).

Abraham obeyed. The biblical narrative does not relate what he thought and felt, or what Isaac felt when he asked his father, "Here are the firestone and the wood; but where is the sheep for the burnt offering?"—only to be told, evasively but more prophetically than Abraham knew, "God will see to the sheep for his burnt offering, my son." The narrative also does not give Isaac's age, though the Rabbis deduced that he must have been at least ten because he was able to recognize the implements of a sacrifice and to ask an intelligent question. It is even possible that Isaac understood what was about to happen. Yet the narrative says, twice, that "the two of them walked on together."

When they reached the place on Mount Moriah that God had indicated, Abraham built a sacrificial altar, piled the wood on it, and then bound Isaac and laid him on the wood. Then he picked up the knife.

The Talmud elaborates on this moment: The angels in heaven began to weep, and as they wept, their tears flowed down to earth and fell upon Isaac's eyes. So moved was the Lord by his angels' grief that he instantly sent the archangel Michael down to earth to prevent the sacrifice. The angel called to Abraham and said, speaking for God, "Do not raise your hand against the boy, or do anything to him. For now I know that you fear God, since you have not withheld your son, your favored one, from Me" (*Genesis* 22:12). Abraham then looked up, noticed a ram caught in the thicket, and offered the ram instead of Isaac. The biblical narrative closes with a reaffirmation of God's blessing to Abraham and to his descendants through Isaac. The binding of Isaac is thus connected to God's promises and their fulfillment; for that reason, the narrative of the binding of Isaac is read traditionally on Rosh Hashanah, the Jewish New Year.

The binding of Isaac is one of the most problematic passages in the Bible because it raises questions concerning God's sense of justice. For centuries, Jewish scholars have been troubled by the passage because of its seeming cruelty. What kind of God, they asked, would demand the sacrifice of a son? Many scholars interpreted the fact that the sacrifice was called off at the last moment as an injunction against the practice of child sacrifice prevalent at that time. Yet the binding of Isaac became, for later generations of Jews, the supreme example of self-sacrifice in obedience to God's will, as well as the symbol of Jewish martyrdom.

David Establishes Jerusalem as His Capital

990 B.C.E.

Shepherd, poet, military genius, and king, David became the first monarch of all the tribes of Israel. He conquered Jerusalem and made it the capital of a united kingdom; Jerusalem is still known as the City of David. David is considered the Jewish people's most popular and successful king, and for over two thousand years Jews have looked back to David's reign as a golden age.

David, born sometime in the eleventh century B.C.E. in Bethlehem, was the great-grandson of Boaz and Ruth, the Moabite woman whose loyalty to her mother-in-law, Naomi, led her to follow Naomi back to Israel and convert to Judaism. David was the eighth and youngest son of Jesse, from the tribe of Judah. After God's rejection of Saul, the first king, the prophet Samuel, instructed by God, visited Jesse secretly in order to anoint one of Jesse's sons as the next king. Not finding the requisite qualities in Jesse's older sons, Samuel asked Jesse, "Are these all the boys you have?" Jesse replied, "There is still the youngest; he is tending the flock" (*1 Samuel* 17:11–12). David was called from the field, and Samuel anointed him.

Despite God's rejection, Saul continued to rule. He became subject to bouts of depression. One of Saul's courtiers suggested that music might help and recommended David as a skilled musician; the courtier added, "He is a stalwart fellow and a warrior, sensible in speech, and handsome in appearance, and the Lord is with him" (*1 Samuel* 17:18). Soon afterward, David displayed these qualities in his well-known encounter with the Philistine giant, Goliath. Relying on God's help and on his own courage,

which had enabled him to rescue his father's sheep from wild animals, he rejected Saul's offer of armor and slew his enemy with a slingshot aimed at the giant's head. David was acclaimed as a hero. He became Saul's armor-bearer and, later, one of his commanders.

David married Saul's daughter Michal, who had fallen in love with him. His relationship with King Saul's son and heir, Jonathan, became an archetypal example of male friendship. Saul, already mentally disturbed, however, became jealous of David's growing popularity and made repeated attempts on his life. Warned by Jonathan, David fled and lived as an outlaw. Finally, he took refuge among the Philistines. He was prepared to join the Philistines in their planned attack on King Saul; they, however, were suspicious of him and ordered him to leave the battlefield. In the battle on Mount Gilboa, the Philistines were victorious, and Saul and Jonathan were killed. Upon hearing of their deaths, David mourned his king and friend:

> Your glory, O Israel,
> Lies slain on your heights;
> How have the mighty fallen!
> Tell it not in Gath,
> Do not proclaim it in the streets of Ashkelon . . .
>
> Saul and Jonathan,
> Beloved and cherished,
> Never parted
> In life or in death!
> They were swifter than eagles,
> They were stronger than lions!
> *2 Samuel* 1:19–23

David's laments over the deaths of Jonathan and Saul, and, later, over his son Absalom are some of the most poignant verses in the Bible.

Returning to Judah, David settled in Hebron, where he remained for seven and a half years. He was publicly anointed king by the men of Judah and eventually by all the tribes of Israel. After rewarding the men who had rescued Saul's body and buried it, David declared himself Saul's successor. An attempt was made to make Saul's son Ish-bosheth king in David's place, but it was unsuccessful, partly because of infighting and defections among Ish-bosheth's followers. David consolidated his rule over the tribes of Israel and also over the neighboring peoples. The walled city of Jebus had remained in Canaanite hands since the time of Joshua; it belonged to none of the tribes of Israel. The Israelites had been unable to conquer Jerusalem even though it was centrally located and, strategically, the most important city of the region. David captured it, however, and he made it his capital. He then opened a crucial corridor that connected the northern and the southern tribes, thus physically uniting the nation Israel.

King Hiram of Tyre immediately recognized David's ascendancy; he sent ambassadors with a gift of cedar logs, and the envoys were accompanied by skilled craftsmen, who built a palace for David. David then turned his attention to the Philistines and ended their threat to the now-unified kingdom.

Although politically the union of northern and southern tribes was tenuous, David strengthened it by making Jerusalem the religious as well as the political capital. He sent for the Ark of the Covenant, the Jews' most precious religious relic and the symbol of their unity, which had remained at Kiriat Yearim, northwest of Jerusalem, for twenty years, and had it brought to the City of David. Amidst a procession of Levites, throngs of people danced as the Ark was transported to Jerusalem. "David whirled with all his might before the Lord; David was girded with a linen ephod. Thus David and all the House of Israel brought up the Ark of the Lord with shouts and with blasts of the horn" (2 Samuel 6:14–15). David wanted to build a temple for God. He said to Nathan the prophet, "Here I am dwelling in a house of cedar, while the Ark of the Lord abides in a tent!" (2 Samuel 7:2). Though Nathan's immediate response was to agree with David, he received instructions from God that night to tell David that God would establish David's house and that it was David's son, not David, who would build a temple for God.

During the forty-year rule of King David, Jerusalem developed into the seat of power. David is given credit for being an able administrator, organizing the country into districts, appointing a competent group of officials, and reorganizing the army. After defeating the Philistines, David began campaigns against other hostile neighbors, including the Moabites, the Edomites, and the Ammonites. He also defeated the Arameans and captured Damascus; his territory extended from the Mediterranean to the Euphrates. What made David special in a Jewish context was his recognition that the king was subject to the law—specifically, to the laws of the Torah. During the war against the Ammonites, David committed a grave sin, adultery—with Bathsheba, the wife of one of his warriors. When David discovered that Bathsheba was pregnant by him, he arranged to have Uriah, Bathsheba's husband, sent into the fiercest fighting against the Ammonites, so that the Ammonites would kill him in battle; David then married Bathsheba. Nathan the prophet confronted David and denounced his behavior. Instead of punishing Nathan for his boldness, as the neighboring kings would have done, David admitted his misdeed: "David said to Nathan, 'I stand guilty before the Lord'" (2 Samuel 12:13). David's punishment was the death of his and Bathsheba's first child and, because he had used the Ammonites' swords to kill Uriah, the constant presence of warfare in his own house. But Bathsheba's next son was Solomon, David's successor.

The feud between the northern and southern parts of the kingdom continued, as did the infighting in David's palace. David's son Absalom led a rebellion against his father. It was put down, but only after serious fighting. Absalom died in the battle, and his father mourned him—"My son, Absalom!. . . If only I had died instead of you! O Absalom, my son, my son!" (2 Samuel 18:33)—until the army commander persuaded him to stop, out of loyalty to the troops who had restored him to the throne.

In old age, David witnessed another fight over the succession. His son Adonijah, who was next in line for the throne after the death of Absalom, also attempted to become king in his father's lifetime. He was supported by the army commander and by one of the two leaders among the priests, but not by the other, or by David's own guard, or by Nathan the prophet, all of whom remained loyal to David. Nathan informed Bathsheba of Adonijah's coup attempt and intrigued with her to persuade David to declare her son Solomon his successor. Thus, Solomon was anointed king during his father's lifetime. During his last days, David advised Solomon concerning the steps he would need to take to eliminate his opponents and consolidate his rule. The precise site of David's burial is unknown, but it is believed to be in the City of David—Jerusalem—probably southeast of the present Siloam region.

David has been admired in Jewish, Christian, and Islamic traditions for his courage, wisdom, energy, and abiding trust in God. Because the *Book of Psalms* was attributed to him, he has been called the "sweet singer of Israel." He occupies an especially important place in the Jewish imagination. The traditional liturgy includes prayers for the restoration of the Davidic monarchy, and there is a tradition, reflected in one of the blessings said after readings from the Prophets, that the Messiah would be a descendant of King David.

Solomon Builds First Temple

950 B.C.E.

> *Solomon's reign, approximately 967 to 928 B.C.E., was marked by extensive construction projects. The most important was the building of the Temple in Jerusalem. The Temple became the focus of Jewish worship and is still central in Jewish memory.*

Solomon was the third king of the united Israelite monarchy. The son of David—the second son of David and Bathsheba—he was named David's heir and anointed during his father's lifetime after coup attempts by his older brothers and court intrigue. He ruled for forty years over a region that extended from the Euphrates to Gaza. His reign was a period of peace, largely because both Egypt and Assyria were weak and Solomon possessed a large army. He used marital alliances as an instrument of diplomacy; his most important marital alliance was with the daughter of the Egyptian Pharaoh, who brought the town of Gezer as a dowry. According to the biblical account, Solomon had seven hundred wives and three hundred concubines. The Bible mentions only three of Solomon's children, his son and successor, Rehoboam, and two daughters married to provincial governors.

Solomon's reign was renowned for its magnificence. In addition to the Temple, he also built a massive palace that took thirteen years to complete. Artisans, laborers, timber, and gold for both projects were provided by Solomon's ally, Hiram of Tyre. The two leaders, Solomon and Hiram, also established a commercial fleet at the Sea of Reeds port of Ezion-Geber (later, Eilat).

On dedicating the Temple, Solomon offered a moving prayer praising God as the sole ruler of the universe and begged for his blessing on the people of Israel.

In addition to his magnificence, Solomon was famed for his wisdom. One of his best-known legal cases was that of two women who insisted they were the mother of the same child. When Solomon decided that the solution was to divide the child in two, one woman responded that she would renounce her claim to prevent the child's being killed. Because she showed compassion for the child, Solomon ruled that she was the mother (*1 Kings* 3:16–28).

Solomon also composed proverbs and songs and had a deeper knowledge of natural history than anyone else in his time. Many people visited Solomon to hear his wisdom, among them the Queen of Sheba, who "came to test him with hard questions." Impressed by his answers, she gave him gold, precious stones, and "a vast quantity of spices" (*1 Kings* 10:1–10). Three biblical books are traditionally attributed to Solomon: *Proverbs*, *Ecclesiastes*, and the *Song of Songs*.

Solomon's most important achievement, from the perspective of later generations of Jews, was his fulfillment of his father's dream of building a temple to God in Jerusalem. We know how Solomon's Temple looked only from the description of it in chapters 6 and 7 of *1 Kings*. Nothing visible is left of Solomon's Jerusalem. One explanation of its disappearance is that what he built may have been submerged beneath the enormous Temple buildings later erected by Herod the Great. Another theory is that the Romans might have demolished Solomon's building and used the stones for their own projects.

Archaeological excavations at Lachish and Beth

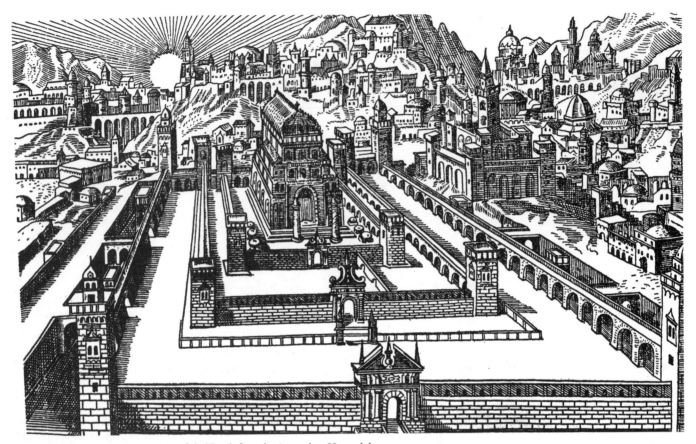

A seventeenth-century reconstruction of the Temple from the Amsterdam Haggadah.

Shean suggest, however, that Solomon's Temple was similar in appearance to Late Bronze Age Canaanite temples at those sites and to a later ninth-century B.C.E. temple excavated at Tel Tainet in Syria. Like these temples, the one Solomon built had three rooms, each thirty-three feet wide, on an axis; the *ulam*, or porch, was sixteen feet long; the *heikhal*, or main holy room, was sixty-six feet long; and the inner shrine, or Holy of Holies, which was kept totally dark, like the inner sanctum in an Egyptian temple, was thirty-three feet square.

The Temple was built of stone, cedar, and cypress. Phoenician masons dressed the stone ashlars. Hiram of Tyre sent a specialist in bronze to cast the Temple's ceremonial vessels. These included ten bronze lavers on stands with wheels, and the great Brazen Sea, or tank, which stood on twelve bronze oxen; the tank contained two thousand baths of water and was used by the priests for their presacrificial cleansing rituals. Two bronze pillars, each nearly forty feet high, protected a gold-covered altar and the gold table for the bread of display. Ten gold lampstands stood on either side.

The inner shrine, the Holy of Holies, was built to house the Ark of the Covenant, which contained the tablets Moses had received at Mount Sinai. (The Talmud, however, records a tradition that the Holy of Holies contained not only the Ark of the Covenant but also Moses' and Aaron's rods, the manna jar, and the stone on which Jacob's head had rested at the time of his dream about the ladder.) On either side of the Ark was an olivewood cherub overlaid with gold; the wings of the two *cherubim* were outstretched and touched above the Ark, in the center of the chamber. The Holy of Holies was overlaid with gold, as was its altar. Its door screen was made of hanging gold chains.

Solomon's Temple, in its size and magnificence, and in its location within the fortified walls of a royal upper city, represents a departure from the religion the Israelites had practiced during their wanderings in the wilderness. Solomon had built the Temple in the hope of achieving a royal absolutism in which the king controlled a single, centralized shrine. It seems, moreover, that although the Ark and the tablets it contained were not worshiped, the Israelite people believed, or felt, that God lived in the Ark. Solomon echoed this feeling im-

THE ISRAEL MUSEUM, JERUSALEM.

"Inauguration of Solomon's Temple" by an unknown Dutch artist.

mediately after the dedication service, when he declared, as the priests were leaving the sanctuary:

> I have now built for you
> A stately House,
> A place where you
> May dwell forever.
> *1 Kings* 8:13

In his blessing of the congregation, however, he addressed a God whom he recognized as symbolically rather than physically present: "But will God really dwell on earth? Even the heavens to their uttermost reaches cannot contain you, how much less this house that I have built!" (*1 Kings* 8:27). Later generations continued

to experience the tension between these two positions; the concept of God's presence in the Holy of Holies as a divine emanation, the shekhinah, was one attempt at resolution.

The second half of Solomon's reign did not live up to the promise of the first, for his glory contained the seeds of its decline. His building projects were paid for by high taxes and a system of forced labor that caused disaffection among the people; four months of labor a year were required of every Israelite male. Moreover, in addition to his Egyptian wife, Solomon had entered into marital alliances with the Moabites, Ammonites, Edomites, Phoenicians, and Hittites; he antagonized strict monotheists by building shrines at which his foreign wives could worship their native deities. The growing discontent exacerbated the old north-south rivalry and led to the secession of the north after Solomon's death.

Nevertheless, Solomon's reign is remembered for its period of glory. Focusing on the spiritual significance of Solomon's reign for later generations rather than its political history, the well-known biblical scholar Adin Steinsaltz wrote in *Biblical Images* (1984):

> Temperamentally, David and Solomon seem to have been almost complete opposites. David was an adventurous spirit and much of his life was spent in wandering and in battle . . . Solomon . . . conveys a vivid, enchanting quality. He seems, however, to have been a man of peace, preferring to install himself firmly in a position of authority from which he could build and create.

Solomon's famed wisdom not only enabled him to follow the path of peace but also guided him to build the holy Temple, the great achievement that helped to turn the man into a magnificent myth. When he died, it was as though a Messianic age of peace, prosperity, and splendor had passed from the world.

Cyrus Permits Jews to Return to Zion

538 B.C.E.

Cyrus, who founded the Persian empire and conquered Babylonia in 539 B.C.E., has an honored place in Jewish history. He became the prototype of the just Gentile ruler, for it was his edict of 538 B.C.E. that gave the Jews the opportunity to return to Zion and rebuild the Temple.

When they first arrived in Babylonia, the deportees from Judah were overwhelmed by grief. For a while, the exiles of the first deportation, in 597 B.C.E., entertained false hopes of a quick return to Judah, despite Jeremiah's letter advising them to establish homes in Babylonia. In 586 B.C.E., the destruction of Jerusalem and of the Temple put an end to their hopes. The exiles of the second deportation found friends and relatives in Babylonia, but their sense of loss—expressed in *Psalm 137*—was no less great:

> By the rivers of Babylon,
> there we sat,
> sat and wept,
> as we thought of Zion.
> There on the poplars
> we hung up our lyres,
> for our captors asked us there for songs,
> our tormentors, for amusement,
> "Sing us one of the songs of Zion."
> How can we sing a song of the Lord
> on alien soil?

After a while, having no other choice, the Jews followed Jeremiah's advice and grew more accustomed to life in exile. They lived in their own communities, where they were allowed to control their internal affairs. They maintained their religious customs, including the newly instituted fasts mourning the destruction of Jerusalem, and they heard the teachings of the prophet Ezekiel, who not only rebuked them but also kept alive the vision of return and of a rebuilt Temple. Gradually, the position of the Jews improved. Though the Babylonians taxed the Jews heavily, they allowed them to own land, and farming was easy, for the soil, irrigated by canals, was more fertile than that of Judah, which depended entirely on rainfall. Moreover, the Jews experienced in Babylon, the capital, the attractions of a prosperous, cosmopolitan commercial center. It is likely that they eventually exerted some influence at court, for one of the first recorded acts of Nebuchadnezzar's son and successor was the release of Jehoiakin, the penultimate king of Judah, who had been brought to Babylon in the first deportation and imprisoned.

The position of the Jews was radically transformed by the sudden collapse of the Babylonian empire. The two-year reign of Nebuchadnezzar's successor was followed by a period of revolt. Though Babylonia's internal situation stabilized, the last king of Babylonia was mainly engaged in trying to repel attacks by the Medes. When Cyrus, a hitherto unknown chieftain, revolted against his Median overlord and founded the Persian empire, he continued the Medes' policy of hostility to Babylonia. After conquering Lydia and the Greek-speaking Ionian city states in what is now Turkey, Cyrus moved against Babylon and conquered it with little difficulty in 539 B.C.E. With the fall of Babylonia, Palestine and Syria became part of the Persian Empire and re-

Seed of Cyrus (left) with his Xerxes.

mained under Persian control until Alexander the Great conquered Persia approximately two hundred years later.

By the standards of his time, Cyrus was a remarkably enlightened ruler. His policy toward conquered peoples differed markedly from that of the Babylonians and that of the Assyrians before them. Instead of the large-scale deportations by which his predecessors had sought to destroy not only strongholds of resistance but even the national identities of the vanquished and to create, instead, a subject people of indeterminate nationality, Cyrus respected the national, ethnic, and religious identities of his subjects and allowed them to remain in their original homelands, which he granted local autonomy and administered as provinces within the regions, or satrapies, of his empire. In this way, he succeeded in gaining their gratitude and loyalty.

In 538 B.C.E., probably as the result of an appeal by leaders of the Jewish community in Babylon, Cyrus issued an edict permitting those Jews who wished to do so to return to Judah and rebuild the Temple. His declaration is recorded in the last verse of the Hebrew Bible:

Thus said King Cyrus of Persia: The Lord God of Heaven has given me all the kingdoms of the earth, and has charged me with building Him a house in Jerusalem, which is in Judah. Any one of you of all His people, the Lord his God be with him and let him go up.

(2 *Chronicles* 36:23)

The Jews were overjoyed at this unexpected turn of events. Only two years earlier, their future had seemed hopeless; now they had a chance to revive their nation, resettle their land, and rebuild the destroyed Temple. Many of them prepared for the return. The degree of their exultation is known from the poetry of a nameless prophet often called Deutero-Isaiah, whose words appear in the last twenty-seven chapters of the *Book of Isaiah*. His universalist view of God allowed him to see God working through Cyrus, the just Gentile ruler, whom he calls the Lord's "anointed one" and the man to whom God says, "He is My shepherd; he shall fulfill all My purposes" (*Isaiah* 45:1, 44:28).

Reaffirming the relationship between God and Israel, Deutero-Isaiah portrays Zion as a mourning woman whom God loves and comforts, and as a bereaved woman whose children are restored to her. In a well-known passage, the prophet depicts the arrival of the news of her restoration, stage by stage:

How welcome on the mountain
Are the footsteps of the herald
Announcing happiness,
Heralding good fortune,
Announcing victory,
Telling Zion, "your God is king!"
Hark!
Your watchmen raise their voices,
As one they shout for joy;
For every eye shall behold
The Lord's return to Zion.
Raise a shout together,
O ruins of Jerusalem!
For the Lord will comfort His people,
Will redeem Jerusalem. . . .

Isaiah 52:7–9

Though the unknown prophet welcomes the rebuilding of the Temple, his understanding of God's nature transcends the relationship between God and Israel:

Tomb at Pasargadae, traditionally thought to be that of Cyrus' final resting place.

Thus said the Lord:
The heaven is My throne
And the earth is My footstool:
Where could you build a house for Me,
What place could serve as My abode?
Isaiah 66:1

He envisions God's power radiating out from Zion and becoming manifest throughout the world.

Despite Cyrus's permission to return to Zion, only a minority of the Jews in Babylonia traveled to Palestine—less than a half million in the first wave, led by King Jehoiakin's son Sheshbazzar, who had been appointed governor. They were men of conviction and purpose, "whose spirit had been roused by God . . . to build the house of the Lord that is in Jerusalem." Those who stayed behind "supported them with silver vessels, with gold,

with livestock, and with precious objects" (*Ezra* 1:5–6). They also brought back to Jerusalem the Temple vessels captured by Nebuchadnezzar, which Cyrus had ordered his treasurer to return to them.

The early years of the restoration were disappointing. Though the returning exiles redistributed to the various clans the land of the small territory allotted to them and built a temporary altar on the site of the Temple, they could do little more during the first years of settlement, for they suffered from drought and heavy taxation. The death of Cyrus in 529 B.C.E. was followed by a period of disorder in the Persian empire that was reflected in the new settlement. Cyrus's successor, Cambyses, conquered Egypt in 525, in a campaign that threatened the fragile peace of the Jewish settlers in Judah. After Cambyses' death in 522, the line of succession was unclear, for much of the empire followed a pretender claiming to be Cambyses' murdered brother. The Persian empire was not firmly established until the reign of Darius I, which began in 521.

King Jehoiakin's son Sheshbazzar, who had led the return, is not mentioned again in the biblical account. According to some historians, he probably died soon after the initial settlement and was succeeded by his nephew Zerubbabel; others consider the two to be the same person. The prophets Haggai and Zechariah encouraged Zerubbabel to begin the rebuilding of the Temple. The community had appointed the high priest, Joshua ben Jozadak, as its leader, but the royalist faction, supported by the prophet Haggai, encouraged Zerubbabel to claim the throne. Zechariah, however, discouraged his ambition—"Not by might, nor by power, but by My spirit" (*Zechariah* 4:6)—and advised him to govern jointly with the high priest. Though Zechariah's advice was followed, Zerubbabel's name disappears from biblical accounts of the restoration soon after the beginning of the rebuilding of the Temple, perhaps because reports of his ambition had reached the Persian authorities.

The foundation of the Temple was laid in 520 B.C.E. Describing the occasion, Ezra, the scribe who led the second return, wrote:

> Many of the Priests and Levites and the chiefs
> of the clans, the old men who had seen the first
> house, wept loudly at the sight of the founding
> of this house. Many others shouted joyously
> at the top of their voices. The people could not
> distinguish the shouts of joy from the people's
> weeping, for the people raised a great shout,
> the sound of which could be heard from afar.
>
> *Ezra* 3:12–13

The rebuilding soon encountered obstacles, however. When the tribes of Judah and Benjamin rejected at-tempts by the Samaritans to join in the building, the latter denounced the builders to the Persians. Moreover, several of the previously independent nations under Persian control had taken advantage of the disorder to rebel. Immediately after his accession to the throne, Darius put down two attempted revolts in Babylon. In this atmosphere of uncertainty, Persian distrust was aroused by the rumors of royalist sentiment in Judah, and even by the rebuilding of the Temple. The satrap (chief administrator) of the western provinces, of which Judah was a part, was sent to Jerusalem to investigate. To allay his doubts about the advisability of rebuilding the Temple, the Jews showed him Cyrus's edict; a copy of it, found in the royal archives, corroborated the satrap's report. Darius confirmed Cyrus's edict, for he did not believe the Jews strong enough to regain their independence and wished to retain their friendship. He ordered that the completion of the Temple be funded by the royal revenue collected from the Jewish community and that the same source should also provide the daily sacrifices for the welfare of the Persian king and his sons.

The Second Temple was finished in 516 B.C.E., seventy years after its destruction. Therefore, according to tradition, it is the completion of the Temple, not the arrival of the first Jews to return under Cyrus's decree, that marks the end of the Babylonian exile, which is considered to have lasted for the full seventy years predicted by Jeremiah.

As Jacob Neusner and other scholars have noted, only a small number of Jews in Babylonia made the journey to Judah. Most of the Jewish community remained in Babylonia and supported the new community financially. In time, Babylonia was to become a major center of Jewish learning and culture. Yet it is because of the minority who made the journey that Jews have come to understand the central movement of their history as one of exile and return.

Ezra Leads Second Return

457 B.C.E.

> *The rebuilding of the Temple could not, in itself, overcome the difficulties encountered by the community of Jews who had returned from exile in Babylonia or guarantee its cultural and spiritual health. The spiritual guidance needed by the community was provided by Ezra, the scribe who led the second return and established the religious life of the Jewish people on a firm foundation of Torah.*

The Second Temple, completed in 516 B.C.E., became the focus of the Jewish people's religious and cultural identity until its destruction by the Romans in 70 C.E. Its dedication was an occasion of great rejoicing. Yet life in Palestine was harsh and bitter. The returning exiles had attempted to distribute the land fairly to the various clans, but the new community was soon troubled by social inequality, as poor harvests and high taxation forced farmers to sell their land and even their children. War was always a threat, for the small territory of Judah was troubled by hostile neighboring kingdoms. In the north, the Samaritans took up the old north-south rivalry. The Samaritans were an ethnically mixed people that had developed, after the Assyrian destruction of the northern kingdom, from intermarriage between the few members of the northern Israelite tribes who had avoided deportation and the foreign colonists whom the Assyrians had forcibly introduced at that time. The Samaritans considered themselves Israelites, but, because they practiced a diluted monotheism, the Jews refused to allow them to participate in the rebuilding of the Temple in Jerusalem. Out of resentment, they presented frequent complaints about the Jews to the Persian authorities.

Though the rebuilt Temple remained a treasured Jewish symbol and descendants of Joshua ben Jozadak—the first High Priest of the restoration, whom the community had named its leader—continued to serve as high priests, the priesthood soon became corrupt; thus, the Temple did little to improve the people's lives. In general, religious observance—especially of the Sabbath—became lax. Intermarriage was widespread, for, in an era in which arranged marriages were the norm, the leaders of the community found it expedient to improve relations with hostile neighbors by contracting marital alliances with them; the foreign wives brought their own religious customs with them. The pious few in the Jewish community in Judah seem to have withdrawn from worldly life and practiced asceticism. From these few came the prophetic voice of the time, that of the author of the last prophetic book, the *Book of Malachi*. His personal identity is unknown; "Malachi" is a Hebrew word meaning "my messenger." To right the evils of the time, he looked, not to human action, but to a day of judgment announced by the prophet Elijah.

The Jewish community of Babylonia was distressed by the news from Judah and obtained permission from the Persian king, Artaxerxes, to send an emissary to look into conditions there. They chose Ezra, a Torah scholar and scribe from a priestly family; he was an example of the new type of leader that was beginning to replace the prophets as the religious guides of the community. Ezra received from the king a decree granting him authority to appoint judges and to enforce the laws of the Torah by fining, imprisoning, banishing, or executing offenders. The decree also granted the Temple priests exemption from taxation, and the king and his council sent gifts for the Temple. Most important of all, Ezra was permitted to bring funds and additional settlers from the Jewish community in Babylonia.

In 457 B.C.E., in the month of Av, Ezra arrived in Jerusalem with eighteen hundred men (women and children were not included in the count). He brought with him a scroll of the Torah written by Babylonian scribes. Ezra spent the first four months examining the situation. Appalled at the extent of intermarriage, he fasted and mourned publicly. He prayed in front of the Temple, where he attracted a large crowd. After an influential man in the crowd expressed solidarity with him, Ezra called an assembly, which voted by a large majority to require men who had intermarried to divorce their wives. A committee was appointed to draw up a list of the men in question. The committee worked through the winter. In the spring of 457, the resolution was carried out, and foreign wives and their children were sent back to the wives' families of origin. *The Book of Ezra* ends at this point, with the triumphant moment of Ezra's early career.

Needless to say, the Samaritans and the other peoples affected by the decree were furious, since they interpreted the dissolution of the marriages as dissolution of the alliances the marriages were intended to cement. In the face of their anger, Ezra realized how vulnerable Jerusalem was to sudden attack; the city needed to be fortified. Ezra prepared to rebuild the walls, exceeding the authority given to him by the Persian king. The neighboring peoples denounced him, and the governor of Samaria sent the king a petition expressing the Samaritans' complaints. In response, the king ordered work on the walls of Jerusalem to be stopped at once and the completed portion to be razed.

News of the king's order reached Nehemiah, a high-ranking Jewish official at the Persian court who held the title—perhaps honorary—of King's Cupbearer. He appealed to the king and obtained permission to go to Jerusalem and rebuild the walls. The king also appointed

The priest and scribe Ezra reading the Torah to the people. From the menorah outside the Israeli Knesset by Benno Elkan.

Nehemiah governor but, unwilling to lose the services of an unusually competent official, made him promise not to settle permanently in Jerusalem but to return to the Persian court. Nehemiah's term as governor was limited to twelve years.

Nehemiah arrived in Jerusalem in the summer of 445 B.C.E. Three days after his arrival, he went out at night and secretly surveyed the walls. The next morning, he summoned the people to begin the work. Inspired by his enthusiasm, they completed the walls in fifty-two days, despite opposition, both open and secret, from the Samaritans and other neighboring peoples. At the same time, Nehemiah tried to remedy some of the social inequities in the Jewish community in Judah by canceling debts and restoring land to those who had been forced to sell it; because the governor's salary came from the people's taxes, he refused the allowance due him and paid for the expenses of his position out of his own considerable wealth.

Nehemiah next turned his attention to the community's religious life and sought out Ezra, whose life between the failure of his own attempt to rebuild the walls and Nehemiah's success many years later is not known. Some say he returned to Babylonia for a while. It is more likely, however, that he remained in Judah as a private citizen, studying, teaching, and writing. In addition to the book that bears his name, Ezra is credited with writing the genealogies of the *Book of Chronicles* and with a role in compiling the *Book of Psalms*. It was Nehemiah's success as governor, however, that gave Ezra the scope he needed to give the entire people firm grounding in the Torah.

An assembly was called on the first day of Tishrei in 445 B.C.E. From dawn until noon, Ezra read the Torah to the entire people—all men and women capable of understanding it—while the Levites provided explanations. The twenty-fourth of Tishrei was observed as a public fast day on which the people assembled to confess their personal and collective sins and to renew the covenant. A formal document of ratification was signed by Nehemiah, as governor, and by representatives of the priests, Levites, and ordinary Israelites. This document emphasized topically important Torah commandments such as avoidance of intermarriage with the surrounding peoples, remission of debt and rest for the land in the sabbatical years, payment of tithes, and the prohibition of business transactions on Sabbaths and festivals.

Nehemiah was recalled to the Persian court at the end of his term as governor but returned to Jerusalem for a brief second term to correct—at least temporarily—relapses into some of the conditions that had prevailed before the renewal of the covenant. The religious reforms that endured were those of Ezra, whose importance for Jewish history lies not only in his leading the second return but in his bringing the Torah—physically and spiritually—with him to Jerusalem. Indeed, he was so zealous in teaching the Torah that the rabbis said of him, "If Moses had not anticipated him, Ezra would have received the Torah." Ezra instituted regular Torah readings on the Sabbath, and on Mondays and Thursdays as well; because Mondays and Thursdays were market days on which the country people came to town to trade, the readings on those days gave them as well as the residents of Jerusalem opportunities to hear the Torah. These are still the days on which the Torah is read in the synagogue. Beyond his establishment of public Torah reading, however, it was Ezra's insistence on Torah as the basis of Jewish religious life that laid the foundation for traditions of Torah study and religious observance that have endured to this day.

Judaism Thrives in Southern Russia

740 C.E.

> *Around the year 600 C.E., a warlike Turkish tribe conquered what is now southern Russia. Within a short time, the domain of this people, known as the Khazars, stretched from the Caspian to the Black Sea. The Khazar empire, which flourished more than a thousand years ago, was the largest Jewish state ever. For two hundred years, between the eighth and tenth centuries, their empire was ruled by kings with Hebrew names like Menasheh and Hanukkah. The Khazars claimed descent from the biblical tribe of Simeon.*

During the fifth century, a group of warlike tribes known as the Khazars settled near the Caspian Sea during a major migration. They were of Hun or Turkish stock. The Khazars occupied a large stretch of territory north of the Caucasus that included all of the Volga region and, by the year 600, had conquered what is now southern Russia. Before long, the kingdom of the Khazars stretched from the Caspian to the Black Sea; its capital city, Ityl, was at the mouth of the Volga River.

The Khazar kingdom had significant commercial and military influence. It became, in effect, an "empire of the steppe," a continental bridge crossed by wandering merchants. The Khazars mingled with the native Slavic population, and Jewish, Christian, and Muslim merchants visited them and influenced their culture.

Sometime during the eighth century, the Khazar king and nobility decided to abandon their pagan worship and adopt a monotheistic religion. The merchants from the Byzantine (Eastern Roman) empire urged Christianity upon them. The merchants from Persia urged them to adopt Islam. Apparently, each of these religions was successful in gaining a large number of followers among the Khazars, but the royal family and many of the nobility were impressed with the Jewish faith and converted to Judaism about 740 C.E. Though the actual reasons for their choice are not clear, the story of the conversion of the Khazar king to Judaism formed the basis for Judah Halevi's famous philosophical dialogue *Kuzari*.

The *khaqan*, or king, who converted to Judaism was named Bulan. The story accepted by the Khazars is that Bulan decided to become a Jew after listening to a disputation concerning the relative merits of Islam, Christianity, and Judaism by an Islamic mullah, a Christian priest, and a rabbi. A later *khaqan*, Obadiah, in an effort to give the Khazars' Judaism a firm doctrinal and practical foundation, invited rabbis and talmudic scholars from either Babylonia or the Crimea. These rabbis founded synagogues and religious schools and taught the Torah to the Khazar people, who clung to their Judaism tenaciously for a long time.

Later scholars have tried to determine more accurately why the Khazars converted to Judaism. According to one theory, there had long been Jewish settlers in this region, and their numbers rose as migrants fled from Byzantium. The Jews instructed their nomadic neighbors in advanced techniques for cultivating the soil. They probably also taught the previously illiterate Khazars the art of writing in Hebrew. Because the Khazars used Hebrew, some scholars consider it plausible that they felt a certain affinity toward the Jewish religion as well.

Since the Khazari rulers were separated from the major centers of Jewish learning, they knew little about talmudic law and tradition. Nevertheless, in the major dispute of the era between the Karaites—who rejected the Oral Torah—and the adherents of rabbinic Judaism, who regarded both the Oral and Written Torah as the basis of Jewish practice, the Khazars, for the most part, supported the latter.

For several centuries, the Jewish kingdom of the Khazars continued to rule over southern Russia. At its height, the kingdom covered a territory hundreds of times larger than the modern state of Israel, though the actual Jewish population in the Khazar kingdom probably never was larger than thirty-five thousand. During the eighth century, the Khazars were able to act as a buffer between Byzantium and the expanding Islamic powers. Later, therefore, they were caught in the middle between Islam and Christianity. In the tenth century, as the Abbasid Empire decayed and Byzantium grew more powerful, the Byzantine empire was able to threaten the Khazar kingdom, which lost its ability to act as a buffer state. The Byzantine rulers in Constantinople made it clear to the Russians that they would not stand in the way if the Russians chose to invade the Khazar state. Nevertheless, despite being defeated and occupied, the Khazars remained a nominally Jewish state until the invasion of the Mongols in the middle of the thirteenth century.

A letter in Hebrew dated 950 C.E. from a Khazar Jew. The letter mentions incidents that led to the conversion of the Khazars and to the events that occurred in the Khazar empire during the tenth century.

The descendants of the Khazars reached eastern and central Europe. There is substantial evidence that some of them settled in Slavic lands, where they took part in establishing the major Jewish centers of eastern Europe. It is also significant that Tshagataish, the Turkic dialect that was the language of the Khazar Jews, is still spoken in Poland, Hungary, and Lithuania by the Karaites. It is also widely believed that many Khazar Jews fled to Poland to avoid forced baptism.

Moreover, some of the groups that migrated from eastern to central Europe have been called Khazars and may have originated in the former Khazar empire. Some apparently fled into northern Hungary, where, to this day, there are villages that bear such names as Kozar and Kozardie.

It was only with the translation of Yehudah Halevi's *Kuzari* into Latin in 1660 that the story of the Khazars became known in the Western world. The *Kuzari* is a fictitious dialogue imagined to have taken place between the king of the Khazars and Hisdai ibn Shaprut, a well-known rabbi of Muslim Spain in the tenth century. From this book, and especially from the reports of Arabs and Jews from tenth-century Constantinople, the existence of the Khazars and a general outline of their history became clear. The Khazars themselves left little physical evidence of their history and culture. Archaeological digs have yielded few artifacts, and most of what is known comes from Arabic sources.

Ba'al Shem Tov Founds Hasidic Movement

1736

The founding of the Hasidic movement was the result of the efforts of a pious man named Israel ben Eliezer, who was born in 1700 in Okop, Podolia, then southeastern Poland, now the western Ukraine. He became known as the Ba'al Shem Tov (Master of the Good Name). In the eighteenth and nineteenth centuries Hasidism spread among Jewish communities in Poland, Russia, and Austria-Hungary. The Ba'al Shem Tov was the movement's first tzaddik ("righteous" or "proven man").

Born in Okop, in southeastern Poland, to poor and elderly parents, Israel ben Eliezer was orphaned while still a child. When he was twelve years old, he became a teacher and caretaker at a *heder*, a religious elementary school. He preferred the wooded outdoors to school, however, and resisted acquiring a talmudic education.

At eighteen he married, and over the next eighteen years Israel worked at a number of different kinds of jobs, including kosher slaughterer and school assistant. It was during this phase of his life that, according to disciples, he acquired a reputation as a healer. According to one story, a miraculous wall of fire arose and saved him from thieves who had promised to take him to the Holy Land through an underground tunnel.

While in his twenties, Israel and his wife lived in seclusion in the Carpathian Mountains. Sometimes, to earn money, Israel would work as a lime digger. In the mountains, he later told his followers, he communicated with the biblical prophet Ahijah the Shilonite, who taught the prophet Elijah. As a healer, Israel used folk remedies combined with spiritual powers to work his cures.

A portrait of the Ba'al Shem Tov.

In 1736, when he was thirty-six years old, Israel ben Eliezer settled in Medzibozh, Podolia, where followers, sometimes numbering in the thousands, gathered to bask in his presence. His reputation grew. Eventually he was considered a great spiritual figure and was known as the Besht, an acronym for Ba'al Shem Tov, Master of the Good Name.

The Ba'al Shem Tov preached that God was accessible to all Jews. He told stories and parables that even the least sophisticated Jew could understand. When the Besht taught that the way to God did not require great learning, uneducated Jews responded to his message.

Dressed like a peasant, smoking a pipe, the Besht told his stories in the marketplace or chatted with other Jews while evening prayers were being recited. The common people gathered around him were cheered by the message that it was possible to be a pious Jew without the rationalist-based talmudic learning.

Influenced by the mystical thought of the sixteenth century Kabbalist Isaac Luria, the Ba'al Shem Tov argued that the most important goal of religious life was spiritual communion with God. The constant focusing of the mind upon God could be achieved not only through prayer but in each and every part of daily life including eating, drinking, and conversation. Seeking ways to enhance popular participation, he developed a new theory of prayer that he hoped would bring more devotees into the fold. Prayer, he asserted, was more of a supernatural act than a human effort—with man breaking down the barriers of his natural existence, trying to gain access to the divine world. The best way to gain such access, the Besht insisted, was to concentrate one's mind on the letters in the prayer book, rather than reading the prayer. In this way, the shapes of the letters dissolve, and the divine attributes hidden in the letter can be "seen." The Besht called this act "entering into the heavenly halls." The Ba'al Shem Tov's critics, known as Mitnaggedim ("opponents"), regarded his teachings as a threat to their own belief system—that all that mattered spiritually was the study of Torah.

The Besht opposed the kind of Messianism that had been discredited by the apostasy of Shabbetai Tsevi and argued that his followers could experience cycles of ecstasy within their own lives. The Ba'al Shem Tov did not believe that one's attitude toward faith was dependent upon a messianic redeemer. In a famous letter to his brother-in-law, the Besht wrote that the Messiah had spoken to him in a dream to say that he would enter the world "only when all Israel is capable of uniting the lower and upper worlds through prayer and meditation."

The Besht wrote no scholarly treatises; only letters. It was his chief disciples, Jacob Joseph of Polonnoye and Dov Ber of Mezhirech, who recorded his teachings in writings. Dov Ber of Mezhirech succeeded the Ba'al Shem Tov as the leader of Hasidim.

It was the Besht's hope to reinvigorate Judaism. Within a generation, Hasidism spread throughout many Jewish communities in Eastern Europe. In the modern day, thousands of Jews kept the Hasidic movement alive in the former Soviet Union with many of them eventually reaching the United States and Israel. One of the greatest Hasidic leaders in the world was the Lubavitcher Rebbe, Menachem Mendel Schneerson, who established his headquarters in Brooklyn, New York. though they encourage study far more than did the early followers of the Besht, several hundred thousand Hasidim around the world, serving God with their merriment and singing, still carry out the legacy of the Ba'al Shem Tov.

Rebecca Gratz Introduces
First Sunday School

1838

> *Rebecca Gratz, who was born on March 4, 1781, in Philadelphia, Pennsylvania, was a social welfare activist. The most eminent Jewish woman of antebellum America, she introduced the first Jewish Sunday school in the United States and founded a number of other key Jewish welfare institutions.*

Rebecca Gratz's father, Michael, was born in Langendorf, Germany, immigrated to the United States, and with his brother, Barnard, operated a prominent shipping and trading business. Rebecca's mother, Miriam, was the daughter of Joseph Simon, a leading merchant of Lancaster, Pennsylvania. Miriam had twelve children, ten of whom survived to adulthood; Rebecca was the seventh child. She lived with her family in Philadelphia. Her father traded with Indians and shipped kosher meat.

Practicing Jews, the Gratz family clung enthusiastically to their Judaism, and observed the Jewish dietary rules in their home. When Rebecca's aunt, her mother's sister, married a non-Jew, Rebecca's mother broke off relations with her sister.

Rebecca always dressed neatly in plain black with thin white collars and cuffs and a close-fitting bonnet over her dark brown curls. Although she received little formal education, she was an elegant, cultured, good-natured woman, who established her own identity.

Moving in the best social circles, she counted among her acquaintances such well-known personalities as author Washington Irving and politician Henry Clay; well read, Rebecca loved to write letters. Both of her

Thomas Sully's portrait of Rebecca Gratz.

parents met early deaths, and Rebecca accepted the responsibility of running the household, which included the nine children of her sister Rachel, who had died very young. Taking care of her many nieces and nephews, Rebecca was easily drawn into the world of social work.

Rebecca fell in love with a young promising attorney named Samuel Ewing. He proposed to her, but with vivid memories of the pain her aunt and two brothers had inflicted on the family by marrying outside the faith, Rebecca turned down his offer. She never married.

She immersed herself in charitable works. In 1801, she served as the secretary of the Female Association for the Relief of Women and Children in Reduced Circumstances. In 1819, she founded the Female Hebrew Benevolent Society, which took care of the many Jewish immigrants flocking to the United States. The first full-fledged Jewish philanthropic institution in America, it was the inspiration for all other Jewish-American welfare agencies. The Philadelphia Orphan Asylum, which Rebecca Gratz also founded, was the first Jewish foundling home in the United States. She was its secretary for forty years.

True recognition came to Rebecca Gratz for founding the first Jewish Sunday school system in America in 1838. She realized that the growing population of Jewish children in Philadelphia needed a great deal more religious training than it was receiving. An earlier attempt to establish a Jewish private school for children had proved completely unsuccessful. Rebecca, after following the Christian model, drew up plans for the first Hebrew Sunday School in America, called the Hebrew Sunday School Society, located in Philadelphia. She served as its president and supervisor for twenty-six years.

Realizing that time was short, she limited instruction to the general principles of the Jewish religion. A series of questions and answers were prepared on religious subjects and pupils were expected to learn them by heart. Little time was given over to the study of Hebrew or Jewish history. Rebecca was assisted by a number of young women from the Mikveh Israel Congregation. Her school succeeded in creating strong Jewish loyalties on the part of the children who attended.

Efforts were made to open more advanced schools. The establishment of the Hebrew Education Society was encouraged in 1849 as a Jewish all-day school. Maimonides College, which opened in 1867, was designed to provide a broader Jewish education and to serve as a rabbinical academy, but it closed after six years.

A room over the Phoenix Hose Company on Zane Street (later Filbert Street) near Seventh was the site of the first Jewish Sunday school in Philadelphia. On a table stood a hand bell and a contribution box for the poor of Jerusalem. Oddly, the first Sunday school had a decidedly Christian atmosphere at first. Some of the early textbooks were Christian, with the words "Jesus" and "Christ" appearing. Because it was the only edition in print at the time, the King James Version of the Bible was used as well. When the school opened, the only Jewish texts available in English were older theological works published in London and elsewhere.

Rebecca Gratz's efforts proved a huge success. The Sunday school movement spread to Richmond, Charleston, Savannah, Baltimore, and New York. By the 1890s no other type of Jewish educational effort was as important as the Sunday school. It continues in synagogues today.

Oddly enough, it was in a non-Jewish context that Rebecca Gratz attained a certain historical significance. Often, she visited Saratoga Springs, New York, with her brother Joseph; there, she met Washington Irving. When she learned that his fianceé, Matilda Hoffman, was seriously ill, Rebecca nursed Matilda during her final days. Beyond her beauty and charm, it was Rebecca's devotion to Matilda that especially impressed Irving, who, during a visit to England in 1817, recounted her behavior to his friend, Sir Walter Scott, who was writing his novel *Ivanhoe*. So impressed was he with what he heard, that Scott modeled his heroine in the novel after Rebecca Gratz. Following *Ivanhoe's* publication, Scott wrote to Irving in 1819: "How do you like your Rebecca? Does the Rebecca I have pictured compare well with the pattern given?"

Rebecca Gratz, who died at the age of eighty-eight, is described as the matriarch of Jewish-American women.

Reform Temple Founded in New York

April 6, 1845

Beginning in a rented room in 1845, New York City's Temple Emanu-El blossomed into the largest synagogue in the world. Today it stands as a center of American Reform Jewry.

As early as 1830, some Jews in America advocated reforms in synagogue ritual similar to what was being instituted in Germany. Increasingly, as more and more Jews arrived from central Europe, the number of Reform Jewish sympathizers rose. But it was only after the wave of German-Jewish immigrants to the United States in the 1840s that Reform Judaism began to flourish in the new world.

In September 1844, a cultural society was established on New York's Lower East Side, comprising liberal German Jews who came together out of a wish to develop religious roots in America. In April 1845 thirty-three members of the cultural society raised thirty dollars to establish a Reform congregation. It was the first New York Reform congregation and the third such liberal congregation in America. At the time there were only 15,000 Jews in the United States.

The Jews who founded Temple Emanu-El strove to adjust their lives and institutions to American society. Caught between the crosscurrents of assimilation and religious observance, wishing to be neither totally assimilated nor entirely observant, they searched for a middle road.

At first congregants used a traditional prayer book. Men sat in the front rows of the small rented synagogue, women in a section behind them. Men wore hats as well as prayer shawls. Many of the congregants observed the dietary laws. The only significant addition to the service was the presence of a choir.

Decorum was insisted upon. Both days of two-day Jewish festivals were observed. A German hymnal was introduced so that those who understood no Hebrew could still participate in the service. The sermon, which soon became part of the weekly Sabbath service, was used to educate the laity in the tenets of Judaism.

The material resources available to the founders of Temple Emanu-El were limited. Their first house of worship was a rented room on the second floor of a building at the corner of Grand and Clinton Streets. The synagouge was in the heart of the Orthodox Jewish community. The founding members called their new home Temple Emanu-El, Hebrew for "God is with us."

In 1848, outgrowing the rented room, Temple Emanu-El moved to Chrystie Street, a few blocks to the west. The congregation still could not afford to erect its own edifice, so it purchased a building that had previously been used as a Methodist church. In time, male congregants discontinued wearing hats in the synagogue, and the second day of festivals was no longer observed.

Congregation Emanu-El began serving as the center for Reform Jewish sentiment in the United States, providing a model that inspired bursts of Jewish reform in other American cities.

One of the distinguishing aspects of Emanu-El was its upper-crust membership which, by the 1860s, included New York's most prominent bankers, lawyers, tradesmen, and their families. These were New York City's German-Jewish elite: the Lehmans, the Goulds, the Bloomingdales, and the Morgenthaus.

In 1868, the congregation moved into a domed brownstone on Fifth Avenue at Forty-third Street. A critic called it "the finest example of Moorish architecture in the Western world." The *New York Times*, reporting on the dedication of the synagogue's new building, noted that the Temple spoke for a new era—a "universal communion" of reason and "a Judaism of the heart, in which the spirit of religion was more important than the letter."

In 1873, services at Temple Emanu-El were conducted in English for the first time, as German was replaced as the synagogue's language of choice.

If Temple Emanu-El was a focal point for Reform Jewry, most American Jews remained unaffiliated. Fewer than 10 percent of American Jews belonged to a synagogue.

Emanu-El became known throughout New York City as "The Temple."

Louis Marshall, the president of the congregation from 1916 to 1929, was the driving force behind the decision to merge with another important institution of Reform Jewry, Temple Beth-El, and move further northward on Fifth Avenue to Sixty-fifth Street, purchasing the Astor mansion. A majority of the congregation's membership lived uptown.

Construction of the new building began in 1927, and work was completed by the autumn of 1929 at a cost of 7.5 million dollars. Louis Marshall died on September 29th of that year; his funeral was the first service held in the new building. The formal dedication ceremony took place on January 10, 1930; Temple Emanu-El calls itself the largest Jewish house of worship in the world.

Temple Emanu-El as it looked shortly after it was founded.

Temple Emanu-El provides the unusual amenity of transmitting Friday night prayer services over radio station WQXR, owned by the *New York Times*. The structure of Temple Emanu-El is cathedral-like, with a limestone facade and a combined seating capacity in all sanctuaries of four thousand people. It is the third-largest house of worship in New York City, ranking behind the Church of St. John the Divine and St. Patrick's Cathedral.

Temple Emanu-El celebrated its one hundred fiftieth anniversary in April 1995 by dedicating a Torah commissioned for the event.

Ellis Island Receives Jews Arriving in America

1891

To the hundreds of thousands of Jews who poured into the United States at the end of the nineteenth century, Ellis Island became a symbol of their new lives, both a positive and negative one, the excitement of arrival tempered by the rigorous questioning and examination of immigration officers. To help ease the transition, immigration aid organizations helped the arriving immigrants, merging in 1902 into the Hebrew Immigrant Aid Society (HIAS). It tried to smooth the path for immigrants both at Ellis Island and in the immediate period after as they settled into their new lives.

By the late 1800s, faced with worsening poverty and oppression, Russian Jews had more and more reason to leave their homeland and seek a better life. Between 1800 and 1881 two hundred fifty thousand Jews emigrated from eastern Europe to western Europe and the United States. Between 1881 and 1899, that figure rose to four hundred fifty thousand—an average of twenty-four thousand Jews a year.

Whole families came, sometimes entire communities. Improved ocean transportation aided emigration. Some 1.75 million Jews arrived from Bremen and Hamburg on German liners; another 750,000 Jews left Liverpool on the Cunard lines. These huge ships carried hundreds of passengers at a time. Each person received a bed, towel, soap, and life preserver. Cabins were shared, sometimes with up to six people in a room; married couples were given private rooms. Thanks to Jewish philanthropic organizations, kosher food was available.

When the immigrants sailed in sight of American shores, the hardships of the voyage receded, and thoughts of a new life became uppermost in their minds. Mary Antin, in her autobiography, *From Polotz to Boston*, wrote: "America was in everybody's mouth. Businessmen talked of it over their accounts, the market women made up their quarrels that they might discuss it from stall to stall... children played at emigrating...all talked of it." Arriving in New York was a dream come true for immigrants such as the editor of the *Jewish Daily Forward* and novelist Abraham Cahan, who was so glad to see "The tender blue of sea and sky, the dignified bustle of passing craft—above all those floating, squatting, multitudinously-windowed palaces which I consequently learned to call ferries. It was all so utterly unlike anything I had ever seen or dreamed of before. It unfolded itself like a divine revelation."

For many decades the immigration station for New York Harbor was Castle Garden, under the supervision of the State of New York. Then, in 1890, a celebrated Supreme Court decision gave the Federal government jurisdiction over immigration. Soon thereafter, the United States Treasury Department transformed Ellis Island in New York Harbor into its main inspection port for newcomers.

Once owned by the heirs of Samuel Ellis, this three-acre sandbank was located just northeast of Bedloe's Island and the Statue of Liberty, and was in fact closer to New Jersey than to New York.

Like Castle Garden, the main staging area at Ellis Island was a large enclosure on the ground floor. Here immigrants were numbered and tagged, then placed in groups of thirty for an initial medical examination and processing. If a newcomer failed to satisfy an in-

COURTESY OF THE ELLIS ISLAND/LIBERTY PARK MUSEUM

Immigrants awaiting examination.

spector, he or she was sent to examining rooms on the second floor.

Up to five thousand immigrants each day routinely passed inspection at Ellis Island. Few were kept overnight. The ones who did stay the night were given decent food and clean beds in dormitories that were nicely lit and well ventilated.

Generally speaking, however, the immigrant found being at Ellis Island a rather unpleasant experience. The name Ellis Island evoked painful memories to immigrants long after they had settled in America. They remembered the seemingly endless red tape.

Physicians had been instructed to check for granuloma, trachoma, and other communicable diseases common to eastern Europe. An infected immigrant could be returned to his or her point of origin.

Then there were the endless questions:

- Have you ever been arrested for a crime involving moral turpitude?

- Have you got a job in America? (To reply yes was an invitation to be deported—for American law prohibited anyone from contracting for foreign labor.)

- Are you an anarchist?

- Are you willing to live in subordination to the laws of the United States?

- Are you a polygamist?

- Have you any friends in New York? Give me the address.

- How much money have you got? Show me, please.

"They are not a bit better than Cossacks," novelist Abraham Cahan's hero, David Levinsky, remarked to his friend in *The Rise of David Levinsky* (1917). "But they neither looked nor spoke like Cossacks," he reflected, "so their gruff voices were part of the uncanny scheme of things that surrounded me."

The fresh-off-the-boat immigrants navigating this maze were in need of advice. A number of immigrant aid groups, armed more with goodwill than resources, sought to smooth the immigrants' arrival at Ellis Island; these volunteer, makeshift groups merged in 1902 into the Hebrew Immigrant Aid Society (HIAS), whose representatives helped immigrants locate relatives, lodging, employment, even negotiate the purchase of railroad tickets to other cities.

HIAS, which received occasional donations from Jacob Schiff and other uptown German Jews, became the most important Jewish immigration agency in the

United States. Its agents acted as interpreters and lawyers, trying to protect the newcomers from being exploited by officials who might misinterpret law and abuse the discretionary powers vested in the Board of Special Inquiry. HIAS maintained responsibility for the immigrants until relatives and friends could take over their care and handling. HIAS even advertised in the Jewish daily newspapers in an effort to find the relatives of new immigrants. It ran an employment agency as well as a temporary shelter in New York.

United Hebrew Charities in New York took on the task of handling newcomers who required long-range relief and rehabilitation after passing through Ellis Island. Many immigrants needed such aid. Even as late as 1907, 40 percent of the Jews arriving in America from eastern Europe were poor, having spent all their funds to cover the cost of passage.

America signified for thousands of Jewish immigrants the opportunity to escape a past freighted with poverty and despair. For all the difficulties immigrant procedures posed to new arrivals, Ellis Island was a gateway that held out the promise of a better life, one that was more economically secure, more tranquil, and full of possibilities.

Herzl Organizes First Zionist Congress

AUGUST 29, 1897

On August 29, 1897, Theodor Herzl convened the First Zionist Congress in Basel and afterwards wrote in his diary, "At Basel I created the Jewish State. If I were to say this out loud everybody would laugh at me. In five years, perhaps, but certainly in fifty everybody will agree." His words proved prophetic.

Theodor Herzl.

The man who created the modern Zionist movement by organizing the First Zionist Congress in Basel, Switzerland, was Theodor Herzl. Born in 1860 in Budapest, he was an author and journalist. As a correspondent in Paris in the early 1890s, Herzl had covered the Dreyfus trial and was struck by how widespread anti-Semitism had become. He searched for solutions to the "Jewish question" and thought the best one was the establishment of a Jewish state.

To gain support from the major powers, Herzl engaged in active diplomacy, meeting with an assortment of European leaders as well as organizing several Zionist congresses. He died forty-four years before the United Nations approved the creation of a Jewish state in Palestine, the dream he, more than anyone else, had helped to bring about.

Theodor's father was a wealthy merchant. A fledgling writer even in high school, Theodor published his first newspaper article anonymously. When in his final year of high school, his eighteen-year-old sister Pauline died, his mother suffered a severe psychological setback and his father moved the family to Vienna.

Theodor studied law at the University of Vienna. He joined a fraternity but left abruptly when it adopted a resolution barring Jews from becoming members. In 1884, when he was twenty-four, Herzl obtained a doctorate in law. Working gratis as a clerk in a judge's office, Herzl occasionally traveled to Salzburg where he began writing plays.

In 1891, he joined the staff of the *Neue Freie Presse,*

Delegates' card at the First Zionist Congress at Basel.

which was the mouthpiece of the assimilated Jewish-Viennese bourgeoisie, and became its Paris correspondent. Even before he covered the Dreyfus Affair for the paper, Herzl had begun to think about how to solve the Jewish question. At one point, he suggested that all Jews convert to Christianity. The Dreyfus trial, however, turned him into a fiery Zionist.

Herzl began in 1895 to pour his ideas into a pamphlet that he called *Der Judenstaat,* "The Jewish State." Later that year he returned to Vienna to become the literary editor of the *Neue Freie Presse.* Published in February 1896, *Der Judenstaat* argued that Jews are a nation, not simply a community of believers. Neither civil emancipation nor cultural assimilation were adequate solutions to the problem of Jewish identity. In this era of nationalism, the Jewish problem, because it was "political," required a political solution.

Herzl advocated the establishment of a Jewish commonwealth or state; its population would include all the Jews who were not wanted elsewhere. The existence of the commonwealth would serve to normalize the lives of

Jews left behind in the Diaspora. At first Herzl was not definite about whether the commonwealth should be located in Palestine or in some other territory, perhaps in North or South America. In time, however, he concluded that Palestine was the logical choice because only the Land of Israel would appeal to large numbers of Jews.

Herzl used his connections to seek support for his ideas. An admirer, the Zionist writer Max Nordau, introduced Herzl to the British writer Israel Zangwill; in turn, Zangwill had Herzl speak to London's Maccabean Club, whose members were sympathetic to Herzl's Zionist urgings.

To his surprise and regret, Herzl soon realized that most of the Jewish lay and spiritual leadership in Europe were not enthusiastic about the notion of Jewish peoplehood and thus disapproved of the establishment of a Jewish state. Still, he was not discouraged. Herzl was tremendously popular and able to gain entrance into the inner sanctums of the most powerful leaders of Europe. In June 1896, for example, he managed an audience with the grand vizier in Constantinople.

On July 18, 1896 Herzl met with Baron Edmond de Rothschild, who had founded farming settlements in Palestine. The baron and his *Hovevei Zion* (Lovers of Zion) movement rejected Herzl's ideas, because Rothschild doubted that the Jewish masses would rally to support a state. But the baron's rejection, more than anything else, prompted Herzl to consider the need for organizing the Jewish people in order to achieve the creation of a Jewish state in Palestine.

At a preliminary conference on March 6, 1897, delegates from *Hovevei Zion* societies in Germany, Austria, and Galicia adopted Herzl's idea to convene a general Zionist congress. Herzl founded and financed the weekly *Die Welt* in order to disseminate the Zionist idea; the first issue appeared on June 4, 1897.

Herzl had high hopes for the congress that he was organizing for the late summer; perhaps the major powers would take a greater interest in Zionism. Maybe the Jews would be offered a territory. He was concerned, too, that with the world's press focusing on the meeting, hopes would be dashed and nothing would come of the sessions.

On August 29, 1897, Herzl convened the First Zionist Congress, the first international gathering of Jews on a national and secular basis. It set up the World Zionist Organization as the political organization of the "Jewish people en route." Herzl chaired the First Congress (he would go on to chair the congresses until his death) and was elected president of the World Zionist Organization.

In Basel Herzl called to order two hundred four delegates who represented nearly every country in which Jews lived.

One delegate arose and recited the ancient Hebrew benediction for first occasions, "Blessed art Thou, O Lord our God, King of the Universe, for keeping us alive, preserving us, and permitting us to attain this day." The delegates were all conscious of the great historic importance of the occasion. Herzl's unflagging optimism seemed to pervade the crowd.

Herzl and Max Nordau reported on different aspects of Jewish life. They then accepted the task of organizing a Zionist movement. The Congress approved the creation of a Zionist organization in every country.

Most important, the Congress decided on a set of Zionist aims that came to be known as the Basel Program: "Zionism seeks to establish for the Jewish people a publicly recognized, legally secured home in Palestine." To attain that end, the Congress contemplated:

- The promotion by appropriate means of the settlement in Palestine of Jewish farmers, artisans, and manufacturers.
- The organization and uniting of the whole of Jewry by means of appropriate institutions, both local and international, in accordance with the laws of each country.
- The strengthening and fostering of Jewish national sentiment and national consciousness.
- Preparatory steps toward obtaining the consent of governments, where necessary, in order to reach the goal of Zionism.

Deciding to meet again the following year, the Congress adjourned. Delegates left the meeting feeling very enthusiastic. After the Congress Herzl wrote in his diary: "At Basel I created the Jewish State. If I were to say this out loud everybody would laugh at me. In five years, perhaps, but certainly in fifty everybody will agree." On May 14, 1948, fifty years and eight months later, David Ben-Gurion proclaimed the birth of the new state of Israel.

Ben-Yehuda Revives Hebrew Language

1897

Through the extraordinary efforts of one man, Eliezer Ben-Yehuda, Hebrew became the everyday language of Palestinian Jewry. The Lithuanian-born Ben-Yehuda was a Hebrew writer and lexicographer; he had become convinced that Hebrew should again be the main language of the Jews. He made his way to Paris and then to Palestine where he became the catalyst for the modern revival of Hebrew, the biblical language that many Jews refused to speak, as the everyday language of Jews in the Land of Israel.

Born Eliezer Yitzhak Perelman, Eliezer used the pseudonym Ben-Yehuda in his literary efforts and officially adopted the name when he traveled to Palestine in 1881. Eliezer's father, a follower of the Lubavitcher Rebbe, died when his son was five years old.

At age thirteen, Eliezer was sent to an uncle so that he could attend a yeshiva in nearby Polotsk. The yeshiva's director, however, introduced Eliezer to secular literature, including a Hebrew-language translation of Daniel Defoe's *Robinson Crusoe*. Thus began Eliezer's commitment to the use of Hebrew for secular as well as religious purposes.

Eliezer's uncle was concerned that his nephew had strayed from traditional Jewish studies so he sent Eliezer to a yeshiva in the Vilna district where he met a Lubavitcher Hasid named Samuel Naphtali Herz Jonas, a writer for Hebrew-language periodicals. Jonas convinced Eliezer that he should continue formal study so that he could graduate from high school. Jonas's eldest daughter, Deborah, taught Eliezer Russian, French, and German. A year later, Eliezer entered the Dvinsk Gymnasium, graduating from the school in 1877, at the age of nineteen.

Ben-Yehuda sympathized with the Russian revolutionary movement, which distanced him further from traditional Jewish life. When Russia and Turkey went to war in 1877, the struggle of the Balkan nations for their independence convinced Ben-Yehuda that Jews, too, ought to strive for a national homeland. Ben-Yehuda traveled to Paris in 1878 to study medicine, hoping to settle later in Palestine.

In 1879, Ben-Yehuda wrote an article called *"She'elah Lohata"* ("A Burning Question") for the Hebrew-language magazine *Ha-Shahar*, using the name E. Ben-Yehuda in print for the first time. In the article he urged Jews to immigrate to Palestine, contending that only in a country with a Jewish majority could a living Hebrew literature and a distinct Jewish nationality develop and thrive. He encouraged Jews to speak Hebrew as their everyday language.

While studying medicine in Paris, Ben-Yehuda had developed tuberculosis and was hospitalized at the Rothschild Hospital, where he met a Jerusalem scholar, A. M. Luncz. The scholar pointed out to Ben-Yehuda that Jews in Jerusalem used the Sephardic pronunciation in speaking Hebrew.

Ben-Yehuda routinely sent articles promoting Jewish settlement in Palestine to a Jerusalem-based, Hebrew-language journal called *Havatzelet*, ("The Lily"), but he became increasingly concerned that people would brand him a hypocrite for urging that Jews immigrate to Palestine while he remained behind in Paris. "In those days," he wrote, "it was as if the heavens had suddenly opened, and a clear, incandescent light flashed before my eyes, and a mighty inner voice sounded in my ears; the renaissance of Israel on its ancestral soil."

In 1881, dropping his medical studies, Ben-Yehuda decided to immigrate to Palestine. While en route, in Vienna, he was reunited with Deborah Jonas; they were married in Cairo and reached Jaffa later that year. Ben-Yehuda announced to his new wife that they would speak only Hebrew to each other. Deborah agreed. Her husband decided that they would use the Sephardic pronunciation because he was convinced that it was closest to biblical Hebrew.

At the time, only a few Jews spoke Hebrew in Jerusalem. Because they thought it to be a holy language, Orthodox Jews did not dare utter Hebrew in simple conversation outside of the synagogue. Hebrew should be used only in reading from the Bible and in prayer, they believed. The few secular Jews in Palestine, who were of European descent, also had no interest in speaking Hebrew. But once he was appointed the associate editor of *Havatzelet*, Ben-Yehuda imposed upon himself the task of making Hebrew the language of Palestinian Jewry.

When Ben-Yehuda learned that his wife was pregnant, he asked her to promise that their child would be the first in centuries to hear only the Hebrew language at home.

A portrait of Eliezer Ben-Yehuda.

Deborah acquiesced to her husband's wishes. Their son, Ben-Zion (later called Itamar Ben-Avi), became the first modern Hebrew-speaking child. Ben-Yehuda's decision to use Hebrew exclusively in the home imposed a great burden on his five children, for they were now deprived of the opportunity to play with friends, having no language in common with other children.

Ben-Yehuda ingratiated himself with the Orthodox Jews of Jerusalem, believing that they would be the easiest segment of the Jewish community to convert to speaking modern Hebrew—even if they didn't want to speak the language, at least they were familiar with it. He grew a beard and earlocks and convinced his wife to wear a *sheytl* (wig), but the Orthodox Jews reviled Ben-Yehuda, charging him with debasing the holy tongue through everyday use. They threw stones at him

and denounced him to the Turkish authorities. He even was jailed briefly by the Turkish authorities for sedition.

Ben-Yehuda refused to abandon his mission. He founded the Hebrew Language Council in 1890, the forerunner of the Academy of the Hebrew Language, and created the first Hebrew-language newspaper for children. He also encouraged Jews to take a Hebrew-language surname, as he had done by exchanging Perelman for Ben-Yehuda, a practice adopted by many Israelis in later years.

Tragedy struck the Ben-Yehuda household in 1891, when Deborah died at age thirty-seven. Within the next three months, three of their children also died. Ben-Yehuda soon married his wife's sister, Hemdah, who aided her new husband in his literary work and, after his death in 1922, devoted herself to the continued publication of his Hebrew-language dictionary.

By 1897, Ben-Yehuda's dream was materializing. Hebrew was increasingly accepted as the everyday tongue of Jews in Palestine. The real breakthrough came in the isolated farming communities in rural Palestine, not in Jerusalem, where Orthodox Jews continued to oppose Ben-Yehuda's dream. By convincing village schools to use Hebrew exclusively, Ben-Yehuda ensured that Jewish youngsters, as they grew up and married, would use the language in their homes.

Books and plays began to appear in Hebrew. Ben-Yehuda started working on his *Dictionary of Ancient and Modern Hebrew* and remained at the task for the rest of his life. His goal was to make Hebrew literature simple and concrete, to do away with the florid rhetoric that had long characterized the Hebrew language.

Ben-Yehuda's dictionary included not only established Hebrew words but also new words he coined to describe aspects of modern life unknown in biblical times. The first word he improvised was *millon*, "dictionary," from the word *millah*, meaning "word." He also coined the word *leumiut*, which means "nationalism." He introduced these words and many more into his everyday speech and into his writings; he also encouraged his family to use these newly coined words. Ben-Yehuda died in 1922 at the age of sixty-four. The greatest testament to his mission, his dictionary, was completed by others, the last of the seventeen volumes appearing in 1959.

When World War I began in 1914, Ben-Yehuda was forced to flee to the United States. Returning to Palestine after the war, he was greeted by the British governor of Jerusalem with the phrase, *Shalom aleichem*, or "Peace be unto you." Ben-Yehuda was overjoyed that a British official had welcomed him back to Palestine using Hebrew.

At the time of Ben-Yehuda's death, Hebrew had become the main language of the Jewish community in Palestine. Under the British Mandate, Hebrew was recognized as one of the country's official languages.

Henrietta Szold Founds Hadassah

FEBRUARY 24, 1912

Henrietta Szold, among the greatest Jewish women of her generation, founded Hadassah, the Women's Zionist Organization of America, which became one of the foremost institutions of international Jewry. With three hundred fifty thousand members today, Hadassah is the largest women's organization in the world.

Henrietta Szold was born on December 21, 1860, shortly after her family arrived in the United States from Hungary. She was the oldest of the eight daughters of Rabbi Benjamin Szold. Though few young women received more than a basic Jewish education, Henrietta's father, a prominent leader of the Baltimore Jewish community, taught her Hebrew, Bible, Talmud, and Jewish history. She had an incredible intellect, a nearly perfect memory, wide-ranging Jewish and basic knowledge, and was fluent in Hebrew, German, and French, with a working knowledge of Yiddish.

The flood of Jewish immigrants who settled in Baltimore, having fled the pogroms in the early 1880s, was a major influence on Henrietta Szold. She eagerly helped them adjust to their new lives. Henrietta was concerned that being female might handicap her efforts to assist the Russian immigrants. In a letter she wrote at that time, she expressed concern for "my Russians": "I have gone back to my early childhood longing to be a man...I am sure that if I were to be, I could [mature] plans of great benefit to them."

Henrietta became a correspondent for the *New York Jewish Messenger* and signed her articles "Sulamith." Szold

Henrietta Szold plants first tree in Ha'amisha Forest.

CENTRAL ZIONIST ARCHIVES, JERUSALEM

Henrietta Szold with Hadassah personnel in Jerusalem in 1922.

taught at a female academy in Baltimore, but she conceived of a night school where adults could learn English and the basics of American life. In 1888, renting a room above a store in the cheaper section of town, Henrietta Szold started classes with thirty immigrants. In 1898 the public school system would take over the program.

In 1893, Henrietta became secretary to the editorial board of the Jewish Publication Society. Her main task was editing the *American Jewish Year Book.* In time she became the society's dominant figure, functioning as editor until 1916.

When her father died in 1902, Henrietta had wanted to gather, edit and publish his scholarly writing. Sensing that she required further education for such a task, she applied to the Jewish Theological Seminary in New York. At the age of forty-three, Henrietta Szold was the first female student to study there but was permitted to attend only on the condition that she not aspire to accreditation for her studies.

Henrietta was incredibly industrious. She began helping Jewish Theological Seminary scholar Louis Ginzberg

with his major literary effort, *The Legends of the Jews.* Her affection for him grew, but when he returned from a vacation in Germany with a much younger wife, she felt betrayed and suffered a severe mental breakdown. Slowly she recovered.

Shortly after that, in July of 1909, she and her mother made their first visit to Palestine. Henrietta wrestled with the question of whether to stay in Palestine or return to the United States. "If I were ten years younger," she wrote, "I would feel that my field is here. I think Zionism a more difficult aim to realize than I ever did before . . .[but] if not Zionism, then nothing . . .then extinction for the Jews." Although she returned home early in 1910 and resumed work at the Jewish Publicatation Society, the sight of Jews suffering from malaria and trachoma, and the absence of basic hygienic standards in Palestine, gnawed at her.

Back in the United States, she spoke to members of a Jewish study circle to which she belonged. Two years later, meeting with a group of forty women in the vestry rooms of the old Temple Emanu-El in New York City, she founded Hadassah, becoming the organization's first president, a post she would hold until 1926. Appropriately, the date, February 24, 1912, was the Jewish festival of Purim, the holiday that celebrates Queen Esther's victory over Haman. Hadassah is the Hebrew name for Esther.

Said Szold: "If we are Zionists, as we say we are, what is the good of meeting and talking and drinking tea? Let us do something real and practical—let us organize the Jewish women of America and send nurses and doctors to Palestine."

In 1913, the organization began its activities by sending two visiting nurses to organize a maternity center and dispense treatment to children with trachoma, a contagious and debilitating eye disease. Three years later Federal judge Julian Mack became a key benefactor to Szold. In order to allow her to devote all of her time to Jewish philanthropy, Mack and other friends gave her a lifetime stipend to cover her living expenes. She resigned as secretary of the publications committee of the Jewish Publication Society but continued to proofread its English translation of the Bible.

Putting in sixteen hour days, she complained that part of her life was empty. "I have always held that I should have had children, many children." In 1918, World War I ended, and Palestine was liberated from Ottoman occupation, coming under British authority. That same year Hadassah inaugurated the American Zionist Medical Unit, and subsequently sponsored a network of clinics and hospitals throughout Palestine.

In 1920, Henrietta returned to Palestine to supervise the Zionist Medical Unit. There she encountered great difficulties: during her first week forty-five doctors resigned and seventeen student nurses went on strike. She quickly brought calm to the situation, both by her strong presence and her willingness to improve the Jewish community's health services. Soon a network of welfare stations, dispensaries, and laboratories was operating efficiently throughout the Yishuv. It was supported by Hadassah and the Jerusalem Nurses' Training School —the entire effort operating under Henrietta Szold's aegis. This network provided health services to both Jews and Arabs and taught them preventive medicine in homes and schools.

In 1934, Henrietta laid the cornerstone for the Hospital on Mount Scopus in Jerusalem. In April 1948, as tensions between Arabs and Jews increased with the approaching end of the British Mandate, seventy-eight doctors, professors, and nurses were massacred by Arabs while driving in a convoy through the Sheikh Jarrah neighborhood in Jerusalem on their way to the Mount Scopus hospital. The hospital was lost to the state of Israel from the War of Independence until the 1967 Six-Day War, when Israel regained control of Mount Scopus.

In 1975, the original hospital was rededicated and committed itself to renovating the facility in its entirety. The restored building reopened in 1978. In time, Hadassah's two medical centers, at Ein Kerem and on Mount Scopus, became the largest in the Mediterranean region. The centers included a medical school, a school of dentistry, a nursing school, and schools in community health and occupational therapy.

Henriettz Szold remained vigorous to the end. She died on February 13, 1945 at the age of eight-five. Her greatest legacy was Haddassah, the Women's Zionist Organization of America, which is the largest Zionist organization in the United States and the largest Jewish women's organization in the world.

Weizmann Helps Launch Modern Jewish State

NOVEMBER 2, 1917

A special moment for the Jewish people occurred toward the end of World War I, which provided the first glimmer of hope that a Jewish state was in the offing. On November 2, 1917 the British issued the Balfour Declaration, the first time that a world power had expressed support for the idea of a Jewish homeland.

Chaim Weizmann, a research chemist and a young leader of the Zionist movement, engineered the first major diplomatic victory for the movement when he convinced foreign secretary Arthur J. Balfour to convey a statement of British policy to Lord Walter Rothschild, the son of Nathaniel Mayer Rothschild on November 2, 1917. That statement expressed British support for a Jewish homeland in Palestine and brought Theodor Herzl's dream of a Jewish state closer to fruition.

What motivated the British to issue the Balfour Declaration? Much of the answer has to do with the personality of Chaim Weizmann.

Chaim Weizmann was born in 1874 in Motol, Russia, one of fifteen children. Weizmann's father, Ozer, was a timber merchant, floating logs along the Vistula River to Danzig for processing. Although few of the children of Motol had the opportunity to advance beyond the village classroom in their studies, Chaim showed special talent in science.

In 1885, Weizmann, only eleven years old, wrote a letter in which he asked why Jews should look to England to take compassion on them and "give us a resting place?" He ended it with: "In conclusion, to Zion: Jews—to Zion let us go."

When he was eighteen years old, Weizmann enrolled at Darmstadt Polytechnic in Berlin to study chemistry (later he would enroll in Freiburg University, in Switzerland, to complete his doctorate). During this time he was profoundly influenced by Zionist leader Theodor Herzl. Weizmann became one of the new young leaders of the Zionist movement, receiving recognition for his organizational and fund-raising abilities.

Weizmann attended his first Zionist Congress in 1898 and in 1901 became the leader of the Democratic Fraction, which sought to introduce Jewish traditions, culture, and heritage into the Zionist movement. In contrast, Theodor Herzl emphasized diplomacy and organizational efforts.

Herzl focused on attracting wealthy patrons to donate money to develop agriculture in Palestine. Weizmann, on the other hand, stressed the importance of getting the common man to lend his support to Palestine. Influenced by his training as a chemist, Weizmann advocated what he called "synthetic Zionism," combining diplomacy to achieve a Jewish homeland and Jewish efforts to build the land for themselves. A strong believer in educating the Jewish community in Palestine, Weizmann wanted to build a university there and promote Jewish culture.

Weizmann worked in a German chemistry laboratory before being appointed lecturer in chemistry at England's Manchester University in 1906. Weizmann began publishing scientific papers and pursuing his research in the field of chemistry.

Weizmann was deeply involved in the effort to scuttle the plan for Jews to establish a homeland in Uganda. British foreign secretary Lord Lansdowne had offered the Jews some territory in the British protectorate of Uganda. Willing to accept the offer, Theodor Herzl ran into heavy opposition at the Sixth Zionist Congress in August 1903. Weizmann was against the Uganada plan and helped to defeat it. As a result, Herzl agreed to renew his efforts to promote a Jewish homeland in Palestine.

In 1916, while World War I raged on, England was having problems producing munitions. As a research chemist, Weizmann developed a new process, based on ordinary chestnuts, plentiful in England, for producing acetone, which was essential to the making of cordite, an explosive used by the navy.

Weizmann had befriended several British politicians, including David Lloyd George, who became prime minister of England, and Arthur Balfour, who served as foreign secretary. These influential British friends were so grateful for Weizmann's discovery that they wanted to make him a knight. He politely declined and instead asked that the British government proclaim its readiness to support the idea of a Jewish homeland in Palestine.

The British were not prepared to go as far as the Jews would have liked. Rather than endorse the notion of a state, the declaration spoke only of a "national home" for the Jewish people. It made no mention of carving out an autonomous area or even a protectorate for the Jews, nor did it define the way in which a national home might be achieved.

As if to indicate their less-than-enthusiastic attitude toward Jewish nationalism, the British chose to issue carefully phrased sentences known as the Balfour Declaration not in an official government decree or even in a statement to the Zionist Organization, but rather in a letter addressed to Lord Rothschild, almost as if the declaration were a private communication.

Moreover, the British did all that they could not to offend the Arabs. While earlier drafts of the Balfour Declaration had avoided mention of the "existing non-Jewish communities in Palestine," a euphemism for the Arabs, the sentence referring to those communities in

A portrait of Chaim Weizmann.

AMERICAN JEWISH ARCHIVES, CINCINNATI, OHIO

the final version read: "His Majesty's Government view with favour the establishment in Palestine of a national home for the Jewish people, and will use their best endeavors to facilitate the achievement of this object, it being clearly understood that nothing shall be done which may prejudice the civil and religious rights of existing non-Jewish communities in Palestine, or the rights and political status enjoyed by Jews in any other country."

The British hoped that issuing the statement would win the support of American Jews for American entry into World War I. The British also hoped to persuade Russian Jews to support Bolshevik Russia's continued participation in the war and to forestall any German effort to gain Jewish support by issuing a similar declaration.

The statement was issued several weeks before British troops started their successful conquest of Palestine. The British hoped that the Balfour Declaration would help them retain control of Palestine after the war. Because of its proximity to the Suez Canal, Palestine was a vital strategic asset, and the British had no wish to see another European power control the canal.

The Balfour Declaration elicited great excitement in the Zionist world but drew the wrath of anti-Zionist Jews, pro-Arab British politicians and soldiers, and Arabs who contended that the land promised by the British to the Jews did not belong to the Jews.

Weizmann's achievement in attaining the Balfour Declaration from the British established him as a leader of the Zionist movement. He was elected president of the Zionist Organization at a conference in London in July 1920 and served in that position until 1931. He was president again from 1935 to 1946.

The Balfour Declaration did not fulfill all Zionist expectations, inasmuch as the British did not promise to help in the building of a Jewish state. It did, however, pave the way for widespread Jewish settlement and development in Palestine. Had that not occurred, a Jewish state might not have been established.

Weizmann advocated the establishment of a Jewish state throughout the 1930s and 1940s. After the Jewish state was founded in 1948, Weizmann served as president until his death in 1952.

Dead Sea Scrolls Are Discovered

1947

One day in 1947 a Bedouin boy entered a cave on the north-western tip of the Dead Sea and came across a set of documents that would prove to be the greatest archaeological find of the twentieth century. These and subsequent documents uncovered in the Judean Desert became known as the Dead Sea Scrolls, the oldest Biblical manuscripts ever found, which demonstrate the accuracy with which the Bible has been copied down through the ages as well as provide extensive insight into Jewish life during the Second Temple period.

In the winter of 1947, a Bedouin boy, pursuing a runaway goat along the cliffs on the northwestern shore of the Dead Sea, came upon a cave. He threw a stone into the cave, and when he heard the sound of clay breaking, he entered the cave and discovered a set of documents encased in clay jars, which he, or an acquaintance to whom he showed his find, then turned over to an antiquities dealer in Bethlehem.

Just a few days before the United Nations adopted the historic November 1947 partition resolution, archaeologist E.L. Sukenik, of the Hebrew University learned of the ancient Hebrew manuscripts that had come into the possession of the Bethlehem antiquities dealer. Shown a fragment of one of the documents, Sukenik grew convinced that they were of great archaeological significance. Despite the danger, on November 29th, the day of the UN partition decision, he traveled in an Arab bus from Jerusalem to Bethlehem, purchased three of the documents from the antiquities dealer, and carried them back to Jerusalem wrapped in a newspaper under his arm.

ISRAEL GOVERNMENT PRESS OFFICE

One of the caves of Qumran where the Dead Sea Scrolls were found.

The Dead Sea Scrolls as they are in the Israeli Museum.

Upon close examination of the scrolls in Jerusalem, Sukenik concluded that they were approximately two thousand years old. Included was a copy of the biblical book of Isaiah, which was older by at least one thousand years than any previously known Hebrew manuscript of that book. Sukenik also had purchased the War Scroll and the Thanksgiving Hymns.

In February 1948, Sukenik secretly negotiated for the remaining four scrolls—another copy of Isaiah, the Rule of the Community, the Pesher Habakkuk, and the Genesis Apocryphon—which had been sold to the Syrian Metropolitan Athanasius Yesha Samuel in Jerusalem. Sukenik was deeply disappointed when he was unable to raise the money needed to buy the scrolls from the Metropolitan. In 1954, Sukenik's son Yigael Yadin, also

an archaeologist at the Hebrew University, was able to acquire the four scrolls.

Archaeologists were able to locate the cave in which the first manuscript had been discovered. Additional texts were uncovered in Cave 1, and in the 1950s hundreds of manuscript fragments were excavated from other caves at Qumran and other Judean Desert sites.

No one knows for certain who collected the Dead Sea Scrolls and stored them at Qumran. Many identify the Dead Sea sect with the Essenes, a pietistic group whose tenets and practices were similar to those outlined in the scrolls. The Essenes thought of themselves as the true and ideal congregation of Israel, a small remnant that had remained faithful to the covenant between God and Israel, assuring the survival of God's people.

The Dead Sea sect lived in the Judean Desert on the western shore of the Dead Sea between approximately 150 B.C.E. and 68 C.E. Their founder and leader was the Teacher of Righteousness.

Archaeological discoveries at Qumran include the remains of a two-story building, a large kitchen and communal dining room, a water system, and ritual baths. The largest collection of manuscripts come from Cave 4, which is thought to have been the sect's library. Scholars believe the site was destroyed by the Tenth Roman Legion, which had been dispatched to suppress the First Jewish Revolt (66–70 C.E.).

The Qumran scrolls include all the books of the Bible, with the exception of the *Book of Esther*. The variations between the Dead Sea Scrolls and the extant Masoretic Texts are very meager. The scrolls prove that the Bible had been faithfully copied and remained largely unchanged for over one thousand years.

The discovery of the Dead Sea Scrolls attracted worldwide interest. The slow and laborious publication of the scrolls has engendered much controversy.

The original seven Dead Sea Scrolls are housed in the Shrine of the Book at the Israel Museum in Jerusalem.

ISRAEL GOVERNMENT PRESS OFFICE

Restoring the Dead Sea Scrolls.

United Nations Votes to Establish Jewish State

NOVEMBER 29, 1947

Thirty years after the Balfour Declaration was issued, the General Assembly of the United Nations voted in favor of partitioning Palestine into two states, one Jewish, the other Arab. Though the Jews considered the passage of the resolution a great achievement, it was rejected by the Arabs, who declared war to prevent a Jewish state from coming into being. Five months after the resolution was adopted, the state of Israel was founded.

In April 1947 the General Assembly of the United Nations appointed an eleven-member group, the United Nations Special Committee on Palestine (UNSCOP), whose purpose was to figure out how to resolve the conflict between Jews and Arabs over who should control Palestine. After a first-hand look at the problems, the UNSCOP committee issued its report on August 31, urging that the British mandate be canceled and Palestine partitioned into Jewish and Arab states. The Jewish state would consist of the Eastern Galilee, the coastal plain, and the Negev; the rest of Palestine would go to the Arabs, except for Jerusalem which would fall under UN administration.

The proposed Jewish state would embrace fifty-five million square miles, or some 55 percent of the land area of Palestine. There were 1.2 million Arabs, 650,000 Jews, and 150,000 others living in Palestine at the time.

UNSCOP's majority report stated: "Only by means of partition can these conflicting national aspirations find substantial expression and qualify both peoples to take their places as independent nations in the international community and in the United Nations." With the

United Nations' plan favoring states for both Jews and Arabs, and with the American and Soviet support for the idea of a Jewish state, the UN was ready to vote on a resolution.

The vote was scheduled for November 29, 1947.

Jews and Arabs bargained up to the last moment to improve the wording of the resolution that would be placed before the United Nations General Assembly. The Americans and the Soviet Union had committed themselves to partition. So had Norway, Canada, and Guatemala. So, too had a number of the smaller nations. Against partition stood the Moslem bloc, India, Yugoslavia, and Greece.

It was unclear how the French would vote. A Jewish state in the Middle East undoubtedly would strengthen the position of the pro-French Maronites in Lebanon. Even so, the French delegation was ambivalent. Its chairman, Alexandre Parodi, feared antagonizing the North African communities and undermining a large network of French Catholic institutions in the Moslem world. Less than two hours before the vote, the French delegation received instructions from its government to support partition. Chaim Weizmann, the Zionist leader, had phoned Léon Blum in France. Blum, who was Jewish and a former premier of France, still had considerable influence with the French government, and Blum's intervention worked.

As the time for the vote neared, journalists from around the world gathered in the lobby outside the General Assembly. Delegates took their seats. The visitors' gallery was packed. On the podium were the President of the Assembly, Oswaldo Aranha, Trygvie Lie, the UN Secretary General, and Assistant Secretary-

General Andrew Cordier. Aranha called the meeting to order and invited the representative of Iceland to the rostrum.

Abba Eban, a member of the Jewish Agency's delegation to the United Nations, had visited Ambassador Thor Thors of Iceland that morning at New York's Barclay Hotel to urge his support for the resolution. Eban's visit paid off. The Iceland delegate spoke warmly in favor of partition.

Camille Chamoun, the delegate from Lebanon, tried to secure a postponement on the partition vote, but he was ruled out of order by Aranha and opposed by Andrei Gromyko, the Soviet delegate, and Hershel Johnson, the American representative on the Palestine Committee. The United States and the Soviet Union were clearly upset with the delaying tactics employed by the Arab and British delegations.

As for the Philippines, General Carlos Romulo, who had spoken against partition two days earlier, had been replaced by a new delegate who backed partition. Liberia, Belgium, Luxembourg, and the Netherlands were in favor of partition as well.

Israelis dancing in the streets in celebration of the United Nations vote to establish a Jewish State.

Finally, the speechmaking came to an end. There was silence. Aranha announced that it was time for the delegates to vote. Cordier called out the names of the countries; votes were recorded in alphabetical order.

Afghanistan? No.
Argentina? Abstain.
Australia? Yes.
Belgium? Yes.
Bolivia? Yes.
Byelorussia? Yes.

When France loudly said "Oui," applause broke out. Aranha put a stop to the cheering. By the time the M's had been polled, Jewish delegates knew that the partition resolution would carry.

Finally, after the announcement of Yugoslavia's "abstain," came the historic words: "Thirty-three in favor, thirteen against, ten abstentions, one absent. The resolution is adopted."

Other than Cuba and Greece, all the states voting against the measure were either Moslem or Asian. The pivotal bloc of votes in favor of the resolution—comprising 40 percent of the United Nations membership—came from the Latin American delegation.

When the partition vote was announced in the General Assembly, the Arab delegates rose and walked out of the hall, threatening that they would engage in violence against the Jews. "The partition line shall be nothing but a line of fire and blood" was all that the Secretary-General of the Arab League, Azzam Pasha, could say.

Abba Eban went out into the lobby, where the Jewish delegation was greeted by enthusiastic supporters. Eban later wrote: "There were Jews in tears, and non-Jews moved by the nobility of the occasion. Nobody who lived that moment will ever lose its memory from his heart."

Eban and his wife Suzy got into one of the delegation's cars and drove to New York's Plaza Hotel to see Chaim Weizmann, who in no small measure was responsible for the passage of the resolution. The Ebans persuaded the veteran Zionist leader to join them at a Labor Zionist rally in Madison Square Garden, where he was greeted warmly.

In Jerusalem it was evening. Crowds gathered near the Jewish Agency building in Rehavia to hear the results of the vote. Upon learning of the outcome, the crowds burst into song and dance. Inside, David Ben-Gurion, the effective prime minister of the planned Jewish state, sat at his desk with his head buried in his hands. If the moment was historic for the Jews, it was also fraught with peril, and Ben-Gurion knew that.

What ultimately helped the Jews win victory more than anything else was the unexpected and unprecedented fact that the Soviets and Americans had taken the same side on the issue. Their collaboration in support of partition gave the resolution unstoppable impetus.

Beyond that, the General Assembly had offered little else that might have been an alternative to the partition plan. Both Arabs and Jews were against a federalized Palestine, while partition claimed the support of at least one of the parties [the Jews] in the dispute. That morning before the vote Arab delegates had announced that they would support a federal solution in principle. Yet it was clear that Jewish immigration was still unacceptable to them. Another major reason for the passage of the resolution was the appeal the Jews had in the West. They were deeply admired for trying to rebuild themselves into a nation after being brutalized during World War II. Excitement attached to the Jews, and the Arabs could not neutralize the feeling.

Ben-Gurion Proclaims Israel's Independence

MAY 14, 1948 • 4:32 P.M.

Aware that seven Arab states were about to attack them, the Jews of Palestine declared the establishment of the state of Israel on May 14, 1948, in a moving ceremony at the Tel Aviv Museum, during which the new prime minister, David Ben-Gurion, declared: "We hereby proclaim the establishment of the Jewish State in Palestine, to be called Medinat Yisrael *(the State of Israel)."*

The dawn was bright and clear on the momentous Friday morning of May 14, 1948. Having agonized over whether to proclaim their new state, then concluding that they had no choice but to proceed, the Yishuv now felt a mixture of elation and fear. The six hundred fifty thousand members of the Jewish community in Palestine were thrilled at the prospect of establishing the first Jewish state in 1,878 years but anguished that the armies of seven neighboring Arab countries, poised to invade Palestine, would destroy them and their fledgling state. Forcing a decision was the plan of the British Mandatory authorities to depart Palestine on that day.

The decision to establish the Jewish state had been taken at the last minute, leaving little time to prepare for the ceremony set for that afternoon. The English-language *Palestine Post's* headlines reflected the Yishuv's indecision over whether to press on with statehood: "Britain Pleads for Arab-Jewish Compromise as Mandate is Given Up;" "U.S. Still Seeks to Postpone Partition." With much understatement, a last-minute bulletin noted: "Jewish State Begins Today."

At his Tel Aviv home, the evening before, David Ben-Gurion, who was about to become the prime minister of the new state, had experienced another sleepless night. Earlier, the text of the new state's Declaration of Independence had been shown to the National Council, the thirty-seven member ruling body of the Yishuv, which Ben-Gurion headed. With Arabs already attacking Jewish communities, declaring a Jewish state may have seemed a luxury, or an irrelevancy. But Ben-Gurion was determined to declare statehood.

To ceremony organizers, secrecy was crucial. If word leaked about when and where the historic occasion would occur, Arabs might plant a bomb or launch an attack at the site. The ceremony was scheduled for 4:00 P.M. at the Tel Aviv Museum, a low, white, concrete building on Rothschild Boulevard. Though editors of Yishuv newspapers promised not to divulge the planned ceremony, the morning newspapers disclosed that the new state radio planned to initiate its broadcasting service by transmitting the event at 4:00 P.M. At least the location remained a secret. In gleeful response to the planned ceremony, Jews in Tel Aviv placed blue and white flags outside their homes.

The audience for the ceremony was kept small, again to preserve secrecy. Invitees were urged to keep the contents of the written invitation as well as the time of the meeting to themselves. In deference to the solemnity of the event, guests were asked to wear "dark festive attire."

Foreign journalists were barred by Jewish censors from reporting that the Jews planned to proclaim statehood that afternoon, despite what had appeared in the morning newspapers. Associated Press reporter Aryeh Dissentchik found a clever way around this re-

David Ben-Gurion reading the Declaration of Independence.

striction, cabling his home office in New York early that morning: "Tonight in Palestine the Sabbath prayer over the candles, 'May we worship You in the rebuilt Temple as we worshipped You in ancient times,' will have, in part, come true." The staff of the AP cables desk in New York astutely figured out that Dissentchik, referring to the rebuilt Temple, was in fact alluding to a rebuilt Jewish state. A story was filed disclosing that the Jews planned an announcement of statehood very soon.

Even at 1:00 P.M. when the National Council met, its members could not agree about the wording of the proclamation of statehood. Some demanded that it spell out the new state's frontiers. Ben-Gurion said no. Observant Jews wanted a reference to "the God of Israel." Secularists balked. Compromising, Ben-Gurion decided that the word "Rock" would appear instead of "God." What about a name for the new state? How about Judea, suggested one member? How about Zion, proposed another? Again Ben-Gurion broke the impasse: the new state would be called Israel.

A few minutes before 4:00 P.M. a fleet of rented American limousines pulled up at the Tel Aviv Museum, igniting the crowd into wild cheer. Last among the members of the National Council to enter the museum was Ben-Gurion, all five-feet, three inches of him. His craggy face, fringed with strands of white hair, bore little expression. "Now we are responsible for our destiny," he thought to himself.

Inside, the three hundred and fifty invitees were crowded, and the room was packed from wall to wall. Some sat in brown wooden chairs in a semicircle. Seated at a table—with a portrait of Zionist pioneer Theodor Herzl peering down at them—were Ben-Gurion and ten other members of the thirteen-member provisional cabinet. The fourteen other members of the National Council sat at a right angle to the main dais. Throughout the country, thousands of new Israelis were listening to the radio broadcast of the ceremony. At 4:00 P.M. Ben-Gurion rapped his walnut gavel three times, and the crowd sang the national anthem *Hatikvah*. Then Ben-Gurion declared, "I shall now read to you the Scroll of

David Remez signing Israel's Declaration of Independence.

the Establishment of the state, which has passed in first reading by the National Council."

Ben-Gurion raised his voice when he read: "Accordingly, we, the members of the National Council, representing the Jewish People in Palestine and the World Zionist Movement, are met together in solemn assembly today, the day of termination of the British Mandate for Palestine; and by virtue of the natural and historic right of the Jewish People and the Resolution of the General Assembly of the United Nations, we hereby proclaim the establishment of the Jewish State in Palestine, to be called *Medinat Israel* (the State of Israel)." With those words, the crowd inside the hall went wild. Some applauded, some shouted, some cried. Everyone smiled. It had taken Ben-Gurion seventeen minutes to read the 979-word document.

The entire audience rose to show its approval. A rabbi pronounced the traditional blessing thanking the Lord for allowing one to reach a celebration—the *Shehecheyanu*. Ben-Gurion then announced the first decree of the new state: the British White Paper of 1939, hated by the Jews for its curbs on Jewish immigration and land sales, was null and void. Council members then signed the Declaration of Independence. A future prime minister, Golda Myerson, wept uncontrollably when she signed. Moshe Shertok, another future prime minister, affixed his signature, feeling like "a man might feel while standing on a cliff, ready to leap into a yawning chasm."

The Palestine Philharmonic Orchestra played *Hatikvah*, and at 4:32 P.M., new Prime Minister David Ben-Gurion declared that "The State of Israel is established. The meeting is ended." Stepping down from the dais, Ben-Gurion was surrounded by a mob; he broke out in a child-like grin and said to a British reporter, "You see, we did it!"

Truman Recognizes Israeli State

MAY 14, 1948 • 6:11 P.M.

Despite pressure from others in the American government, the president of the United States, Harry Truman, gave early recognition to the state of Israel on May 14, 1948, and played a crucial role in the formation of the new Jewish state. Ignoring the wishes of senior officials in the State Department, who were unsympathetic to Zionism, not to grant recognition, Truman was determined to give a boost to the Zionists.

In the years leading up to Jewish statehood, it was Zionist leader Chaim Weizmann's friendship with President Harry Truman that proved of critical importance in securing early American recognition of the new Jewish state.

After World War II, Chaim Weizmann traveled to the United States to solicit Truman's help in fighting the newly announced British ban on further Jewish immigration to Palestine. The two men met, and as a result, Truman developed a warm, close relationship with Weizmann. The American president pleaded with the British to rescind their ban but to no avail.

Weizmann was, however, successful in his pleas for support from the United Nations, which, on November 29, 1947, voted to support a plan to partition Palestine into two states, one Jewish, one Arab.

Five and a half months later—in the late afternoon of May 12th—on the verge of the expiration of the British Mandate over Palestine—a new Jewish state appeared about to rise. Jewish leaders of the Yishuv knew that the new state would get a tremendous boost if the United States granted it immediate diplomatic recognition. That same day a letter from Weizmann arrived at the White House asking the United States government to recognize Israel when the new state came into existence.

President Truman, wavering about whether to grant recognition, met with his senior advisers to help him reach a decision. Truman had seemed to be leaning toward recognition when, on April 23rd, he told Judge Samuel Rosenman, who had served as an adviser to Franklin Roosevelt and had close ties to American Jewish leaders: "I have Dr. Weizmann on my conscience."

Truman asked his political adviser, Clark Clifford, to enunciate the arguments in favor of recognition. To grant that recognition, Clifford reasoned, would preempt the Soviets who also were planning to extend recognition to the new Jewish state. It would strengthen the United Nations and increase respect for American integrity and faithfulness. Robert Lovett, the under-secretary of state, countered that granting recognition would be "buying a pig in a poke," for how could anyone predict what kind of state the Jews would establish? Besides, Lovett added, Clifford's favoring recognition "was a very transparent attempt to win the Jewish vote." Secretary of State George Marshall concurred with Lovett.

Truman gave no indication of which way he was leaning. With his aides sharply disagreeing on what to do about the new state, Truman adjourned the meeting.

Over the next twenty-four hours, Marshall and Lovett softened their opposition to American recognition of the new Jewish state. Marshall had no desire for a confrontation with the president; Lovett, for his part, began to sense that Clifford might have been speaking with Truman's blessing.

Chaim Weizmann presents President Truman with a Torah in 1949.

Lovett met at his downtown Washington, D.C. club with Clifford on May 14, the day that the state of Israel was born. Sensing that Lovett was backing down from his strong opposition to recognition, Clifford took a more low-key approach. He insisted that President Truman appreciated his arguments; because of Marshall and Lovett, Clifford explained, Truman had put off an announcement in favor of recognition of the new state.

Time was short, however, and Truman was eager to make the announcement. Clifford hinted strongly to Lovett that the American president wanted to make sure that he obtained proper credit with American Jews for what he was about to do. Timing, said Clifford with great candor, was "of the greatest possible importance to the President from a domestic point of view. The President is under unbearable pressure to recognize the Jewish state promptly." When Lovett recorded Clifford's comments in a memo for the State Department's files, that memo eventually became the basis for later suggestions that the American president had decided to recognize Israel only to woo the American Jewish voter.

In the hours just before the new state of Israel was declared, Clark Clifford went to work in preparing the government's act of recognition. With an eye on laying to rest the "pig in a poke" argument raised at the May 12th session, Clifford got in touch with the special emissary of the Jewish Agency in Palestine, Eliahu Epstein, and asked him whether David Ben-Gurion and his colleagues planned to proclaim a "provisional" government and what would be the boundaries of the new state. Answers to these questions would go far toward calming the fears of those who wondered what kind of a state the American government would be recognizing.

Epstein turned to Benjamin Cohen, the New Deal's master legal draftsman, for help in formulating the "official" Zionist request for recognition. Cohen produced the appropriate draft only two hours before the scheduled 4:30 P.M. declaration of statehood. Cohen then rushed over to Clifford's office with the document. Finally at 6:11 P.M., the White House announced de facto recognition of the provisional government of the Jewish state. "The old doctor will believe me now," the President murmured, referring to Claim Weizmann.

A few days later, Weizmann, who became the first president of the state of Israel, visited President Truman in Washington. "You will never know what this means to my people," he told the President. "We have waited and dreamed and worked for this moment for two thousand years." Weizmann assured Truman that the President's support for the Jewish people would not be forgotten.

When American Zionist leader Abba Hillel Silver and his political organizers grasped the qualified nature of Truman's gesture and asked for immediate de jure recognition, the president ignored their demands. The Jewish Agency office in Washington became the Embassy of Israel. Lovett was now firmly on the side of recognition. To Truman, he observed: "Well, Mr. President, they [Lovett's State Department colleagues] almost put it over on you."

Only in January 1949, after the first Israeli elections were held, did Washington extend de jure recognition. Meanwhile, the embargo on American arms shipments to Palestine remained in effect through all the fighting during Israel's precarious first months.

Truman wrote later: "I was told that to some of the career men of the State Department this announcement [of recognition] came as a surprise. It should not have been if these men had faithfully supported my policy . . . I wanted to make it plain that the president of the United States, and not the second or third echelon in the State Department, is responsible for making foreign policy."

Years after the state was founded, David Ben-Gurion met with Truman. Ben-Gurion noted: "I told him . . . his courageous decision to recognize our new state so quickly and his steadfast support since then had given him an immortal place in Jewish history. As I said that, tears suddenly came to his eyes And his eyes were still wet when he bade me good-bye. Later a correspondent came up to me to ask, "Why was President Truman in tears when he left you?"

Brandeis University Founded

1948

In 1948 Brandeis University, the only nondenominational institution of higher learning in the United States under Jewish aegis, was founded in Waltham, Massachusetts. The school was named for Louis Brandeis, the first Jewish justice on the United States Supreme Court.

I n the late 1800s, the Reform, Orthodox, and Conservative movements all founded institutions of higher learning: Hebrew Union College (1875), Yeshiva University (1886), and the Jewish Theological Seminary of America (1887), respectively. However, for years the Jewish community was the only religious community in the United States that had not established a nondenominational college or university. There was a certain irony in this, for, since World War I, far more Jews had attended college than any other religious or ethnic group in the United States.

In 1946 a group of Jews from Boston and New York, led by a Conservative rabbi active in Jewish communal life, Israel Goldstein, decided to pursue the dream of founding a nondenominational college. The president of Middlesex University, a failing medical school in Waltham, Massachusetts, nine miles west of Boston, offered to donate its ninety-acre campus and buildings to any interested educational institution. Goldstein negotiated with Middlesex and reached an agreement; control changed hands on February 7, 1946. The new institution became Brandeis University, in memory of Justice Louis Brandeis.

Lacking capital, Goldstein arranged for a committee of public figures, among them Albert Einstein, to help

The campus of Brandeis University today.

BRANDEIS UNIVERSITY

dards; rigid objectivity in teaching and research; and an unambiguous policy of nondiscrimination on racial, religious, or national grounds in selecting students and faculty. He devoted himself to building the school's endowment and soon attracted to Brandeis widely recognized scholars in their fields. Among them were psychologist Abraham Maslow, writers Albert Guerard, Irving Howe, Stanley Kunitz, and Ludwig Lewisohn, sociologists Lewis Coser and Philip Rieff; historians E. H. Carr, Frank Manual, Geoffrey Barraclough, Leonard Levy, and Merrill Peterson; musicians Leonard Bernstein and Irving Fine; and physicist Leo Szilard.

in fund-raising. Einstein stipulated that no major decisions were to be taken without his agreement.

Rabbi Stephen Wise, a longtime friend of Einstein's, asked the physicist to drop his stipulation. Instead, in 1947, Einstein resigned from the board, since he lacked faith in the new chairman, George Alpert, a Boston attorney. Resigning along with Einstein were most of the important New York public figures.

Plagued by infighting, Brandeis University in early 1948 seemed a project in serious trouble. Nonetheless, the school opened in the fall with a starting class of 107 freshmen.

The board proposed that Abram L. Sachar, who had just retired as director of the B'nai B'rith Hillel Foundation, become president of the University. David K. Niles, who served as President Truman's "Jewish adviser" in the White House, urged Sachar to take the job, and in April 1948 he did. Sachar, then forty-nine years old, was a well-known educator and historian, a major figure in the American Jewish community with a wide public following. It was hoped that Sachar's selection would give the school a needed lift out of its financial difficulties.

Sachar, in his inaugural address, pledged a commitment to high stan-

Brandeis became fully accredited in 1954, the same year in which it inaugurated a graduate studies program.

During his twenty years as president of Brandeis, Sachar raised $200 million for the school. Some of those funds were earmarked for new buildings, endowed departments, professorships, and scholarships.

While Brandeis remained nondenominational, the school's board promoted the highest quality of Jewish studies. Brandeis's School of Near Eastern and Judaic Studies became a significant center of scholarship, led by its directors Simon Rawidowicz and later Nahum Glatzer. The Jacob Hiatt Institute of-

fered undergraduate and graduate programs in Israel. In 1966 the American Jewish Historical Society moved its headquarters and large research library from New York to the Brandeis campus.

In 1996, Brandeis had an enrollment of thirty-eight hundred students, including one thousand graduate students, and a student-to-faculty ratio of nine to one. Among the visiting professors who have been brought to the campus are Natan Sharansky, the well-known Russian dissident; composer Marvin Hamlisch; authors Saul Bellow, Gloria Naylor, and Alice Walker; and Sumner Redstone, chairman of the board of Viacom International Inc.

BRANDEIS UNIVERSITY

Among Brandeis's notable alumni are: *New York Times* columnist Thomas L. Friedman (class of '75); Christie Hefner (class of '74) of Playboy Enterprises; television producer Marshall Herskowitz (class of '73); and Edward Witten (class of '71), Professor of Physics, Institute of Advanced Studies, Princeton University.

The renowned historian Howard Morley Sachar, son of Abram Sachar and the founder of the Jacob Hiatt Institute in Israel, has called Brandeis University "American Jewry's most impressive communal achievement."

Schneerson Revives Lubavitch Movement

JANUARY 17, 1951

It was the Ukrainian rabbi and spiritual leader Menachem Mendel Schneerson, who, by dint of his charisma and perseverance, revived the Lubavitch Hasidic sect in the United States, after it had been devastated by the Nazis in Europe, and made it the most dynamic phenomenon in Orthodox Judaism. Schneerson was beloved by his followers, many of whom looked toward him as the Messiah.

Menachem Mendel, son of Rabbi Levi Isaac and Channah Schneerson, was born in 1902 in Nikolayev, a port on the Black Sea in the Ukraine. Menachem was a great-grandson of the third Lubavitche *rebbe*.

When Menachem was five years old, his family moved to Yekaterinoslav, where his father had been appointed chief rabbi. Menachem briefly attended a religious primary school—*heder*—but primarily was educated at home by private tutors. He was considered a Torah genius, an *ilui*. By the time he was seventeen, he had mastered the entire Talmud, some 5,894 pages in its Hebrew edition.

Menachem was always interested in helping others. When he was nine years old he saved a boy from drowning. At age twenty, he helped organize relief during a typhus epidemic and came down with the disease himself.

Chabad Hasidism, today the Lubavitch movement, was founded by Rabbi Shneur Zalman of Lyady in the eighteenth century. In 1923, Menachem Mendel Schneerson met the sixth Lubavitcher *rebbe*, Joseph Isaac

Menachem Mendel Schneerson.

Schneersohn, a distant relative. In 1929, Menachem married Chaya Moussia, one of the *rebbe*'s daughters. Menachem took the nearly unprecedented step of entering the secular world by studying engineering at the University of Berlin and at the Sorbonne in Paris.

In 1940 Schneerson was almost arrested for trying to smuggle religious materials to Jews in occupied France. Two years later, after Nazism had spread throughout Europe, Schneerson and his wife were given refuge in the United States. In 1944, he was named director of Lubavitch publishing and educational activities.

Rebbe Joseph Schneersohn, disheartened that so many American Jews had disavowed Orthodox Judaism, and heavy-hearted over the destruction of European Jewry in the Holocaust, created a new, modern organizational structure for Chabad. But when he died in 1950, a struggle ensued over who would become the new Lubavitcher *rebbe* Menachem Schneerson or Rabbi Gourary, another son-in-law of Rebbe Joseph. Menachem Schneerson was selected on January 17, 1951, and became the movement's seventh Grand Rabbi.

Chabad is an acronym formed from the Hebrew words for wisdom, understanding, and knowledge. Through his charisma and perseverance, Menachem Mendel Schneerson disseminated Orthodox Judaism throughout North America and the world. Under his leadership, the Lubavitch movement became the most outward-looking of the Hasidic groups, most of which looked inward, seeking to strengthen their own adherents instead of seeking new ones. Schneerson zealously championed the idea that all Jews are responsible for one another. Schneerson delivered lengthy talks on such subjects as Hasidism, rabbinic thought, and politics; some of his speeches were broadcast by satellite. He wrote numerous volumes of commentary.

Accordingly, his emissaries traved in "Mitzvah Mobiles," stood on street corners to ask Jewish men to put on *tefillin*—phylacteries—and went door-to-door urging Jewish women to light Sabbath candles. The Lubavitch movement became well known for erecting huge Hanukah menorahs for public celebrations.

By 1990 over two hundred fifty Chabad houses had been set up throughout the United States. These serve as synagogues, schools, and drop-in counseling centers. Lubavitch has been especially active in the former Soviet Union. Estimates of Lubavitch membership range from the tens of thousands to as high as one million.

Schneerson's followers in Israel built an exact replica there of his New York headquarters at 770 Eastern Parkway in Crown Heights, Brooklyn. Curiously, Rabbi Schneerson never visited Israel. (In fact, he only left Brooklyn to visit his father-in-law's grave in Queens.) He did, however, play a major role in Israeli politics, waging an (ultimately unsuccessful) attempt to change Israel's Law of Return to invalidate conversions performed by non-Orthodox rabbis. Schneerson took a hard-line view on relinquishing Israel's occupied territories, firm in his belief that the Torah commanded Israel to keep all captured land.

In 1977 Schneerson suffered a heart attack, but he was in good health for years after that. President Jimmy Carter proclaimed Rabbi Schneerson's seventy-eighth birthday "Education Day, U.S.A.," and President Ronald Reagan declared the rabbi's eightieth birthday a "National Day of Reflection."

When Rabbi Schneerson, childless, died on June 12, 1994, at the age of ninety-two, he left no designated successor. Many of his acolytes, convinced he was the Messiah, refused to mourn his passing.

At the time of his death *The New York Times* called Schneerson "perhaps the best known Jewish leader in the world." In October 1994 he was posthumously awarded the Congressional Gold Medal. According to the resolution, he "inspired people to a renewal of individual values of spirituality, cooperation, and love of learning."

Menachem Mendel Schneerson's ability to reach out and inspire so many, particularly the young, to return to Judaism is a great legacy.

Israeli Soldiers Rejoice at Western Wall

June 7, 1967 • 10:30 a.m.

When the Jews of the Old City of Jerusalem were forced to
surrender in the early phases of the 1948 Israeli War of Independence, they relinquished perhaps their greatest treasure, the
sacred wall that encircled the Temple Mount, site of the two
ancient, destroyed Jewish Temples. The capture of the Western Wall by Israeli soldiers almost twenty years later, during
the June 1967 Six-Day War, represents one of the most significant moments of modern Jewish history.

On the third day of the 1967 Six-Day War, Israel launched one of its most significant and
dramatic attacks, aiming to recapture the Old
City of Jerusalem nineteen years after it had been conquered by the Jordanians during Israel's 1948 War of
Independence.

At 8:30 a.m., Mordecai "Motta" Gur, the commander
of the Israeli paratroop brigade and a future chief of
staff of the Israel Defense Forces, ordered his troops to
storm the last remaining Jordanian high point overlooking the Holy City, the Augusta Victoria Church, which
fell without a struggle. Next, the paratroopers used their
tanks and infantry for a frontal assault on the Lion's Gate,
one of the main entry points to the Old City.

Into the Old City they streamed, swarms of helmeted
soldiers, eighteen and nineteen years old, who had
dreamed all their lives of touching the Western Wall.
Part of the periphery of the ancient Temple Mount, upon
which the First and Second Temples had been built and
destroyed, the Western Wall was the Jewish people's
most poignant connection to its ancient roots.

As the young soldiers broke through the gate and

poured on to the Via Dolorosa, Gur's men headed directly for their precious target: the Western Wall.

Captain Yoram Zamush led his company of soldiers
toward the Temple Mount. They faced no opposition.
Motta Gur reached the top of the holy mount. It was
deserted. He announced over the radio, "Temple Mount
is in our hands. Temple Mount is ours. Temple Mount is
ours." It was 10:00 a.m. Uzi Narkiss, head of the central
command, responded, "Message received. Great show.
Great show."

No moment of conquest during the Six-Day War
was as sweet for the Israelis as this one. After a nine-
teen-year absence they had regained the Jewish Quarter, which had been surrendered to the Arabs in May
1948.

Gur met Zamush. The two men silently embraced.
Zamush sent soldiers to bring two rabbis from their
homes. One was Zvi Yehuda Kook, son of the former
chief rabbi of Israel. The other, David Cohen, father-
in-law of Israeli army chaplain Shlomo Goren, had been
known as the "monk rabbi" because he had vowed, after
being expelled from the Old City in 1948, that he would
never leave his home until the Western Wall once again
was under Jewish control. Now that the wall again was
in Jewish hands, Rabbi Cohen agreed to travel to it along
with Rabbi Kook.

The soldiers still needed to secure the Western Wall.
Zamush and Major Moshe Stempel, the deputy commander of the parachute brigade, searched for a route
down to the base of the Western Wall. Paratroopers
were placed along the way to mark the path.

Shortly before 10:30 a.m., Zamush and Stempel came
upon an elderly Arab man and asked him if he knew the

way. Answering in Hebrew, he said he would take them to the spot. Then he removed a large key from his pocket and opened the Mughrabi Gate; its stone stairs led directly down from the Temple Mount to the base of the last vestige of the containment wall built by Herod the Great around the Temple in 20 B.C.E.

Suddenly a truck towing an antitank gun emerged across from the stairway. Several Jordanian soldiers alighted and opened fire on the Israelis. The paratroopers returned fire, forcing the Jordanians to dive under the truck. When the gas tank blew up, all the Jordanian soldiers were killed.

Zamush and three soldiers proceeded to the base of the Western Wall. Because houses had been built quite close to it, the soldiers had almost no room to stand and gaze at the stones rising up in the air.

Zamush had touched the stones of the Wall for the last time when he was four years old. He became the first Israeli to stand at that spot in almost twenty years. A few minutes later, he donned his *tefilin*, the leather-bound cases, which contain holy scripture, and straps that observant Jews wrap around their forearms and drape from their foreheads when they recite the morning prayers. Zamush and five other soldiers began to pray at the Wall.

Moshe Dayan, the defense minister, wanted to be there and have his photograph taken, leading Israeli soldiers into the Old City and to the Western Wall. He knew that the capture of the Western Wall would be the highlight of the war.

Dayan sent a message to Uzi Narkiss, that he would arrive at the Lion's Gate at 1:00 P.M. "Wait for me," Dayan commanded Narkiss, who had trouble complying with the order. He had already been inside the Old City with Israeli forces, but he agreed to be at the gate to greet Dayan.

Accompanying Dayan as they headed for the Western Wall were Chief of Staff Yitzhak Rabin, other offic-

Army Chaplain Shlomo Goren carrying the Torah scroll with soldiers at the Western Wall.

ISRAEL GOVERNMENT PRESS OFFICE

ers, and a number of civilians, including photographers, newspaper reporters and radio broadcasters.

Once inside the Old City Dayan and his entourage proceeded to the Temple Mount. Dayan was unpleasantly surprised to find that an Israeli flag had been hoisted on the spire of the Dome of the Rock. It was an act of religious insensitivity, in his view, and he ordered the flag taken down at once. Reaching the Western Wall, Dayan found some flowers growing out of a crevice and took some as a personal souvenir. Following an old custom, he wrote a note on a slip of paper and stuck it between the stones.

Moshe Perlman, Dayan's assistant, had asked him what he had written.

Dayan was reluctant, but then he showed him the note: "Would that peace descend on the whole house of Israel." Later, Dayan described to his wife the strange experience of being at the Western Wall: "I was there, and yet I looked on as if I wasn't there."

Yitzhak Rabin remembered that day as the "peak of my life." As soldiers raced up to embrace him at the Western Wall, he spoke:

It is with affection and pride that the whole nation salutes you today for the decisive victory you have brought us . . . It was not handed to us on a silver platter. The fighting was savage and hard. Many of our comrades in arms have fallen in action. Their sacrifices shall not have been in vain . . . The countless generations of Jews murdered, martyred, and massacred for the sake of Jerusalem say to you 'Comfort yet, our people; console the mothers and the fathers whose sacrifices have brought about redemption.'

In addition to those at the Wall, thousands were listening to Rabin's words over the radio. He reminded his listeners that he had been in the city and fought for it during the War of Independence; his entry into the Old City on this occasion was "for me perhaps the most important event that has occurred during these fifty-five hours."

As Dayan walked out of the Old City, he turned to Chaim Herzog, the newly appointed military governor of the West Bank and later president of the state of Israel: "It's your baby, now you take over."

Israel did indeed take over, prepared to return much of its newly won territory but determined to hold on to

Goren blows shofar at the Western Wall.

its sacred Jerusalem, including the cherished Western Wall, forever. The euphoria that Israelis felt in the immediate aftermath of the Six-Day War over reuniting Jerusalem under its control and perhaps winning peace with the Arabs eventually gave way to a more sober realization, that a resolution of the Israeli-Arab conflict remained elusive.

First Woman Rabbi Ordained

JUNE 3, 1972 • 11 A.M.

On June 3, 1972, Sally Priesand became the first woman in the United States to be publicly ordained as a rabbi. She confronted resistance at first to the idea of her holding a pulpit; in time she gained acceptance and paved the way for other women rabbis. Today she is the rabbi at Monmouth Reform Temple in Tinton Falls, New Jersey. The Reconstructionist Rabbinical College ordained its first woman rabbi in 1973; the Jewish Theological Seminary of America ordained the first Conservative woman rabbi in 1985.

Sally Priesand was born in Cleveland, Ohio, on June 27, 1946, the daughter of Irving Priesand, a construction engineer, and his wife Rose. She credits her parents with giving her a wonderful gift, the courage to dare and to dream: "That was really important in helping me to remain focused on my goal of becoming a rabbi even though no woman had become a rabbi before." While attending Reform Temple Beth Israel in West Cleveland, she learned "what it means to be a Temple family and how central to Jewish life is the concept of *tikkun olam* (repairing the world)."

Throughout childhood she wanted to be a teacher. At age sixteen, she decided that she wanted to teach Judaism. It seemed only natural for her eventually to think about becoming a rabbi.

She received a Bachelor of Arts degree in English from the University of Cincinnati in 1968; throughout college she took courses at the Hebrew Union College-Jewish Institute of Religion (HUC-JIR) in Cincinnati, enabling her to enter the seminary as a second-year student. Sally entered HUC-JIR soon after the president of the school, Professor Nelson Glueck, announced that he was prepared for the school to ordain a woman. On her way to ordination, she received a Bachelor of Hebrew Letters in 1971 and a Master of Arts in Hebrew Letters in 1972, both from HUC-JIR.

When Sally Priesand entered the Hebrew Union College she did not dream of being a pioneer in Jewish life; she simply wanted to become a rabbi. The school's leadership, she assumed, thought she was there for other reasons. "They probably thought I was more interested in marrying a rabbi than being one," she told a reporter in September 1997." There were thirty-five men in my class and me."

Her parents supported her enthusiastically. "My decision," she said, "was an affirmation of my belief in God, in the worth of each individual, and in Judaism as a way of life. It was a tangible action declaring my commitment to the preservation and renewal of our tradition." With no dorm rooms for women, Sally was permitted to live off campus. It took four years before people began to realize that she was serious about entering the rabbinate. She believed that, to be fully accepted as a serious candidate for the rabbinate, she had to outshine her classmates in her studies; that way no one would question her academic ability. One indication of her growing acceptance came during her final year in rabbinical school: when off making speeches about what it was like to be the first woman rabbinical candidate, fellow students taped lectures she had missed for her.

She found her professors fair but decided that some would not have been upset if she had failed.

Sally Priesand served as a visiting student rabbi—a requirement of rabbinical students at HUC-JIR—at synagogues in Hattiesburg, Mississippi, and Jackson, Michigan. She spent her final year at rabbinical school as a rabbinic intern at Cincinnati's Isaac Mayer Wise Temple, the same historic Plum Street temple where she was later ordained.

When she was ordained on June 3, 1972, Sally Priesand became the first woman rabbi in the United States. She was also the world's first publicly ordained female rabbi of the Reform movement. (One woman had preceded her, German-born Regina Jonas, who completed her studies for the rabbinate at the Berlin Academy for the Science of Judaism in the late 1930s. Denied ordination, Jonas did receive a Hebrew rabbinate diploma from Rabbi Max Dienemann of Offenbach. She was able to work only briefly as a rabbi before the Nazis killed her at the Theresienstadt concentration camp in the early 1940s.)

Classmates gave Rabbi Priesand a standing ovation when she was ordained. As she sat waiting to receive ordination, Rabbi Priesand reflected on the significance of what she had accomplished. "For thousands of years

Sally Priesand in 1973.

THE JEWISH WEEK

women in Judaism had been second-class citizens," she wrote later. "They were not permitted to own property. They could not serve as witnesses. They did not have the right to initiate divorce proceedings. They were not counted in the minyan. Even in Reform Judaism, they were not permitted to participate fully in the life of the synagogue. With my ordination all that was going to change; one more barrier was about to be broken."

She insisted, however, that she had no feminist motives in mind, suggesting that "I didn't decide to do this so that I would be the first woman rabbi or to carry a torch for the feminist movement. I had always wanted to teach, and simply realized that what I wanted to teach was Judaism."

Upon ordination, she was offered the post of assistant

rabbi at the Stephen Wise Free Synagogue in New York City; later she became an associate rabbi there; fulfilling all rabbinic functions, she presided over weddings and funerals, conducted worship services, gave a sermon each Shabbat, and taught in the adult institute; she also supervised the youth program, lectured the Golden Age Club, and attended all committee meetings.

Attaining her own pulpit did not come easily. Synagogues routinely refused to interview a woman for the post of rabbi; most were only willing to hire women as assistant rabbis. Of the twelve synagogues to which Rabbi Priesand applied, nine rejected her without even granting an interview.

In August 1979, Rabbi Priesand took the pulpit of Temple Beth El in Elizabeth, New Jersey, and served there for two years. She also served as chaplain at Manhattan's Lenox Hill Hospital.

Despite her own success as a rabbi, she knew that a good deal more had to be accomplished before women felt equal to men within Judaism.

The most challenging part of being a rabbi, she suggests, is confronting the joys and sorrows that befall a synagogue on a daily basis and, as she told a reporter in 1993, "the need to change emotions at a moment's notice. On a single day, I may officiate at a funeral, a wedding, and then counsel a potential suicide. It's sometimes so draining, and difficult to handle all that..."

Since 1981, she has served as the full-time rabbi of the Monmouth Reform Temple in New Jersey. The Monmouth congregation, numbering three hundred fifty families, "taught me a lot about the meaning of success. We're taught that if you don't move up and take a larger post, you're not successful. This congregation taught me that the real measure of success is doing better today than you were doing yesterday."

She has written numerous articles and authored a book called *Judaism and the New Woman* (1975). She is single and resides in Eatontown, New Jersey.

As a result of her own personal illness and the suffering she has witnessed among some of her congregants, she has changed the way she thinks about God. "In rabbinical school I always believed in an all-powerful God," she told a reporter in 1993. "But when you start dealing with real people who suffer, that's not the kind of God you can believe in. I've started to believe in a God who is not all-powerful but loving. Who is with us, helping us to cope, sometimes disappointed in us, not able to prevent tragedies from happening to us—a God who weeps with us."

Since 1972, the Hebrew Union College-Jewish Institute of Religion has ordained nine hundred and ninety rabbis, of whom two hundred sixty-one are women. Beginning in the early 1990s, half of the entering HUC-JIR rabbinical students were women.

On March 12, 1997, Rabbi Priesand was honored for twenty-five years of service to the Jewish people when HUC-JIR presented her with an Honorary Doctor of Divinity. At the Cincinnati ceremony marking the occasion, Rabbi Sheldon Zimmerman, president of HUC-JIR, noted that "Rabbi Priesand has contributed so much to the life of the rabbinate and of the Jewish people."

Celebrating the milestone of twenty-five years of women in the rabbinate, the Women's Rabbinic Network and HUC-JIR began to campaign to raise five hundred thousand dollars in order to establish the Rabbi Sally Priesand Visiting Professorship of Jewish Women's Studies at HUC-JIR.

Asked whether she still encountered problems being a woman rabbi, Rabbi Priesand shrugged off the query. "I've never dwelt on the issue. It gets blown out of proportion. People have seen that I was serious. I maintained my sense of humor and never argued with anyone who told me that a woman shouldn't be a rabbi. Today we have still not provided women opportunities to be rabbis of large congregations, but in the last few years we've made progress in getting women into leadership positions at the higher levels of the Reform movement. I experience no real problems at my congregation. I'm accepted as the rabbi, not as the first women rabbi."

In 1974, the Reconstructionist Rabbinical College in Philadelphia ordained its first woman rabbi, Sandy Eisenberg Sasso. In 1985 the first Conservative woman rabbi, Amy Eilberg, was ordained by the Jewish Theological Seminary of America.

First Right-Wing Prime Minister Elected in Israel

MAY 17, 1977 • 10 P.M.

> *Menachem Begin's right-wing Herut party lost eight elections to the Labor party. Finally, on May 17, 1977, Begin was elected prime minister of the state of Israel as head of the Likud bloc, marking the first time that the left-wing Labor party would not rule Israel and the right-wing Likud bloc would govern.*

For twenty-nine years Menachem Begin had been in the political wilderness. On the eve of elections in May 1977 it appeared likely that Begin, age sixty-three, would lose again, and since he had suffered a serious heart attack only seven weeks before, his political career appeared at an end.

Prime Minister Yitzhak Rabin, a decided favorite to win re-election in May, had been forced to resign as premier in April when it was discovered that his wife Leah had kept an illegal bank account in Washington, D.C. Shimon Peres took over as the new Labor party leader and candidate for prime minister. Labor led the public opinion polls, despite the blame heaped on the party for its failure to have prepared the nation sufficiently for the 1973 Yom Kippur War. Might Begin benefit from post war malaise and the Rabin scandal and pull off an upset?

Although well known to Israelis as the country's leading political hard-liner, few outside of Israel knew Menachem Begin because he was not one of Israel's key rulers. To ruling Labor party politicians, Begin seemed dangerous, abrasive, and uncompromising; they feared he would lead the country into another war. This super-hawk, they said accusingly, attached more impor-

tance to the Bible than to the exigencies of diplomacy. He hated the Arabs. He would never give up an inch of precious Israeli-occupied Arab territory. Indeed, Begin hoped to witness one day the reestablishment of Jewish sovereignty over *Eretz Yisrael*, the biblical name for the land of Israel stretching from the Mediterranean Sea to the Jordan River. To that end, Begin had campaigned in the spring of 1977 in favor of continued Israeli rule over the Golan Heights, the West Bank, the Gaza Strip, and the Sinai Peninsula, territories captured by Israel from the Arabs during the 1967 Six-Day War.

Begin knew that his reputation as a warmonger had hurt him with the voters, so he campaigned as a peacemaker. Early in 1977, at his party's convention he said that "if the Likud is asked to form a government, then its first concern will be to prevent war. A Likud government will adopt a number of peace initiatives." He was, however, unable to relinquish his sacred principles. The key plank in the Likud platform was the principle that *Eretz Yisrael* would never be partitioned again and that a Likud-led government would do its utmost to extend Israeli law throughout the West Bank. His campaign speeches were fiery and to the point.

On election night crowds packed into Tel Aviv's Bet Jabotinsky, Likud's headquarters; they seemed to sense that victory was theirs. "Begin, Begin, Begin," they chanted enthusiastically. When they tired of that they switched to "Begin to the government."

At 10:00 P.M. Israel Television anchorman Haim Yavin, relying upon exit polls, announced that a "revolution" had occurred, that Likud indeed had won the election, and that Menachem Begin was to be Israel's next prime minister. The crowd inside Likud headquarters went wild.

Israel Government Press Office

Menachem Begin casts his ballot.

Finally, at 2:15 A.M., Begin's car, trapped in traffic snarled from the mad frenzy, made it to Bet Jabotinsky. Begin emerged slowly, a wide smile on his face. He hugged and kissed friends and colleagues, patiently absorbing their pats on the back. Inside the building, Begin slowly made his way to the large hall, decorated profusely with purple and orange Likud posters. Large pictures of Theodor Herzl, the founder of modern Zionism, and Ze'ev Jabotinsky, the spiritual founder of Herut and the Likud, hung on one wall. There were more kisses, embraces, and smiles. Israel Television wanted to interview Begin. He asked for an hour's delay "so I can meet my friends."

Later that morning Begin thanked everyone, including his eight grandchildren, one of whom had said proudly that he was "for Begin because he's a good grandfather." Begin proposed a national unity government, his way of beginning the healing process in the hope of uniting the country behind what would surely be a controversial prime ministership. Begin extended an offer of peace to Arab leaders. He wondered why Shimon Peres had not yet sent a telegram conceding defeat.

In a separate victory speech Begin made it clear that he still believed as strongly as ever that all of the West Bank should be in Israeli hands. He paid tribute to Aliza, his wife of thirty-nine years, with a paraphrase from Jeremiah, "I remember thee, the kindness of thy youth, the love of thine espousals, when thou went after me, in a land that was not sown."

Begin did not wait long to assert his authority. Throwing down the gauntlet on May 19 at Kaddum, a Jewish settlement on the West Bank, he promised that such Jewish settlements would blossom all over the West Bank. Said Begin, "There is enough room in the beautiful and holy land for Jews and Arabs."

Egyptian President Visits Israel

NOVEMBER 19, 1977 • 7:58 P.M.

When Anwar Sadat, President of Egypt, set foot on Israeli soil on that historic Saturday evening of November 19, 1977, it marked the first time that an Arab leader genuinely seemed willing to make peace with the state of Israel. Sadat's visit to Jerusalem that weekend, capped by his speech to the Knesset urging Israelis to make peace with Egypt, began a process that led to the first peace treaty between the state of Israel and an Arab country.

Ever since the founding of the state of Israel, the Arab nations on its borders had refused to make peace with her. Wars were fought, Israel winning each one—yet paying a tremendous price in the number of lives lost—but the Arab leaders persisted in their hope of conquering Israel, refusing to recognize the Jewish state and to meet publicly with any Israeli official to negotiate peace terms. After the 1967 Six-Day War, Arab leaders insisted that, before any peace negotiations could begin, Israel had to withdraw from the land it had conquered during the war.

A decade later, Egyptian president Anwar Sadat had a change of heart toward the state of Israel. Addressing Egypt's parliament on November 9, 1977, he stated his willingness to travel to the ends of the earth if that would help prevent a single Egyptian son from being killed or wounded in battle. In the past no one believed him. Yet on this occasion he indicated that he would even go to "the Knesset itself" to talk with the Israelis.

Sadat had to repeat the statement a number of times before others were willing to trust his sincerity. He even said he was prepared to leave for Israel in a few days. To test the Egyptian president, Prime Minister Menachem Begin issued a formal invitation for him to come to Jerusalem to conduct peace talks. In response, Sadat said he would arrive in Israel on November 19th.

Large segments of the Arab world branded Sadat a traitor and engaged in economic and political warfare against Egypt to isolate him. Sadat argued that he was serving Arab interests by seeking peace with the Israelis.

Sadat's journey that historic Saturday evening, November 19, took no more than twenty-eight minutes, a blink of an eye in historical perspective. But its effect on the Middle East was shattering: suddenly, the conflict between Israeli and Arab, marked by four bloody wars and thousands of battle dead, seemed open to resolution. Attesting to the worldwide interest in Sadat's peace mission, television journalists Walter Cronkite and Barbara Walters accompanied President Sadat from Egypt to Israel. During the flight, Sadat seemed determined to make history. "What I want from this visit," he told *Time* magazine reporter Wilton Wynn, who accompanied the Egyptian president to the Jewish state, "is that the wall created between us and Israel, the psychological wall, will be knocked down." Sadat's sleek Boeing 707 landed in Israel at 7:58 P.M.

Israeli political figures crowded next to one another at Ben-Gurion International Airport near Tel Aviv, standing at the foot of the plane waiting for the first glimpse of Sadat. Among the colorful trappings for the formal state welcome were the freshly-cleaned red carpet; the military band, new sheet music of the Egyptian national anthem clipped to their instruments; and the soldiers standing near the awesome-looking cannon ready to fire a twenty-one-gun salute reserved for heads of state.

Menachem Begin welcomes Anwar Sadat.

Euphoria and suspicion vied with one another in the minds of those assembled on the tarmac. Would Sadat indeed land? Was it all some kind of Arab trick?

Yet there he was, emerging from the door of the plane, standing on top of the ramp, moist eyes surveying the scene that lay before him, hand waving, nervously it seemed, to the hundreds of Israeli officials and guests down below. A slight smile wreathed the face upon which millions of eyes were transfixed, a smile that appeared to say, "Well, you want to talk; here I am." Whatever followed, nothing could compare to this supreme moment when Anwar Sadat's plane touched down on Israeli soil.

Sadat's journey marked a major milestone in modern diplomacy. Rarely had a single act captured the imagination of the entire world, and rarely had one deed marked such an obvious turning point in a major world trouble spot.

As Sadat waded into the crowds near the plane, one of the first Israelis to greet him was Moshe Dayan, who

had led Israeli armies to victory against Egypt in 1956 and 1967. "Don't worry, Moshe. It will be all right," Sadat said, as if he had read Dayan's secret concerns that somehow Sadat was intent on tricking the Israelis. Trailing behind Sadat was Deputy Prime Minister Hassan Tuhami, who did not greet Dayan like a long lost friend. "You said you were waiting for a phone call," Tuhami told Dayan, referring to their previous, secret meeting in Morocco on September 16. "Here we are."

As Sadat neared Golda Meir, she asked him, "Why didn't you tell me when I was prime minister that you wanted to come to Jerusalem? I would have you here in a moment." Golda later told friends, "he's not as ugly as I thought."

The highlight of Sadat's dramatic visit to Jerusalem was his appearance before the Knesset at 4:00 P.M. on Sunday, televised live around the world. "I have not come here for a separate agreement between Egypt and Israel," he said. He had not come to seek a partial peace—merely to terminate the state of belligerency. Sadat promised an

Yitzhak Rabin, Mordecai Gur, and Golda Meir greet Anwar Sadat at Ben-Gurion Airport.

end to the fighting. "Tell your sons that the past war was the last of wars and the end of sorrows."

The next day, the Egyptian leader's meeting with Israeli political leaders in the Knesset was carried live on Israeli television and beamed around the world. Golda Meir's banter with Sadat ranked as one of the most memorable moments of the Egyptian president's visit. Golda rose to the occasion with a touch of grand theater. She chided Sadat for calling her the "Old Lady" and praised him for his *zechut rishonim*, the privilege of being the first, inasmuch as he was the first Arab leader to come to Israel and say, "Let us have peace."

The Israelis and Egyptians were hardly on the verge of signing a peace agreement. Negotiations had begun, however, punctuated with a number of ups and downs. In September 1978 President Jimmy Carter brought Sadat and Begin together in the United States for face-to-face talks at Camp David, resulting in an agreement that established a framework for an eventual treaty. Fur-

ther negotiations were required, but they culminated in the signing of the first peace treaty between the state of Israel and an Arab state on March 26, 1979.

That peace treaty has stood the test of time and remains in force. Anwar Sadat was assassinated in October 1981 while watching a parade in Cairo. Although the assassins' motives were never fully clear, many believed that he had paid with his life for the historic visit to Jerusalem.

For many years the Israeli-Egyptian agreement constituted a separate peace, but the dream of a comprehensive Middle East peace seemed closer to realization when, in September 1993, and again, two years later, Israel and the Palestinians signed agreements that foresaw an end to Israel's occupation of the Gaza Strip and the West Bank, establishing Palestinian autonomy in those areas. In October 1994 Israel and Jordan signed a peace treaty as well.

Sharansky Crosses Bridge to Freedom

FEBRUARY 11, 1986

> The most famous Russian-Jewish dissident, Natan Sharansky conducted a long battle for the rights of Soviet Jews to leave for Israel and was arrested in 1976, charged with being an American spy. After being held in jail for eighteen months, he was convicted and sentenced to thirteen years in prison. Sharansky became the object of an international campaign, led by his wife Avital, to win his release, a campaign that brought immense sympathy to the Russian-Jewish cause. On February 11, 1986, after serving nine years, he was released in a dramatic prisoner exchange as he walked across the Glienicke Bridge to West Berlin. He settled in Israel and, in 1996, became Israel's Minister for Commerce and Industry.

Natan Borisovich Sharansky was born in Donetsk, in the Ukraine, on January 20, 1948. Since his parents sought to downplay their Jewish background and were afraid to use a Hebrew first name, they called him Anatoly. Natan's father, a Communist, was a journalist for a party newspaper. Natan's mother, Ida Milgrom, was an economist.

Natan showed a talent for mathematics. He was the chess champion of his school and then of his home city. In 1972 he graduated from the Moscow Physical-Technical Institute, where he studied mathematics and computers and began to work for the Oil and Gas Research Institute. The official reason Sharansky would later be denied an exit visa, Soviet authorities would insist, was because his job gave him access to state secrets.

During his childhood, Natan's parents made every effort to shield him from anti-Semitism. As a result, the youngster knew little about Judaism. That would change when he was nineteen years old and Israel triumphed in the Six-Day War of June 1967.

That war had a profound impact on numerous Russian Jews. Suddenly Sharansky no longer felt he had to hide his Jewish roots; he was openly proud to be Jewish, proud to identify with the state of Israel. Six years later, in April 1973, he sought an exit visa to immigrate to Israel. But the journey would take much longer than he anticipated.

Not only was Sharansky's visa denied on the basis of his "knowledge of state secrets," but government officials began to build a criminal case against him, alleging that the reason he wanted to go to Israel was so that he could kill Soviet soldiers fighting for Egypt.

As part of his growing involvement in the dissident movement, Sharansky became friendly with Misha Stieglitz, who also wanted to immigrate to Israel. In October 1973, Sharansky met Misha's sister Natalia outside the Moscow Synagogue, where Jews had gathered to hear news of the Yom Kippur War. They soon fell in love and made plans to marry.

Like Sharansky, Natalia Stieglitz had applied for an exit visa. Unlike him, she was granted one. On July 4, 1974 she and Sharansky were married. The very next day she left for Israel, at which time she began to use her Hebrew name Avital. She was sure that her husband would be close behind.

It was not to be. Unable to leave for Israel, Sharansky stepped up his dissident activities, traveling to outlying towns and provinces to collect information on the experiences of other "refuseniks," as those who were refused visas were called. He took part in letter-writing campaigns and protest demonstrations: at one such rally that he attended on the steps of Moscow's Lenin Library on February 24, 1975, two of the organizers were arrested, tried, and sentenced to five years in Siberia.

Early in 1977, Sharansky, then twenty-nine years old, was accused of spying for the CIA. Toward the end of March he was arrested. More than a year later, on July 14, 1978, Sharansky was convicted of treason, espionage, and anti-Soviet agitation and was sentenced to thirteen years in prison and labor camp. He would serve nine years of that sentence, four hundred three days of which he would spend in isolation cells, including one one-hundred-thirty-day stretch. Often deprived of food and exposed to the cold, he suffered from severe headaches,

Natan Sharansky and his wife, Avital, arrive in Israel.

ISRAEL GOVERNMENT PRESS OFFICE

problems with his vision, and chest pains. Proclaiming his innocence, he never considered "confessing" his crimes or asking for a medical pardon in order to gain his freedom. He was often on hunger strikes, once for more than one hundred days in protest against the Soviet refusal to let him write to Avital. On the one hundred tenth day, he was allowed to write to her again.

Writing to his mother from prison in 1980 upon learning of his father's death, Sharansky said: "The day after I received your telegram telling me of Papa's death, I decided, in his memory, to read and study all hundred and fifty Psalms of David in Hebrew...It will be as if I had erected a memorial stone to him in my heart."

From the moment she arrived in Israel in 1974, Avital had worked tirelessly to secure her husband's release. Following his imprisonment she traveled around the globe, meeting with world leaders, speaking at rallies and demonstrations. Thousands joined her and together kept the pressure on the Soviets to free Natan and other Jewish dissidents. She founded the Association for the Release of Anatoly Sharansky. In 1984, just before their

tenth wedding anniversary, she said, "Anatoly is so optimistic in his whole life that he makes people believe he will be free. I have no doubt that he will come. Not too soon, but he will be here."

Finally, on February 10, 1986, Sharansky was stripped of his Soviet citizenship and expelled from the Soviet Union. He was then flown to East Germany and led across the Glienicke Bridge to West Berlin and to freedom. Greeting Avital in Frankfurt, West Germany, seeing her for the first time since she had left Russia in 1974, Sharansky said simply, "Sorry I'm a little late."

Arriving in Israel hours later, he was given a hero's welcome. Spotting fellow dissidents in the crowd at Ben-Gurion International Airport, he quipped: "I am very glad to have an opportunity to speak to an audience in which my criminal contacts are represented so widely." In New York a few months later, Sharansky was warmly greeted at a rally attended by three hundred thousand people. The following week he met with President Ronald Reagan in the Oval Office at the White House.

The Sharanskys settled in Jerusalem. Natan found

Avital more sophisticated, more knowledgeable than twelve years earlier. "In Russia, when I discussed politics with friends, she was almost bored. Now she is my chief adviser. She knows everybody."

Sharansky's mother, Ida Milgrom, arrived in Israel in August 1986, as did his brother Leonid, and Leonid's wife and two sons. In November of that year, Avital and Natan had their first child, a girl named Rachel. The Sharansky's second child, Hannah, was born in 1988.

In 1996, Sharansky agreed to head a party appealing to Russian immigrants called the Yisrael B'Aliya party, which roughly translates as "Israel on the ascent," the Hebrew word for ascent (*aliyah*) also meaning "immigration." On May 29 of that year, the party garnered seven (out of one hundred and twenty) Knesset seats, and Sharansky became Minister for Commerce and Industry in the new government formed by Prime Minister Benjamin Netanyahu.

On January 27, 1997, saying that he had made the trip to close the circle, Sharansky returned to Russia for the first time since leaving there in 1986. He went on official business as Israel's Minister for Commerce and Industry, in an effort to increase Israeli trade with the former Soviet Union. But, undeniably, there was much emotion attached to his return to Russian soil. Upon landing in Moscow, he told reporters: "When I was in prison, I often dreamed of landing in Israel in an El Al [Israel's national airline] plane...but I never dreamed of landing in Moscow in an El Al plane." He was accompanied on the trip by his eighty-nine year old mother and Avital. He visited his father's grave for the first time. And he signed an economic cooperation agreement with Moscow Mayor Yuri Luzhov to boost trade between Israel and the city of Moscow. The ceremony occurred in a magnificent hall, next door to the building where Sharansky had been arrested twenty years earlier.

Rabin and Arafat Shake Hands

SEPTEMBER 13, 1993

Few believed that the state of Israel and its long time enemy, the Palestine Liberation Organization, (PLO) led by Yasser Arafat, would ever make peace. The century-old conflict between Jews and Arabs had been punctuated by frequent violence, deepening an enmity between the two peoples that appeared irreconcilable. Yet on September 13, 1993, the Israelis and the PLO (in the name of the Palestinian people) reached an accord that called for Palestinian self-rule in the Gaza Strip and in the West Bank town of Jericho. Sealing the deal, Israel's Prime Minister Yitzhak Rabin and PLO Chairman Arafat met at the White House where they signed the Declaration of Principles and sealed it with the most famous handshake of the modern era. Israelis and Palestinians alike hoped that their long war for political control over the land of Palestine had finally ended.

By the time Israel's prime minister, Yitzhak Rabin, and Palestine Liberation Organization chairman Yasser Arafat, arrived at the South Lawn of the White House on that sunny, September 13 morning in 1993, it was clear that the two archenemies had decided to embark upon a revolutionary course of peacemaking. They were about to affix their signatures to a document that marked the beginning of the joint quest for peace between Israelis and Palestinians. Yet, it was not the Declaration of Principles as much as it was their handshake, so much anticipated, so shocking to the eye, that sealed the historic occasion.

Eight months of delicate, highly secret negotiations in Oslo, Norway, had led to the signing of the Declaration of Principles, a framework for interim Palestinian self-government in the Gaza Strip and on the West Bank. The document called for Palestinian autonomy to begin in the Gaza Strip and the West Bank town of Jericho, and then to widen to include the rest of the West Bank.

One of the key peacemakers felt the weight of the hour. Bill Clinton, the president of the United States, who would play host to Rabin and Arafat on the White House lawn later that day, rose at 3:00 A.M, roamed the White House corridors, and read the *Book of Joshua*, reminding himself to make the point in his speech that this time the trumpets "herald not the destruction of that city but its new beginning."

No one was certain that Rabin and Arafat would shake hands. The Declaration of Principles did not call for it, nor did any written or unwritten diplomatic protocol. Neither the Israelis nor the Palestinians had sent a formal request through diplomatic channels for such a handshake. Rabin asked Clinton to tell Arafat that the Israeli prime minister did not want the Palestine Liberation Organization chairman to give him one of those Arab-style bearhugs; their "friendship" had not evolved to that point. On the prospect of a Rabin-Arafat handshake, the prime minister said nothing, but he sensed that Clinton might insist upon one. He deferred the decision of whether to shake Arafat's hand until the time came.

Rabin had been reluctant to attend the White House ceremony, let alone to shake the hand of the man his country had for years branded a murderer and a terrorist. Arafat, however, was eager to be on hand for the signing, because his presence, he believed, strengthened his claim to be the leader of the entire Palestinian na-

Yitzhak Rabin and Yasser Arafat shake hands as U.S. President Clinton looks on.

ISRAEL GOVERNMENT PRESS OFFICE

tion, rather than merely the chairman of an organization. Arafat's original wish had been to appear on the White House lawn wearing his Smith & Wesson pistol and, with a flourish, to unstrap the gun and hand it to the American president. Such theatrics were vetoed by Clinton. An hour before the ceremony, the Israelis and the Palestinians were still wrangling over details of the event. Arafat insisted on wearing his military-style uniform and on having the phrase "PLO" (as opposed to just the word "Palestinians) appear in the peace accord. At the last minute, Rabin swallowed his objections and allowed the ceremony to go forward.

At a reception inside the White House just before the ceremony, Rabin and Arafat avoided each other; but leaving the Blue Room, the two men looked at one another for the first time. Both seemed to realize that, if

the peace accord was to work, they would have to get used to talking to one another. Until that moment, they had not met or even talked to each other by telephone. Their communications during the secret Oslo negotiations had been through aides.

Rabin was the first to speak. "You know," he said to Arafat, "we are going to have to work very hard to make this work."

"I know," replied Arafat, "and I am prepared to do my part."

Seconds later, there were Rabin, Arafat, and Clinton, walking across the White House lawn, approaching the three thousand invited guests, a scene that many Israelis and Palestinians thought they would never witness in their lifetimes.

The two Middle East leaders were a study in con

trasts as they stood on the dais with the world watching. Arafat, dressed in his well-pressed brown khakis and trademark black-and-white kaffiyeh, smiled constantly. Rabin, on the other hand, squirmed, wriggled, cocked his head at the sky, the ground, anywhere, just to avert Arafat's eyes.

The image of that morning etched in people's minds was not the affixing of signatures on the documents, not the speeches. After the signing Arafat, to the far right, Clinton, in the middle, and Rabin, to the far left, stood for a few seconds with no one telling them what to do next. Arafat made the first gesture, extending his right hand to Rabin. Eager for the two men to seal their accord with a handshake, Clinton placed his right hand behind Rabin's back, as if to encourage the prime minister to move closer to Arafat. Rabin gave one of his customary expressions, as if to say, "Oh, all right, I'll do it," and then grasped Arafat's hands. The crowd broke into applause and, as they did, Arafat reached across

Rabin to shake the hand of Foreign Minister Shimon Peres. "Now it's your turn," Rabin mumbled to Peres, as if to say, "Well I managed to do it. You'll have to also."

The Rabin-Arafat handshake took on special significance. In a violent world, where conflict seemed to be the rule and peaceful resolution the rare exception, here were two men, representing one of the world's most enduring conflicts, reaching out to one another. Their handshake gave the world something positive to think about: If these two implacable foes could cross such a huge and seemingly unbridgeable chasm of hatred, perhaps other adversaries might find the strength and courage to do the same.

No one believed that the Rabin-Arafat handshake augured a quick and painless peace between Israelis and Palestinians. Indeed, as both sides sought to implement the Declaration of Principles, it became clear that shaking hands was far easier than establishing a durable peace.

Catholic Church Reconciles with Jews

JUNE 15, 1994

In June 1994 Israel and the Vatican agreed to establish full diplomatic relations. The announcement, no surprise after the two sides had agreed six months earlier on a historic reconciliation, was the best evidence of the Catholic Church's slow but steady putting aside of ancient hatreds and suspicions against the Jewish people.

When Israel and the Vatican announced in mid-June 1994 that they had agreed to establish diplomatic relations, the pronouncement did not seem earth-shaking. After all, in the wake of the famous handshake on the White House Lawn the previous September between Israel's Prime Minister Yitzhak Rabin and Palestinian Liberation Organization leader Yasser Arafat, Israel was moving toward establishing diplomatic relations with all sorts of countries that hitherto had refused to recognize the Jewish state.

Yet the Israeli-Vatican agreement was different from all the others, for it marked a moment of reconciliation between the Catholic Church—and its nine hundred million members—and the Jewish people, the people from which Jesus emerged. While the Arabs had been hostile to the Jews "only" for the past one hundred years, the Catholic Church's enmity toward the Jewish people had lasted nearly two thousand years.

During the Middle Ages, the Catholic Church promulgated charges of blood libel against Jews, accusing Jews of hunting down and killing Christians in a ritual murder designed as a reenactment of the Passion of Jesus. Following the alleged murder, the Jews, according to the blood libel charge, supposedly used the blood of the victim to make matzahs for the Jewish festival of Passover. During the same period, Jews were forced into public disputations, over which presided kings and bishops, to defend their holy books—and their religion. The whole point of the exercise was to humiliate the Jews, prove that the Jewish religion was inferior to Christianity, and make the Jews convert. In the twentieth century, the Church adopted a passivity toward Nazi behavior that was consistent with its centuries-long hostility toward the Jewish people.

Signing the historic document in Jerusalem were Deputy Foreign Minister Yossi Beilin and the Vatican's Archbishop Andre de Montezemolo.

Rabbi David Rosen, former chief rabbi of Ireland, one of the key negotiators of the Israeli-Vatican accord, said the agreement affirmed the great improvement in Catholic-Jewish relations. "It will affect the way Jews are viewed within the Catholic world and the way Jews feel they are viewed within the Catholic world," said Rosen.

Back on December 30, 1993, Israel and the Vatican had agreed to establish full diplomatic relations within four months. Since the founding of the Jewish state in 1948, the Vatican had refused to establish diplomatic relations with Israel, always appearing to side with the Arab view that the Jewish state had no right to exist. Now, the Vatican had dropped its aversion to the Jewish state and was ready to deal with it.

The Israeli-Vatican agreement of December 30 said that the two sides were to exchange special envoys immediately and that a full ambassador and nuncio—the highest ranking papal emissary accredited to a civil government—were to assume their posts the following April.

Monsignor Celli, representing the Vatican, shakes hands with Yossi Beilin, Israel's Deputy Foreign Minister after the signing.

The preamble to the agreement was not composed in the customary language of international diplomacy: "Mindful of the singular character and universal significance of the Holy Land, aware of the unique nature of the relations between the Catholic Church and the Jewish people and the historic process of reconciliation and growth in the mutual understanding and friendship between Catholics and Jews . . ."

The rapprochement between Israel and the Vatican came about in large measure because of *Nostra aetate*, the Church's ecumenical council's historic 1965 document on religious attitudes toward non-Christians. That document permitted the church to banish anti-Semitism from Catholic teaching and to build a new, "fraternal" religious dialogue based on respect and separate religious identities.

More progress had been made between Jews and Catholics in the negotiations leading up to the signing of the December 30, 1993, document than in the past ninety years. It was in January 1904, for example, that

Theodor Herzl tried to introduce Pope Pius X to political Zionism. The pope, however, replied that he could not take this movement seriously— "as the Jews did not recognize our Lord, we cannot recognize the Jewish people."

It was only on May 27, 1954, six years after the Jewish state was founded, that Pope Pius XII received an Israeli political official for the first time, Foreign Minister Moshe Sharett. A month later, when the Israel Philharmonic Orchestra performed Beethoven's Seventh Symphony for the pope, the Vatican reported that "Jewish musicians of fourteen different nationalities" had performed for His Holiness.

Pope John XXIII, as one of his first acts, ordered that the expression "perfidious Jews" be expunged from Good Friday prayers. Greatly influenced by the French-Jewish Holocaust survivor and philosopher Jules Isaac who was devoted to the study of Christian anti-Semitism, Pope John XXIII insisted that the ecumenical council address the attitude of the Catholic Church to the Jews, which would later result in *Nostra aetate*, approved by Paul VI, John XXIII's predecessor.

On January 4, 1964, Pope Paul VI became the first pope to visit the state of Israel. The Vatican billed the visit as a trip to the "Holy Land" and not to the state of Israel. After the visit, the pope sent a telegram of thanks to "President Shazar, Tel Aviv."

Still, the 1965 *Nostra aetate* was flawed from a Jewish perspective, especially in stating so ambiguously "Moved not by political motives but by religious, evangelical charity, the church deplores hatred, persecutions and all manifestations of anti-Semitism directed against Jews at any time and by any person." It was noted that the verb "deplore" was used rather than the stronger verb "condemn."

Relations appeared to be improving when on January 15, 1973, Israel's Prime Minister Golda Meir met Pope Paul VI. Still the Vatican spokesperson went out of his way to explain that the visit was not "a gesture of preference or exclusivity," making sure to note that the Vatican had close, friendly relations with many Arab personalities and countries. And, in case anyone had any doubts, the spokesperson noted that the Holy See's "attitude towards Israel remains unchanged."

Pope John Paul II went far toward reconciliation by becoming the first pope to visit a synagogue, which he did when he visited the Main Synagogue of Rome and addressed Jews as "our dearly beloved older brothers"

in 1986. He declared in 1992, this time much more forthrightly, "Anti-Semitism is a sin against God and against man."

In January 1993, Pope John Paul II told members of the Anti-Defamation League of B'nai B'rith that "the Holocaust was the greatest trauma, the greatest tragedy of our century, and we (Jews and Christians) must work together to prevent anything similar from happening again. This is in God's design."

The great stumbling block to Israeli-Vatican reconciliation had always been the slow pace of the Middle East peace process; but starting in November 1992 with the Madrid peace conference, attended by all of the main parties to the Arab-Israeli conflict, it was increasingly difficult for the Arabs to protest the warming up of Israeli-Vatican relations. When asked how the Palestine Liberation Organization would react to the creation of an Israeli-Vatican bilateral commission in July 1992, Vatican press spokesman Joacquin Navarro noted, "Palestinians and other Arabs cannot protest against our starting a process leading to diplomatic recognition of Israel when they themselves are sitting at the negotiating table with Israeli authorities."

With the announcement of diplomatic relations in June 1994, there was ample rejoicing on the part of Vatican and Israeli officials, yet few were willing to predict that the anti-Semitism and enmity that had prevailed against Jews for so long would be eradicated over night.

MOMENTS
of
DESPAIR

Solomon's Empire Is Divided

925 B.C.E.

With the death of Solomon in 925 B.C.E., his empire split into two separate kingdoms—Israel in the north and Judah in the south. Never without internal strife, Israel was ruled by short-lived dynasties. Israel was larger and wealthier than Judah, however, and may have made Judah into a vassal for a while; both kingdoms eventually became vassals of Assyria, which conquered the northern kingdom in 722 B.C.E. and forcibly resettled the inhabitants. Lacking a sense of national identity, they were lost among the surrounding peoples.

The division of Solomon's kingdom began even before his death in 925 B.C.E. Northerners resented the concentration of religious power in Jerusalem and the disparagement of the older shrines in the north as heterodox. The guilds of prophets and other religious purists objected to the worship of foreign deities introduced by Solomon's wives. Heavy taxes and forced labor were also increasingly unpopular, especially in the north, since the men of Judah were partly exempt.

The revolt of the north began when Jeroboam, an administrator of forced labor from the tribe of Ephraim, left one day and encountered the prophet Ahijah outside Jerusalem; Ahijah was from Shiloh, in the north. The prophet accompanied Jeroboam on his way. According to the biblical account, Jeroboam "had put on a new robe; and when the two were alone in the open country, Ahijah took hold of the new robe he was wearing and tore it into twelve pieces. 'Take ten pieces,' he said to Jeroboam. 'For thus said the Lord, the God of Israel: I am about to tear the kingdom out of Solomon's

hands, and I will give you ten tribes. But one tribe shall remain his—for the sake of my servant David and for the sake of Jerusalem'" (*1 Kings* 11:29–32). Solomon tried to apprehend Jeroboam and have him killed, but Jeroboam fled to Egypt and remained with the Pharaoh, Shishak, until Solomon's death.

The northerners refused to accept the coronation of Solomon's son and successor, Rehoboam, in Jerusalem; they insisted that he also travel to Shechem (today's Nablus), which he did, to be crowned in the north. The people presented their grievances to Rehoboam, but he rejected the advice of his senior advisers to make concessions and, instead, threatened even greater repression. At that, the northerners declared that they would secede. Rehoboam sent Adoniram, the chief administrator of forced labor, to deal with them, but they stoned him to death, and Rehoboam fled in haste back to Jerusalem. Meanwhile, Jeroboam had returned from Egypt, and the northerners crowned him king in Shechem, which became the first capital of the northern kingdom, Israel. In the south, only the tribe of Benjamin remained loyal to Judah.

To break the affection and loyalty most of the people felt toward the Temple in Jerusalem, Jeroboam reestablished the religious decentralization that had prevailed before the Davidic monarchy and restored the shrines of Dan and Bethel, at opposite ends of the northern kingdom. Unfortunately, he antagonized the prophets who had helped establish him on the throne by setting up miniature golden calves in these shrines as a focus for popular religious feeling. Like the Israelites in the desert who had made the original Golden Calf, Jeroboam did not intend to promote the worship of

Jewish captives from Judah before Pharoah Shishak, c. 930 C.E. from a relief, Temple of Amon, Karnak.

other deities but to represent the one God through an image. "He said to the people, 'You have been going up to Jerusalem long enough. This is your God, O Israel, who brought you up from the land of Egypt!'" (*1 Kings* 12:28). The calves, however, resembled the images of deities worshiped by the surrounding peoples. Thus, Jeroboam's largely political act, in the long run, caused the people of the northern kingdom to lose their sense of religious and national identity.

In Judah, Rehoboam continued to treat the secession of the north as a rebellion, and war with the northern kingdom continued throughout his reign. Rehoboam's military success led Jeroboam to call on his Egyptian patron, the Pharaoh Shishak, for help. Shishak, the founder of a new Egyptian dynasty, was only too eager. He invaded Judah and reached the gates of Jerusalem. A hieroglyphic inscription in the Temple of Karnak records his triumphs against Judah. He reduced many fortified towns to heaps of stones and drove his chariots as far north as the valley of Jezreel. He also deported many of the people of Judah to Egypt and stripped the Temple and Solomon's palaces of their gold and treasure. Moreover, both the northern and southern kingdoms were obliged to pay him a heavy annual tribute.

Rehoboam protected Judah against any possibility of another Egyptian invasion by strengthening fortifications in the southern cities of his kingdom. His son and successor, Abijah, tried to protect Judah against the northern kingdom by entering into an alliance with the Arameans, to the north of Israel.

Jeroboam reigned in the north for twenty-two years and was succeeded by his son, who was killed after two years by one of his generals. A series of short-lived dynasties followed, the longest of which lasted for five generations. They included, however, a few outstanding rulers, such as the former army officer Omri and his son Ahab. Omri moved the northern capital to Samaria, an easily fortified location on a hill six miles northwest of Shechem that remained the capital for the duration of the northern kingdom. Like Solomon, he formed an alliance with the Phoenicians, an alliance cemented by Ahab's marriage to Jezebel, daughter of the king of Tyre.

Jeroboam had risen to power as champion of the people, but neither he nor any of his successors in the north established a just government. Though most of Ahab's reign was a period of prosperity and relative peace, it is most noted for Ahab's and Jezebel's stormy relations with the prophet Elijah, who confronted Ahab concerning his idolatrous worship of the Phoenician Ba'al and, especially, the judicial murder of a private citizen, engineered by Jezebel to allow Ahab to expropriate a piece of land he coveted. Elijah—and his successor, Elisha—were instrumental in the overthrow of the dynasty.

The other outstanding ruler was Jeroboam II, during whose forty-year reign Damascus was recaptured and the northern kingdom reached the height of its strength. Judah, too, enjoyed a long period of prosperity. The two kingdoms were allies—though it is possible that Judah may have been Israel's vassal during this time—and their rulers worked together to extend the territory that had once been Solomon's.

Ultimately, however, the greatest threat to the region—not merely to Israel and Judah but to the Phoenicians and Arameans as well—was from Assyria, which, from its capital on the Tigris River, was relentlessly extending its empire southward. From the end of Ahab's reign on, Israel participated in military coalitions against the Assyrians that fell apart as soon as their short-term goals had been accomplished. Eventually, all the smaller kingdoms—Israel, Judah, Ammon, Moab, and Edom, and Damascus as well—became vassals to the Assyrians. They paid tribute and, thereby, were able to keep some autonomy. After a while, relying on an understanding with Egypt, the king of Israel refused to continue paying tribute to Assyria. When Egypt went back on its word, the Assyrian ruler, Sargon II, captured the king of Israel and laid siege to Samaria, which fell in 722 B.C.E.

Though the northern kingdom came to an end at that time, opposition to the Assyrians continued. To quell it, the Assyrians undertook a massive transfer of populations, a practice then considered routine when territory was captured. According to his own records, Sargon carried off twenty-seven thousand two-hundred ninety Israelites—probably the upper classes and skilled artisans—and resettled them elsewhere. He then brought new settlers from Babylonia and Syria into the evacuated areas. Many of them intermarried with the local population and became the ancestors of the present-day Samaritans. In their new homes, the deportees from the kingdom of Israel were also assimilated into local populations. Though its history is preserved in the Hebrew Bible, the northern kingdom is remembered mainly for the books of the prophets Hosea and Amos, who foresaw its downfall. The future of the Jewish people lay with the small kingdom of Judah in the south.

Lasting another one hundred thirty-five years, the southern kingdom of Judah managed to survive for the most part because of the ongoing struggles between Assyria, which was moving into decline, Babylonia, which was reviving, and Egypt, which was trying to regain its empire.

By 612 B.C.E., the Assyrian capital, Nineveh, fell to the Babylonians. Seven years later the Babylonians defeated the Egyptians, at Carchemish in Northern Syria.

Nebuchadnezzar, who was the greatest and most powerful of the Babylonian kings, now marched his Babylonian army to the Mediterranean Sea and in 597 B.C.E. captured Jerusalem. Both the northern and southern kingdoms would wither away, but the process would take several centuries.

The First Temple Is Destroyed

AUGUST 587 B.C.E.

The destruction of Solomon's Temple by the Babylonians in 586 B.C.E. is perhaps the archetypal Jewish tragedy. The anniversary of the destruction is still observed as a major fast. Even though, under the monarchy, many Jews were not strict monotheists in practice, the Temple in Jerusalem, with its centralized worship of the one God, had symbolized the Jewish people's national and religious identity for more than four hundred years. Its loss, therefore, was traumatic. Both before and after the event, the Prophets gave the destruction meaning for the Jewish people by interpreting it as the consequence of the people's violations of their own ideals of monotheism and social justice.

The beginnings of the defeat of the southern kingdom can be traced to the unrest of the eighth century B.C.E. The people of Judah and Jerusalem lived a fragile, unsettled life, caught between Assyrian domination of the region and the shifting alliances of the northern kingdom and its immediate neighbors. Though both kingdoms, on the whole, experienced some prosperity, their people were divided by conflicts between nationalism and regionalism and by extreme inequality in the distribution of wealth. Fear of conquest and awareness of its eventual probability were widespread. The priests in Jerusalem hoped to placate God through the Temple rituals and avert disaster. The late-eighth-century prophet Isaiah, however, in a passage of rebuke read yearly on the Sabbath before the anniversary of the destruction, declared the Temple rituals offensive to God because they were not accompanied by ethical behavior and social justice.

Your rulers are rogues
And cronies of thieves,
Every one avid for presents
And greedy for gifts;
They do not judge the case of the orphan,
And the widow's cause never reaches them.
Isaiah 1:23

Isaiah accused the Jews of deserting God; he compared the people to children rebelling against a parent and the rulers of Judah and Jerusalem to those of Sodom and Gomorrah. Yet he also taught that there was time to repent and that, if the Jews changed their behavior, God would forgive them. He also prophesied the future restoration of Jerusalem, as well as a time of peace in which

. . . they shall beat their swords into plowshares
And their spears into pruning hooks:
Nation shall not lift up
Sword against nation;
Neither shall they learn war anymore.
Isaiah 2:4

Isaiah continued to warn the people—"Watchman, what of the night? Watchman, what of the night?" (*Isaiah* 21:6)—and he rebuked those who, despite the impending disaster, held feasts and said, "Eat and drink, for tomorrow we die!" (*Isaiah* 22:12–13). Though his first vision—of God enthroned above the Temple and the seraphs declaring God's holiness (*Isaiah* 6:1–7), followed immediately by his first clear premonition of the destruction to come (*Isaiah* 6:8–13)—took place in the

Temple itself, he aroused the priests' disdain by speaking, not to them, but directly to the Temple worshipers. He was consulted, however, by four successive kings of Judah. The last was Hezekiah, during whose reign the Assyrians overthrew the northern kingdom and besieged Jerusalem. They did not capture it, however, but abruptly lifted the siege, apparently because of an epidemic in the army and news of attacks on other fronts.

Isaiah was the first to realize, even before the Babylonians defeated Assyria in 612 B.C.E., that Judah would eventually be conquered by the Babylonians, not the Assyrians. The Bible twice reports his response to King Hezekiah's overly favorable reception of ambassadors from Babylon (2 *Kings* 20:16–19, *Isaiah* 39:5–8). The ambassadors had brought gifts to Hezekiah to congratulate him upon his recovery from a serious illness. Elated, Hezekiah showed them all his treasure. Isaiah then confronted him and asked where the men had come from and what they had seen. Hezekiah told him, and Isaiah replied, "Hear the word of the Lord: A time is coming when everything in your palace that your ancestors have stored up to this day will be carried off to Babylon; nothing will remain behind, said the Lord. And some of your sons, your own issue, whom you will have fathered, will be taken to serve as eunuchs in the palace of the king of Babylon." Unable to imagine the magnitude of the disaster, which was not to take place for several generations, Hezekiah replied, "'The word of the Lord that you have spoken is good.' For he thought, 'It means that safety is assured for my time.'"

The writers of the biblical books of *Kings* and *Chronicles* considered Hezekiah one of the best kings of Judah because of his devotion to monotheism; his son Manasseh was considered one of the worst because of his revival of Canaanite and foreign cults and his arbitrary executions of political enemies. Manasseh was succeeded by his son Amon, who was assassinated after reigning for two years. The coup was suppressed, however, and Amon's son Josiah was made king at eight years of age. In 621 B.C.E., when Josiah reached maturity, he gave orders for the repair of the Temple. As the work proceeded, the high priest Hilkiah discovered a "scroll of the teaching" and gave it to Josiah's chancellor, the scribe Shaphan, who read it to the king. Scholars are not sure what the text was. Some think it might have been the original text of the Pentateuch, whereas others think it was the *Book of Deuteronomy*. Whatever it was, the king was deeply moved by its predictions that national disaster would be the consequence of disobeying

God's commandments. He ordered Hilkiah, Shaphan, and his ministers to inquire of the prophetess Huldah, who confirmed the predictions but reassured the king that, because he had taken the message to heart, the disaster would not happen in his time. The king then read the scroll to the assembled people of Jerusalem, who were also moved, and he renewed the covenant with God. Josiah ordered a total reform of the cult. All images were to be destroyed; provincial shrines—the "high places"—were to be shut down, and pagan, heterodox, and heretic priests were slain. As worship was centralized, the Temple gained greater authority.

After Isaiah, the next powerful prophetic voice was that of Jeremiah, who followed the tradition of Hosea and, to some extent, of Isaiah. He began his prophetic career during the thirteenth year of Josiah's reign, prophesied throughout the southern kingdom's final decades, and attempted to guide the people through the destruction of Jerusalem and the beginning of the Babylonian exile. He was soon disappointed by Josiah's reforms, for it proved impossible, especially in the countryside, to eradicate popular pagan practices, such as household offerings of cakes to the Queen of Heaven, by royal decree. In the Temple itself, the priests controlled the official prophets, with the power to censor those they did not approve. Jeremiah focused his wrath on this establishment: "The prophets prophesy falsely,/And the priests bear rule accordingly;/And my people like it so./But what will you do at the end of it?" (*Jeremiah* 5:31). Like Isaiah, he denounced the establishment's conviction that Temple ritual alone, without ethics and without faithfulness to God, would protect Judah from conquest:

> Thus said the Lord of Hosts, the God of Israel: Mend your ways and your actions, and I will let you dwell in this place. Don't put your trust in illusions and say, "The Temple of the Lord, the Temple of the Lord, the Temple of the Lord are these [buildings]." . . . Will you steal and murder and commit adultery and swear falsely, and sacrifice to Baal, and follow other gods whom you have not experienced, and then come and stand before me in this house that bears my name and say, "We are safe"?
>
> *Jeremiah* 7:3–10

Contradicting the official prophets, Jeremiah warned that God would destroy the Temple in Jerusalem and "make this House like Shiloh" (*Jeremiah* 26:6), once the religious center of the northern kingdom. He was almost sentenced to death for this prophecy and for others as well. Yet he persisted. Though some saw in Jeremiah's prophecies a treasonable defeatism, he was actually offering his people a blueprint for survival, for he taught that the relationship between God and Israel, the basis of the Jewish people's religious identity, would survive a military defeat and continue even in exile. Moreover, far from being a prophet of defeat, he continued to emphasize God's promise of restoration. Just before the final destruction, while he was in prison, he redeemed a field belonging to his family as a sign that "fields shall again be purchased in this land," and he foresaw that "Again there shall be heard in this place . . . the sound of mirth and gladness, the voice of bridegroom and bride" and that the Temple would be rebuilt (*Jeremiah* 32, 33:10–11). He knew, however, that the restoration would not take place for many years.

During the last years of Josiah's reign, the Babylonians staged a successful revolt against the Assyrian empire, which had been weakened by attacks by nomad peoples on its northern borders. The Babylonians conquered Nineveh in 612 B.C.E. The Assyrians responded by forming an alliance with Egypt. In 609, the Assyrian and Egyptian armies marched into Syria to take Haran, and then into the Jezreel Valley. Josiah tried to stop them and was killed in battle at Megiddo. The "people of the land," that is, the council of landed nobility, named Josiah's second son, Jehoahaz, to succeed him. Jehoahaz, who supported his father's policies, was dethroned by the Assyrian-Egyptian alliance a few months later and sent in chains to Egypt, where he died. The Egyptians then enthroned his brother Jehoiakim, who was sympathetic to their cause.

Four years later, the Egyptians made a final attempt to cross the Euphrates. Under Nebuchadnezzar, who was soon to become king, the Babylonians destroyed the Egyptian army in the critical battle of Carchemish. Babylon became the greatest power in the Middle East. Though he had been placed on the throne to serve Egyptian interests, Jehoiakim soon acknowledged Babylonian power. Like the other states in the region, Judah became a vassal of Babylon, a relationship that at first did not appear to threaten the internal autonomy of Judah. Yet, nationalism reasserted itself in Judah. In 598 B.C.E., Jehoiakim broke away from Babylon and tried to reestablish his alliance with Egypt as a step toward independence. Judah was invaded by Babylonian troops stationed in neighboring countries, and Jehoiakim was

killed. He was succeeded by his eighteen-year-old son Jehoiakin.

In 597 B.C.E., Nebuchadnezzar himself arrived to direct the siege of Jerusalem. Jehoiakin surrendered at once and was deported to Babylon with his mother, harem, and court, as well as much of the nobility. The *Second Book of Kings* relates that Nebuchadnezzar "exiled all of Jerusalem: all the commanders and all the warriors— ten thousand exiles—as well as all the craftsmen and smiths; only the poorest people in the land were left" (2 *Kings* 24:14). He also carried off the Temple and palace treasures. This was the first Babylonian deportation.

Wishing to maintain a subordinate but stable entity in Judah, Nebuchadnezzar appointed Jehoiakin's uncle Zedekiah, a son of Josiah, as the new king over those who remained behind. He bound Zedekiah by a strong oath to maintain his allegiance to Babylon. Yet, three years later, Zedekiah broke his oath and joined a coalition of small states opposed to Babylon; by 590 B.C.E., he had allied himself with Egypt. The anti-Babylonian party in Jerusalem predicted a short captivity and a quick end to Babylonian power. Jeremiah, however, had consistently taught that the Jewish people's survival depended on peaceful cooperation with the conquering power, both at home and in exile. He predicted a period of captivity lasting seventy years; about this time, he sent a letter to the exiled community in Babylon advising:

> Build houses and live in them, plant gardens and
> eat their fruit. Take wives and beget sons and
> daughters. . . . Multiply there, do not decrease.
> And seek the welfare of the city to which I have
> exiled you and pray to the Lord in its behalf; for
> in its prosperity you shall prosper.
>
> *Jeremiah* 29:4–7

He also counseled against the Egyptian alliance, advice Zedekiah did not heed.

Nebuchadnezzar reacted swiftly to Zedekiah's defection. He established his headquarters at Riblah, led his main force to Jerusalem, and laid siege to the city. Because the walls were strong and well defended, he built a rampart around them in order to subdue the inhabitants by starvation, a strategy that proved successful. When an Egyptian army advanced toward Jerusalem in 587 B.C.E., Nebuchadnezzar temporarily raised the siege to combat it. He easily defeated the Egyptian army and resumed the siege on the tenth day of the month of

Tevet in 586 B.C.E., a day Orthodox Jews still observe as a minor fast, from sunrise to sunset. On the seventeenth of Tammuz, also observed as a minor fast day, the Babylonians succeeded in making a breach in the city wall. Zedekiah tried to flee across the Jordan but was captured at Jericho and brought to Babylonian headquarters at Riblah, where he was forced to watch the slaughter of his sons. Then his eyes were put out, a typical punishment at the time for a vassal who broke his oath, and he was carried in chains to Babylon.

The destruction of Jerusalem is also recorded in the Babylonian Chronicle. According to a fragment now housed in the British Museum, "In the seventh year, in the month of Kislev, [Nebuchadnezzar] mustered his troops, and having marched to the land of Hatti, besieged the city of Judah, and on the second day of the month of Adar took the city and captured the king. He appointed therein a king of his own choice, received its heavy tribute and sent [them] to Babylon." The date was August 587 B.C.E.

On the seventh of Av, the Babylonian commander-in-chief arrived with orders from Nebuchadnezzar to destroy Jerusalem. The Babylonians plundered Jerusalem and set fire to the Temple, the royal palace, and the houses of the nobility. They carried off the remaining Temple vessels and bronze, razed the walls of Jerusalem, and led the remaining population as captives to Babylon in the second Babylonian deportation. Presumed lost in the Temple's flames was the Ark of the Covenant, though the absence of any reference to the Ark has fostered speculation that it may not have been destroyed at this time. Even the rabbis of the Mishnah debate whether the Ark was hidden (rather than destroyed), or whether it went into exile with the people.

The very day the Temple was destroyed, the Babylonians, who wished to maintain at least some strength in the area against possible attacks from Egypt, set up an autonomous Jewish community with its center at Mizpah. It was made up of Jews friendly to Babylon—for the most part, the poorer Jews who remained after the deportations. The Babylonians appointed as governor a moderate nobleman named Gedaliah, who was not of royal lineage but, rather, the grandson of Josiah's chancellor. Jeremiah, still in a position to offer guidance to the new community, was given a pension.

Gedaliah's attempts to establish peace and stability after the siege and deportations lasted less than two months. A fanatical descendant of the royal house, with support from the neighboring kingdom of Ammon, assassinated Gedaliah in the month of Tishrei and slaughtered the Babylonian garrison at Mizpah; the third day of that month, the day after Rosh Hashanah, is still observed as a minor fast to commemorate the assassination, which put an end to any possibility of Jewish life in the territory of Judah. The assassin and his followers fled to Ammon. Fearing reprisal, the remaining leaders of the Jewish community, with many of their followers, fled to Egypt, against Jeremiah's advice, carrying Jeremiah off with them against his wishes. Thus, Judah was left without a government, without religious guidance, and with few inhabitants. As *Deuteronomy* and the Prophets had foreseen, the land was desolate. In the words of the *Book of Lamentations*, a series of poems traditionally attributed to Jeremiah that describe and mourn the siege of Jerusalem and the destruction of the First Temple,

> Alas!
> Lonely sits the city
> Once great with people!
> She that was great among nations
> Is become like a widow;
> The princess among states
> Is become a thrall.
> Bitterly she weeps in the night,
> Her cheek wet with tears.
> There is none to comfort her
> Of all her friends. . . .
>
> *Lamentations* 1:1–2

The anniversary of the destruction of the Temple is observed as a major fast; like Yom Kippur, the fast of the Ninth of Av lasts from sunset to sunset. Many of the customs associated with mourning are observed, and the *Book of Lamentations* is chanted. Moreover, the destruction of the First Temple is not the only tragic event that occurred, and is commemorated, on the Ninth of Av. That date is also the anniversary of the destruction of the Second Temple by the Romans in 70 C.E. The fast, therefore, commemorates the destruction of both Temples. Over the centuries, many other tragic events experienced by the Jewish people also came to be commemorated on the Ninth of Av. Only the Holocaust, different in character from the earlier catastrophes, has been given its own day of remembrance.

Zealots Commit Suicide at Masada

73 C.E.

> *The rhomboid fortress known as Masada, located on the Dead Sea, served as the last outpost of the Jewish Zealots during the Jewish war against Rome. After Jerusalem fell to Titus in 70 C.E. Jewish patriots fled to the granite outpost. When a Roman force, after a three-year siege, succeeded in capturing the fortress, the Romans found that the Jewish defenders, rather than be taken captive, had committed suicide. Especially after the archaeological excavation of the site in 1963, the mass suicide at Masada became a symbol of Jewish resistance.*

Aerial photo of Masada.

Twenty miles north of Sedom on the Dead Sea, where the high ground recedes from the water's edge, lies the flat-topped rock called Masada, whose plateau is half a mile across. Masada is a natural, nearly impregnable stronghold at the edge of the Judean Desert and the Dead Sea Valley, 15.5 miles (25 kilometers) south of Ein Gedi. On the eastern side, the rock drops sharply some thirteen hundred feet to the Dead Sea shore.

The first to fortify this rock was Jonathan, the youngest brother of Judah Maccabee, in the second century B.C.E. The ruins that can be seen there today are of fortifications built by Herod the Great, a son of the Idumean (Edomite) chief minister of one of the last Hasmonean rulers, Hyrcanus II. Though the younger son, Herod succeeded his father and gradually took over the political authority that the Hasmoneans still retained under the Romans. When Mark Antony's long stay in Egypt allowed the Parthians to take Jerusalem in 42 B.C.E., Herod sent his family to Masada. More than the Parthians, however, Herod feared the Hasmoneans, who had allied themselves with the Parthians in an attempt to regain their dynasty's position as rulers of Judea. Herod himself, therefore, fled to Petra in Arabia, then to Alexandria, and, from there, traveled to Rome. After the Roman Senate confirmed his title as king of Judea in 37 B.C.E., Herod retook Galilee and Jerusalem and reestablished his power; he remained in power until his death in 4 C.E. To defend himself against both Jewish opposition and the Egyptian queen, Cleopatra, who sought to annex Judea to Egypt, he maintained Masada as a refuge for himself and spent the next six years transforming the rock into a highly defensible fort, designed to withstand a long siege. He erected a defense wall, with thirty-seven watch towers, around the plateau, and at the northern corner, looking out across the Dead Sea, he constructed a semicircular palace, which was cut into the rock-face below the top of the mountain.

A Roman garrison was probably stationed on Masada for sixty years, from 6 to 66 C.E. In 66 C.E., as Jewish resistance to the Roman occupation intensified, a band of Zealots attacked Masada and captured it. They were led by Menachem, the son of a Galilean named Judah, whose father had been executed by Herod. When Herod died, Judah had assumed the leadership of the Jewish resistance fighters, who became known as Zealots (*Kannaim*). Though the Romans defeated and executed Judah, his followers continued to look to his family for leadership. After Menachem was murdered by Jewish rivals in Jerusalem, his nephew Eleazar succeeded him.

The Jewish resistance was defeated by the Roman general Vespasian, soon to become emperor, who conquered Jewish towns one by one and isolated Jerusalem. When Vespasian's son Titus conquered Jerusalem in 70 C.E. and burned the Temple, Eleazar escaped to Masada, where he took command of a band of Jewish patriots, a thousand strong, who also had fled to the mountain fortress with their women and children. Masada was the last fortress that remained in Jewish hands.

Our only significant source of information concerning the fate of Masada is *The Jewish War*, written by the Jewish historian Josephus Flavius, a Jewish general, originally named Joseph ben Mattathiah, who defected to the Romans and spent his later years in Rome writing histories of his people in the manner of the Greek and Roman historians. Josephus records that the Jewish defenders on Masada held out against the Tenth Roman Legion for three years while a Roman force under General Flavius Silva encircled the mountain, laid siege to it, and tried in vain to storm the fortress. By 73 C.E., the besieging army had grown to ten thousand men, bivouacked in eight camps in the valley. Standing atop Masada, one can still make out the remains of the encampments. The Romans built an earthen rampart on the western side nearly to the summit. They mounted torch-throwers and were able to set the inner defense wall of Masada, with its framework of wood, on fire. When the wind carried the flames all along the wall, the Romans, according to Josephus, "returned to their camp with joy, and resolved to attack their enemies the very next day." That night, however, Eleazer gathered his people together and told them that the end was near. Josephus records—or composed, in the classical manner—the moving speech to the gathering in which he reminded the people of their resolution "never to be servants to the Romans, nor to any other than to God himself." Rather than be taken captives by the Romans, they decided to take their own lives. Josephus continues:

> They then chose ten men by lot out of them, to slay all the rest, every one of whom lay himself down by his wife and children on the ground, and threw his arms about them, and they offered their necks to the stroke of those who by lot executed that melancholy office; and when those ten had without fear, slain them all, they made the same rule of casting lots for themselves, that he whose lot it was should first kill the other nine, and after all, should kill himself.

When the Romans, coming in full armor for the attack, eventually took control of Masada, they "were met with a terrible solitude on every side. . . as well as a perfect silence." They discovered that nearly all of nine hundred sixty of the Jews who had held out there for those three years, had committed suicide. Two women and five children, who had hidden in a cave, came out and "informed the Romans what had been done as it was done." Josephus adds that the Romans could only "wonder at the courage of their resolution and the immovable concept of death, which so great a number of them had shown, when they went through such an action as that was." Though suicide, which the Romans considered noble in such circumstances, is largely frowned upon in Judaism, that of the Zealots at Masada has usually been interpreted as an act of martyrdom.

Byzantine monks lived on Masada during the fifth

Masada

and sixth centuries; however, the site was largely ignored until American explorers identified and visited it in the mid-nineteenth century. It was not extensively explored until 1963, when Yigael Yadin, who was Israel's second chief of staff and later Professor of Archaeology at the Hebrew University, managed to convince Prime Minister David Ben-Gurion that excavating Masada would help strengthen Israel's ties to the land. Ben-Gurion was skeptical and remained disenchanted with the notion of mass suicide. At first, he refused to visit Masada, but thousands of volunteers arrived from around the world. Once, they found on the floor the skeletons of a young man, woman, and boy, lying in dark bloodstains, that confirmed Josephus's report.

Israeli attitudes toward Masada have changed over the years. At first, the mountain fortress symbolized Jewish heroism, plain and simple. The Israeli army held swearing-in ceremonies on top of Masada to make sure that soldiers identified with a great moment in Jewish history. In 1967, however, after the Six-Day War, in which Israel captured large areas of Arab-held land, the Zealots' mass suicide seemed to many Israelis a sign

of Jewish desperation rather than of heroism. Israeli right-wing politicians argued that, by giving up Arab-held land, Israel would endanger its security and could find itself forced into the same desperate situation as Masada's Zealots. Israeli Prime Minister Golda Meir told a 1973 press conference that "we do have a Masada complex, and a pogrom complex, and a Hitler complex." She meant that the experiences of Masada, the Russian pogroms, and the Holocaust had taught Israelis that it was better to fight to the end than simply to submit to the enemy. She avoided the question of whether Israelis, if they were in a situation like that of the Zealots, should follow the Zealots' example of mass suicide; she obviously doubted that Israel would ever face such a decision.

The mass suicide at Masada, one of the most controversial moments in Jewish history, raises a difficult question for Jews: Does one admire the behavior of the Jewish Zealots or pity them? We do both, if we are honest with ourselves, for, as little as we would want to be in their situation, we can have nothing but respect for their final act of defiance against their enemy.

Bar Kokhba Leads Revolt Against Rome

132 C.E.

Angered beyond endurance by the Roman emperor Hadrian's anti-Jewish policies, which included increased repression of Jewish religious observance, the Jews mounted their most unified revolt against Roman repression. With the support of Rabbi Akiba, the Jewish warrior Simeon bar Kokhba led a Jewish revolt against the Romans that began in 132 C.E. Victorious at first, he inflicted considerable damage on the Roman legions and briefly conquered Jerusalem, but he was killed three and a half years later during the last stand of his forces in the town of Betar, southwest of Jerusalem. After his defeat, Rabbi Akiba was martyred, and the Romans consolidated their rule.

Jewish resistance against Rome, which continued to smolder after the destruction of the Second Temple, flared up again under the emperor Hadrian (117–138 C.E.), who sought to rebuild Jerusalem as a pagan city, with a Roman temple dedicated to Jupiter on the Temple Mount. When he revived an old Roman law forbidding mutilation of the body, the Jews realized that it prohibited circumcision; they felt the law to be directed primarily against them and, therefore, intensified their resistance.

Hadrian spent the years between 128 and 132 C.E. visiting the eastern provinces of the empire. As long as Hadrian remained in the east, the Jews thought it unwise to rebel. They used the period, however, to build secret fortifications and to store arms within them. When Hadrian returned to Rome, the Jews prepared for battle. They felt they had a chance to succeed because there were few Roman legions in the region.

The leader of the Jewish revolt was known as Simeon Bar Kokhba. His original name, learned from two of his letters discovered in 1959 by the Israeli archaeologist Yigael Yadin, was Simeon bar Kosiba. The name "Bar Kokhba"—"son of the star"—was given to him by the eighty-year-old Rabbi Akiba, the leading scholar of his day, who, in a break from the usual rabbinic policy of aloofness from military endeavors, had traveled throughout Judea organizing Jewish resistance to Rome and believed he had found in Bar Kokhba the military leader he was looking for. The name was derived from Numbers 24:17, "A star rises from Jacob," which Rabbi Akiba interpreted as a messianic prophecy.

Because Roman repression made it unsafe for anyone to write about the revolt—and also because there was no Jewish historian of the caliber of Josephus to record the events—little is known about Bar Kokhba, though he has become an important Jewish folk hero. He is said to have been uncompromising, arrogant, and hot-tempered. According to legend, his recruits had to cut off a finger to prove their courage; when the rabbis disapproved of this practice of self-mutilation, he required instead that the men uproot a cedar. According to another legend, Bar Kokhba kept a lighted blade of straw in his mouth, which he fanned to create the impression that he was spewing out flames. Though he claimed to have been divinely inspired, it is also said that he relied more on his own strength than on God; when he was welcomed with the greeting "God will help" on going into battle, he replied, "God will neither assist nor weaken." The popular festival of Lag ba-Omer appears to commemorate Bar Kokhba's revolt, but no one can trace the precise link between them.

In this network of Judean desert caves overlooking the Dead Sea, the first manuscripts of the Bar Kokhba period were found in April 1960.

The revolt broke out in 132 C.E., after Hadrian's return to Rome. Despite their lack of formal military training, Bar Kokhba's fighters inflicted heavy casualties on the Romans and succeeded in capturing Jerusalem, from which Bar Kokhba minted coins dated according to the year of "Jerusalem's liberation" and "Israel's redemption." The Romans quickly brought in reinforcements; eventually, Rome deployed twelve legions against the Jewish revolt.

Bar Kokhba's reverses began when Hadrian appointed as commander one of his ablest generals, Julius Severus, whom he recalled from Britain; there, Severus had had considerable experience against the untrained guerrilla fighters of an indigenous population. Severus refused to meet Bar Kokhba in battle. Instead, he took advantage of Bar Kokhba's lack of military training to fight what has been called a war of attrition; though the Romans continued to suffer heavy losses, Severus systematically divided the Jewish forces, cut their supply lines,

and starved the isolated pockets of resistance into surrender. Within two years, he had retaken Jerusalem.

Bar Kokhba withdrew to Betar, a fortified town southwest of Jerusalem, which the Romans surrounded and besieged for weeks until their spies discovered a secret entrance to the town. Exhausted by famine, thousands of Jewish fighters, Bar Kokhba among them, fell to the Romans. The revolt ended in 135 C.E., two and a half years after its beginning. The date is traditionally said to be the ninth of Av, the anniversary of the destruction of both the First and Second Temples. Jewish casualties, estimated at five hundred thousand, were heavier than those incurred at the time of the destruction of the Temple in 70 C.E. Roman losses were also heavy, however, and Hadrian, who had supervised the early stages of the campaign in person, omitted in his report to the Roman Senate the usual opening phrase, "I and my army are well."

The Roman victory was complete. Very few of the Jewish rebels were spared. Those who survived were taken to the slave markets of the East or to the gladiatorial arenas in the major cities of the West. Rabbi Akiba was executed and died with the Shema on his lips.

Other important rabbis also became martyrs as Hadrian's suppression of Jewish religious teaching and observance became more intense. Hadrian carried out his plans to build a temple in honor of Jupiter Capitolinus on the site of the Temple and to turn Jerusalem into a pagan city, called Aelia Capitolina, which Jews were forbidden to enter on pain of death. The name "Judea" was discarded, and the troublesome province was renamed Syria and Palestina.

Professor Yehoshafat Harkabi of Jerusalem's Hebrew University developed a controversial theory in the early 1980s called the Bar Kokhba syndrome; it referred to the question of realism in Israel's foreign and security policy. He defined the syndrome as "the admiration of rebelliousness and heroism detached from responsibility for their consequences." Harkabi believed that Bar Kokhba took unreasonable risks that put Jewish national existence in jeopardy, since the Bar Kokhba revolt led to the death of hundreds of thousands of Jews and to the second banishment of the Jewish people from the Land of Israel. In his view, therefore, the revolt reflected an unrealistic assessment of historical and political circumstances. For that reason, Harkabi argued, it would be folly for Israelis to adopt Bar Kokhba as a national symbol of heroism and the Bar Kokhba revolt as a model for national policy.

"The problem," said Harkabi, "is not how Bar Kokhba committed a mistake—that can be explained—but rather how we [Israelis] have come to admire his mistake, and how it influences our national thinking. By admiring the Bar Kokhba rebellion we Israelis enmesh ourselves in the predicament of revering our people's destruction and rejoicing at an act of national suicide." Nevertheless, it is possible to see how the longing for political restoration—and, in the second century C.E., a literal messianic hope as well—led many Jews, including the greatest rabbinic scholar of the time, to support Bar Kokhba.

Crusades Reach Holy Land

MAY 1099

In 1099, after two years of storming through Europe, Christian forces reached the Holy Land and conquered Jerusalem, initiating two centuries of Crusader rule. Popular history has viewed the Crusaders as legendary, almost heroic in dimension, a procession of knights in armor who rode gallantly off to the Holy Land. In fact, both the cavalry and the common soldiers were an unruly lot who killed thousands of innocent Jews in both Europe and the Land of Israel. After conquering the Holy Land, they fought among themselves over the division of the spoils.

The Crusades were Christian military campaigns, initiated by the Roman Catholic Church and undertaken by Western European powers, to liberate the Holy Land from Muslim domination and place it under Christian control. Indeed, the most popular explanation of why the Crusades took place is that they were organized to assert the supremacy of Christianity. By the eleventh century, the Roman Catholic Church had come to dominate all of the Western world, but that was not enough. Pope Urban II searched for a way to deliver a final blow to the Byzantine Church and to extend the sphere of influence of the Roman Catholic Church to the Middle East—to Turkey, Syria, and Palestine. Thus arose the Crusades, in which the Christian powers attempted to recover territory they claimed had been taken from them by the caliphs of the Muslim Umayyad Dynasty, who had established themselves in Damascus and, from there, presided over an empire that extended from Spain to Indonesia. The Muslims considered Jerusalem a holy city of Islam because they believed that Muhammad had been transported from there to heaven on his horse. To commemorate the episode, a beautiful mosque, the Dome of the Rock, was built where the Temple of the Jewish people had stood. After a brief but bloody Byzantine invasion of Palestine in the middle of the tenth century, followed by a period of Egyptian rule, the country was conquered in 1071 by Seljuk Turkish tribes, who oppressed both Jews and Christians.

It was at this juncture that the Roman Catholic Church and the major powers of Western Europe began a Christian counteroffensive, the Crusades, to regain one of the major Christian holy places in Jerusalem, the Holy Sepulcher, from the Muslim "unbelievers." A major victim, however, was the Jewish people. In 1095, Pope Urban II, preaching at Clermont, appealed to the French to recover the Holy Land for Christianity. The response was immediate and positive. The Crusaders were all too conscious, however, of the great distance between Europe and Jerusalem. Accordingly, before attacking Muslims—and the Jews of Jerusalem—they first moved against the Jews of Europe. Godfrey of Bouillon, one of the French military leaders of the Crusades, declared, "I will avenge the blood of little Jesus on the blood of the Jews—and, God willing, leave not one of the cursed lot alive." "Kill a Jew and save your soul" became the battle cry of the Christians. The massacres began in the French town of Rouen; property was looted, and houses were burned. Many Jews died as martyrs, reciting passages from Jewish prayers. Others, also choosing martyrdom, killed one another and themselves to avoid being tortured by the Crusaders—and in the case of women, raped—before being killed. A few Jews chose baptism,

Crusaders attack Jerusalem.

though even some of them did not escape with their lives. Advancing mobs menaced Jews in northern France and in the Rhineland. The Jewish communities of Metz, Speyer, and Mayence were all wiped out, though Rashi's community in Troyes was not harmed.

Supporters of King Richard of England, called the Lion-Hearted, began killing the Jews of England in Lynn, Stanford, and Colchester, and then in Thetford, Ospringe, and York. Influenced by the tirades of Peter the Hermit, a Fleming from Amiens, fanatical bands of peasants moved eastward; passing through southern Germany, Hungary, and the Balkans, this first mob "army" destroyed the Jewish communities in their path but failed to reach the Holy Land; it was wiped out by the Turks in October 1096.

The Christian cavalry set out for the Holy Land in 1097. Along their way, they captured Nicea and Antioch and defeated a great army of Seljuk Turks near Mosul. They reached the Holy Land in May 1099. From Lebanon, they moved south to Caesarea, then to the center of Palestine, and finally westward to Jerusalem. After a month of siege, Godfrey of Bouillon's troops broke through the northern wall of the Old City, and the soldiers of Raymond of Toulouse broke through to the Old City at Mount Zion. Jerusalem was captured on July 15, 1099; much of its Jewish population, which numbered between twenty and thirty thousand, was slaughtered that very day. Many Jews were thrown into synagogues and burned alive. Others were taken captive and sold into slavery in Italy. Only a few managed to escape south to Ashkelon and Egypt. After a day's slaughter of Jews, the Crusaders assembled at the church of the Holy Sepulcher inside the Old City and declared the establishment of a Latin kingdom in Jerusalem. The aim of the Crusaders had been attained: the capture of the Holy City. The Crusaders then proceeded to occupy the rest of Palestine; the residents of Bethlehem, south of Jerusalem, had surrendered even before the Crusader conquest of the Holy City.

Once firmly established in Palestine, the Crusaders created several small feudal principalities close to the new kingdom of Jerusalem. Acre, situated in northern Palestine on the Mediterranean coast, was the main stronghold of the Crusaders in Palestine.

Toward the end of the twelfth century, the Crusader hold on the Holy Land was broken temporarily when the Saracen leader Saladin defeated them at a ridge, called the Horns of Hittin, overlooking the Sea of Galilee, and proceeded to occupy Jerusalem. The Church called for new Crusades and encouraged participation by canceling the soldiers' debts to Jews, thereby reducing many Jewish communities to poverty. Once contact with the Middle East was established by the First Crusade, the anti-Jewish economic motives of the Eu-

ropean powers became more obvious; French feudal leaders and shipowners, combined with Italian feudal leaders, shipowners, and bankers, had concluded that once they dissolved the Muslim hold over trade in the Middle East, they could destroy what they perceived to be the Jewish monopoly of such trade in Europe.

During the Second Crusade, a new Crusader army under King Richard of England recaptured Acre. Richard then marched south and won another battle where the Israeli town of Herzlia now stands. Rather than attempt to recapture Jerusalem, however, he spent the winter in Jaffa, along the Mediterranean coast. A generation later, during the Fifth Crusade, the Holy Roman Emperor Frederick II, of Germany, reconquered Jerusalem for the Christians and was crowned its king.

Ultimately, the Crusaders' attempts to make Jerusalem a Christian city and to maintain a European military and political presence in the Middle East proved futile. Toward the end of the thirteenth century, a new Muslim enemy arose in Egypt. Calling themselves the Mamelukes, they were former Circassian slaves who had taken control of Egypt in 1291. The Mamelukes conquered Acre, finally ending the Crusader rule over the Holy Land; they controlled Palestine for the next three centuries.

First Blood Libel Unleashed

1144

Christian hatred of Jews in the Middle Ages used as its justification the blood libel, the mistaken belief that Jews ritually murdered Christians to reenact the crucifixion of Jesus and then used the victim's blood to make matzah for Passover. The blood libel resulted in the deaths of many Jews and the destruction of many European Jewish communities. Despite Jewish and educated Christian efforts to refute it, the blood libel persisted until the early years of this century.

During the Middle Ages, the Jews sought to survive in an increasingly hostile and threatening world. Christian leaders in Western Europe were determined to convert them to Christianity. From the twelfth century onward, Christian hostility to Jews had a more obvious economic motive, since many Jews with whom Christians had dealings seemed to be in the money-lending business, and hence were thought to be robbing Christians of their money through exaggerated lending rates. A new religious motive for Christian hostility, however, developed as well. Toward the end of the Middle Ages, Christians created an image of the Jew as an enemy of God who sought Christian blood and devoured Christian children. It was a powerful image that was hard to refute.

Under the influence of the blood libel, Christians tortured and killed many Jews. Mobs slaughtered entire communities. From time to time, popes and educated secular leaders issued declarations suggesting that the blood libel was a false accusation, but the mobs refused to listen.

The first recorded blood libel occurred in Norwich, England, in 1144. A boy named William had disappeared, and Christians sent out an alarm. Theobald of Cambridge, an apostate Jew, approached the authorities and charged the Jews with having murdered the boy. He told them that the Jews had been following an ancient custom of sacrificing a Christian child during the Passover festival and that representatives of Jews throughout the world had assembled in Narbonne, France, to decide who would carry out the murder. According to his story, the assembly at Narbonne had cast lots, and the "honor" of carrying out the ritual murder had fallen to the Jews of Norwich. When the boy's body was found in Norwich, however, it showed no evidence of murder; therefore, no one was punished. Nevertheless, the boy, William of Norwich, was declared a martyr and canonized by the Church, and a memorial chapel and shrine were erected in his honor in Norwich.

Another early accusation of ritual murder occurred in Blois, France, in 1171. It resulted in the burning alive of all the Jews of the town. Offered one avenue of escape, baptism, the Jews refused, and died singing the *Alenu*, which often served as a martyr's prayer during the Middle Ages.

The next English ritual-murder accusation of consequence occurred in 1255 in Lincoln. The incident was part of the increasing popular Church, and state anti-Semitism that led, in 1290 to the expulsion of the Jews from England. The most vivid account of the Lincoln incident comes from a contemporary English chronicler, Matthew Paris, who wrote in his *Historia Major*:

> . . . about the feast of Peter and Paul, the Jews of Lincoln stole a child called Hugh, being eight years old; and when they had nourished him, in

the most secret chamber, with milk and other childish aliments, they sent to almost all the cities of England wherein the Jews lived, that, in contempt and reproach of Jesus Christ, they should be present at their sacrifice at Lincoln. . . . And coming together, they appointed one Lincoln Jew for the Judge, as if it were for Pilate. By whose judgment by the consent of all, the child is afflicted with sundry torments. He is whipped even until blood and lividness, crowned with thorns, wearied with spitting and strikings. . . and after they had derided him in diverse manners, they crucified him.

The report of little Hugh's supposed crucifixion produced massive hysteria among the English Christian population. To prevent further disorder, the authorities arrested all the Jews of Lincoln. When the murdered child was found in the well of a Jew named Jopin, where Jews believed he had been secretly deposited by the real murderers, Jopin was tortured until, finally, he confessed to whatever he was asked to say, encouraging Christians to believe even more in the blood libel. Besides Jopin, eighteen leading Jews of Lincoln were tortured and forced to confess to being part of the plan to murder the boy. They were publicly hanged, and their property was confiscated. Twenty other Jews were imprisoned in the Tower of London but were freed after the Jews paid a large ransom to King Henry III. The ceremony marking the funeral of little Hugh was solemn. His body was borne to the cathedral for burial. Shortly after, he was canonized as Saint Hugh of Lincoln. A shrine was erected over his tomb in Lincoln Cathedral, at which many thousands came to worship. Geoffrey Chaucer's "Prioress's Tale," written about ninety years after the expulsion of the Jews from England, helped perpetuate the blood libel.

The ritual-murder tale took on epidemic proportions, particularly in Germany. Moving through the towns of Franconia, blood-libel hysteria spread to Bavaria, and then to Austria and other parts of Europe. Pope Innocent II and the Fourth Lateran Council of the Church did nothing to stem the hysteria.

By the thirteenth century, several leaders of the Church, as well as Emperor Frederick II, attempted to refute and forbid the blood libel. In 1245, Pope Innocent IV issued a bull forbidding the blood libel, which, he said, was groundless; he declared it a mockery of Christ's teachings that led only to evil. Pope Gregory X banned the accusation in another bull in 1274. Other popes also denounced it. Unfortunately, their decrees were ineffective, since the blood libel was an easy way for anti-Semitic demagogues to manipulate mobs. By the seventeenth century, ritual-murder accusations had spread to Eastern Europe and Russia, where they continued until the early years of this century.

Christians Debate Jews at Tortosa

FEBRUARY 1413

During the Middle Ages, Jewish scholars were sometimes forced into public debates with Christians—called disputations—at which kings and bishops presided, to defend their religion and their traditional religious literature, especially the Talmud. The point of these exercises was to humiliate the Jews by proving Judaism inferior to Christianity and, thereby, making Jews convert. Though the intended outcome was clear, the Jewish scholars, trained in debate, treated the disputations as opportunities to show their religion in the most favorable light. One of the best-known disputations occurred at Tortosa, in Spain.

Sixteenth-century wood art showing a dispute between Jews and Christian clergy.

As late as the Reformation, Martin Luther complained, "It is as easy to convert the Jews as the Devil himself." During the Middle Ages, the Catholic Church had two main ways of proselytizing Jews. One was through sermons delivered by Christian preachers, in synagogues or churches, at which attendance of all Jews twelve years old and over was mandatory. The other was the holding of public disputations between rabbis and Christian theologians. These disputations were called "tournaments for God and Faith." They were "contests" Jews almost always lost.

In the year 1240 the king of France ordered a public disputation between Nicolas Donin, a learned Jewish convert to Christianity, and four prominent rabbis, including the celebrated talmudist Rabbi Yehiel of Paris and Rabbi Moses of Coucy. Present at the disputation were the queen, the archbishops and bishops of the realm, and many theologians and nobles. Rabbi Yehiel strove in vain to expose Donin's accusations against Judaism as inventions and slanders. Eventually, however, the Talmud was condemned. With other Hebrew books, it was burned in Paris in a great public ceremony arranged by the Dominicans. Moreover, Donin persuaded Pope Gregory IX to issue a bull ordering the burning of the Talmud everywhere and establishing censorship of other Jewish writings, a practice that haunted the Jews for many years.

Like the Muslims before them, Spanish Catholics held religious disputations. At first, the debates in Spain took place in an atmosphere of mutual respect. In June 1263, Pablo Christiano, a Christian convert from Judaism, prevailed upon the king of Aragon to order Nahmanides, the famed talmudist and philosopher, to dispute with him before the court and clergy in Barcelona. Nahmanides' own report indicates that he had complete freedom of speech. At the end of the disputation, impressed by Nahmanides' skill in argument, the king awarded him a prize and declared that never before had he heard "an unjust cause so nobly defended."

In time, the intellectual climate of Spain became harsher. At the beginning of the fifteenth century, Vincent Ferrer, an itinerant Dominican preacher noted for his dramatic proselytizing of Jews, urged the king of Aragon to stage a public disputation. Accordingly, the king summoned the most learned rabbis in his kingdom to Tortosa to debate Christian theologians. The proceedings took place in the presence of the antipope Benedict XIII, many cardinals and bishops, and a large audience. Threatened with fines, imprisonment, and expulsion, the leading Jewish scholars of Spain reluctantly agreed to appear. Foremost on the Christian side was the physician of the antipope Benedict XIII, a former rabbi and convert to Christianity, named Joshua Lorki, who functioned as prosecuting counsel. Among the twenty-two Jewish defenders was the noted philosopher and talmudist Joseph Albo. The Jewish spokesman, Vidal Benveniste, replied in Latin to Lorki's opening speech.

Benedict announced at the beginning that the purpose of the discussion was to prove from Jewish sources that Jesus was the true Messiah. In effect, Judaism was on trial. Moreover, while the rabbis were in Tortosa,

Vincent Ferrer and other Christian preachers gave sermons in the rabbis' leaderless communities and made converts, who were brought to Tortosa for display.

The disputation was conducted in sixty-nine sessions and lasted twenty-one months. Rabbi Astruk ha-Levi protested against the conditions in which the Jews were forced to debate:

> We are away from our homes. Our resources are diminished and are almost entirely gone. In our absence great damage has occurred to our communities. We do not know the fate of our wives and children. We have inadequate maintenance here and even lack food. We have been put to extraordinary expenses. Why should people suffering from such woes be held accountable for their arguments, when contending with [Christian opponents] who are in the greatest prosperity and luxury?

He questioned the value of religious disputation and stated that the time had come when no further purpose was served by repeating familiar arguments. "A Christian living in the land of the Saracens," he said, "may be defeated by the arguments of a pagan or a Saracen, but it does not follow that his faith has been refuted." During the final stages of the disputation, the Jews resorted to a form of passive resistance. They claimed that they did not understand the questions and tried, whenever possible, to preserve a dignified silence.

To no one's surprise, the Christian theologians were declared the winners of the unequal disputation. Benedict ordered the Jewish participants to accept baptism, but none would. Angered by their refusal, he banned Jewish study of the Talmud. Subsequent anti-Jewish decrees by the antipope and by the government of Aragon and Castile weakened the fabric of Jewish communal life in Spain.

Jews Expelled from Spain

As King Ferdinand and Queen Isabella consolidated their power in Spain, they took increasingly drastic measures against the Jews. King Ferdinand lent his full support to the Inquisition, under which Jews were tortured, imprisoned, and publicly executed. Early in their reign, the Catholic monarchs considered expelling all Jews from Spain. They hesitated, however, because several Jews served as advisors to the Spanish government. Finally, after their victory over the Moors in 1492, the royal couple issued the expulsion decree. They signed it on March 30 of that year and established August 1 as the deadline for departure, though the last Jews did not leave until the following day.

The banner of the Inquisition.

The marriage of Isabella of Castile and Ferdinand of Aragon in 1469 led to the unification of the two kingdoms and the growth of Catholic power in what is now Spain. Because certain Jews held important positions in the government, Ferdinand and Isabella promised to provide "care and protection" to the entire Jewish community of Spain. Nevertheless, the campaign to convert the Jews continued.

It soon became clear that many forcibly converted Jews, popularly known as Marranos ("pigs"), continued to practice Judaism in secret and were aided by unconverted members of the Jewish community. In 1478, a group of Marranos was caught celebrating the seder on the first night of Passover. Shocked by the incident, Isabella and Ferdinand agreed to the establishment of the Inquisition in Spain. The Spanish monarchs insisted, however, that the Inquisition be under their control, and not under the control of Rome. After two years of negotiations the Church agreed; Ferdinand and Isabella appointed Inquisitors and began to carry out their anti-Jewish policies.

rical executions staged in the public squares of Spanish towns. An execution of this type, usually by fire, was known as an auto-da-fé, or act of faith.

Because they had authority only over Christians, the inquisitors tried to control recently converted Jews by separating them from unconverted relatives and friends in the Jewish community. Therefore, the clergy urged Ferdinand and Isabella to expel the Jews. Influential recent converts to Christianity objected strongly. Ferdinand and Isabella also still needed the resources and skills of Spanish Jews in the effort to conquer the Moorish kingdom of Granada, which was held by the Muslim Arabs and Berbers who had conquered Spain in the eighth century. On January 2, 1492, Granada surrendered to the army of Ferdinand and Isabella. For the first time in more than seven hundred years, the Iberian Peninsula was ruled entirely by Christians. Having defeated the Muslims, the Spanish rulers were now ready to expel the Jews.

On March 30, in the Alhambra—the palace of the kings of Granada—Ferdinand and Isabella signed a decree ordering the Jews to leave Castile and Aragon by August 1. They were allowed to take their furniture and household goods but were not permitted to take gold, silver, or other precious metals. Thus, their wealth was greatly diminished. More than poverty, however, the decree meant homelessness and uncertainty, since the Jews did not know where to go and which nations would receive them. They also feared the journey, which might bring death to those too weak to tolerate it.

The Chief Inquisitor Tomás de Torquemada oversees the torture of the Jews.

A terrible period ensued, as the conduct of newly-converted Christians was scrutinized by their neighbors. Those who observed Jewish customs, even the wearing of clean clothes on the Jewish Sabbath, became suspect and were brought before Inquisitors. Some were merely fined; others suffered confiscation of property and torture. The rack was used not only to extract confessions from the accused but to force them to inform against others. Many of the accused were put to death in theat-

The Jewish community tried desperately to have the edict repealed. A delegation consisting of Abraham Senior and Isaac Abrabanel obtained an audience with Ferdinand and Isabella. Senior, called the chief rabbi of Castile, was, in effect, the leader of Spanish Jewry. Isaac Abrabanel, a scholar and philosopher, was the financial adviser whose skill had enabled Spain to conquer Granada.

They appealed to the royal couple for mercy and, to

strengthen their case, they offered a substantial payment in exchange for revocation of the decree. According to one version of this meeting, the delegation placed the bag of money on the table. Moved both by the power of their arguments and by the sight of the gold, Ferdinand and Isabella hesitated. Just then, the Grand Inquisitor, Tomás de Torquemada, entered the room. He approached the table, set the cross he held in his hand near the bag of gold, and said, pointing to the figure of Jesus on the cross, "Here he is; sell him."

The royal couple's doubts vanished. They rejected the delegation's pleas and ordered the Jews to prepare for departure. Abraham Senior converted to Christianity—some say under duress. Ferdinand and Isabella were willing to allow Abrabanel to stay in Spain as a Jew, but he chose to join his people in exile.

The deadline for the departure of the Jews of Castile and Aragon was August 1, though some left the following day, August 2. In 1492, August 2 was also Tishah b'Av, the ninth of Av—the fast day that commemorates the destruction of the First and Second Temples. August 2, 1492, was also the date on which Christopher Columbus and his expedition set sail out of the harbor near Seville, past the ships upon which Jewish exiles were embarking. His voyage of discovery was financed, to a great extent, by money confiscated from Jews. As his three ships moved past the others, he noted this fact in his diary.

Venetian Ghetto Is Created

MARCH 1516

From medieval to Napoleonic times, and even beyond, one of the greatest humiliations suffered by Jews in Europe was compulsory segregation. Jews were forced to live in designated districts and forbidden to live elsewhere. Though not the first, the district that gave the institution its name was established in Venice in 1516. Called the Ghetto, probably after a nearby iron foundry, it became the archetype for all such Jewish districts, and for districts occupied by other minorities as well.

The existence of a section of a city in which the Jewish population was con-centrated, preceded the institution of the ghetto by centuries. Though the term originated in Renaissance Italy, the institution itself, without its compulsory aspects, dates back to the Byzantine and early medieval periods. It was given various names in different languages: *Vicus Judaeorum*, the Jewish quarter, in Latin; *judiaria* in Portuguese; *juive-rie* in northern France; *carrier des Juifs* in Provençal; Jews' Street in English; *Judenviertel* or *Judengasse* in German.

In medieval Europe, even before they were physically segregated, Jews had already been cut off from the mainstream of political, social, and cultural life. Treated as a separate class, denied the rights of citizenship, the next step was to compel them to live only in specific areas of towns and cities. The Catholic Church prohibited Christians and Jews from living together in 1179, though the decree was not always enforced. During the thirteenth century, compulsory Jewish districts were established in London, in Breslau in what is now Poland, and in France.

The first compulsory Jewish quarter to be given the name ghetto was established in Venice in 1516. Though Venice had not enforced earlier laws mandating the segregation of Jews, Venetian authorities were alarmed by the growth in Venice's Jewish population following the expulsion of the Jews from Spain in 1492. The ghetto was established in a district far from the center of the city near an iron foundry called *getto*, or *gheta*, in the Venetian dialect from which, it is thought, Venice's Jewish quarter got its name. Other suggested derivations include the Italian words *borghetto* ("small burgh" or "district") and *guitto* or *ghito* ("dirty"), as well as the German word *gitter* ("bars"). According to a bitter Jewish joke, *ghetto* was derived from *get*, the Hebrew word meaning "divorce," since the institution of the ghetto divorced Jews from the life and culture of the people around them. *Ghetto* soon became the general term for the districts in which Jews were compelled to live.

Though ghettos varied in appearance, there was little variation in the frustration and misery experienced by the Jews who were forced to inhabit them. Poverty and overcrowding made life unpleasant for, though the Jewish population increased, the original area of the ghetto remained constant. Since the houses could expand only upwards, buildings in the ghetto were often taller than those around them. Their masonry was crumbling. The streets were narrow and gloomy. Little sunlight penetrated into the ghetto.

Often, ghettos were surrounded by high walls and a large gate, secured at night by heavy chains and locks. No Jew was allowed to leave the ghetto between dusk and daybreak; if discovered outside the walls at night, Jews were subject to harsh penalties. Yet the walls and gates also served to keep enemies out; this protection proved particularly valuable at Easter time, when Jews dared not show their faces outside the ghetto walls for fear of the blood libel.

Within the ghetto, Jews were granted a high degree of autonomy and developed a vigorous communal life, the synagogue becoming its focus. Second to the synagogue were the schools associated with it. The Jews had their own courts and administrative offices in some ghettos, as well as prisons to enforce the decisions of their courts; in some ghettos, they even had a town hall. They administered the communal institutions necessary for religious and secular life, including kosher slaughterhouses, bathhouses, cemeteries, bakeries, and inns. Jews were legally barred from owning real estate but developed a system, based on traditional Jewish laws of proprietary right, that prevented arbitrary evictions; under it, prospective tenants were forbidden to offer landlords higher rents than those paid by the current occupants.

Though ghettos were re-used by the Nazis in the Holocaust to channel Jews to the concentration camps, in general, ghettos were abolished in Western Europe by Napoleon and in Russia and the areas under its control by the revolution of 1917. Today, the word ghetto often is used as a generic term for a section of a city in which any minority group lives.

The entrance to the Cracow Ghetto, one of the many ghettos of Eastern Europe.

Shakespeare Reinforces Negative Image of Jews

1596

Throughout the Middle Ages, religious indoctrination taught many European Christians to despise Jews. As Jews were forced to become moneylenders, a secular motive for Christian hatred was added to the religious motive. Jewish moneylenders were accused of charging usurious interest, and the venom of anti-Semites was directed at the moneylending trade. No less a figure than the English playwright William Shakespeare reinforced the negative image of the Jew by portraying the character Shylock as a vengeful moneylender in his 1596 play The Merchant of Venice.

From the twelfth century on, the growth of a Christian merchant class, the barring of other professions to Jews, and Church decrees against the charging of interest among Christians increasingly forced European Jews to earn their living by moneylending. Though the high rates of interest prevalent during the Middle Ages and Renaissance were determined mainly by the scarcity of money at the time, they exacerbated Christian hatred of Jews and helped produce the literary stereotype of the greedy, antisocial Jewish moneylender whose primary motivation was hatred of his Christian clients.

The most famous of these characters is William Shakespeare's Shylock in *The Merchant of Venice*. Though the main plot of the play concerns Bassanio's courtship of Portia, the heiress to Belmont, Shakespeare's delineation of the character of Shylock made him and his subplot the real focus of interest.

Bassanio asks his merchant friend Antonio, to lend him money for his expedition to Belmont. Antonio borrows the necessary sum from the Jewish moneylender, Shylock. Instead of demanding interest, Shylock proposes a "merry bond": if Antonio should default, Shylock would be entitled to a pound of flesh nearest to Antonio's heart. Not only does Antonio suffer unexpected losses and fail to repay the debt, but Shylock finds that his daughter, Jessica, has eloped with Lorenzo, a friend of Antonio, taking with her much of her father's money. A Christian character describes Shylock as lamenting equally—with comic effect—the loss of his ducats and his daughter.

Shylock takes Antonio to court to demand the "penalty and forfeit" of the bond. Portia, however, appears disguised as a lawyer and saves Antonio when she points out that the bond does not entitle Shylock to a single drop of blood. By going after the life of a citizen of Venice, Shylock stands to lose his entire estate. The penalty is reduced to confiscation of half of Shylock's estate, but only if Shylock agrees to convert to Christianity.

Both plots of *The Merchant of Venice* have been traced to various literary sources, primarily Italian, including one in which the Jewish character is the victim. Some scholars believe Shakespeare also was influenced by the 1594 trial and execution of Queen Elizabeth I's physician, a Portuguese Marrano named Rodrigo Lopez, and by Christopher Marlowe's *The Jew of Malta*, a play with a Jewish villain that gained in popularity during performances in the early 1590s. Shakespeare's Jewish character is more three-dimensional than Marlowe's. Shylock is given a plausible motivation that includes anger at his treatment by Venetian Christians, and his famous lines, "I am a Jew. Hath not a Jew eyes? hath not a Jew

Painting of the main Jewish characters in William Shakespeare's play Merchant of Venus, *"Shylock and Jessica."*

likeness of a Jew." Shylock's name has entered the English language as a noun that means "an extortionate creditor or loan shark" and as a verb that means "to lend money at high rates of interest."

Shylock was played as a comic character until 1741, when the Irish actor Charles Macklin created a sensation by portraying him as a tragic figure. Nineteenth-century actors followed Macklin's example and developed a style of performance that acknowledged the full humanity of Shylock's character.

Some have accused Charles Dickens of anti-Semitism for his characterization of the Jewish Fagin as evil incarnate in *Oliver Twist*, setting the tone for the portrayal of Jews in drama for most of the rest of the nineteenth century. The first adaptation of *Oliver Twist* reached the stage in 1838, the same year that the novel was published.

Almost as if to refute accusations that he was anti-Semitic, in *Our Mutual Friend* (serialized in 1864–1865) Dickens created one of his most saintly characters, Mr. Riah, "the gentle Jew in whose race gratitude is deep."

Sometimes it was not clear whether an author or playwright intended to portray a character as a Jew. In Victorian times, Jews often were associated with dingy red hair, and some of the more unpleasant characters in literature possess this attribute: Uriah Heep in *David Copperfield* and the Reverend Obadiah Slope in Anthony Trollope's *Barchester Towers*.

That William Shakespeare and Charles Dickens, two men of such high stature, should create Jewish characters with distinctly distasteful personality traits, did much to perpetuate anti-Semitic stereotypes.

hands, organs, dimensions, senses, affections, passions? fed with the same food, hurt with the same weapons . . . as a Christian is?," temporarily arouse the audience's sympathy. Nevertheless, the Christian characters equate him with the devil.

Launcelot Gobbo, Shylock's servant, tells the audience in a comic malapropism that his master is "the very devil incarnation." Later, one of Antonio's friends, upon seeing Shylock, comments that the devil "comes in the

False Messiah Appears in Poland

1648

Soon after the Chmielnicki massacres in Poland which began in 1648, thousands of Polish Jews believed that the Messiah would materialize and lead them back to the promised land of Palestine. A kind of mass hysteria enveloped Judaism around this time and fraudulent messiahs arose, trying to capitalize on Jewish fears and expectations. The most famous was Shabbetai Tsevi, a Jew from Smyrna (Izmir) in Turkey, who built up the hopes of countless Polish Jews by promising to lead them in a mass return to Palestine.

Bogdan Chmielnicki.

Shabbetai Tsevi was born in Smyrna, Turkey, in 1626, the son of a poultry merchant. A child with a gifted mind, he spent hours involved in study, particularly of the Talmud and, later, Jewish mysticism. He was ordained as a *hakham* ("wise man") at the age of eighteen.

In 1648, Cossack invaders, led by Bogdan Chmielnicki, revolting against Polish rule over the Ukraine, carried out horrific massacres against Polish Jews. Jews who followed the Kabbalah chose to interpret the slaughter as a sign that the Messiah was not long in coming. Kabbalistic calculations appeared to confirm a connection between the massacres and the arrival of the Messiah.

It was against this background that Shabbetai Tsevi contended to have experienced a heavenly voice that identified him as the Messiah. One day he was praying in the synagogue. Traditionally, it had been forbidden for all Jews other than the high priest, and then only on Yom Kippur, to utter the name of God (the Tetragrammaton). Shabbetai Tsevi not only uttered God's name but declared the cancellation of certain fast days, notably the Ninth of Av, the anniversary of the destruction of the Temples. He also noted that the birthday of the Messiah—the Ninth of Av—happened to coincide with his own date of birth. The rabbis of Smyrna exiled him from the city and placed him under a ban of excommunication.

Shabbetai Tsevi journeyed to Salonika, and there, in an act that was meant to confirm that he was the Messiah, he "wed" the Torah in a mystical marriage ceremony. Again, the rabbis of the city expelled him.

He spent a number of years wandering through

Greece and Turkey, shocking the rabbinate wherever he went, yet gaining numerous disciplines. He married twice during this time.

Aiding his efforts was the respected kabbalist hermit he met in Constantinople, who claimed to have discovered an ancient parchment that had predicted the arrival of Shabbetai Tsevi as the Messiah. Along with his large number of disciples, Shabbetai Tsevi decided in 1662 to immigrate to the Holy Land. Upon his arrival he clothed himself in a sparkling robe and prayed at the Western Wall, the holiest site in Judaism. He and his followers also journeyed south to Hebron where they prayed at the tomb of the patriarchs. He was then sent to Egypt as an emissary in order to collect funds for the support of Jerusalem's Jewish community.

While in Cairo, Shabbetai Tsevi met a strikingly beautiful young woman named Sarah, who had gone around telling everyone that she refused to marry anyone who was not the Messiah. Sarah had been a Marrano who had lived in Poland, been raised in a convent in Amsterdam, and earned her living as a prostitute. At his wedding, Shabbetai Tsevi cited the precedent of the prophet Hosea, who married a prostitute named Gomer, and called Sarah "the bride of the Messiah."

On his journey back to Palestine, Shabbetai Tsevi met kabbalist Nathan of Gaza, who asserted that he had experienced a vision in which it was revealed to him that Shabbetai Tsevi was the Messiah. Shabbetai Tsevi adopted Nathan as his "prophet," and Nathan played a significant role in spreading the word that his master was indeed the Messiah. Nathan crowned Shabbetai Tsevi "King Messiah" and sent messengers and leaflets to many parts of the Jewish world announcing the arrival of the Messiah. According to Nathan, Shabbetai Tsevi would soon depose the sultan of Turkey and lead the Jewish exiles of the world back to the Holy Land.

Such talk only angered the rabbis of Jerusalem who decided first to flog Shabbetai, hoping to get him to cease calling himself the Messiah, and then, when flogging failed to budge him, to excommunicate him. Shabbetai Tsevi journeyed, along with his followers, to Turkey where, with an aura of triumph, he entered Smyrna, the town that fifteen years earlier had expelled him. The community now greeted him with shouts of "Long live the Messiah!"

By 1665 a mass frenzy had seized the Jewish world, and Jews from Holland to Yemen started to prepare to

Shabbetai Tsevi anoints a disciple.

return to the Holy Land. Nathan of Gaza declared that, in a second vision, it had become clear to him that 1666 was to be the year of redemption, during which Shabbetai Tsevi would ride into Jerusalem on a lion with a seven-headed serpent as its bridle. Shabbetai Tsevi uttered his own public statement in a synagogue, reiterating that he was the Messiah. Rams horns were blown as part of the performance. Shabbetai, gaining confidence that others now believed him when he said he was the Messiah, issued a series of decrees: he turned fasts into feasts; recited the Tetragrammaton in regular services; ordered that men and women sit together at services; and substituted his own name for that of the Turkish sultan in the prayer for the ruler of the country.

He also announced that he planned to have intercourse with his wife for the first time; the next morning he produced the traditional "evidence" of her virginity! He then announced that he was dividing his territories into twenty-six kingdoms that would be allocated among his colleagues. Each colleague would be given a title found in the Bible.

Shabbetai Tsevi as shown in a 17th-century copper engraving.

Shabbetai Tsevi's behavior increasingly angered the Turkish authorities. Sailing to Constantinople, Shabbetai hoped to depose the sultan. Instead he was immediately arrested and imprisoned in a fortress in Gallipoli. Resorting to bribery, he was able to hold court in prison and continued to preach to his followers, who maintained their faith and spread stories of the miracles Shabbetai Tsevi was able to perform.

The Turkish authorities had Shabbetai Tsevi brought to the sultan's privy council, where he was offered the choice of converting to Islam or being killed. He chose conversion. Standing before the Sultan, he accepted the turban of a Muslim; he emerged from his audience asking to be called Aziz Mehmed Effendi. The sultan gave him a new wife and appointed him royal doorkeeper.

Shabbetai Tsevi now played a double game—trying to strengthen his ties with the Turks by encouraging some of his followers to convert to Islam, yet insisting to the Jewish world that he was indeed the Messiah. It was hard for Jews to retain faith in him once word got out that he had converted to Islam, yet some remained true to him. Converting to Islam, these faithful believed, with the encouragement of Nathan of Gaza, was all part of getting along in the world as the Messiah. Tiring of Shabbetai Tsevi's duplicity, however, the Turks eventually banished him to a fortress in Dulcigno, Albania, though he managed to keep in touch with his disciples. He died on Yom Kippur in 1676 at the age of fifty.

For years afterward, sects adhering to Shabbetainism thrived. One group, the Dönmeh, existed in Turkey well into the twentieth century. Its members continued to believe that Shabbetai Tsevi was the Messiah and that he would return to earth one day.

Many today believe that Shabbetai Tsevi was a severe manic-depressive and that this explains his wild mood swings and bizarre behavior.

Baruch Spinoza Excommunicated

JULY 27, 1656

It was in 1656 that the most famous excommunication in Jewish history was carried out against Dutch philosopher Baruch Spinoza. He was the leading thinker of the seventeenth century; his writings provided the basis for modern biblical criticism. Spinoza was punished for publicly expressing heretical views about Judaism in public, questioning among other things whether God had written the Torah.

Baruch Spinoza's parents, Marranos who had fled Portugal to escape the Inquisition, settled in Holland where Baruch's father, Michael, became a successful merchant. Baruch was born in Amsterdam in 1632; his mother died when Baruch was just six years old.

Young Baruch received a traditional Jewish education. He studied Bible, Talmud, Jewish philosophy, and the Hebrew language, but he delved into such secular subjects as mathematics, physics, and astronomy to expand his horizons.

When Baruch was twenty-two years old his father died. Baruch and his brother Gabriel opened a fruit import and export business. Baruch continued to attend a yeshiva even though he was already beginning to question—and even to doubt—the tenets of the Jewish faith.

Eventually Spinoza enrolled in a private school run by Francis Van den Enden, a former Jesuit with a reputation as a freethinker. Although Latin was associated in Jewish minds with the Inquisition, Spinoza began to study that language. He also immersed himself in the Greek and Roman classics, the physical sciences, and the philosophy of René Descartes.

The leaders of the Jewish community were outraged

A portrait of Baruch Spinoza.

to learn of Spinoza's lessons with Van den Enden. Spinoza had given up many Jewish practices and had even begun to question whether God wrote the Torah and whether natural law shouldn't supersede Mosaic law.

Synagogue authorities gave Spinoza a choice. They would pay him one thousand florins a year in exchange for which he would conform to synagogue rules, or he would be excommunicated. When he failed to submit a formal reply to the synagogue authorities, Spinoza's brother-in-law Samuel de Cacares launched a campaign against Spinoza. In 1656 Spinoza was formally accused of heresy. One month later, on July 27, Spinoza was excommunicated from the Nation of Israel for the "abominable heresies practiced and taught by him" and the "monstrous acts committed by him." The rabbinical pronouncement was signed by Rabbi Saul Levi Morteira, among others. The writ of excommunication read in part: "Cursed shall he be in the daytime, and cursed when he riseth up! Cursed shall he be when he goeth out and cursed when he cometh in! May the Lord forgive his sins. May the Lord's anger and wrath rage against this man, and cast upon him all the imprecations that are written in the Book of the Law! May the Lord wipe his name from under the Heavens; and may the Lord destroy him and cast him out from all the Tribes of Israel with all the maledictions that are written in the Book of Law!" Members of the Jewish community were forbidden to have any contact with Baruch Spinoza.

Spinoza defended his dissident beliefs, but in truth, the excommunication freed him to develop his own philosophy.

While the writ of excommunication seems harsh, the actual ban or *herem*, in Hebrew, was a common enough practice among the Jews of Amsterdam of that time. Indeed, there were a number of grounds for excommunication, quite apart from heresy and blasphemy, including speaking too loudly or carrying weapons in the synagogue, disseminating libelous literature, organizing private prayers, representing the Jewish community without the permission of the elders of the community, and associating with people who refused to pay taxes.

In the wake of the actions taken by the Jewish community, the Amsterdam Municipal Council banished Baruch Spinoza from the city, forcing him to move to a small town in the Dutch countryside called Ouwerkirk, not far from Amsterdam. Spinoza made a modest living as an optician and a tutor of philosophy, and he began working on his *Tractatus theologico-politicus*, in which he would provide the basis for modern biblical criticism.

In 1660, at the age of twenty-eight, Spinoza left Ouwerkirk and settled in Rijnsburg, near Leyden. He changed his name to the Latin Benedictus, joined a Mennonite sect, and delved into Cartesian philosophy, authoring *Principles of the Philosophy of René Descartes*.

In 1664 Spinoza moved to Voorburg, a suburb of The Hague. There he embarked on a work that was meant to explain his whole philosophic system. Two years later, however, he returned to *Tractatus theologico-politicus*. In it he wanted to refute the charges of atheism that had been leveled against him and to defend freedom of speech and thought. He wanted also to expose what he considered to be a series of false religious beliefs, that the Torah could have been the work of Moses, and that none of the events or laws in the Bible should be taken literally. Instead, they should be taken to be parables or morality tales.

When the book appeared anonymously in 1670 it was perceived by both Jewish and Christian theologians as an attack on religion and was banned at once, although it still went through several printings. Spinoza called off the publication of a Dutch edition of the work. He turned down the offer of a chair of philosophy at the University of Heidelberg.

That same year, Spinoza settled in The Hague to be near his patron, Jan de Witt. Spinoza was shocked and outraged when de Witt and his brother were assassinated in 1672 by a mob who blamed them for the French invasion of Holland.

Two years later, Spinoza completed his most important metaphysical literary effort, *Ethics*, providing his original analysis of the role of God. Prior to Spinoza's assertions about God, most philosophers had thought of human beings as functioning within God's all-encompassing universe as discrete, autonomous figures. Rejecting such an approach, Spinoza insisted that all things in the universe were modifications or modes of God. He repudiated the Judeo-Christian idea of the special nature of God's interaction with man, as spelled out in the Bible. To him, God did not have a special feeling for human beings as opposed to other parts of his universe.

Spinoza died in 1677 at the age of forty-five. He was buried in a church in The Hague. In the early 1950s, Israeli Prime Minister David Ben-Gurion tried without success to have the excommunication against Spinoza lifted.

Napoléon Convenes Sanhedrin

FEBRUARY 9, 1807

During February and March 1807 Napoléon permitted French Jews to convene the Sanhedrin, an assembly of leading rabbis and laymen, which had as its purpose the defining of Jewry's relationship to the state. While Napoléon appeared to be providing French Jewry with an independent body through which it could make its own decisions, his hidden agenda seemed to be to tighten his control over them.

The Reign of Terror in France (1793–1794) had caused great suffering in the Jewish community. Synagogues were closed, and the communal organization of French Jewry was abolished. Napoléon Bonaparte, who came to power in 1799, understood nothing about Judaism and knew no Jews. He was suspicious of them, having accepted the long-held prejudices of many in Europe.

Napoléon wanted to carry on the reforms he had instituted for people of other religions and for the Jews of the Netherlands, Italy, and Germany. Those reforms were meant to provide Jews of those countries legal equality with other Dutch, Italians, and Germans. He was disturbed, however, by the Jews' independent spirit. When he visited Alsace and Lorraine, the peasants complained of their dislike for the Jews. The Jews made it hard for them to keep control of the land they had been given during the French Revolution. While what the Jews had done was perfectly legal—loaning money to the peasants—the peasants could not manage their farms and found it difficult to repay the loans with interest.

Napoléon, accepting the claims that Jews could not be easily assimilated and had formed themselves into a "nation within a nation," considered punishing them or deporting them from France. Instead, he gathered the Assembly of Jewish Notables in 1806.

The first session was held on July 26, a Saturday. Napoléon deliberately scheduled the meeting for the Jewish Sabbath, to see whether the Jews would object. No one did; the Jewish representatives avoided traveling and writing on the Sabbath, however.

The Assembly was expected to respond to twelve questions put to it by commissioners appointed by the government. The notables could do little more than answer "yes" or "no" to questions such as: Did the Jews consider themselves Frenchmen? Could they engage in manual labor, or did they insist on living by usury? Could they marry more than one wife at a time? Was it not possible to encourage intermarriage between Jews and Christians?

The Jews had no trouble declaring their loyalty to France; nor did they object to engaging in manual labor. They had more trouble justifying their practice of moneylending and agreeing to intermarriage.

Not entirely satisfied with the answers he received from the Assembly, Napoléon decided to have them formulated into a kind of religious code.

To accomplish that, Napoléon revived the Jewish legislative institution known as the Sanhedrin, the political, religious, and judicial body that had existed in Palestine during the Roman and Byzantine periods. Seventy-one men were selected—including Ashkenazi and Sephardi members from France, Italy, and Germany, among them forty-six rabbis—many of whom were members of the Assembly of Jewish Notables. Napoléon

The French Sanhedrin in session.

wanted to assure that the French Sanhedrin would not oppose any decisions taken by the notables.

The Sanhedrin convened in Paris on February 9, 1807. Joseph David Sinzheim of Strasbourg, a halakhic authority, was appointed its head (*nasi*).

The Sanhedrin reaffirmed the decisions taken by the Assembly of Jewish Notables, agreeing to be bound by the laws of France. Patriotism, declared the Sanhedrin, is "the religious duty of all Jews who were born or who settled in a state, or who are so considered according to the laws and conditions of the state to regard this state as their fatherland." They declared usury illegal. The Sanhedrin refused, however, to sanction mixed marriages. Accepting some key demands of Napoléon's empire, members of the Sanhedrin and Assembly tried to remain within the framework of Jewish law and tradition.

Napoléon dispersed the Sanhedrin suddenly, after only two months, perhaps on the authority of French Jesuit Augustin Barruel. He rekindled old arguments that Jews were intent upon becoming "masters of the world," claiming that an Italian named Simonini had delivered to him the "plans of world Jewry" to turn the churches into as many synagogues, and reduce Christians to utter serfdom.

While the establishment of the Sanhedrin appeared to "save" the French Jews from explusion, in fact it represented little more than clever manipulation on Napoléon's part to make them more French and less Jewish. As Abba Eban wrote in 1968 in *My People: The Story of the Jews*: "The [French] Sanhedrin's renunciation of separate nationhood marked an important turning point in Jewish history and set the tone of Western Jewish life for the next century and more."

A painting depicting Napoleon rehabilitating French Jewry, 1806.

Dreyfus Arrested for Espionage

Alfred Dreyfus, a Jew and an officer in the French army, was falsely accused of espionage. He was tried and found guilty, and the case became a major scandal in France, playing a significant role in encouraging the spread of anti-Semitism throughout Europe.

B orn in 1859 in the French province of Alsace, Alfred Dreyfus studied at the École Polytechnique, joining the army as an engineer with a lieutenant's rank. In 1892 he was appointed a captain, the only Jew on the general staff.

In September 1894 a French counterespionage agent found a suspicious piece of paper in the wastebasket of the German military attaché. Written on the paper in French was a promise to deliver a valuable French artillery manual to the Germans. Although neither Colonel Jean-Conrad Sandherr, chief of French military intelligence, nor handwriting experts could identify the writing, Sandherr's aide, Major Hubert Joseph Henry, suggested that Captain Dreyfus was the spy.

Though the handwriting bore little resemblance to Dreyfus's, he was disliked by the Jesuit-trained staff at military headquarters; he seemed too rich, too snobbish, in short a perfect scapegoat to take the blame for the crime. On October 15, 1894, Dreyfus was arrested, jailed, held incommunicado, then dragged before a military court and formally accused of treason. He faced a court-martial.

Until the Dreyfus case, Jews living in France and elsewhere in Europe had been under the illusion that their growing assimilation into European society meant a

Alfred Dreyfus.

gradual end to anti-Semitism. The eighty-six thousand French Jews, maintaining a low profile and asserting a deep-seated patriotism, thought themselves immune to anti-Semitic pressures. Yet, a number of Frenchmen, from the diplomat Comte Joseph-Arthur de Gobineau to the philosopher Joseph-Ernest Renan, had dwelt in their writ-

Dreyfus is put on trial.

ings on the alleged inferiority of the Jewish people, creating a welcome mat for the anti-Semitism that had arrrived in the country during the Dreyfus Affair.

Because the evidence against him seemed too meager, the court at first was reluctant to find Captain Dreyfus guilty. The influence of the media was extraordinary. Headlines and editorials, arguing that the "international Jewish conspiracy" had prodded Dreyfus to act, convinced the court that convicting Dreyfus would be politically expedient. In mid-December 1894, Dreyfus was found guilty and sentenced to life imprisonment in exile. Two weeks later, on January 5, 1895, he was expelled from the army during a public humiliation in the courtyard of the École Militaire in Paris.

Placed in chains, Dreyfus was then sent to prison on Devil's Island, off the coast of French Guiana, South America, where he continued to protest his innocence.

Sandherr retired as chief of intelligence, and Lieutenant Colonel Georges Picquart replaced him. In March 1896, the same counterespionage agent who had discovered the original paper now found—in the same office of the German military attaché—another piece of paper presumably written by the same French spy and promising new deliveries of French military secrets. The handwriting proved identical to that of another officer, a notorious gambler and playboy, Ferdinand Esterhazy.

The fresh evidence was brought to Picquart's attention, who then revealed these findings to Henry, who was embarrassed at having to admit that the case against Dreyfus was flawed. Fearing exposure as the one who had manufactured evidence against Dreyfus, Henry managed to convince Picquart that the army would tarnish its honor by admitting to being wrong about Dreyfus. Utilizing his connections with Picqaurt's superiors, Henry convinced them to transfer the intelligence chief to Tunisia.

Before his departure, however, Picquart turned over the new information to the liberal vice president of the

Central Zionist Archives, Jerusalem

A portrait of Émile Zola.

French Senate, Auguste Scheurer-Kestner, who, along with his colleagues in the liberal wing of the Senate, started to campaign for reopening the Dreyfus case. Meanwhile, Dreyfus's brother Mathiew submitted a copy of the original paper to some bank officials who speedily identified the handwriting as Esterhazy's, leading to a trial for Esterhazy. Though Esterhazy had motive (his gambling had left him short of cash and he detested his adopted land), he was acquitted: the court found it simply impossible to sully the army's honor by acknowledging that the case against Alfred Dreyfus had been in error.

By 1898, the Dreyfus Affair had reached the proportions of a public scandal. Newspapers contained diatribes from both supporters and enemies of Dreyfus; families and friends were torn apart; some even fought duels over "L'Affaire". The Vatican Secretariat of State organized an anti-Semitic campaign as well. The famous novelist Émile Zola published an open letter attacking the French general staff entitled "J'Accuse" ("I Accuse") in the French newspaper *L'Aurore*, and two hundred thousand copies of the paper quickly were sold. Zola was

found guilty of libel and was forced to flee to England to avoid imprisonment.

During the summer of 1898 the uproar over the Dreyfus case continued. Upon learning from a disgruntled relative of Esterhazy's that the "secret" evidence against Dreyfus had been a fraud, General Cavaignac, the new chief of staff, probed the charge and concluded that Henry's "evidence" was indeed a forgery. Thrown into jail, Henry became drunk and cut his own throat. Henry's suicide enflamed the opponents of Dreyfus: one prelate said he wished to "circumcise the Jews up to the necks." Nonetheless, a retrial for Dreyfus was nearing.

For five years Dreyfus had remained in a vermin-filled cell on Devil's Island, slowly going insane. By day he was permitted to view nothing more than the small beach in front of his hut; at night he was chained to his bed. He grew convinced that everyone had forgotten him. He had no idea that his case had become a major scandal.

Only in June 1899, upon his return to France for retrial, did he learn that his conviction had caused a furor. When he entered the courtroom, now thirty-nine years old, Dreyfus was bent, gaunt, bald but for a small fringe of white hair. Though French army officers used the new trial to spew their anti-Semitic venom, including the warning that Jews faced "mass extermination," the evidence this time overwhelmingly favored Dreyfus. Or so it appeared. Given the proof of Major Henry's forgeries and of Ferdinand Esterhazy's complicity, Dreyfus should have been exonerated. Yet he was not. The army officers who formed the panel at the retrial deliberated only an hour before finding Dreyfus guilty a second time. Their one act of leniency was to reduce Dreyfus's life sentence to ten years because of "extenuating circumstances."

Furious with the court's decision, liberals sought to overturn the verdict. And indeed, the new liberal president of the French Republic, Emile Loubet, pardoned Dreyfus a few days later. It took another seven years, however, for a court of appeals to clear Dreyfus's name entirely.

In 1905 the French government enacted a law separating church and state and reaffirmed the liberal principles of the French Republic.

Dreyfus was reinstated as a major in the army; he retired a year later but reenlisted in the army in World War I. He was promoted to lieutenant colonel in 1916 and given the Legion of Honor, the government's way of signaling French Jewry that the seemingly-official anti-Semitic campaign had ended. He died in Paris in 1935, at the age of seventy-six.

The triumph of French liberals in the Dreyfus Affair did not mean an end to anti-Semitism. The case was a dress rehearsal for an even more frightful campaign against the Jews, this time centered in Germany.

In September 1995, the French military officially recognized that it had framed Dreyfus. General Jean-Louis Mourrut, head of the army's history department, termed the Dreyfus affair a "military conspiracy that led to the conviction and deportation of an innocent man..."

Theodor Herzl covered the Dreyfus case as a correspondent for the Vienna *Neue Freie Presse*. His shock at the anti-Semitism that had infected France was one of the factors that led him to focus on the need for a Jewish state.

Kishinev Pogrom Carried Out

APRIL 6, 1903

They were called pogroms, attacks carried out by street crowds against Jews and their property, sanctioned by the Russian government. The most infamous one occurred in 1903 in Kishinev, the capital of Bessarabia. Once news of the attack reached the West, Kishinev became a rallying cry as Jews around the world were reminded of the virulent forms anti-Semitism could take.

In the Russia of the early 1900s a surge of revolutionary activity led the government to search for scapegoats. It chose the Jews. Labeling the entire liberal movement in Russia one vast conspiracy, the government urged its citizens to save the country from the villainy of those Jewish troublemakers by involving themselves in anti-Semitic acts.

In Kishinev, the capital of the province of Bessarabia, Jews had coexisted with their Russian neighbors for years. The only newspaper in the province, however, the *Bessarabetz*, was actively subsidized by the minister of the interior, Wenzel von Plehve, and spewed out anti-Semitic statements. Plehve not only refused to license any other newspaper but dipped into a special slush fund to keep the *Bessarabetz* going. The newspaper's publisher, Krushevan, was only too happy for the opportunity to ingratiate himself with his patron; early in 1903 the perfect opportunity arose. Some peasants living on the outskirts of Kishinev discovered the mutilated body of a Russian boy. Although the boy's uncle openly confessed to the crime, the *Bessarabetz* unleashed the charge of ritual murder against the Jews.

On the eve of Easter a group of Russian government emissaries arrived in Kishinev to engage in secret conversations with Krushevan and provincial officials. Soon thereafter, handbills, printed by Krushevan on the press belonging to the *Bessarabetz*, were distributed around the city, urging the citizens to inflict "bloody punishment" on the Jews. In the saloons and teahouses of the city open discussion of the approaching pogrom took place.

On Sunday, April 6, 1903, a mob of teenage ruffians, undoubtedly responding to a prearranged signal from the authorities, rushed into city streets, attacking Jews and looting Jewish stores and homes. The police chose not to quash the obviously criminal behavior. By evening, the looting had stopped and the killing had begun. For nearly twenty-four hours, while the local police remained in their barracks, Jews were hunted down and murdered.

It was not until 5:00 P.M. the next day, April 7, that Plehve sent a telegram to the local police, ordering them to detach troops, which they did an hour later. Fully armed, the troops appeared on the central streets to disperse the mobs. By then, of course, the rioters had largely accomplished their task. A total of fifty Jews had been killed, six hundred wounded, and fifteen hundred stores and homes gutted.

Russian eyewitnesses described people torn in two, babies' brains splattered, bellies split open, tongues cut out, women with breasts cut off, men castrated, blinded, hanged, hacked to death.

The news of the massacre spread not only through Russia. Numerous activists in the Russian intelligentsia issued statements of outrage. In the major capitals of Europe and in the United States, mass protests were held, under both Jewish and Christian auspices. The reaction of world leaders was sharp. The German Kaiser protested personally to the czar, as did the Austrian emperor. Resolutions were adopted at mass meetings in Britain, and those resolutions were sent by the British Foreign Secretary to the Russian Foreign Ministry. In the United States, President Theodore Roosevelt sent a personal note of deep concern to Nicholas II. So large, in fact was the international uproar, that the Russian government felt obligated to take a few tentative steps to appease public opinion, that was, to encourage Russians to think more highly of Jews than they had previously.

Plehve replaced the governor of Bessarabia and brought a few of the malefactors of the Kishinev pogrom to trial. But government attorneys who tried to handle the prosecution in good faith were hampered at every turn, and the sentences imposed upon a few convicted rioters were very lenient.

Plehve's violent efforts against the Jews, however, were not over. In August of 1903 a government-instigated pogrom broke out in Gomel, in Belorussia, where twenty thousand Jews comprised half the city's population. There had been some well-organized efforts on the part of the Jews of Gomel to defend themselves. Still, some two hundred fifty Jewish homes were destroyed and twelve Jews were killed in that pogrom. For the remainder of the year pogroms erupted in rapid succession throughout White Russia and the Ukraine.

In January 1904, Plehve summoned a committee of governors and other high officials from the Ministry of the Interior, warning them not to get squeamish about what he was asking them to do against the Jews. The task of these officials, he said, was not to modify Jewish legislation to make it easier for the Jews, but to systematize it so as to make life harder for them.

A few days later, however, the Russo-Japanese War broke out, and anti-Jewish measures temporarily were suspended in Russia, largely because Jewish communal leaders had asked their people to support the war effort and because the government concluded that pogroms might disrupt the economy. Accordingly, Plehve allowed the families of Jewish soldiers to remain at home until the war was over.

In 1906, the United States Congress passed a resolution of sympathy with the Jews of Kishinev. Referring to the mass protest meetings in New York, Philadelphia, and Chicago, and to the joint resolution of protest passed by Congress, President Roosevelt stated on one occasion: "I have never in my experience in this country known of a more immediate or deeper expression of sympathy for the victims...[of oppression] or of horror over the appalling calamity that has occurred."

A group of prominent Jews, including Judge Mayer Sulzberger, leading lawyer Louis Marshall, philanthropist Jacob H. Schiff, and eminent scholar Cyrus Adler decided to establish a nationwide organization to represent Jewish interests before the American public. They invited select individuals from every important Jewish community to join them in the American Jewish Committee, having as its aim the defense of Jewish rights whenever they were threatened.

What is most notable about Kishinev is not so much the degree of brutality exacted against the Jews, but the intensity of the international reaction; after all, the Kishinev pogrom occurred in 1903, forty years before the Nazi program to exterminate the Jews began.

Ford Sponsors Hate Literature

October 1920

One of the worst examples of hatred against Jews was the venom that spewed from the pen of one of the most powerful men in America. That Henry Ford, pioneer of the automotive industry and founder of the Ford Motor Company, thought it important to unleash a wave of anti-Semitism put the Jews of America on the defensive. It was, in fact, one of the worst moments American Jews endured this century.

In the early 1920s a Michigan newspaper, the *Dearborn Independent*, ran a series of articles charging the existence of a secret Jewish plot against the American judicial system. One headline read: "The Jewish Smoke Screen of Falsehood in What Press Dubs the 'American Dreyfus Case.'" The newspaper's publisher was Henry Ford, founder and president of the great Ford Motor Company. Ford hated financiers, especially bankers from the East Coast, because he believed that Jews controlled American banks. Ford's closest aide, Ernest G. Liebold, had purchased the *Dearborn Independent*, an obscure weekly newspaper in 1918, so that Ford could spread his views. By March 1920 Ford had become virulently anti-Semitic and begun an anti-Jewish crusade in the pages of his newspaper.

"International financiers are behind all war," he told an interviewer of the *New York World*. "They are what is called the international Jew—German Jews, French Jews, English Jews, American Jews. I believe that in all those countries except our own the Jewish financier is supreme . . . Here the Jew is a threat."

In May 1920 the *Independent* carried an article entitled "The International Jew: The World's Problem." The ar-ticle warned of a Jewish world conspiracy; it was influenced in part by the appearance of *The Protocols of the Elders of Zion*.

That document, one of the cruelest expressions of anti-Semitism, had its roots in a political satire on Emperor Napoleon III of France, which had been written in 1864 by journalist Maurice Joly. Four years later, Joly's literary effort was plagiarized in a German novel. It spoke of a conspiracy for world domination arising out of an alleged secret meeting of Jewish elders in Prague. In 1917, a group of former Russian Czarist officers living in Berlin published *The Protocols of the Elders of Zion*, based on those earlier works.

The document was brought to the United States in 1919 by some White Russian immigrants and eventually came to the attention of Ernest Liebold. He and his staff published their series on "The International Jew" weekly for two years, then on and off for another five years, relying on the theme in *The Protocols of the Elders of Zion* of a Jewish plot to control American industry.

From week to week Ford's writers aimed their literary assaults at specific Jews who allegedly were part of the Jewish plot to take over the world's financial and political sectors. The writers accused Jews of penetrating churches, labor unions, and colleges and argued that Jewish financial leaders were spearheading efforts to take over American industry. Among the financial moguls targeted by Ford's paper were Jacob Schiff, Felix Warburg, and the Guggenheim family.

With Ford's automobile dealers acting as subscription agents, the *Dearborn Independent's* circulation, which had been only seventy thousand in 1920, skyrocketed to three hundred thousand just two years later and then to seven hundred thousand by 1925.

In October 1920, Ford published a two-hundred-page booklet that contained reprints his newspaper's initial twenty articles on the Jews. Entitled *The International Jew*, and distributed free, in bulk, to public officials, the book was especially well received in rural areas of the country.

Here and there Ford came under attack. Some newspapers assailed him for his "mean and narrow mental attitude" and his "vulgar attacks" on Jews. The Hearst chain called him an ignoramus. A manifesto signed by one hundred nineteen important Americans, headed by Woodrow Wilson and including former President William Taft, excoriated him.

Profoundly affected by Ford's diatribes against the Jews, American Jewish leader Louis Marshall described Ford's assault as "the most serious episode in the history of American Jewry." A conference of national Jewish organizations in November 1920 at New York's Hotel Astor led to the publication of an eighteen-page statement that sought to refute Ford's charges against Jews. While the document won widespread news coverage, it did not stop Ford from carrying on his anti-Semitic crusade.

The growing dissent against Ford did not appear to have any impact on his behavior until 1923, when he considered a run for the presidency. He ordered the anti-Semitic articles in the *Dearborn Independent* to be brought to a halt. When it became clear that Calvin Coolidge had the Republican presidential nomination sewn up, however, the *Dearborn Independent* renewed its anti-Jewish attacks.

Eventually, a one-million-dollar lawsuit in Federal court brought against Ford in 1925 by Aaron Sapiro, a San Francisco lawyer who had helped organize farmers' marketing cooperatives and had been accused by Ford of attempting to seize control of American agriculture, forced Ford to cease his anti-Jewish efforts.

Sapiro and Ford settled out of court. Undoubtedly the boycott of Ford products by Jews and non-Jews alike encouraged Ford to desist in his attacks. Ford was forced to issue an unqualified retraction of all charges against the Jews, Sapiro in particular, along with a complete apology, the text of which would be written by Louis Marshall. All anti-Jewish articles had to cease, and *The International Jew* had to be withdrawn from circulation.

The statement drafted by Marshall explained that Ford had been too busy to monitor the *Independent*'s series of articles. Only when he learned of Jewish resentment did he become "shocked and mortified" by their content. He

A portrait of Henry Ford.

went on: "I deem it to be my duty as an honorable man to make amends for the wrong done to the Jews as fellow-men and brothers, by asking their forgiveness for the harm that I have unintentionally committed, by retracting so far as lies within my power the offensive charges laid at their door by these publications, and by giving them the unqualified assurance that henceforth they may look to me for friendship and good will."

Ford won praise for the statement. "Mr. Ford has shown superb moral courage in his wholehearted recantation," editorialized Adolph S. Ochs in *The New York Times*.

But Ford continued to mistrust the Jews. In 1938, German Chancellor Adolf Hitler presented Ford with the Grand Cross of the German Eagle; two years later Ford informed a Manchester *Guardian* reporter that "international Jewish bankers" had brought about World War II, a view heartily shared by Ford's friend and employee Charles Lindbergh.

Because of Henry Ford's prestige and importance in America, he had caused a major setback to the self-confidence of American Jews in the early part of the twentieth century.

Nazi Terror Presaged on Kristallnacht

November 9, 1938

When a Jew named Herschel Grynszpan decided to seek revenge against the Nazis for brutalizing his family by shooting a Nazi official in the German embassy in Paris, the Nazis exploited the shooting to take action against the entire three-hundred-thousand-strong German Jewish community. The Nazis unleashed a night of terror against the Jews on November 9, 1938, which became known as Kristallnacht, *the night of broken glass.* Kristallnacht *was an ugly harbinger of even worse to come, the Holocaust, during which six million Jews were murdered by the Nazis.*

The Nazis began tightening their hold over the Jews of Germany in the late 1930s, imposing more and more regulations restricting their behavior. By the autumn of 1938, the Jews were facing desperate economic times—tens of thousands had become destitute and over two hundred thousand had fled Germany to find better lives in other places.

Still believing the "Jewish problem" to be unresolved—the problem was that Jews were still in Germany and the rest of Europe—Adolf Hitler, who had been appointed chancellor of Germany in 1933, started to rant and rave in his speeches against the so-called inordinate power of the Jews abroad, especially the power to make war against him.

In October 1938 twenty thousand German Jews were sent to the Polish frontier, but the Poles refused them entrance, forcing these Jews to live in open fields along the border zone, reduced to poverty. At Zbaszyn, a point along the frontier, the Jews were put in stables still filled with horse dung. Finally, a truck with bread arrived from Poznan, but at first there was not enough bread to feed everyone. Zindel Grynszpan decided to send a postcard to his son Herschel in Paris, describing the family's travails.

Herschel Grynszpan, was living with relatives in Paris when he learned that his family was one of those living in this no man's land. Concerned especially at the thought of his sister facing such a perilous situation, he decided to turn her plight and that of the other Jews into an international issue. His plan was to take action that would arouse the world's attention.

Entering the German embassy in Paris on November 7, 1939, to "deliver a package" to the ambassador, he was led by attendants instead into the office of the third secretary, Ernst vom Rath. Grynszpan took out a pistol and shot the Nazi functionary at point-blank range.

As vom Rath lay wounded, the Nazis denounced the deed as part of a Jewish-inspired world conspiracy against Germany. On November 9, vom Rath was dead. The moment the news of the shooting had reached Hitler in Munich, he became enraged, suggesting: "The storm troopers should be allowed to have a fling." Joseph Goebbels, the Nazi propaganda minister, proposed to Hitler—and Hitler agreed—that, if the riots spread, no one would discourage them. It was safely assumed that Goebbels meant for the Nazi party to organize the riots.

The night of November 9, 1938 became known as *Kristallnacht,* the "Night of Broken Glass," named for the glittering shards of broken glass that lined Jewish neighborhoods throughout the German Reich.

Nazi party members smashed and looted the shops of Jewish merchants. Storm troopers rang doorbells and smashed the glass windows in the doors if there was no

YAD VASHEM, JERUSALEM

A synagogue in Berlin consumed by fire on Kristallnacht.

reply, eventually entering the Jewish houses. Bonfires were lit in every neighborhood where Jews lived. On those fires were thrown prayer books, Torah scrolls, and numerous volumes of poetry, philosophy, and history. In hundreds of streets, Jews were chased, reviled, and beaten up. In the course of twenty-four hours, ninety-one Jews were killed. Thirty thousand—fully one in ten of those who remained—were arrested and sent to concentration camps. Hundreds of synagogues were destroyed along with more than a thousand private Jewish businesses and homes.

The Nazis dispatched teams to burn down all synagogues. The SS, under Heinrich Himmler, received the news at 11:05 P.M. Himmler minuted: "The order was given by the propaganda directorate, and I suspect that Goebbels, in his cravings for power, which I noticed long ago, and also in his empty-headedness, started this action just at a time when the foreign political situation is very grave . . . When I asked the Fuhrer (Hitler) about

it, I had the impression that he did not know anything about these events."

Within two hours Himmler had ordered out all his police and SS forces to prevent widespread looting and to place 20,000 Jews into concentration camps.

Hitler had shifted gears and moved to a new level of action against Jews—going from economic and political oppression to overt physical brutality.

After *Kristallnacht*, the Nazi leadership imposed a one-billion-dollar "fine" on Jews still in Germany for "clean up." The fine was levied via the compulsory confiscation of twenty percent of the property of every German Jew. On November 12, three days after the confiscation order, Jewish children were barred from German schools.

The Western press reported *Kristallnacht* in as much detail as it could garner. In the United States, Jewish editorialists called for a day of mourning; on the Sabbath of November 19, most American synagogues heeded the call. Still the important Jewish organizations, including the American Jewish Congress, decided that it would be more useful to protest under "nonsectarian" auspices.

To be sure, the civil organizations and the press responded to *Kristallnacht* with deep revulsion. Former governor of New York, Al Smith, and New York district attorney, Thomas E. Dewey, broadcast protests during special radio programs. On Sunday, November 13, hundreds of ministers and priests gave sermons in opposition to Nazi cruelty. The German ambassador in Washington, Hans Dickhoff, noted that American public opinion "is without exception incensed against Germany."

In New York, on November 23, a mass demonstration organized by the Joint Boycott Council protested against the renewed violence. Two days later, in Chicago, protesters burned the German flag.

Kristallnacht was an ugly harbinger of even worse things to come—the Holocaust, the mass destruction by the Nazis of six million Jews.

Death Camp Built at Auschwitz

JUNE 1940

The extermination camp at Auschwitz in Poland was the most infamous of the thirty death camps built by the Nazis during World War II. The operation of these concentration and extermination camps constituted one of the greatest crimes human beings have perpetrated on one another, and they were aimed largely at wiping out the Jews of Europe. In all, six million Jews were killed, often in large groups, led into "showers" that were in fact massive gas chambers. As many as two-and-a-half-million Jews were gassed at Auschwitz.

In the spring of 1940 the Germans decided to establish a new concentration camp. The site chosen was in Upper Silesia, which had been annexed by Germany. The town selected was called Oswieçim in Polish, Auschwitz in German.

Rudolf Hoess, convicted murderer, was ordered by Heinrich Himmler to establish extermination facilities at Auschwitz in June 1940. Hoess thought that the gas used at Treblinka, another death camp, was not very efficient; so he decided to use Zyklon B, a crystallized prussic acid that took between three and fifteen minutes to kill anyone in the death chamber and that had been marketed as a strong disinfectant.

The camp at Auschwitz had four gigantic gas chambers adjacent to which were crematoria for burning the bodies.

The rail journey that arrivals coming from France, Holland, or as far away as Greece, were forced to endure just to get to Auschwitz was murderous. Locked inside freight cars, they went without food or water for as much as a week.

One survivor of the journey from Paris to Auschwitz, Albert Hollender, is quoted in Martin Gilbert's book *The Holocaust: The Jewish Tragedy* (1986):

> Piled up in freight cars, unable to bend or to budge, sticking one to the other, breathless, crushed by one's neighbor's every move, this was already hell. During the day, a torrid heat, with a pestilential smell . . . We arrived worn out, dehydrated, with many ill. A newborn baby, snatched from its mother's arms, was thrown against a column. The mother, crazed from pain, began to scream. The SS man struck her violently with the butt end of his weapon over the head. Her eyes haggard, with fearful screams, her beautiful hair became tinted with her own blood. She was struck down by a bullet in her head.

Sometimes, the Germans would try to calm the arriving Jews with these salving lines:

> Ladies and gentlemen, we are so sorry. Just look at this mess! How they treat people! Please get out, and please stay away from those criminals [Jewish inmates assigned to collect luggage]. If you've got unmarked luggage and are afraid that it might get lost, just take it with you . . . .We are keeping an eye on the criminals . . . And our German honesty, about which we hope you've no doubt, is a guarantee that all your property will be returned to you . . . Please don't cause

YAD VASHEM, JERUSALEM

Selection. Jews were first ordered to assemble in two groups, one women and children, the other men. Those fit to work were sent to slave labor, the rest were sent to the gas chambers.

any trouble. We can give you water and allow you basic sanitary conditions to be restored after your dismal journey.

One "improvement" over Treblinka, in Hoess's view, was that the victims at that camp almost always knew they were to be exterminated. At Auschwitz he tried to fool the victims into thinking that they were about to go through a delousing process. Further tricks were employed. Some arrivals were given picture postcards marked "Waldsee" that they were to sign and address to relatives back home; each bore the printed inscription: "We are doing very well here. We have work and we are well treated. We await your arrival."

Not everyone arriving at Auschwitz was killed. Two doctors stationed at the railroad siding greeted the newcomers. The doctors examined them and then made spot decisions about who was fit to work and who was not. Children were immediately sent to be exterminated, though women sometimes tried to hide their children under their clothes.

The gassings were called *Sonderaction*, "special action." The gas chambers were underground. Above them were well-kept lawns bordered with flowerbeds. The signs at the entrances to the gas chambers read "BATHS." An inmate orchestra played gay tunes from *The Merry Widow* and *Tales of Hoffman* as Jews were led into what they thought were the showers.

Once inside the "bathhouses," men, women, and children were told to undress and given towels. Since as many as two thousand people were packed into the "shower room," many must have begun to suspect that this was no real shower. Some must have wondered why there were no drains on the floor, only showerheads

YAD VASHEM, JERUSALEM

Disembarkation.

from which no water spouted. Sometimes, when they realized that delousing was just a trick, there were riots. The large door slid shut, hermetically sealed. Orderlies wearing gas masks then dropped the amethyst-blue crystals of Zyklon B into the lids of vents hidden by the lawns and flower beds.

Through heavy glass portholes, the executioners could watch the panicked reaction of the victims, who grew more and more frantic as they began to realize that gas was issuing from the perforations in the vents. They tried to run toward the door, piling one on top of the other in death.

Hoess later testified at the Nuremberg Trials: "We knew when the people were dead because their screaming stopped. We usually waited about a half hour be-fore we opened the doors and removed the bodies. After the bodies were removed our special commandos took off the rings and extracted the gold from the teeth of the corpses."

The bodies, stripped of gold and hair (considered a strategic material by the Nazis) were taken to furnaces. In forty-six days during the summer of 1944 as many as three hundred thousand Hungarian Jews were killed at Auschwitz. Toward the end of the war the camp was gassing a record six thousand victims a day.

While Nazi orders were to carry out the exterminations in secrecy, the nauseating stench of the burning bodies permeated the air. It seems impossible that those living in the surrounding communities did not know exactly what was occurring at Auschwitz.

Nazi Officials Design Final Solution

January 20, 1942

> *No chapter in modern Jewish history is more horrible than the Holocaust, the extermination by the Nazis of six million Jews during World War II. One of the many tragic moments during that period occurred early in 1942 in a suburb of Berlin known as Wannsee where a little-known meeting of Nazi officials set the final solution in motion.*

The setting for the historic Wannsee conference was a villa near Berlin. The meeting had been postponed for almost three weeks because of the Japanese attack on Pearl Harbor on December 7, 1941, and America's entry into the war immediately after that attack.

Reinhard Heydrich began the meeting by telling the gathering of senior civil servants that he had been appointed "Plenipotentiary for the Preparation of the Final Solution of the European Jewish Question."

Attending the meeting were officials from the Ministry for the Occupied Eastern Territories, the Ministry of the Interior, the Ministry of Justice, the Foreign Ministry, and other government offices. The "Final Solution" was an ugly euphemism for the Nazi plan to exterminate all of European Jewry. It was at Wannsee that the execution of that plan was discussed and put into action.

By the time of Wannsee, there was definite anxiety among top Nazi officials. Their failure to conquer Russia, and the entrance of America into the war, had convinced many of them that Germany was bound to lose the fight.

If it was not possible to conquer all of Europe, the Nazis were determined at least to punish their greatest enemy—the Jews. The Holocaust would take priority over the war effort itself, reflecting Hitler's resolve that, whatever the outcome of the war, European Jewry would not survive it.

Heydrich told the gathering at Wannsee that his intention was "to achieve clarity in essential matters." Until then, Heydrich explained to the audience, the Nazi struggle against the Jews had been confined to expelling them "from the living space of the German people." Now it was time to engage in what Heydrich called the "evacuation of the Jews to the East." It was clear that evacuation was meant to be a prelude for the "final solution."

Heydrich noted that the "final solution" referred not only to those Jews who were under German rule, but to eleven million Jews throughout Europe. "In the course of the final solution," he observed, "the Jews should be brought under appropriate direction in a suitable manner to the East for labor utilization. Separated by sex, the Jews capable of work will be led into these areas in large labor columns to build roads, whereby doubtless a large part will fall away through natural reduction." Then Heydrich added: "The inevitable final remainder, which doubtless constitutes the toughest element, will have to be dealt with appropriately, since it represents a natural selection that upon liberation is to be regarded as a germ cell of a new Jewish development."

Heydrich noted some of the problems in rounding up Jews. In Romania, for example a Jew could purchase appropriate documents that officially certified him or her as a foreign national and not a Jew.

Dr. Joseph Buhler, the representative of the General Government, welcomed the start of the final solution:

Jews should be removed from the domain of the General Government as fast as possible, because it is precisely here that the Jews constitute a substantial danger as carrier of epidemics and also because his continued black market activities create constant disorder in the economic structure of the country. Moreover, the majority of the two and a half million Jews [in the territory controlled by the General Government] involved were not capable of work.

Toward the end of the Wannsee conference, as the official notes from the meeting record, there was a discussion of the different types of "solution possibilities." But nowhere in the notes does it mention what those "possibilities" might be. After the conference, recalled Adolf Eichmann, the man who had the responsibility of executing the final solution, "we all sat together like comrades. Not to talk shop, but to rest after long hours of effort."

The Belzec extermination camp became operational a month after Wannsee. The construction of an extermination camp at Sobibor began in March. At the same time Majdanek and Treblinka were transformed into death centers.

Nazi orders, even those written for very limited circulation, often described Jewish genocide euphemistically; at the Wannsee conference Heydrich used code words. All Jews, he said, were to be "evacuated to the East" and formed into labor columns. Most would "fall away through natural decline" but the hard core, capable of rebuilding Jewry, would be "treated accordingly." This last phrase meant "killed."

Most Jews were killed at the six largest death camps: two-and-a-half million at Auschwitz; one million four hundred thousand at Majdanek; eight hundred thousand at Treblinka; six hundred thousand at Belzec; three hundred forty thousand at Chelmno; and two hundred fifty thousand at Sobibor.

Anne Frank's Diary Made Public

1947

The publication of the diary of a teen-age Dutch Jewish girl named Anne Frank, written in hiding before the Nazis carried her off to her death in 1945, brought home to millions of Jews and non-Jews the awful reality of the Nazis' brutality against the Jews during World War II. More than twenty-five million copies of the diary have been printed in fifty-five languages.

The looter grabbed a briefcase, dumping its contents on the floor of the annex at Prinsengracht 263 in Amsterdam. He needed the briefcase to stow the plunder left behind after Anne Frank and her family, having hidden in the annex for twenty-five months during World War II, had been picked up by the Nazis.

One item dumped on the floor was a small book, clothbound, insignificant looking. Sometime after the looter had left the premises, at considerable risk to herself, an employee of Anne's father Otto, Miep Gies, retrieved the book—Anne Frank's diary of her life in hiding. Miep turned the diary over to Otto Frank after he was liberated from Auschwitz.

When the diary was published in 1947, entitled *The Annex*, it became an instant success. Anne Frank's simple, poignant words turned her into a symbol of the persecuted Jewish children in particular and the victims of the Holocaust in general.

Later titled *Anne Frank: The Diary of a Young Girl*, her diary became a literary classic.

With the end of the Holocaust, the world learned of the Nazi attempt to wipe out the Jewish people; but even as the evidence mounted that Hitler had murdered six million Jews, those events remained a distant nightmare, too abstract, too removed for many to understand. Only with the publication of Anne Frank's diary did the Nazis' persecution of Jews bring home to millions what the Holocaust really was like.

Anne Frank was born in Frankfurt, Germany on June 12, 1929. A decade later, she and her family moved to Amsterdam, Holland. Intelligent and insightful, Anne planned to be a writer, but pursuing such hopes was a luxury as long as Hitler's Nazis were victimizing Jews and marching across Western Europe.

Anne and her family were forced into hiding four days after Anne's sixteen-year-old sister Margot was ordered by the Nazis to appear for forced labor. On July 9, 1942, the Frank family's long ordeal began as they chose rooms at the rear of Otto Frank's business premises as their place of hiding. The next day the family moved to the vacant annex of Otto Frank's office.

Anne made sure to take into hiding her curlers, school books, and, most important of all, her dairy, a present for her thirteenth birthday.

Once in hiding, she began to describe her frightening existence to an imaginary friend she called Kitty in her diary. Aware that Jews were being sent to unknown destinations, she assumed they were then murdered and that the same would happen to her and her family, if caught. In Anne's diary entry for April 11, 1944, she vowed to Kitty that she would not weaken: "We Jews mustn't show our feelings, must be brave and strong, must accept all inconveniences and not grumble...If we bear all this suffering and if there are still Jews left, when it is over, then Jews, instead of being doomed, will be held up as an example."

ISRAEL FILM ARCHIVES

Scene from The Diary of Anne Frank.

Life in hiding was precarious. Anne and her family were totally dependent upon Otto's non-Jewish employees, including Miep Gies, to supply them with the necessities of life—and not to betray them. To pass the time, Anne read books, wrote in her diary, and prayed. At times, she stared through her attic window at the blue sky. Living in such crowded conditions—there were eight people altogether, the Frank family, the Van Daan family, and a dentist named Albert Dussel—the residents took to squabbling about petty matters. Anne was aghast: "Why do grown-ups quarrel so easily, and over the most idiotic things?" she wrote in her diary on September 28, 1942. And al-

ways there was the fear of being discovered. When a carpenter suddenly showed up one day she feared that he might uncover their hiding place.

She took refuge in the fact that perhaps she would see daylight again. In her diary entry of February 23, 1944, she wrote: "I looked out of the open window, over a large area of Amsterdam, over all the roofs and on to the horizon, which was such a pale blue that it was hard to see the dividing line. 'As long as this exists,' I thought, 'and I may live to see it, this sunshine, these cloudless skies, while this lasts I cannot be unhappy.'"

On August 4, 1944, the German police discovered the Frank family as the result of an act of betrayal. Along

ISRAEL FILM ARCHIVES

Scene from The Diary of Anne Frank.

with the others, Anne was arrested. She and her sister were sent to Bergen-Belsen where Anne developed a case of typhus and died in March 1945.

In March 1995, to mark the 50th anniversary of Anne's death, Doubleday released *The Diary of a Young Girl: The Definitive Edition*, which contained material from Anne's diary that had been left out of the 1947 published version by Otto Frank. Among the new material was Anne's anger at her mother, her budding feminism, and her sexual yearning.

Anne Frank's diary remains one of the most well-known and moving documents emerging from the Holocaust.

Altalena *Attempts to Land on Israeli Shores*

June 22, 1948

> *Apart from soldiers and weapons, the new state of Israel required harmony among its citizenry. Yet the arrival of the Irgun ship* Altalena *on Israeli shores in June 1948 threatened to undermine that unity. When the dissident Irgun organization insisted that a percentage of the arms brought by the* Altalena *be delivered to Irgun units in Jerusalem, a Jewish civil war—between the new Israeli government and the Irgun—loomed. When the ship dropped anchor, a military battle ensued between Israeli soldiers and the Irgun; the ship went down in flames and all the arms were lost. Fourteen Irgun soldiers died in the battle. Yet civil war was averted.*

From the moment of its founding, the state of Israel was locked in fierce battle against its Arab enemies. Above all else, the small Jewish force fighting seven Arab armies required unity. Yet one incident threatened to undermine that unity.

The incident began just a few weeks after the state of Israel was born. On June 1, 1948, David Ben-Gurion, the Israeli prime minister, had ordered all armed Jewish groups to be absorbed into the new Israeli army.

Though two of these groups, the Irgun and the more radical Stern Gang, had long advocated harsher steps against the Arabs and the British, and had at times acted independently, Israeli leaders were confident that these dissident organizations would willingly fall under the new government's jurisdiction. And indeed, by the time of the June 11 Arab-Israeli truce, the Irgun had already promised to dissolve its military wing. Its members would join the newly created Israel Defense Forces and hand over its weapons to the IDF.

The Irgun had kept its promise by and large. It insisted on rearming its unit in Jerusalem, however, an act of defiance against the new Israeli government's rule, especially after the cease-fire, which included a pledge on the part of Israel and the Arab states not to introduce new arms into the region.

In early June the Irgun ship *Altalena* set sail from southern France for Israel with a cargo of five thousand rifles, two hundred fifty light machine guns and a number of antitank weapons. The ship also carried nine hundred immigrants. The Irgun and the fledgling Israeli government had agreed that the arms would be turned over to the IDF, but the Irgun demanded that some of the arms be earmarked for its units in Jerusalem. Though both Jews and Arabs had secretly violated the agreement not to rearm during the truce, the Israeli government felt that it could not tolerate the disloyalty exhibited by the Irgun. Ben-Gurion ordered the Irgun to turn over the ship, but this demand was met with a staunch refusal.

The offloading of the arms threatened to unleash a civil war. To David Ben-Gurion, the solution, painful as it seemed, was clear. The unloading of arms had to be stopped and the Irgun had to be destroyed as an independent body.

It was not easy to find troops willing to take part in the action; no Jew wanted to take up arms against a fellow Jew. The Alexandroni Brigade refused to participate. Yitzhak Sadeh, commander of the Eighth Brigade, was approached next. He turned to the Eighty-Ninth Battalion to handle the task.

A young officer named Moshe Dayan was called to Sadeh's headquarters, where he was informed about the

Dismantled Altalena *in October of 1949.*

situation. Sadeh concluded simply, "It has to be dealt with. I am no expert in the complicated relations between the Irgun and the government," Dayan replied, "but I do not doubt my obligation to comply with an order."

One of Dayan's troops told him that he had lost all his family in the Holocaust and could not shoot another Jew. "You are a soldier," Dayan said. "You were the one who told me about British army discipline. I am ordering you to go." The soldier, however, was excused by Sadeh.

On June 20 the *Altalena* anchored off Kfar Vitkin, twenty-three miles north of Tel Aviv. When Dayan arrived at Kfar Vitkin with his men, he learned that the Irgun had deployed on the beach, including two battalions that had deserted frontline positions to come to the rescue of the *Altalena*. At first Dayan thought it would be possible simply to surround the Irgun soldiers and force them into a quick surrender. But a gunfight broke out, and two of Dayan's men were killed and another six wounded. When the shooting died down, Dayan

learned where the Irgun leaders were and broke through a barricade in order to reach them. Though he faced tommy guns, Dayan forged ahead. His comrades advised him not to provide such a welcome target. "If they hit me," said Dayan, "then they'll stop this military action."

They did not hit him. Dayan hammered out an agreement with Irgun leaders Menachem Begin and Ya'acov Meridor, by which the Irgun would surrender the *Altalena's* arms, but the accord quickly fell apart, and during the night the ship set sail for Tel Aviv. Dayan, meanwhile, was summoned to Ben-Gurion's headquarters and asked to take on a sad mission, accompanying the body of David Marcus back to the United States for burial. Marcus was a Jewish-American who accidentally had been killed by Israeli soldiers after having just taken over command of Israel's Jerusalem front.

On June 22 the ship anchored opposite the Ritz Hotel, then the headquarters of the Palmach. Yigal Allon, the Palmach's commander, was instructed by headquarters to take command of the situation, but he

The ship Altalena *on fire after being hit by shell near Tel-Aviv.*

was only there for a short time, leaving Yitzhak Rabin, one of the Palmach leaders and commander of the Harel brigade, effectively in charge. Rabin had only forty men under his command, most of whom had been wounded at the front and were convalescing—carrying out duites as military policemen—at Palmach headquarters.

At a certain point, Rabin saw the *Altalena* and two landing craft nearing the shore. He organized his men for battle. When the *Altalena* refused to surrender, Irgun soldiers and Rabin's men exchanged fire, both sides using machine guns, grenades, and rifles. Rabin ordered Moshe Kelman, the commander of the third Palmach Battalion, to bring his unit to headquarters at once.

The fighting lasted ten hours. Eventually the ship was set on fire by a field gun fired from the shore. The ship went down in flames and all the arms were lost.

Civil war was averted when Begin called off his men and gave up the struggle. Passengers and crew were helped to safety by the men of the Israel Defense Forces. Fourteen Irgun men died in the battle. Rabin lost one man, and several were wounded.

On September 20, 1948, the Israeli Government gave the Irgun twenty-four hours to agree to obey all the laws of the infant state. The Irgun and Stern Gang surrendered their weapons and agreed to merge with the IDF.

The *Altalena* affair was one of the most serious tests the new state had to confront, but Rabin and Ben-Gurion never had any doubt about the morality of taking up arms against fellow Jews. To them the principle of statehood was at stake, and the Irgun was threatening that principle.

Israeli Athletes Murdered at Munich Olympics

SEPTEMBER 5, 1972 • 4:30 A.M.

No Arab terrorist attack against an Israeli target attracted more international attention than the one perpetrated at the Munich Olympic games in September 1972. While a group of Black September terrorists (a clandestine unit of the Palestine Liberation Organization—the PLO) killed two Israeli athletes and held nine others hostage at the Olympic Village, the entire world watched via television cameras already in place for Olympic coverage. After the Israeli hostages were killed in a battle waged at a West German airfield, Israel successfully carried out a secret campaign to kill those responsible for the Munich terror attack.

It was 4:30 in the morning on September 5, 1972, at Connollystrasse 31. A man rapped on the door of the apartment at the Olympic Village in Munich, West Germany. In clumsy German, he shouted, "Is this the Israeli team?"

Moshe Weinberg, coach of the Israeli wrestling team, who shared an apartment with other Israeli athletes, was alarmed by the knocks at the door. He opened the door a crack. Sensing danger, he threw his large frame against the door and tried to force it closed. "Boys, get out!" he screamed in Hebrew. "Get out!"

Shocked awake, Gad Zavarj, a wrestler who was Weinberg's roommate, bolted from his bed. The terrorists could not budge Weinberg. But one of them fired a Soviet-made AK-47 at the door; the slugs penetrated Weinberg's chest and neck.

Pushing open the door, the attackers fired at Zavarj, who was fleeing. They missed him. The terrorists ran past Weinberg's bedroom to two connecting apartments.

More Israelis were sleeping there. They shot Joe Romano, the Israeli weight lifting champion, at point-blank range. Meanwhile, other Israelis had heard the shouts and the shooting. They raced wildly to get dressed and flee.

The terrorists captured nine Israelis, bound their hands and feet with rope, and forced them to a third-floor bedroom that their teammates had vacated. Romano's body was dragged into the room as if to remind the hostages of what might be in store for them. At 9:00 A.M., the terrorists dropped a note through the window of the building where they were holding the hostages. In it they demanded the release of two hundred Arab prisoners from Israeli jails as well as two recently captured West German terrorists in exchange for the lives of the nine Israeli hostages.

The terrorists belonged to the Black September Palestinian terror organization. While acts of Palestinian terror had been committed against Israel before, none had the dramatic effect of this deed, played out against the background of the Olympic games with television crews from around the world recording each moment.

The Olympic International Committee decided that the games should be suspended for twenty-four hours. Events in progress, however, were permitted to continue. The Soviet and Polish volleyball teams played a match that afternoon less than one hundred yards from the spot of the terrorist attack.

At 4:30 P.M. one of the terrorists demanded a plane to fly his squad and the hostages to Cairo. Minister of the Interior Hans-Dietrich Genscher demanded to see the Israeli hostages first. Genscher was allowed to visit them. The hostages told him they were well and would be prepared to fly to Cairo as long as the Israeli government agreed to swap Arab prisoners for them there.

Meanwhile, in the early evening hours, the West Germans organized a rescue attempt. More than five hundred West German policemen had cordoned off the building in which the hostages were being held. Three sets of sharpshooters were to lay in ambush along the route from Connollystrasse to the air force base at Fürstenfeldbruck near Munich.

The Israeli government was to fly the two hundred terrorists to an Arab capital to be designated later. The West Germans were to provide three aircraft to fly the terrorists and the hostages to the same capital.

Meanwhile, Israeli Prime Minister Golda Meir sent Zvi Zamir, chief of the Mossad, to Munich as her personal emissary.

At 10:00 P.M., a gray German army bus pulled to a stop in the underground service road beneath the apartment building. The terrorists, still in disguise, carrying their weapons, and surrounding their captives, climbed into the bus and drove ten minutes to a spot where two West Germany military helicopters awaited them. West German sharpshooters had no chance to hit the terrorists. A third helicopter, with West German officials as well as Zvi Zamir in it, took off. The three helicopters flew to Fürstenfeldbruck, fifteen miles to the west. Landing at 10:30 P.M., Zamir and the West German officials rushed to the control tower.

Five minutes later, the other two helicopters put down side by side on the brightly lit apron forty yards from the control tower. Two terrorists, gripping AK-47s, alighted and walked toward the Lufthansa 727 standing one hundred ten yards to their right. Two other terrorists then emerged from the helicopters and motioned for the pilots and copilots of the choppers to get out and head for the 727, despite having promised the crews they would be freed after landing at the airfield.

At 10:38 P.M., a terrorist stepped inside the 727. He quickly recognized that the plane had not been prepared for flight. Lufthansa had been unable to find a crew willing to act as decoys. A West German police

Erroneous caption in The Jerusalem Post *on September 6, 1972 gave Iraelis the false impression that the Munich hostages had been saved.*

official ordered five sharpshooters to fire once the maximum number of terrorists was in sight.

It was 10:44 P.M. Two terrorists, returning from the 727, were halfway to the helicopters. The crack of a sniper's rifle ripped through the air. The shot, aimed at one of the terrorists, missed. Two more shots were fired at the two terrorists standing guard near the helicopters. The two terrorists fell dead.

One of the two terrorists heading toward the helicopters was hit in the first volley and killed in the second. But the second terrorist darted beneath one of the helicopters and began to fire back.

The four terrorists inside the helicopters began shooting. The West German police were badly outgunned; they were firing bolt-action rifles capable of only one shot at a time. From the terrorists came long bursts of fire aimed at the control tower. The field went dark. The fire fight raged on for another six minutes. Then silence.

Lunging from one helicopter, a terrorist tossed a hand grenade back into the craft. Ripped by the explosion, the chopper burst into flames. The five Israeli hostages in the helicopter were already dead, having been shot by the terrorists before the explosion. The four Israeli hostages in the other helicopter had also been shot dead by terrorist bullets. Black September had executed the Israelis at the moment the snipers opened fire.

The coffins of the Israeli athletes arriving in Israel.

At 11:00 P.M., Conrad Ahlers, spokesman for the Federal Republic of Germany, was about to be interviewed on the evening news when he received a phone call from Chancellor Willy Brandt, who had just been informed by the police that the rescue operation had gone according to plan. The German press agency, DPA, had reported the operation's success thirty minutes earlier as well. Accordingly, Ahlers announced on television that the rescue had achieved its purpose. Many people in Israel went to sleep that night in the mistaken belief that the nine Israelis had been rescued. They awoke to the horror of the athletes' deaths.

Flags of the countries participating in the Olympics were flown at half-mast. Some eighty thousand people gathered in the main stadium for a memorial service. The mourning, however, was not universal. Arab teams refused to participate, and even as the memorial service took place, athletes from the USSR and East bloc indifferently kicked soccer balls on nearby practice fields.

The indifference of the international community to Israel's plight was symbolized by the fact that the Olympic games continued despite the death of eleven Israeli participants. Three Arab terrorists who had survived the final battle were permitted to go free by the West German government in exchange for the peaceful conclusion of a 1973 Lufthansa hijacking. For Israel, the Munich attack made rapprochement with the Palestinians less likely. Prime Minister Golda Meir agreed to Zvi Zamir's plan to form killer-commando teams to hunt down and kill those responsible for the Munich terror attack. "Send your men," she ordered, and appointed former military intelligence chief Aharon Yariv as her special adviser in the fight against terrorism. By October 1972 the Mossad teams were ready for action; they executed twelve terrorists deemed responsible for the Munich massacre.

Israelis Surprised by Yom Kippur War

OCTOBER 6, 1973 • 2 P.M.

Israelis awakened on Saturday morning, October 6, 1973, prepared to observe Yom Kippur, the holiest day of the Jewish year, in peaceful reverence and prayer. Yet, along its borders, Egyptian and Syrian soldiers were preparing for simultaneous and massive military attacks that would catch the Jewish state by almost total surprise. The opening hours of the Yom Kippur War were among the most treacherous of modern Jewish history.

Yom Kippur is a day so holy that even many non-religious Jews in Israel will not drive, and many who observe no other religious holidays attend synagogue and observe the fast. Usually there is no traffic on the streets, and Israeli national radio and television do not broadcast. On Yom Kippur 1973, Israelis were largely oblivious to what was happening along the country's frontier, unaware of growing government concern about whether the Arabs were preparing for a full-scale military attack.

No one knew that Mossad chief Zvi Zamir had recently left Israel to try to determine how serious the Arab military threat was. At 4:00 A.M. came his ominous cable—war would break out that very day at 6:00 P.M. Perhaps, Zamir cabled senior members of the Israeli Government, if Israel were to inform Egypt and Syria that their intentions were known, they might postpone their planned attack.

The Mossad chief's dramatic message shocked Israeli leaders into a high state of alert. They realized the terrible truth: If Zamir were correct—and they now assumed he was—the Israel Defense Forces had a mere

Israel's Minister of Defense Moshe Dayan.

ISRAEL GOVERNMENT PRESS OFFICE

fourteen hours to prepare for war. Vaunted, celebrated, legendary, the Israeli army had always had at least forty-eight hours warning before impending war, forty-eight hours it needed to muster its reserve troops.

On October 6, 1973, no matter how it would scramble in the coming hours, the IDF was being forced

ISRAEL GOVERNMENT PRESS OFFICE

Reservists gather at base in the North.

into a war with its pants down, crippled, hardly resembling the dynamic and frightening juggernaut of past years and past military victories.

With this sobering realization Moshe Dayan, minister of defense, and other Israeli leaders, tried to gear up for war. By 6:00 A.M., David Elazar, the chief of staff, had instructed the commander of the air force, Benny Peled, to prepare for a preemptive strike against Syrian airfields. But Dayan opposed the preemptive strike, preferring to wait and see whether the Egyptians and Syrians really meant war. Dayan did not want Israel to be blamed for starting a war.

Dayan favored mobilizing only two divisions of troops, Elazar preferred a general mobilization. The two took their disagreement to Prime Minister Golda Meir at 8:00 A.M. in her office in Tel Aviv. Leaning toward the chief of staff's view, at 10:00 A.M. Golda ordered the mobilization of one hundred thousand troops, not the full mobilization that Elazar urged, but far more soldiers than Dayan had advocated. Suddenly, military jeeps appeared in neighborhoods all over Israel, and soldiers entered synagogues to summon men at prayer to their bases.

Meanwhile, Prime Minister Golda Meir agreed with

Defense Minister Moshe Dayan that a preemptive air strike should be ruled out. At noon the cabinet met and rejected the chief of staff's request for a preemptive air strike while retroactively approving the mobilization order. Near 2:00 P.M. Justice Minister Ya'acov Shimshon Shapira asked: "Is there not a danger that the Egyptian attack would be advanced?"

"This is the most relevant question to be asked at this meeting," Dayan said. "That's a danger that worries us a great deal. The Egyptians can certainly do this." As Dayan spoke, news came that Egypt and Syria had opened attack; the Yom Kippur War had begun. Dayan optimistically told journalists that the real war would start the next evening, when reserves reached the front lines. "We will turn the area into a gigantic cemetery."

This war, however, was different. Along the Suez Canal, Egyptian soldiers fired two thousand field guns at the sixteen hapless, largely indefensible Israeli fortifications. Stretched out at five-mile intervals, in bunkers manned by twenty to thirty troops, Israeli soldiers were passing a quiet Yom Kippur day, war the last thing on their minds.

In the first minute the Egyptians fired some ten thousand shells. At the same time, a wave of two hundred forty Egyptian aircraft flew over the canal. Within fifteen minutes, the first wave of some eight thousand Egyptian infantry began crossing the canal. By Egypt's own estimates, a canal crossing would cost ten thousand dead; in fact the Egyptians would lose only two hundred eight soldiers.

Had the IDF mobilized its tanks correctly, they could have stopped the Egyptian canal crossing in its tracks, according to most Israeli military leaders. Yet the tanks were not there, and Israel would pay a steep price. The IDF only had eighteen artillery pieces along the Suez Canal, three of which were knocked out almost at once. And while the Egyptians were storming across the canal, Syrian forces unleashed a massive artillery and air assault as the first of some one thousand four hundred tanks moved over Israeli lines and headed across the Golan Heights toward Israel's northern heartland.

In those first few hours of war, shock and despair began to set in among the Israeli military leadership. The unthinkable was happening. Egyptian and Syrian soldiers who, according to conventional Israeli wisdom after the 1967 Six-Day War, would not dare to fight, were pushing across Israeli lines—and almost no one seemed to be in their way.

The *mechdal*, or "mishap" as the Israelis termed it later, spread like an infectious disease through the entire IDF. Not only were tanks and men not where they should have been, but an entire tank battalion was without binoculars; vehicles had not been maintained; and reservists were greeted upon arrival at their units with confusion and disorder. All the while, the chief of staff was under the illusion that whole tank brigades were deployed when they were not. Five hundred Israeli soldiers died on that first day of fighting.

Through bitter battle the Israelis managed to keep the Syrians and Egyptians from advancing beyond the territory gained in the early stages of the war. On October 8, using the full might of its air force and armor, Israel pushed the Syrians back to the highway to Damascus, coming within thirty-five kilometers of the Syrian capital. After the first week, the Israelis shifted their efforts to the south. By October 14, Israel had coun-

Reservists waiting for transportation after being mobilized on Yom Kipppur.

ISRAEL GOVERNMENT PRESS OFFICE

tered Egypt's main offensive. Israel retained the initiative for the remaining eleven days of the war. On October 16 Ariel "Arik" Sharon led his men across the Suez Canal, moving behind the Egyptian forces; soon an Israeli bridgehead was established on the canal's west bank, and Israeli troops advanced to within one hundred kilometers of Cairo. While Israel eventually succeeded in repulsing the Arabs, the disastrous surprise attacks at the start and the heavy casualties suffered by Israel throughout the fighting left the country stunned and joyless at the war's end.

The human loss was devastating. More than twenty-five hundred Israelis were killed in battle, and another three thousand were wounded—the country's heaviest losses since the War of Independence.

The first few hours of fighting shattered the myth of Israel's military invincibility. Having firmly believed that its military defeat of the Arabs in 1967 would keep the Arabs at bay for decades to come, the Israelis now had to confront a new reality: the peace and security that seemed so close after the Six-Day War were clearly still very far away.

Iraq Fires Scud Missiles at Israel

JANUARY 18, 1991

Even when the Israel Defense Forces (IDF) distributed gas masks to the Israeli population in the fall of 1990, few Israelis believed that it would ever become necessary to use the masks against an Iraqi missile attack. Yet, after the United States attacked Iraq in January 1991, the threatened Iraqi Scud attacks became very real. There was genuine fear in Israel that the Scuds would carry chemical and biological warheads. The Scuds fell on Israel—forty over a six-week period—but none carried nonconventional weapons.

As the Gulf War approached in the early days of 1991, no one in Israel could quite believe it. The President of the United States, George Bush, had organized a coalition that insisted that Saddam Hussein, president of Iraq, remove his soldiers from Kuwait, which they had occupied the previous summer, by a January 15 deadline. Hussein refused to back down. Worst of all, Saddam was threatening to unleash Scud missiles armed with chemical and biological weapons against Israel should war break out between Iraq and the United States.

The thought of an Arab country using chemical warfare against the Jewish state evoked horrifying reminders of another time—World War II—and another country—Nazi Germany—which had unleashed lethal gas against millions of Jews. That the Iraqi chemical weaponry was manufactured in Europe made Israeli memories all the more nightmarish.

The Israeli government decided that the best civil defense would be to have families prepare rooms at home sealed against chemical weapons. The authorities did not believe that existing air-raid shelters would provide adequate protection against biological or chemical warfare.

On Monday and Tuesday, January 14 and 15, Israelis raced around buying masking tape and plastic sheeting to seal a room in their homes where they could stay if necessary. People bought batteries for radios and jammed the supermarkets stocking up on food and drink. There was a frantic rush to get their sealed rooms ready.

By the time the January 15 deadline passed in New York, it was already Wednesday, January 16 in Israel. That evening Israelis watched a chapter of *War and Remembrance*, on television.

In the middle of the night—at 1:50 A.M.—the Americans began their attack on Baghdad. Half an hour later Israel Defense Forces spokesman Nachman Shai announced over the radio that Israelis should go into their sealed rooms at once, take out their gas masks, and try them on. There were no air-raid sirens, nothing to indicate that the Iraqis were about to launch Scuds against Israel. Mild confusion reigned in thousands of Israeli homes as Israelis, who had thought they would never have to use the masks, were now being instructed to try them on!

Israelis later were permitted to leave their sealed rooms, but by dawn on Thursday, civil defense authorities had ordered everyone to stay home. Throughout the day all was quiet, and many Israelis felt upbeat. Perhaps no Scuds would fall on Israel.

The Thursday evening news reported that the United States was doing well in the fighting. One piece of news particularly excited the Israelis: the Americans had knocked out Saddam's missile launchers; but those reports proved erroneous. The Israeli government spokes-

ISRAEL GOVERNMENT PRESS OFFICE

House in South Tel Aviv following an Iraqi Scud attack in 1991.

man cautioned that the early euphoria Israelis were feeling could prove premature; no one could guarantee that Saddam would not attack Israel. Israelis might have to rush into their sealed rooms any instant.

Indeed Saddam attacked Israel in the early morning hours of Friday, January 18. When the air-raid siren went off throughout Israel at 1:50 A.M. Israelis raced to get dressed and reach their sealed rooms. They had been led to believe that they would have five or six hours warning before an attack; in fact there was no more than two or three minutes. The Scud missiles took only five minutes to travel 800 or 1000 kilometers from western Iraq to Israel.

Israel Radio, which had signed off for the night, did not immediately broadcast any information about the attack. It was approximately ten minutes after the siren had sounded that the radio finally returned to the airwaves; that delay added to the confusion. Even when the radio began to report on the incident, it said nothing except that there had been a "missile attack." Frightening thoughts raced through Israeli minds: missiles might be landing at any second, and even if the missiles were conventional—without chemical or biological warheads—the results could be devastating.

On Israel Radio, Ze'ev Schiff, military commentator for the Israeli newspaper *Ha'aretz* was telling the BBC that some missiles had fallen in southern Tel Aviv and farther north along the coast. He could not add much more information. Finally, a little more than an hour later, at about 3:30 A.M. the army spokesman announced by radio that Israelis could take off their gas masks, but could not leave their sealed rooms. Soon there followed an announcement that seven people (later revised upward to twelve) had been slightly wounded but that the missiles (ten had been fired, it was later learned) carried no chemical weapons. Of ten missiles, two landed in the Mediterranean Sea; the other eight landed along the coast, some in Tel Aviv, others in Haifa. It seemed a miracle that so few people had been hurt.

Thanks to CNN's minute-by-minute live coverage, each time there was a Scud attack against Israel, television cameras showed a worldwide audience how Israelis were coping with the assaults. Interviews were conducted at times with Israeli officials wearing gas masks. Israeli censors, eager not to provide information to the Iraqis that might help them improve the accuracy of their Scud attacks, forbade reporters from identifying the exact locations of where the missiles fell in Israel, other than to say, for example, that "several landed in the Tel Aviv region."

Would Israel retaliate? The Americans urged against such a step, arguing that those Arab states now siding with the American forces would be forced to switch sides and support Saddam. Israel chose not to retaliate—for the time being.

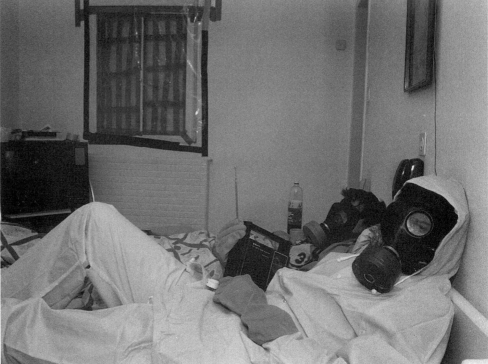

Two boys in gas masks in a sealed room during the Gulf War.

Civil defense authorities issued instructions to stay at home. At 7:40 P.M. that Friday night, the air raid siren went off again. The all clear signal came about thirty minutes later, releasing Israelis from staying in their sealed rooms. Though the radio reported that there had been another missile attack, eventually the IDF spokesman announced that an American satellite had detected signs of Iraqi missile preparations, and that touched off the sirens.

Israelis hoped for a less eventful evening. But the next siren went off at 4:40 A.M., Saturday. Israelis remained in their sealed rooms this time for an hour or so, but it proved a false alarm. At 7:20 A.M. yet another siren went off. This time the missile attack was real, Iraq's second attack on Israel in twenty-nine hours.

After being in their sealed rooms for forty-five minutes, the IDF spokesman announced over the radio that everyone from the town of Hadera and north and everyone from Ashkelon to Kiryat Gat (which was south of Tel Aviv) could take off their gas masks. The rest of the country had to leave theirs on. BBC Radio reported

that Jerusalem had taken four missiles hits, Tel Aviv three. Fifteen minutes later Israelis in the center of the country were told that they were free to take off their masks.

Afterward Israelis learned that ten people had been lightly wounded. Again, there was no evidence that chemical weapons had been used in the attack. Reports that eleven missiles had fallen on Jerusalem proved false.

On Saturday night the United States sent in the first of the Patriots, the most sophisticated anti-missile missile system available. These rockets were meant to shoot down the Scuds before they landed on their targets.

Only five war-related deaths were reported in Israel: three as a result of misuse of gas masks and two from missile hits themselves. In all, Iraq fired forty missiles at Israel between January 18 and February 25, 1991.

Israel's policy of not retaliating against the Scud missile attacks proved correct: the United States and its Arab allies secured its objective of forcing Iraq to remove its troops from Kuwait. Had Israel retaliated, the American-Arab coalition might have disintegrated with unfortunate consequences for Israel.

Violence Erupts in Crown Heights

AUGUST 19, 1991 • 8:20 P.M.

The Crown Heights disturbance of August 1991 represented the most extensive racial unrest in New York City in over twenty years. Although African-Americans and Jews had gotten along with one another for the most part, the Crown Heights affair marked a sharp deterioration in African-American-Jewish relations.

Crown Heights is a Brooklyn neighborhood populated by over two hundred thousand people: African-Americans, Caribbean-Americans, and Lubavitch Hasidim. Though African-Americans and Hasidim lived side-by-side in Crown Heights in relative tranquillity for a number of years, tensions mounted in the late 1980s as African-Americans began to believe that the Hasidim had attained disproportionate political clout and were being given preferential treatment by City Hall.

On the evening of August 19, 1991, at 8:20 P.M., a station wagon that was part of a three-car motorcade carrying the Lubavitcher rebbe reportedly ran a red light at the corner of President Street and Utica Avenue in Crown Heights and then collided into another car. The station wagon struck and pinned two young African-American children beneath its wheels. One of the children, seven-year-old Gavin Cato, died of his injuries; Gavin's cousin, Angelo, was seriously injured.

The police ordered a Hasidic-run ambulance to carry away the station wagon's occupants, igniting a rumor that the ambulance had ignored the two seriously injured children, leaving them to die, and instead helped the occupants of the station wagon. The rumor raced through the crowd like fire, and spectators attacked the station wagon's occupants, shouting: "We don't get any justice . . . we don't get any justice. They're killing our children. We have to stop this . . . Jews get preferential treatment. We don't get any justice." One bystander reportedly said, "Let's go to Kingston Avenue and get the Jews."

The crowd grew in size and moved down President Street, breaking windows and overturning a car along the way. For two-and-a-half hours bottles and rocks flew at the accident scene, as African-Americans and Hasidim shouted racial epithets at one another. At one stage, gunshots were fired.

At about 11 P.M., the disturbance spread as African-American youths wandered through the neighborhood stoning Jewish homes. Around 11:15 P.M., Chaya Sara Popack, a resident of Crown Heights, saw twenty-nine-year old Yankel Rosenbaum, a visiting Hasidic scholar from Australia, walking alone near the corner of President Street and Brooklyn Avenue. She heard someone shout, "There's a Jew. Get the Jews" and saw a group of young African-American males surround Rosenbaum and stab him four times. Three hours later, Yankel Rosenbaum died. Shortly thereafter, police officers in the vicinity saw a large group of people kicking and punching someone, including an African-American male in a red shirt leaning over someone and hitting him with his hands. The crowd dispersed upon hearing the police sirens.

Other police officers, responding to the call for assistance, began a search, locating an African-American male in a red shirt, sixteen-year-old Lemrick Nelson, Jr., A bloodstained folding knife with the word "Killer" inscribed on it was retrieved from Nelson's pants pocket.

Nelson was brought before Yankel Rosenbaum hours

DO THESE PEOPLE GET ALONG TOGETHER? They should. They work together as board members of the Crown Heights Community Corporation, the local anti-poverty agency.

Hassidim and middle class blacks unsigned allies in Crown Heights

(This is the second of a series of three articles on the remarkable achievement of racial and cultural coexistence between shardly contrasting communities in an old area of Brooklyn).

By RAY KESTENBAUM

Stability is the name of the game in Crown Heights by everyone's reckoning, the hassidim, the middle class blacks, the government agencies and the dozens of block associations and organizations, black and white, that have sprung up here over the past decade.

It means preservation - the fight against erosion and crime, against the unabated dumping of welfare families and against roving hostile teenagers like the Jollie Stompers, a nasty fighting gang of 300 who rob, cut up people and occasionally kill. Two of their former members were arrested for the stickup murder of yarmulked grocer Issac Feit. They had this reporter holed in a room, 22 of them, in a local public school, telling him, "We own Crown Heights and pretty soon we're gonna own all of Brooklyn."

Stability means the fight against filth and dope addiction, against unscrupulous landlords and managing agents, against tenant ignorance and apathy and against the influx of agitators and racial polarizers. Stability also means the quieting of people's fears and suspicions, the enabling of diverse ethnic groups to work together even if they don't love each other, the building of confidence and use of government resources so that Crown Heights does not become another Brownsville in 10 years.

Crown Heights the front-line battle

To New York's Jewish community-at-large, Crown Heights represents the frontline battle in the survival of Jewish communities. "If Crown Heights goes," a Brooklynite tells me, "Flatbush and Borough Park are in for a lot of trouble. We're already getting pushed toward the sea." It is not for naught that the Rebbe advised Congressman Mario Biaggi during a campaign visit to secure and hold a threatened Italian neighborhood in the Bronx at all costs.

To the Lubavitch-Chabad community, Crown Heights is the capital of a spiritual movement that numbers in the hundreds of thousands in communities in Israel and the

Soviet Union included. The hassid cannot function as a hassid without a community. It is the domicile of his religious structures - his synagogues, yeshivas, mikvas (ritulariums), glatt kosher markets and beth dins - and, of course, his rebbe. For this reason, the hassidim are less mobile than Reform, Conservative or even Modern Orthodox Jews.

To the middle class black community, Crown Heights is the black man's Westchester and Kew Gardens, a giant step from the ghettos of Bedford Stuyvesant and Harlem, a showcase neighborhood boasting the Brooklyn Museum, Brooklyn's Central Public Library, the Children's Museum, stately churches and cultural centers, tree-lined streets, the Medgar Evers College of the City University system and the lovely Botanic Gardens.

But the hassidic and middle class black area, a 36-square-block enclave of greater Crown Heights, has become washed in with poorer elements, illegal aliens, multi-problem families and persons untrained in apartment living. The Federal census indicates a complete reversal in one decade of Crown Heights' racial composition. Whereas in 1960, the black to white population ratio was 30 to 70, by 1970 it became 70 to 30.

The newcomers have included American blacks, Jamaicans, West Indians, Haitians, Barbadans, Panamanians, Puerto Ricans and a smattering of Hawaiians. While many of these people had resources when they arrived, others were at or near the poverty level and some did not bring with them the know-how of big city living. Within the past 10 years the percentage of welfare recipients in the area rose from six to about 18, hassidim included in the count.

The Caribbean people, with their strong island identities, see themselves as separate from the American blacks, more secure in their sense of identity. They do not

fraternize much with them or with the French-speaking Haitians, who have their own community in Crown Heights and East Flatbush numbering close to 25,000. More than half the Haitian community here are reported by a high government official to be here illegally, unwilling and unable to return to dictatorial Haiti. As a result, they are probably the most exploited group here.

Because of their inbredness and different cultures, the black groups have been either divisive or disinterested in local issues. Former State Senator Waldaba Steward, who says he represents the interests of the poor black people of Crown Heights, blames his shattering re-election defeat to Vander L. Beatty on the voting apathy of his constituency. But Steward, a Panamanian who some hassidim charge is anti-Semitic and the man behind Sonny Carson's 1970 takeover of the Community Corporation, plans to run again in November, especially now with Beatty's reputation on the skids following charges that his wife forged signatures in the recent school board elections.

One asks how come the hassidim, who number only 15,000 out of 230,000 in greater Crown Heights, keep copping the Community Corporation elections and thereby maintain control of the area's anti-poverty structure. The answer is, for one thing, the lower income blacks have been unable to muster a consolidated opinion or vote. For another, the black home-owners don't vote in the poverty elections. They don't want the poverty stigma. In fact, the affluent blacks prefer to have all government structures out of Crown Heights. "Let the poor

(Continued on page 10)

Hasidic and African-American residents of Crown Heights show the tensions of the day on their faces.

had attacked him. "C.T." was later released and never charged. Nelson was arrested, and his clothes were searched. Three dollar-bills that appeared to have blood on them were discovered in the same pocket in which the knife was found.

According to the two detectives who questioned Nelson, Nelson described his participation in the attack on Rosenbaum and admitted that he had stabbed the Jewish man. On August 26, 1991, Nelson was indicted on two counts of murder in the second degree and one count of criminal possession of a weapon in the fourth degree, but at his trial, which lasted from September 22, 1992, to October 29, 1992, he was acquitted of all charges relating to the Rosenbaum murder. The jury included six African-Americans, four Hispanics, and two whites. The fact that not one member of the Jewish community, which accounted for sixteen percent of the population of Brooklyn, served on the jury led some to believe that anti-Semitism was a factor in the verdict. The Jewish community was further troubled when on the evening after the verdict, eleven of the jurors went to a Brooklyn restaurant to meet with the defense counsel, Arthur Lewis. Upon their arrival at the restaurant, the jurors were greeted as well by the defendant, his mother, photographers, and reporters; it appeared that the jurors were celebrating the acquittal. The prosecutors and many members of the public were deeply offended by this gathering.

No one else had been arrested or charged in connection with the Rosenbaum murder. Members of the Jewish community who thought the case against Lemrick Nelson was a strong one took to the streets in protest. Hundreds of Jewish demonstrators closed the Brooklyn Bridge on the evening of the verdict, marching and chanting, "We want justice. We want justice."

Councilwoman Mary Pinkett, an African-American and a Democrat from Brooklyn, stated that she shared the sadness of the Jewish people adding: "There is no

before he died. Other youths had been brought to Rosenbaum, but he had not identified any of them as his attackers. When Nelson was presented to Rosenbaum, Rosenbaum identified Nelson, cursed him, and spat at him. Rosenbaum also identified a fifteen-year-old youth, "C.T.," as a member of the group that pogrom in Crown Heights. We are just as dedicated to finding the murderer of Yankel Rosenbaum [as are the Jews]."

A few days later, on Sunday, November 1, 1991, nearly five thousand people gathered outside Lubavitch headquarters in Crown Heights to protest the verdict in the Nelson case. The victim's brother, Norman Rosenbaum, declared that the murder symbolized anti-Semitic violence permitted in Crown Heights and throughout the United States.

The Crown Heights affair lay dormant for some time until 1994, when Federal officials, responding to public pressure from political leaders and prominent Hasidic Jews, charged Nelson with violating Rosenbaum's civil rights by inflicting at least one of the four stab wounds

he suffered. Convicted in 1997 on those charges, Nelson was sentenced to nineteen years in prison on April 1, 1998. Though Nelson continued to insist on his innocence, "A measure of justice was at last achieved," said Michael Miller, director of the New York Jewish Community Relations Council.

Also convicted was Charles Price, charged with inciting the mob that attacked Yankel Rosenbaum. Price was sentenced in July 1998 to twenty-one years in prison.

New York City mayor Rudy Guiliani apologized to Crown Heights residents and agreed to pay 1.35 million dollars to those residents to settle a civil suit they had brought. The suit charged the city with not protecting them during the August 1991 riots.

Yitzhak Rabin Assassinated

NOVEMBER 4, 1995 • 9:40 P.M.

Israeli prime minister Yitzhak Rabin described the event as one of the happiest evenings of his life. He was referring to a peace rally that was winding down in Tel Aviv on November 4, 1995, at which one hundred thousand Israelis demonstrated their support for his handling of the Middle East peace process. Moments after Rabin left the rally, a lone assassin, twenty-five-year-old law student Yigal Amir, fired three shots at Rabin, killing the prime minister.

It was Saturday, November 4, 1995, 9:35 P.M. and Israel's prime minister, Yitzhak Rabin, was standing on the stage at a Tel Aviv peace rally. The sight of so many enthusiastic supporters of his peace efforts made Rabin feel very good. His Middle East peacemaking over the previous three years had led to two Israeli-Palestinian agreements and an Israeli-Jordanian peace treaty. Israel, however, had become divided over the peace process because so many Israelis had been killed in terror attacks, and Israel seemed willing to relinquish its presence on the West Bank. Some Israelis on the extreme political right called Yitzhak Rabin a traitor, a murderer. Others calmly discussed whether Rabin should be killed in order to prevent him from permitting Israeli troops to pull out from the West Bank and the Gaza Strip. Rabin refused to withdraw from public life or take any special precautions.

Looking into the sea of smiling faces and at the huge, colorful, pro-peace placards at Tel Aviv's Kings of Israel Square, the seventy-three-year-old Rabin felt a new self-confidence; here was proof, despite the disappointing polls showing the peace process in disrepute, that he

Yitzhak Rabin.

and his policies had strong backing. In this buoyant mood, a relaxed, contented Rabin joined the crowd in singing "Shir ha-Shalom," The "Song of Peace," holding the lyrics in his hand.

Just over an hour earlier Rabin had spoken briefly to the crowd:

I was a military man for twenty-seven years. I waged war as long as there was no chance for peace. I believe there is now a chance for peace, a great chance, and we must take advantage of it for those standing here, and for those who are not here—and they are many. I have always believed that the majority of the people want peace and are ready to take a chance for peace.

It was 9:36 P.M. and Rabin, tucking the leaflet with the lyrics into his breast pocket, began saying his farewells. He then walked toward his waiting car.

A tiny segment of the country viewed Yitzhak Rabin as selling out Israel to the Arabs. A tiny fringe of right-wing, religious extremists portrayed Rabin on posters at protest rallies with a red-checkered kaffiyeh on his head, insinuating that he was demonically colluding with the Arabs. A month before the peace rally, someone held up a placard at a protest rally showing Rabin wearing a German SS uniform, suggesting that the prime minister was no better than the Nazis. The Tel Aviv peace rally was designed to marginalize the extremists by providing concrete proof that Israel's peace camp comprised a vocal majority.

Yigal Amir was a third-year law student at Bar-Ilan University in Tel Aviv, who told friends that he felt compelled to stop the peace process. He had been stalking Rabin for months. Amir arrived at the rally at 8:10 P.M., just as Rabin was speaking to the crowd. Though police, soldiers, and guard dogs mixed with the crowds,

Past and present U.S. Presidents stand solemnly before Rabin's coffin.

the armed Amir walked around the huge square undetected. Nearing the stage, he walked down the twenty steps to the area where Rabin's new, heavily fortified Cadillac was parked. When asked who he was, coolly, casually, Amir identified himself as a driver for one of the politicians attending the rally.

At 9:40 P.M., Rabin descended the steps to his car; he

seemed in a hurry. Crowds stood off to both sides. The rear door of the Cadillac was open, and Rabin was about to slide in. From amidst the crowd, a figure ran toward the prime minister.

When he was within two feet of Rabin, Amir aimed his pistol and fired. He got off three shots. Two of the three hollow-point bullets smashed into Rabin. One

Yitzhak Rabin signs the Agreement on the Gaza Strip and the Jericho Area, in Cairo, May 4, 1994.

bullet ruptured the prime minister's spleen; a second severed the major arteries in his chest and shattered his spinal cord, drenching the leaflet with the lyrics in his pocket in blood. The third shot grazed one of the guards. As Amir pulled the trigger, he said: "It's nothing. Nothing. I'm joking. It's not real. It's not real." Rabin gazed confusedly in Amir's direction, clutched his stomach, and fell forward. Menachem Damti, the prime minister's driver, who had been waiting near the car to help Leah Rabin, the prime minister's wife, into it, heard the shots and rushed to the driver's seat.

Yoram Rubin, a security man for Rabin, was lightly wounded in the arm by one of Amir's bullets. Believing that the attack might not be over, Rubin fell on top of Rabin. "Listen to me," the security man shouted at the prime minister, "and only to me. We're going to get up now and get into the car and leave." Rabin did not respond, but somehow the guard managed to pull the prime minister up and push him into the car.

After rushing off in the direction of Ichilov Hospital,

a few minutes drive from the rally, Damti shouted back to Rabin: "Are you hurt? Are you hurt?" Rabin answered: "I think so. But it's not bad. It doesn't hurt so much." But then the prime minister began to breathe with difficulty, and the guard, though wounded himself and losing strength, gave the prime minister artificial respiration.

Within seconds of the shooting, a swarm of police and soldiers grabbed Yigal Amir and thrust him against an adjacent building, forming a human wall around him.

Rabin's car arrived at Ichilov Hospital at 9:45 P.M. Israel Television interrupted its broadcast at 10:20 P.M. to inform the country of the shooting. A few minutes after 11:00 P.M. the doctors who had been operating on Rabin looked at one another, tears in their eyes, and stopped. The prime minister was dead. Dr. Gaby Barbash, head of the hospital, approached Rabin's family: "I'm sorry, the prime minister is no longer with us." At 11:15 P.M., Israel Television anchorman Haim Yavin interrupted an interview to announce to the nation that the prime minister had died.

Leah Rabin wanted to see her husband. The doctors told her it would not be easy for her to view the body, but she insisted. The doctors agreed. She was accompanied by her daughter Dalia and Dalia's husband, Avi, as well as Shimon Peres, who became the acting prime minister immediately and, soon after, the prime minister. Leah approached her fallen husband first. His body was draped with a white sheet that reached up to his shoulders. His lips were swollen, his forehead bright red from the hemorrhaging. Leah kissed him on the forehead and then spoke to him. Peres gave Rabin a long kiss on the forehead.

The next day Rabin's body lay in state in the plaza in front of the Knesset in Jerusalem. Over the next twenty-four hours, one million Israelis, one quarter of Israel's Jewish population, filed past the coffin. Leaders from eighty-five countries assembled in Jerusalem for the funeral, among them American president Bill Clinton; Egyptian president Hosni Mubarak, making his first visit to Israel; and Jordan's King Hussein, making his first journey to Jerusalem in twenty-eight years.

Two days after the shooting Rabin was buried at Mt. Herzl cemetery in Jerusalem.

"Look at the picture," said President Clinton, towering over the other leaders and wearing a yarmulke; he was referring to the sight of red-checkered kaffiyehs, flowing Arab robes and the Western-style dress of other leaders who were joined by some four thousand mourners. To anyone who wanted to know what Yitzhak Rabin had done for his country, the answer could be found in this sea of world leaders, many of whom came from countries that had refused to have political relations with Israel until only recently. The most memorable eulogy of the eleven offered that day was delivered by Noa Ben-Artzi, Rabin's eighteen-year-old granddaughter, who fought back tears to say: "Grandpa, you were the pillar of fire in front of the camp and now we are left in the camp alone, in the dark; and we are so cold and so sad . . . "

MOMENTS
of
CREATIVITY

Judah ha-Nasi Edits the Mishnah

200 C.E.

> Judah ha-Nasi—Judah the Patriarch—was the leader of the Jewish community of the Land of Israel during the early third century C.E. The leading religious scholar of his time, he is best known for his compilation of the Mishnah, the written codification of rapidly developing oral traditions. The Mishnah solidified the work, begun by Yohanan ben Zakkai at Yavneh after the destruction of the Second Temple, of transforming Judaism from a religion focused on cultic worship to a religion centered on law and learning. It quickly became an authoritative text, the basis of commentary in its own right in a process that eventually generated the Talmud.

The period that followed the Bar Kokhba revolt was rich in oral rabbinic scholarship and also, for the first few years, dangerous for scholars. After Bar Kokhba's defeat, the Romans executed many of the best scholars, among them the greatest rabbi of the time, Rabbi Akiba, who had publicly supported Bar Kokhba. After Hadrian's death in 138 C.E., however, conditions became easier for the Jews of the Land of Israel. Hadrian's successor, Antoninus Pius, revoked Hadrian's suppression of Jewish observance and teaching and practiced a policy of tolerance. He gave the Jews under Roman domination, both in the Land of Israel and in the diaspora, internal autonomy under a re-established patriarchate.

The students of Rabbi Akiba emerged from hiding and established a center of study and teaching at Usha in the Galilee, where they continued the development of the Oral Torah; Rabbi Akiba's initial steps toward a systematic arrangement of oral traditions were contin-

ued by his disciple, Rabbi Meir. A descendant of Hillel, Simeon ben Gamaliel, was appointed to the office of patriarch (nasi). Thus, the foundation was laid for the editing of the Mishnah under Simeon ben Gamaliel's son and successor, Judah ha-Nasi.

Judah ha-Nasi was not only the patriarch but also the foremost scholar of his day. So outstanding was his scholarship that he was known simply as Rabbi; because his religious observance and piety equaled his scholarship, some called him Rabbenu ha-Kadosh, our holy teacher. He was held in such esteem that it was said of him, "From the time of Moses to the time of Rabbi, Torah and greatness were never so concentrated in one person."

Judah ha-Nasi held office for fifty years. After studying under disciples of Rabbi Akiba, in the Galilee, he set up his academy at Bet Shearim, not far from what is now the Israeli port city of Haifa. Because of his health, he spent the last seventeen years of his life in the higher altitude of Sepphoris. During his final years, he was confined to bed. He told his disciples near the time of his death that he had given all of his strength to the Torah but was pleased to say that he had never acquired anything material in return. He died in 217 C.E. and was buried in Bet Shearim. His tomb became a site of Jewish pilgrimage.

Judah ha-Nasi's authority extended throughout the Jewish community of Palestine, in both the north and south, as well as to those areas of the diaspora under Roman control. As leader of the Sanhedrin, he appointed judges and teachers. Because he saw his task as the economic as well as religious rebuilding of the Jewish community, his interpretations of laws that affected the economic life of the community, laws concerning farm-

Sculpture of Judah ha-Nasi being lifted by angels to heaven. Sculpture by Milton Horn located at the West Suburban Temple Har-Zion in River Forest, Illinois.

Hebrew to his family, friends, and students; to Roman officials, he spoke Greek. It was said that even his maidservants knew Hebrew and could explain the meanings of rare words. He valued education above all else, stating, "It is the unlearned who bring trouble into the world." One historian has called him "an intellectual elitist of the most uncompromising kind." Yet he can also be seen as a precursor of Eliezer Ben-Yehuda, who almost single-handedly introduced the modern Hebrew language into the Jewish community of Palestine in the early twentieth century.

According to legend, Judah ha-Nasi became a close friend of one of the Antonine emperors—Caracalla or, more plausibly, Marcus Aurelius. It is hard to believe that such a personal relationship could have occurred, though the former emperor visited Palestine in 199 and 215 C.E. The legends were probably created to indicate that Judah ha-Nasi and the Roman emperor were equals.

Unquestionably, Judah ha-Nasi's crowning achievement was the compilation of the Mishnah, which preserved in writing a wide range of oral teachings by earlier and contemporary rabbis and teachers and determined which legal decisions were authoritative. Though scholars in Jewish studies today cite references to later teachers as evidence that closure of the Mishnah was not complete in Judah ha-Nasi's lifetime, they credit him with the major work of editing. The word *mishnah* means "to repeat" because its teachings were—and still are—studied through repetition, memorized, and then recited from memory.

The Mishnah is organized under six broad categories, or "orders" (*sedarim*), each of which is divided into tractates. The six categories are: Zera'im (seeds), which deals with agricultural laws (the first tractate, *Berakhot*, deals with prayers and blessings and serves as an introduction to the Mishnah); Mo'ed (appointed times), the laws of the Sabbath, feasts, and fast days; Nashim (women), the laws governing marriage, divorce, and

ing, for example, tended to be lenient. A wealthy man with large landholdings, he opened his private storehouses to the Jewish community in times of famine, though it is said that he gave preference to scholars.

Indeed, he used his wealth mainly to support scholars, the best of whom were rewarded with places at the most important table in his hall. Scholars were also exempted from paying taxes. Though Aramaic was the vernacular of the Jews of Palestine, Judah ha-Nasi wrote the Mishnah in Hebrew and insisted on speaking only vows; Nezikin (damages), civil and criminal law; Kodashim (holy things), the laws of sacrifices and consecrated objects; and Toharot (purities), the laws of ritual purity and impurity.

The order Nezikin contains the popular tractate *Avot* ("Fathers"), which is included in the prayer book (*siddur*). *Avot* sets forth the basic principle of the Oral Torah—that is, the chain of transmission from Moses to the Mishnah—and offers, for the guidance of both ordinary Jews and scholars, statements on ethics and studies by major teachers. Rabbi Simeon ben Gamaliel, for example, said, "The world is established on three principles: truth, justice, and peace" (*Avot* 1:18). Chapter 6, known as "Praise of the Torah" (*kinyan Torah*), is now considered to be a later addition and not really part of the Mishnah; it attributes seven qualities to the righteous—beauty, strength, wealth, honor, wisdom, longevity, and children—and asserts that they "were all realized in Judah ha-Nasi and his sons" (*Avot* 6:8).

The Mishnah is not a commentary on the Bible but for the most part a code of laws, arranged by topic. It gives detailed instructions for carrying out biblical laws originally stated only in general terms. For example, in the section on farming (Zera'im), one tractate deals with the precise regulations for observing the biblical command that a farmer leave the border of his field unharvested in order that the poor might be free to gather whatever is left there. The Mishnah gained its authority through its use as a legal code by Judah ha-Nasi's government, though it also contains sections of nonlegal material, or *aggadah*, such as narratives about rabbis and elaborate scriptural interpretations. Yet it is more than a code of laws. As Jacob Neusner has pointed out, the Mishnah soon became "a principal holy book of Judaism," studied, memorized, and subjected to close analyses in a continuation of the Oral Torah that culminated in the Palestinian and Babylonian Talmuds.

Babylonian Talmud Is Finalized

500 C.E.

> *The Babylonian Talmud has set the standards by which Jews have lived throughout the diaspora. Its study has been the means of educating Jewish leaders and maintaining a high degree of learning even among ordinary Jews. According to Jacob Neusner, the Babylonian Talmud "has formed the definitive statement of Judaism from the time of its closure to the present day."*

Far from bringing closure to the Oral Torah, the compilation of the Mishnah marked the beginning of a new period of creativity in which the Mishnah itself became the focus of study in a process that, several centuries later, produced the Palestinian and Babylonian Talmuds. That the Mishnah would be memorized was taken for granted. What distinguished the new methods of study is that the Mishnah was discussed and analyzed, section by section, to determine its meaning and formulate new legal interpretations. This dialectical method of study, conducted and eventually written in the spoken language of the people, Aramaic, resulted in the commentary on the Mishnah known as the Gemara—a word that, in Babylonian Aramaic, means not only "to complete," as in Hebrew, but "to learn"; together, the Mishnah and Gemara constitute the Talmud. Teachings of rabbis dating from the time of the Mishnah or earlier, but not collected in that work, also continued to be transmitted; known as *baraitot*, they were often cited to explain passages in the Mishnah.

In the Land of Israel, there were major academies in Tiberias, Caesarea, and Lydda, in addition to Judah ha-Nasi's own academy at Sepphoris. Gradually, however, the centers of scholarship became independent of the patriarchate, for, though the patriarchate grew in political power, the later descendants of Judah ha-Nasi failed to equal his high level of scholarship. At Sepphoris, therefore, Judah ha-Nasi's successors as heads of the academy were not his descendants but his students. The first was Rabbi Efes, from southern Judea; he was succeeded by Rabbi Hanina bar Hama, a student of Judah ha-Nasi who, in his middle years, had come to Palestine from Babylonia.

Other notable Palestinian rabbis were Rabbi Yohanan bar Nappaha—"the blacksmith's son," usually referred to simply as Rabbi Yohanan—and his brother-in-law, Rabbi Simeon ben Lakish (usually called Resh Lakish), a fierce debater whom Rabbi Yohanan had converted from a gladiator's to a scholar's career. Rabbi Yohanan, who died in 279 C.E., taught at Sepphoris and later at Tiberias. Because he developed and disseminated the basic method to be used in analyzing the Mishnah, his scholarship gained recognition in Babylonia as well.

By the fourth century C.E., the academies of the land of Israel were in decline. Even in Judah ha-Nasi's time, there had been frequent comings and goings of scholars between the Land of Israel and Babylonia; indeed, Judah ha-Nasi had trained (but refused to ordain) one of the most influential Babylonian teachers, Abba Arikha ("the tall"), usually called Rav. After the generation of Rabbi Yohanan, most of the noted rabbis who taught in the Land of Israel either had studied for a while in Babylonia or were Babylonians by birth.

Moreover, Jewish life as a whole was in decline in the Land of Israel. Though it had no immediate effect, the Roman empire's adoption of Christianity as the state religion in 312 eventually led to new forms of intolerance. The patriarchate was also in decline, and there was renewed friction between the Jews of Palestine and the Roman military that led to the destruction of the academies of Tiberias, Sepphoris, and Lydda. Many Jews immigrated to Babylonia, which replaced the land of Israel as the center of Jewish learning.

The editing of the Palestinian Talmud is traditionally ascribed to Rabbi Yohanan bar Nappaha; because of his attention to problems of method, he can be credited with laying the groundwork for it. It is more probable, however, from the dates of the rabbis and historical events mentioned in it, that the final editing took place in the first half of the fifth century, probably in Tiberias. The Palestinian Talmud contains Gemara for only thirty-nine of the sixty-three tractates of the Mishnah; there are also many inconsistencies and repetitions. Therefore, it has been considered inferior to the Babylonian Talmud, has never had the latter's authority, and is seldom studied. Many modern academic scholars maintain, however, that despite appearances the Palestinian Talmud was systematically edited, though not by easily recognizable principles.

As learning declined in the Land of Israel, the Babylonian academies continued to grow in quality and importance. The academy at Nehardea was one of the earliest. After studying with Judah ha-Nasi, Rav taught for a time at Nehardea and served briefly as its head. Rav did not remain at Nehardea, however, but appointed as head of the academy his friend Samuel, a native of Nehardea who was also known for his knowledge of medicine and astronomy. Rav went on to found the academy at Sura, where he established the months of Adar and Elul as periods of gathering, or *kallah*, during which students from many areas of the Jewish world joined his students in their study of the Mishnah. The academy at Sura remained, for several centuries, the most influential academy in Babylonia. When the city of Nehardea was destroyed in the third century, during a period of conflict between Persia and Rome, its academy found a new home in Mahoza under one of Samuel's students; it never regained its former prominence, however, but was eclipsed by the newer academy at Pumbedita, which soon acquired a reputation for subtlety and became Sura's chief rival.

By the fifth century C.E., the need to put the oral traditions of the Babylonian academies into written form became apparent, especially in the face of increasing intolerance of other religions by the Zoroastrian rulers of Persia. According to traditional accounts, the editor of the Babylonian Talmud was Rav Ashi, who presided over the academy at Sura for fifty-two years until his death in 427 C.E. During this period, it is said, he used the months of *kallah* to review the entire Mishnah twice. According to tradition, Rav Ashi's successors used these discussions as the basis of the Babylonian Talmud, to which they added Rav Ashi's own opinions and those of subsequent teachers. The work is presented as a record of oral discussions. Modern scholarship suggests that several generations of anonymous editors succeeded Rav Ashi—a probability that makes the final form of the Babylonian Talmud less of a "moment," perhaps, but more strongly the collective effort of an entire rabbinic culture.

The Babylonian Talmud contains Gemara for thirty-six and a half of the Mishnah's sixty-three tractates—two and a half fewer than the Palestinian Talmud. Nevertheless, the Babylonian Talmud is a much longer work than the Palestinian Talmud, both more detailed in its commentary and more inclusive of nonlegal material. It consists of approximately one-third *halakhah*, or legal rulings, and two-thirds *aggadah*; the latter includes material that might be introduced as digressions in halakhic discussions, such as *midrash*—stories and legends that elaborate on and interpret biblical stories; biographical and anecdotal material about rabbis; theological discussion; and information about medicine and other sciences in Babylonia and about Jewish and non-Jewish customs.

The Babylonian Talmud has gained its supremacy over the Palestinian Talmud partly because of its relevance to diaspora Jews. For example, it deals extensively with commerce, a common occupation of Jews in Babylonia; such topics as prayer, the holidays, and family life are also discussed in terms relevant to daily life in the diaspora. Several of the Mishnah tractates without Gemara in the Babylonian Talmud deal with laws that could be practiced only in the Land of Israel, such as those relating to agriculture; the main exception is Kodashim, which contains laws relating to the Temple sacrifices. It has a Gemara in the Babylonian Talmud because, in the absence of the Temple, studying the sacrifices is traditionally held to be the equivalent of performing them.

Over the centuries, the Babylonian Talmud has served to unify Jews living in many cultures and has helped them become a homogeneous community in both study and practice. Its two languages, Hebrew and Aramaic, became the literary languages of later Jews, and its halakhic rulings made them a homogeneous community of religious observance. The stories, parables, and ethical maxims found in talmudic discussions helped shape Jewish values. Jacob Neusner describes the Babylonian Talmud as "the Torah par excellence, the Torah through which Israel would read both Scripture and Mishnah."

Masoretic Text Is Introduced

900 C.E.

As anyone who has prepared to become a Bar or Bat Mitzvah knows, the Torah scroll contains only the letters of the words, without divisions into chapters and without the vowel signs, punctuation, and notation for cantillation that must be known if the text is to be read correctly. Ancient scrolls of the Prophets and Writings also lacked this information, which was transmitted orally. The Masoretes, who worked from the seventh to the early tenth century, are responsible for our knowledge of these traditions in written form. Thanks to the revival of interest in their textual scholarship during the Renaissance, when the first Hebrew Bible was printed, the annotations necessary for correct reading appear in printed texts of the Bible today.

The Hebrew word *masorah* means "tradition," from a root meaning "to transmit." The Masoretes, who established the text of the Hebrew Bible almost as we know it today, were preservers of tradition. They were the heirs of the *soferim*, or scribes, who not only copied the text onto parchment scrolls and preserved special features of the writing, such as letters that are smaller or larger than the others or have dots over them, but also transmitted orally instructions concerning the correct pronunciation and cantillation, which are not apparent from the scroll. The Masoretes wrote the text of the Hebrew Bible in parchment codices in which they indicated the vowel signs, punctuation, and cantillation signs; the last, based for the most part on the sentence structure, served as the basis for the later study of Hebrew grammar. The Masoretes also added marginal notations on the textual variants of the

many manuscripts they examined and indicated which were correct. The oldest text to contain masoretic annotations is the Saint Petersburg Codex of 916 C.E.

The Masoretes worked mainly in Palestine between the seventh and early tenth centuries, after the Muslim conquest of Palestine between 636 and 638 C.E. brought peace to the land and allowed the academies in Galilee to reopen. Tiberias became their main center of activity. Masoretic schools also arose within the Jewish academies of higher learning in the Babylonian cities of Sura and Pumbedita, but the Babylonians were quick to acknowledge the superiority of the Palestinian scholars in establishing the correct text of the Scriptures.

In Tiberias, there were two prominent schools of Masoretes—the Ben Asher school and the Ben Naphtali school. Moses ben Asher and his son Aaron were the two most famous members of the Ben Asher family. Moses ben Asher's codex of the second and third parts of the Bible, the Prophets and Writings, was discovered in the Karaite Synagogue in Cairo; the colophon indicates that it was written in 896 C.E. Aaron ben Asher also edited the Hebrew Bible and provided it with vowel points, cantillation signs, and masoretic notes in the text. Aaron's codex, because it contained the entire Bible, including the Torah, is of major significance. Known as the *Keter of Aleppo*, or "Crown of Aleppo," it came into the possession of the Jewish community in Aleppo, Syria; it is also known as the Aleppo Codex. Maimonides, in the twelfth century, declared it to be the best version and incorporated its annotation into his own copy of the Torah—a fact that was sufficient to establish the prestige of the Ben Asher text. Since then, the Bible editions of the Ben Ashers have been adopted by the

Jewish community at large. The complete Ben Asher text, on which the family worked for five generations, was copied about 1010 by a Masorete named Samuel ben Jacob; it is found in Saint Petersburg.

The preeminent member of the Ben Naphtali school of Masoretes was the tenth-century scholar Moses ben David ben Naphtali. Unfortunately, his work and the other edited versions of the Bible produced by the Ben Naphtali school have, for the most part, disappeared. Only fragments have been discovered; these reveal differences from the system of punctuation and accentuation advocated by the Ben Ashers. An 1105 C.E. manuscript by the Ben Naphtali family, known as the Reuchlin Codex, is now in Karlsruhe, Germany.

The masoretic text again became an object of attention during the sixteenth century, when Daniel Bomberg, a Christian printer in Venice, printed the first Hebrew Bible. He decided to include the masoretic annotations but found that the manuscripts contained copyists' errors that had been introduced between the tenth century, when the Masoretes completed their work, and his own time. He commissioned a Tunisian Jew, Jacob ben Hayyim ibn Adonijah, to examine the manuscripts and produce a definitive version of the masoretic text. This version, which Bomberg included in his second edition, in 1525, remained, for many centuries, the standard masoretic text. Most contemporary biblical scholars believe that there is no single version of the Bible that can be accurately identified as the standard masoretic text. Nevertheless, Jacob ben Hayyim's edition remains the model for printed Bibles today.

Set in columns in the Aberdeen Bible, Italy, 1493, are the masoretic differences between the Ben-Asher and Ben-Naphtali schools.

Rashi Composes Biblical Commentaries

1100

Solomon ben Isaac, the medieval French rabbi known as Rashi, wrote commentaries on the Bible and the Babylonian Talmud that are consulted by both scholars and ordinary Jews even today. His concise, lucid explanations of the plain meaning of the text have made both works accessible despite their difficulty. Translated into Latin, his commentary on the Bible influenced Christian scholars as well.

Rabbi Solomon ben Isaac, best known by the acronym Rashi, was born in Troyes, France, in 1040. On his mother's side, he was a descendant of the mishnaic sage Rabbi Yohanan the Sandalmaker. Rashi's father was a scholar whom he cited in his writings. Though little is known of his childhood, Rashi's fame as an adult made him the subject of several legends. According to one, he cast a precious gem into the sea to avoid giving it to Christians who wanted it for what he considered to be idolatrous purposes. Another legend relates that a heavenly voice told Rashi's father he would have a son who would enlighten the world with his intelligence. According to yet another legend, Rashi's mother was miraculously rescued while she was pregnant with him. When a stranger threatened her on a narrow street, she pressed herself against a wall and was saved by a niche that suddenly formed to conceal her.

Legends aside, Rashi was educated in Worms and then in Mainz. His education centered on the basics: Bible, Talmud, midrash; he also studied those works of grammar and lexicography that were available in Hebrew. He was married at age sixteen, while he was still a student; he and his wife had three daughters.

Medallion with the likeness of Rashi.

Rashi returned to Troyes when he was twenty-five years old. Despite his youth, he was appointed the religious judge of the community. Like the rabbis of earlier times, however, Rashi earned his living from a secular trade; he was a wine merchant and the owner of several vineyards. It is no surprise that Rashi's commentaries often refer to details of medieval commerce, technology, law, and social custom. He founded his own talmudic academy around 1100 and attracted students from far and wide, but his best students were his relatives. All three of his daughters married important religious scholars and are said to have had, in their own right, a degree of scholarly attainment unusual among women of that era. His sons-in-law and grandsons completed the commentaries Rashi left unfinished at the time of his death. His grandsons, with other French and German scholars, belonged to the school of talmudic interpreters known as the tosafists ("supplementers"). Their annotations, based on Rashi's commentary but often modifying it, are printed opposite Rashi's commentary on pages of the Talmud.

Rashi was the first to write unified commentaries on the Bible and on the Babylonian Talmud. His concise, lucid style made both texts accessible to ordinary Jews who were not scholars but for whom study was an important aspect of religious observance. Even today, many Jews study the weekly Torah portion by reading a line or two from the text and then consulting Rashi's commentary. Rashi's biblical commentary focuses on the plain sense of the text, the *peshat*. He did not oppose the use of symbolic interpretations—the *derash*—but he resorted to it only after he was satisfied that he had adequately explained the ordinary meaning. "As for me," he once wrote, "I am concerned only with the literal meaning of the Scriptures and with such *aggadot* as explain the biblical passages in a fitting manner." He appears to have relied to a great extent on Targum Onkelos, a second-century Aramaic translation of the Bible. Other sources include a wide range of midrashic texts of the same period, as well as the teachings of his immediate predecessors in Worms and Mainz and Rabbi Moses the Maggid ("preacher") of Narbonne.

Rashi's method was to introduce a topic and then to explain the text phrase by phrase, giving the meaning, context, and practical relevance of the passage in question. For example, in the phrase, "You shall love the Lord your God with all your heart," Rashi explains "You shall love" as meaning that people should perform God's commandments out of love, not fear. His commentary on the much-disputed opening verse of Genesis is of special importance. He focuses on the syntax of the opening verse and concludes that the first words are not to be construed as "In the beginning, God created. . . " but, instead, as "When God began to create. . . . " Thus, Rashi maintained a neutral position in the theological debate over whether the biblical creation coincided with the origin of the universe.

The reputation of Rashi's commentaries quickly spread throughout Europe. The first dated Hebrew-language book to be printed (as opposed to being a manuscript) was a Bible with Rashi's commentary; it appeared in Italy in 1465. The typography used for Rashi's commentary is known as Rashi script, but Rashi did not invent it; it was invented by Italian printers to make a visual distinction between the commentary and the text, and it is the typeface now used for most Hebrew-language commentaries. His commentary on the Bible was translated into Latin, and Christian scholars used it as a source for their own works. Because he translated approximately ten thousand difficult Hebrew and Aramaic words into French, his work is also an important source for the study of Old French.

Though intended merely as a commentary, Rashi's treatise on the Babylonian Talmud introduces original interpretations of legal issues. Rashi also wrote *responsa*—that is, replies to inquires on issues of Jewish law—that are accepted as authoritative. They reflect Rashi's flexibility and humility. Rashi ruled, for example, that it is acceptable to interrupt the grace after meals to feed one's animals. He derives his ruling from the talmudic injunction—based on the mention of cattle before people in Deuteronomy 11:15—that people feed their animals before themselves.

His modesty was legendary. Unlike many other commentators, he was willing to admit that he did not understand the meaning of the passage in question. He once told a questioner, "I was asked this question before, but I realized that my answer then was wrong and I welcome the opportunity to correct my mistake."

During Rashi's final years, Jews in France and Germany experienced the turmoil of the First Crusade of 1095–1096. Before the Crusades, Jews in the Champagne district had lived much like their Christian neighbors; they spoke French, and mixed freely with their neighbors. Troyes itself was untouched, but many other communities were totally destroyed. Rashi lost relatives and friends in the massacres that occurred at the beginning of the First Crusade. Tradition has it that Rashi correctly predicted that the expedition of Godfrey of Bouillon would be defeated and that Godfrey would lose his entire army and return to his native city with only three horses.

Rashi died in 1105, at the age of sixty-five, on 29 Tammuz in the Hebrew calendar. It is reported that, at the moment of his death, he was sitting at his desk writing the Hebrew word *tam* ("complete," "pure") in his commentary to the talmudic tractate *Makkot* (19b). No one knows where he is buried. His scholarship, however, lives on and influences Jews everywhere.

Maimonides Composes Mishneh Torah

1178

Moses ben Maimon, better known as Maimonides or by the acronym Rambam—was probably the greatest Jewish thinker of the Middle Ages and the most influential in the world at large. Among scholars of Jewish law, he is best known for his Mishneh Torah, *a comprehensive Jewish legal compendium written in Hebrew. His best-known philosophical work is his* Guide of the Perplexed; *written in Arabic, it is an attempt to reconcile Jewish religious belief with Aristotelian thought. Maimonides' thirteen principles of faith are included in the daily prayer book.*

Maimonides.

Moses Maimonides was born in Cordova, Spain, in 1135. His father was a well-known Talmud scholar, mathematician, and astronomer. When Moses was thirteen, the Almohads, a fanatical Islamic sect, captured Cordova. Escaping the expected persecution, the boy's family wandered throughout Spain during the next ten years and eventually settled in Fez, Morocco. Because the Almohads had also captured Morocco, Maimonides and his father, like many of their contemporaries, appear to have been secret Jews, professing Islam in public. While still in Fez, he wrote his *Letter on Forced Conversion*, in which he advised Jews not to live in a place in which conversion was required. The family soon followed his advice. In 1165, with the situation worsening, Maimonides and his family sailed for Palestine, which was under the Crusaders' control at the time. For several months, the family lived in Acre, on the Mediterranean coast. They also visited Jerusalem and Hebron. Because of the harsh living conditions, however, they did not consider remaining permanently;

the family traveled to Egypt, where Maimonides spent the rest of his life. He eventually became the leader of the Egyptian Jewish community.

In Cairo, Maimonides and his brother David started a business that dealt in precious stones. In fact, David

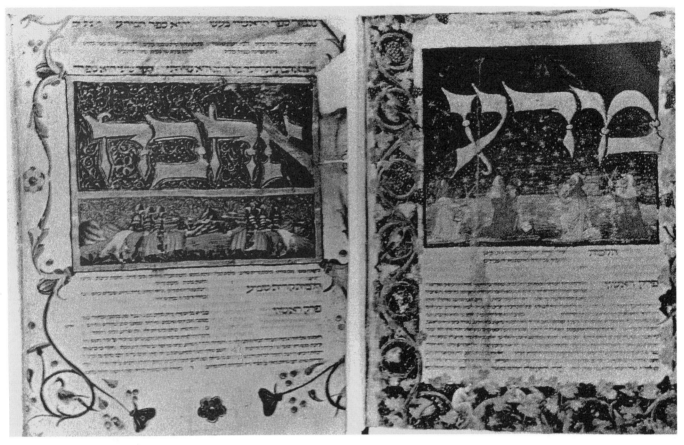

Title pages from illustrated manuscripts of Maimonides' work.

ran the business and left Moses free to pursue his intellectual and community interests. The family suffered a serious reversal, however, when David drowned in the Indian Ocean on a business trip. The family fortune was lost with him. Maimonides was numbed by the loss and also suddenly impoverished. Yet, he refused either to take charity or to use the Torah as a means of livelihood. Therefore, he became a physician.

Maimonides took his medical career extremely seriously, in both its practical and theoretical aspects. He treated both Jews and non-Jews and wrote and lectured extensively on diet, drugs, physiology, and methods of treatment. He was regarded as one of the world's leading doctors, with a special ability to treat what we now call psychosomatic illnesses. So renowned was he that he eventually became the grand vizier's physician. From Maimonides' writings a vivid portrait of his life has emerged—full days at court and at home, taking care of patients, and Sabbaths devoted to the Egyptian Jewish community, whose leader he was. Somehow, he also found time to pursue his studies and to write.

Maimonides' intellectual gifts were apparent even in his youth. He was an excellent Talmud student and widely read in the sciences; he claimed to have read every work on astronomy then available, and he also studied medicine. By the time he was twenty-three, he had written treatises on the Jewish calendar and on logic. That same year, he began work on the *Siraj*, or *Luminary*, a reference work on the Mishnah written in Arabic; relying on his masterly knowledge of the Talmud, he continued to work on it during the family's wanderings even when books were not available. He completed it in Egypt in 1168. It includes a systematic commentary of the contents and constuction of the Mishnah and to the work as a whole. In an eight-chapter introduction to the tractate *Avot* ("Fathers"), Maimonides reconciles the ethical values of *Avot* with Aristotelian ethics, as explained by Muslim philosophers.

This work also contains, in Maimonides' discussion of the tractate *Sanhedrin*, the thirteen principles of faith now included in the daily prayer book, each of which begins with the words, "I believe." The thirteen principles were the first attempt to base Judaism on correct doctrinal belief as well as correct practice. The penultimate statement—of belief in the coming of the Messiah—was often chanted by inmates of the Nazi concentration camps as an expression of their faith.

The same year Maimonides completed the *Siraj*, he began work on the *Mishneh Torah—Repetition of the Torah*—which he completed ten years later, in 1178. The title is a reminder that authority still rests in the Torah. The work, also known as *Yad ha-Hazakah—Strong Hand* (a play on the numerical equivalent of the word *yad* [fourteen]) contains fourteen volumes. *The Mishneh Torah* begins with an affirmation of God as the primal Being and ends with a citation of the prophetic vision of messianic time. Written in Hebrew, the *Mishneh Torah* is a compendium of all known halakhic material from the written Torah to Maimonides' own time, organized by subject matter and including clear statements of Maimonides' conclusions concerning the correct rulings.

The major flaw of the *Mishneh Torah*, which Maimonides himself acknowledged, was that he had not identified the sources of the final legal decisions that he provided. Because this omission meant that readers had to trust Maimonides, the work became the object of the Maimonidean Controversy. Nonetheless, it became a classic. According to the eminent Orthodox American-Jewish scholar Isadore Twerksy, "the *Mishneh Torah* was like a prism through which practically all Talmudic study had to pass"; he describes it as "the flower of Jewish jurisprudence."

Heinrich Graetz, the nineteenth-century scholar of Jewish history, thought the Talmud was a maze, but the *Mishneh Torah* had, in his view, a clearly-defined plan, and one could use the text without guidance. Of that

A page from Maimonides' Mishneh Torah.

work, Graetz said: "Only a mind accustomed to think clearly and systematically, and filled with a genius of orders could have planned and built a structure like this."

Maimonides' other major literary effort, the *Guide of the Perplexed*, (*Moreh Nevukhim*), was written in Arabic between 1185 and 1190. Intended for Jewish intellectuals familiar with Arabic translations of Aristotle and with Arabic philosophical and scientific writings, the *Guide* is essentially an attempt to reconcile the Bible with the

Middle Ages. In it, Maimonides deals with such issues as the nature of God, God's relationship with the world and with humanity, and the nature of prophesy, ethics, and free will. Following in the tradition of Onkelos, the second-century translator of the Bible into Aramaic, Maimonides insists that God cannot be described in human terms; he explains biblical anthropomorphisms—as well as such practices as the sacrificial cult—as concessions to the weakness of human understanding.

The Egyptian Jewish community gave Maimonides the title of *nagid*, or leader, and considered him their guide. Their respect for Maimonides was so great that they conferred the title on his descendants as well; they became leaders of the Jewish community in Egypt for several generations, and Maimonides was considered the outstanding Jew of his time. Jews throughout the world mourned him when he died, in 1204, at the age of sixty-nine. In Fustat, the town near Cairo where he had lived, Muslims as well as Jews mourned for three days. He was buried in Palestine, and his grave became a pilgrimage site. On his tombstone is written, "From Moses [of the Bible] to Moses [Maimonides], there never arose another like Moses."

Maimonides occupies a unique position in Jewish history. Even today, nearly a millennium after he lived, all branches of Judaism regard him with deep reverence. For the ultra-Orthodox Jew who avoids the philosophical *Guide of the Perplexed*, Maimonides' legal commentaries carry all the authority of the Oral Torah, whereas the liberal Jew, who may be less interested in works on religious law, regards Maimonides' philosophic writings with respect.

Moses de Léon Creates the Zohar

THIRTEENTH CENTURY

Jewish religious thought has both rational and mystical traditions. The talmudists, representing the rational tradition in Judaism, interpreted God's law, as written in the Bible, using methods of logic and reason to apply those laws to all areas of life. Mysticism, on the other hand, has been embodied in the literature of the Kabbalah, which delved into the hidden nature of God and bordered on the supernatural. The Zohar is the book that best exemplifies the Jewish mystical tradition.

Kabbalah is not just one book, but an entire body of occult knowledge. The word Kabbalah means "that which is received." The average person could not acquire its knowledge; only the "elect of heaven" could learn its secrets and only by the mystical illumination of the spirit.

While many works constitute the Kabbalah, the two most prized books are the ancient *Sefer Yetsirah* (Hebrew for "Book of Creation"), which dates from the third or fourth century, and the Zohar (Hebrew for "brilliance"). The Zohar, which is sometimes erroneously used interchangeably with the word Kabbalah, was compiled by the Spanish mystic Moses de Léon (c. 1240–1305).

In the middle of the thirteenth century, Moses de Léon announced that he had come across a commentary on the Pentateuch written by the well-known second-century tanna Shimon ben Yochai. Shimon ben Yochai and his son had hidden in a cave from the Roman government for thirteen years, following the unsuccessful Bar Kokhba Revolt.

According to legend, during Ben Yochai's years in hiding, angels revealed to him the divine meanings of the Torah text. Rabbi Shimon wrote a book, in effect a commentary on the Pentateuch, in which he revealed some of these mysteries. The book was the Zohar.

Only a select few people knew of the existence of the book until it came into the hands of Moses de Léon; in publishing the book, de Léon seemed to be suggesting that it uncovered the divine light that the average reader of the Bible could not see. The Zohar became the point of departure for the whole field of Jewish mysticism.

An encyclopedia of occult lore, a mystical commentary on the Torah, the Zohar deals with astronomy, the creation of the world, angels and demons, physiognomy, and—perhaps most significantly—with the mystical science of numbers.

The Zohar assigns numerical values to the Hebrew letters in various scriptural words. Kabbalists arranged the Hebrew Biblical texts in squares and in other geometric forms. Sometimes they read the lines vertically, sometimes backwards or even upside down, all in the belief that they might uncover the hidden meaning of God's words.

Besides the Bible, kabbalistic writings were revered beyond all other sacred Jewish literature by its devotees.

The Kabbalah had two purposes. The first was to help in the redemption of the suffering Jewish people; through a process of spiritual purification, the kabbalists hoped to hasten the coming of the Messiah. The second purpose was to overcome the unendurable difficulties Jews suffered in their daily lives and to frustrate the designs both of human enemies and of evil spirits and demons. The kabbalists thought it possible to alleviate this suffering through the use of magic. Great piety, the rapturous discovery of new mystical formulas, and delirious kabbalistic dreams provided the perfect means of escape from the unpleasant realities of Jewish life.

With the compilation of the Zohar at the end of the thirteenth century, kabbalists defined God as the "primal will," which contained within itself all that was and is and will be of the universe, a total continuum of time. The finite existed only as part of the infinite; the will of God could be understood as an infinite light or radiation. Such thoughts were meant to give Jews the confidence that they could experience the radiance and nature of God. The kabbalists had an unusual interpretation for the anatomy of the human body. They believed there were ten bodily *sefirot*, or *spheres*, forming the divine attributes in man. The head, brain, and the heart were the first three spheres. The head represented the world of thought; the arms and the chest , the world of the spirit; and the legs, sexual organs, and the rest of the body, the material world.

Between the fourteenth and eighteenth centuries, the kabbalistic movement took an enormous hold upon the Jewish people. After the Jews were expelled from Spain, Kabbalah grew and developed in Poland—where prayer itself became a means of inducing a condition of ecstasy. Many Jews in Spain and central Europe welcomed the new mysticism as it proved a potent antidote to the suffering they experienced as Jews. They looked to the Zohar to answer the questions why had they been made to suffer so much and what would they have to do to be redeemed?

By the sixteenth century, the Zohar had become the sourcebook for the Jewish mystic. It was filled with veiled, puzzling, and ambiguous statements, along with profound reflections on the universe and many deeply religious ideas. The Zohar appealed to those who sought the causes of things that had happened in the past and what would happen in the future. Even Christian scholars esteemed the Zohar; they had no trouble believing that, if properly understood, the book could help solve many mysteries.

Joseph Karo Compiles Shulchan Arukh

1564

Born in 1488, apparently in Toledo, Castile, Spain, Joseph Karo is best known as the author of the Shulchan Arukh ("Prepared Table"), which, soon after it was written, became the most widely consulted source-book among Jews. The first commonly accepted code of Jewish law since the period of Maimonides, the Shulchan Arukh retains that exalted status to this day among Orthodox Jews.

Joseph Karo.

Joseph ben Ephraim Karo, born just before the Jews were expelled from Spain in 1492, was part of a family of eminent Spanish scholars. It is thought that soon after the Spanish Expulsion, Joseph, then a boy of four, and his family, departed for Turkey or Portugal. Some suggest, however, that the family may have left for Portugal even prior to the expulsion of Jews from Spain, in which case Joseph might have been born in Portugal.

After the Jews were expelled from the Iberian Peninsula in the 1490s, many of them settled in the Ottoman Empire; Joseph Karo lived in Turkey, then a center for Jewish learning, for forty years. After his father, who was an expert on the Talmud, died, Joseph was raised by his uncle, Isaac. As a teenager, Joseph met Solomon Molcho, a kabbalist who had numerous followers and thought of himself as the Messiah. Molcho was martyred at the stake in 1532, an event that had a significant impact on Karo, who aspired to die a martyr.

In 1521 or 1522 Karo moved to Adrianople, then Nikopol, then Salonika. While living in Nikopol, Karo began writing a four-volume codification of Jewish law. It took him twenty years to complete the work. Called the *Beit Yosef*, it helped to make Karo the most respected talmuic scholar of his age. Karo's purpose in writing the work was to bring order to Jewish law. A variety of codes had been composed over the years that catalogued a bewildering number of local customs. But Karo believed that the various points of view that comprised Jewish

Title page of the Shulchan Arukh.

Karo's *Shulchan Arukh* helped to democratize Judaism. Until the *Shulchan Arukh*, Jewish law had been available only to a select few; now everyone could delve into it.

Karo was insistent upon making his commentary accessible to the Jewish world at large. Indeed, the *Shulchan Arukh* was written in simple, uncomplicated sentences. Karo deliberately chose to keep the code brief so that its study would take no more than thirty days. A pocket edition appeared in 1574 "so that it could be carried in one's bosom," as Karo put it, and "referred to at any time and any place, while resting or traveling." Because printing was gaining popularity at the time, the *Shulchan Aruch* enjoyed a tremendous circulation within the first few years of its publication.

Past efforts to codify Jewish law, including the Mishnah and the Talmud, had not removed the ambiguities in the law. One of Karo's main purposes in publishing the *Shulchan Arukh* was to promote Jewish unity. He believed that the Jewish people was created to serve God. In order to serve God, Jews needed an outline of their duties for every moment of the day—a "Prepared Table," in Karo's phrase, on which all of the commandments were laid out like a feast upon which the soul could nourish itself.

The *Shulchan Arukh* came to be recognized as the basic guide to Jewish religious practice and remains the most popular book of Jewish law ever written.

Yet, Karo was less impressed with it than were future Jewish scholars: he trivialized it as merely a digest for his young students. To him the *Beit Yoseph* was far more authoritative; hence, he quoted from that work, and not the *Shulchan Arukh*, when he offered his *responsa*, those replies that often become Jewish law written by rabbinic authorities to questions posed to them.

In its original version, the *Shulchan Arukh* dealt only with Sephardic custom and practice. The sixteenth-century religious scholar Moses Isserles wrote a supplement and called it *Mappah* ("Tablecloth," a play of words on "Prepared Table"), adding Ashkenazi customs and practices, thus enabling the *Shulchan Arukh* to become the standard code for all of the Jewish people.

Joseph Karo married at least three times. He had six children: five sons and a daughter. Two of his sons and his daughter died young, however. Sketches of Karo that survived show a man with a thin face, a long flowing white beard, and a turban-like covering on his head. Joseph Karo died in Safed at the age of eighty-seven and was buried there.

law needed to be taken into account. He blamed the authors of existing codes of Jewish law for being too superficial in their scholarship.

Joseph Karo investigated each law, tracing it back to its source in the Talmud. He discussed each stage of a law's development and sought to take into account all of the divergent opinions; only then did he make a ruling. He did not produce a new work of commentary; there was enough commentary in his view. Instead, he wrote commentary on existing codes, focusing on the work of three men, Isaac Alfasi, Maimonides, and Asher ben Yehiel (1256–1328). Comparing the codes that these men had written, he decided that whenever the three disagreed, he would accept the majority view. *Beit Yoseph* was studied by many, but it was not as significant as Karo's later work, the *Shulchan Arukh*, which was a shortened version of *Beit Yoseph*.

Mapu Writes First Hebrew Novel

1853

Abraham Mapu is the father of the modern Hebrew novel. During the 1840s and early 1850s the stress in Jewish literature shifted from the rationalism of the Haskalah to an increasing appreciation of the beauties of the world outside the confining Pale of Settlement. Romantic literature, the kind provided by Abraham Mapu, provided the Jewish reading public an escape from life's difficult realities.

Born in Kovno (Kaunas), Lithuania, in 1808, Abraham Mapu was the father of the modern Hebrew novel. His family was poverty-stricken, his father a scholar who worked for meager pay as a Hebrew teacher. Young Abraham was highly intelligent and one of his father's best students. At age twelve, being so advanced, he left his father's class to study on his own. Three years later, under his father's tutelage, Abraham started to probe the Kabbalah, Jewish mysticism.

Married at age seventeen, Abraham continued his studies in the home of his father-in-law. Abraham's parents were disappointed when he came under the influence of Hasidic scholars. His mother sought to extricate him from these circles, but to no avail. He continued to visit the home of the kabbalist Elijah Ragoler.

In Ragoler's home, Abraham Mapu came across a Latin translation of the book of *Psalms*, a book that he later called the critical influence on his secular education. He started to teach himself Latin, unheard of in the circles in which Abraham moved. Studying French, Russian, and German, he turned to the writings of the European romanticists: "I was raised to live in the atmo-

sphere of the dead, and here I am cast among people who lead a real life, in which I am unable to take part."

Abraham's teaching assignment was in the home of a Jewish farmer. Although his physique and his disposition kept him from laboring in the fields, Abraham thought it important to be in close communion with nature.

His father-in-law's financial condition took a turn for the worse. Abraham lived the simple life. At the age of twenty-four, in 1832, Abraham was appointed tutor to the children of a wealthy merchant in a small town called Georgenberg, not far away from his home. He was exposed to modern Hebrew literature for the first time and was deeply influenced by the Haskalah—Enlightenment—movement.

Several years later Abraham moved with his wife and children to Rossieny, which was then the center of the Haskalah movement. He lived there for seven years, and it was there that he started to develop an interest in ancient Jewish history and the Hebrew language.

Returning to Kovno in 1844, he resumed teaching and stayed on for three years. He and his family lived in poverty, and in 1846 his wife died. The next year he moved to Vilna, still working as a tutor. His employer was physically abusive toward him. Making matters worse, Mapu had no great love for the scholars whom he met there. Accordingly, he took a position as a teacher in the government school in Kovno. The year was 1848. Finally, Abraham had stopped wandering.

In 1851, Mapu remarried and started to earn slightly more money. His writing began to win him fame, as he sought to create the heroic existence of Biblical times.

His first novel, *Ahavat Ziyyon* "Love of Zion," which

Central Zionist Archives, Jerusalem.

A portrait of Abraham Mapu.

was published in 1853, was a historical romance that represented a turning point in the development of modern Hebrew literature. The first Hebrew-language novel, *Ahavat Ziyyon* also was the first novel with a biblical setting and dealt with ancient Israel in the days of Isaiah. Well-received, the book went through sixteen editions and was translated into numerous languages.

The plot recounted the wars and loves of King Ahab of ancient Israel. Critics found the novel contrived and implausible, with characters who seemed one-dimensional. The novel had an enormous effect upon the younger generation of Lithuanian Jews, however, who read it in deep secrecy, often hiding it inside the pages of their Talmud texts. It opened a whole new world of love and romance and violence that thousands of Jews had not known about before.

Mapu worked on *Ahavat Ziyyon* for over twenty years. Apparently he lacked self-confidence and was afraid of rejection.

The success of that first novel encouraged him to write more. His second novel, *Ayit Tzavu'a* "The Hypocrite" comprised five parts, the first of which was published in 1855. The second and third parts were published three years apart. All five volumes were published in one edition posthumously in 1869. Like his first novel, this one was widely acclaimed even though it did not sell many copies.

He wrote a third novel called *Hozei Hezyonot* "The Visionary." By this time he had become the target of sharp criticism by adversaries within the pietist and Hasidic movements who were successful in suppressing the publication of *Hozei Hezyonot.* The manuscript disappeared, and only a few chapters remain.

The first part of Abraham Mapu's fourth novel, *Ashmat Shomeron* "The Guilt of Samaria," appeared in 1865; the second part was published a year later.

Mapu published several textbooks as well, which were aimed at improving contemporary educational techniques. In 1860, Mapu became ill. His right hand, with which he wrote, was affected with palsy, so he wrote with his left hand. Even though his fingers caused him great pain, he kept on writing until his death in 1867.

Schechter Recovers Genizah Documents

1896

It was in Fostat, Egypt, that the great Jewish scholar Solomon Schechter recovered the documents that would teach the world so much about Jewish life between the seventh and twelfth centuries. The documents discovered by Schechter were housed in the genizah, a kind of storage room for books and ritual objects that contained the name of God and therefore could not be destroyed. Schechter's find led to a new understanding of Jewish history.

Because of the upheavals, turmoil, and disasters faced by the Jewish people, very few primary sources from the period between the second century C.E. and the early modern age have come down to us. Here and there a good deal is known about certain Jewish figures who lived centuries ago. That is the case with Maimonides, whose life illuminated twelfth-century Egyptian Jewry.

All synagogues contained a room called a *genizah*. This was a place that was earmarked for storing old ritual objects and prayer-books that were too old to use but that, under Jewish law, could not be discarded or destroyed because they contained the name of God. In some cases these semisacred places also contained masses of historical documents, including secular ones. Within a generation or two, however, the documents fell victim to the cold and damp and began to rot, making them all but unreadable.

Only in Egypt, (and later in the Judean Desert), which has an incredibly dry climate, could scholars expect to encounter fragments of papyrus or paper dating back two thousand years or more. And so, not surprisingly, it was at Fostat that a great discovery was made.

The Ezra Synagogue, where Maimonides worshipped and taught and where the Cairo *Genizah* was found, was built in 882 on the ruins of a Coptic church that had been sold to the Jews. It was rebuilt in 1890, but the attic, at the end of the women's gallery, was left untouched. The synagogue's *genizah* was located in the attic, and a multitude of medieval documents remained largely undisturbed in it. The only way to reach the attic, which had no doors or windows, was by ladder through a large hole at the side.

It was at the end of the nineteenth century that the great Jewish scholar Solomon Schechter, who was born in Romania in 1850 (his father was a Habad Hasid) and who would become president of the Jewish Theological Seminary of America, began to systematically recover documents from the Cairo *Genizah*.

The Cairo *Genizah* had been seen by several people before Schechter, but they had not examined its contents because of a local superstition that disaster would befall anyone who touched the repository's holy documents. Still, assorted pages had, without permission, been removed from the *genizah* and sold to interested parties.

Two Christian visitors purchased some Hebrew fragments from the Cairo *Genizah* in 1896. When they returned to England they showed them to Schechter, who identified them as part of the *Book of Ben Sira*. The Hebrew original had long been lost and was known only in Greek translation until then.

Toward the end of 1896, Schechter journeyed to Cairo. After a stay of several months, he was permitted to remove some one hundred thousand pages from the

Solomon Schechter in a Cambridge University attic amid his collection of genizah fragments.

genizah, which he and Charles Taylor, the master of St. John's College, who had provided financial backing for Schechter's trip to Cairo, presented to Cambridge University. Other researchers discovered another one hundred thousand pages, which were deposited in major libraries around the world.

Schechter's greatest find was the Hebrew *Book of Ben Sira*, similar in style to the *Book of Proverbs*. Other treasures from the Cairo *Genizah* included fragments of Aquila's Greek translation of the Bible; the Damascus Document; ancient Palestinian, Babylonian, and Spanish sayings; Jewish historical documents from the time of the Islamic conquest through the First Crusade; and documents relating to the Karaites.

The Cairo *Genizah* contained at least twelve hundred business letters, which demonstrated that Egyptian Jews, including Maimonides' younger brother David, traveled huge distances and handled a remarkable variety of products. The documents confirmed that dyes were a Jewish trading specialty but that Jewish merchants also dealt in textiles, medicaments, precious stones and metals, and perfumes. The immediate trading area was Upper and Lower Egypt, the Palestine coast and Damascus.

Schechter and Taylor jointly published the newly-discovered *Ben Sira* (*The Wisdom of Ben Sira*, 1899). Forty years later the well-known scholar S. D. Goitein would use Cairo *Genizah* documents to great effect in recreating the eleventh and twelfth century society that served as the backdrop to Maimonides' works and ideas.

In 1896 Solomon Schechter wrote:

> It is not the mere revealed Bible that is of first importance to the Jew, but the Bible as it repeats itself in history, in other words, as it is interpreted by Tradition . . . Since then the interpretation of Scripture or the Secondary Meaning is mainly a product of changing historical influences, it follows that the center of authority is actually removed from the Bible and placed in some living body, which by reason of its being in touch with the ideal aspirations and the religious needs of the age, is best able to determine the nature of the Secondary Meaning. This living body, however, is not represented by any section of the nation, or any corporate priesthood, Rabbihood, but by the collective conscience of Catholic Israel, as embodied in the Universal Synagogue.

First Kibbutz Is Founded at Degania

1909

In 1909, Jewish settlers organized the first kibbutz in a region just south of Lake Kinneret in what is now northern Israel. The settlers called their experimental community Degania (cornflower). In time, hundreds of kibbutzim were established, first in Palestine, then in the state of Israel. The uniqueness of the kibbutz lies in its being a geographical and communal enclave whose members enjoy social and economic equality. The members are assigned work according to the immediate needs of the community.

The Jewish men and women who built farming settlements in Palestine hoped both to provide themselves with a livelihood and to establish the underpinnings of a future Jewish state. The first serious proposal to build Jewish settlements came in 1896 when Theodor Herzl, founder of modern Zionism, established the World Zionist Organization in the hope that it would become a powerful vehicle in aiding Jews to settle in Palestine and create a Jewish state.

One early boost for the settlement movement came that same year (1896) when the Jewish philanthropist Baron Maurice de Hirsch provided the financing, through his Jewish Colonization Association, for the nurturing of several colonies in Palestine, among them Hadera and Mish-mar ha-Yarden.

In 1907 and 1908 members of Bar-Giora, forerunner of the self-defense organization Ha-Shomer (which was, in turn followed by the Haganah), were given an opportunity to cultivate a tract of land collectively. Though the commune lasted only a year and a half, it did prove that collective farming was feasible.

In 1908 the World Zionist Organization opened a Palestine office in Jaffa, under Dr. Arthur Ruppin. He was made the head of the Palestine Land Development Corporation and authorized to buy land with money raised by the newly created Jewish National Fund. Ruppin traveled extensively around Palestine, urging that Jewish farming settlements be established and arranging for contiguous areas of land to be purchased.

One early attempt to settle the land was the Sejera (Ilaniayah) training farm run by the Jewish Colonization Association. For seven years it had been controlled by outside interests, but in 1908 it was handed over to Jewish farm laborers who guarded the settlement themselves and shared the profit from their work.

With Sejera's success, the Palestine office became emboldened and established the Kinneret Farm near Lake Kinneret, for the training of agricultural workers.

On October 28, 1910, Jewish settlers organized the first kibbutz in a region just south of Lake Kinneret in what today is northern Israel. The region is six hundred fifty feet below sea level, and summer temperatures sometimes reach above 100 degrees Fahrenheit. The settlers called their experimental community Degania. Its first members were two women who did the cooking and washing, six young men who worked the fields with mules, two youths who stood guard, one young man who served as secretary and treasurer; and one young man who was reserved for ad hoc tasks.

It was Arthur Ruppin who had suggested that the group cultivate the land known as Umm Juni near the Sea of Galilee, east of the Jordan River. He wanted to give the workers at Degania the chance to prove that

October 9, 1980 at the 50th anniversary celebration of Degania.

jointly. We knew that we needed one another's close and constant help because in the harsh and dangerous conditions of the new country, neither an individual nor a family could stand alone."

The training farms at Kinneret and Merhavia also were transformed into kibbutz settlements after Degania had demonstrated how successful the collective arrangement could be.

In 1911, when Shemuel Dayan, father of Moshe Dayan, arrived at Degania, the entire settlement comprised only two stone buildings: a two-story building with eight rooms where the settlers lived, and a single-story building that housed the dining room, kitchen, bakery, showers, and storehouse. For the twelve members of the first kibbutz, Degania was as much an idea as a place, requiring the tiny settlement to place the group above the individual, extolling egalitarianism and collective decision making. The goal was less creating a utopia, more physical survival.

At Degania, the essential traits for a model kibbutznik were hard work and congeniality; they also philosophized about Zionism and talked about remaking themselves into New Jews. The favored tongues on the kibbutz were Hebrew and Yiddish. Degania by then had grown to fifty settlers. Someone consigned to less pleasant farming chores might be asked to patch old sacks, root up weeds, or work on the threshing floor. More desirable was the task of baking bread for the residents of the kibbutz.

When someone wanted to get married on the kibbutz (as did Moshe Dayan's parents Shemuel and Devorah), a *shochet*, or ritual slaughterer, came by cart from the nearby settlement of Menahamiya to perform the wedding. The marriage canopy was a blanket tied to poles usually used for holding up orange trees. The ceremony took place on the banks of the Jordan River.

Moshe Dayan was the first baby born in Degania and the first baby born on an Israeli kibbutz—but he was not the first kibbutz child. That distinction went to Degania's Gideon Baratz, who had been born two years earlier in Tiberias.

Joseph Busel defined the kibbutz as "a form of settlement that obliges us to perform the work ourselves, not by others, and without outside management." Even today members of kibbutzim work according to a schedule set by a work steward. The position of work steward rotates frequently. Kibbutz members are not paid wages for their labor but instead are provided with housing, school, food, cultural activities, and medical care.

they could work the land collectively, and more efficiently, without outside control.

The ten young men and two young women who composed the group had come from the Ukraine and already had been working communally on the Kinneret Farm and in Hadera for two years before they undertook to farm the Umm Juni land together.

Though the new settlers intended to move to a new site after two years, as was common, Joseph Busel, the leader of the group, proposed remaining where they were. His proposal was accepted, setting the stage for the establishment of the first kibbutz.

Joseph Baratz, a founder of Degania, noted that "We were looking for a particular answer to our needs...what we wanted was to work ourselves, to be as self-supporting as we could and do it not for wages, but for the satisfaction of helping one another and tilling the soil

The oldest building at Kibbutz Degania.

Kibbutz children were raised in "children's houses" from birth, not in their parents' homes; they spent only a few hours in the afternoon and on the Sabbath with their parents. Meals were eaten in a communal dining hall, and living quarters had small kitchens in which nothing more than light refreshments could be prepared. Kibbutz members were not paid wages for their labor but instead were provided with housing, school, food, cultural activities, and medical care.

The patterns of life and work at Degania have stood the test of time. Though down through the years the nature of the kibbutz has been modified (more industry, less farming; more time for kibbutz parents with their children), the basic structure of the kibbutz remains intact. Kibbutz life, however, did not become a way of life for the majority of Israelis. The percentage of Israelis living on kibbutzim was never more than three to four percent of the population. But members of kibbutzim were influential in key Israeli institutions, especially the Israel Defense Forces and the government.

Kaplan Founds Reconstructionist Movement

1920

In founding the Reconstructionist movement, religious thinker Mordecai Kaplan brought forth a new stream of Judaism that he hoped would allow it to survive in a world of growing anti-Semitism and assimilation. Rejecting Orthodox, Conservative, and Reform Judaism as too narrow and inclusive, he argued that someone need not attend a synagogue faithfully to be a good Jew; taking part in life outside the synagogue was just as important. Hence, Kaplan inspired and validated many of the American Jewish community's cultural and educational activities.

Mordecai Kaplan, one of Judaism's most luminous intellectuals in the twentieth century, served as a teacher and preacher at a time when American Jews were striving to become American without entirely giving up their Jewish identity. As American Jews struggled in the early part of the twentieth century with the issues of how to be both Americans and Jews, and whether to focus Jewish life around the synagogue, Mordecai Kaplan offered a much more expansive view of Judaism, insisting that Judaism should embrace every aspect of one's life. Following Kaplan's thinking, one could be a good Jew by taking part in the activities of a local Jewish community center, rather than the more traditional way of regularly attending synagogue. Accordingly, Kaplan's thinking led many American Jews to broaden their synagogues into centers for Jewish living and to create a whole network of Jewish community centers.

Born in Lithuania on June 11, 1881, at the age of seven Kaplan immigrated with his parents to New York where his father served on the New York rabbinical court. The Kaplan family was observant, and Mordecai Kaplan attended a yeshiva. In 1900 he received his bachelor's degree from the City College of New York; two years later he was ordained a rabbi at the Jewish Theological Seminary of America. In 1906, he married Lena Rubin, the daughter of a prominent New York Jewish community.

Although he was raised in an Orthodox environment, it was Kaplan's hope to furnish Jews with an alternative, more appealing, kind of Jewishness. In 1934 he summed up his "Copernican revolution in my understanding of Judaism" in the preface to his most important book, *Judaism as a Civilization: Toward a Reconstruction of American-Jewish Life*" ... The Jewish religion existed for the Jewish people and not the Jewish people for the Jewish religion." He also wrote that "the Jewish people are not here to maintain Torah. Torah exists for the sake of the Jewish people." Judaism, he insisted, should be interpreted as a civilization, which encompasses "language, folkways, patterns of social organization, social habits and standards, and spiritual ideals, which give individuality to a people and distinguish it from other peoples."

The turning point for Kaplan's intellectual journey came in 1912 when, at the invitation of Solomon Schechter, the man who established Conservative Judaism in the United States, Kaplan was appointed dean of the newly opened Teachers Institute at the Jewish Theological Seminary. For the previous nine years Kaplan had served as rabbi of the prestigious Orthodox Kehilath Jeshurun synagogue in New York City. But he found that he was drifting away from traditional thinking about Judaism; his appointment to the Jewish Theological Seminary came at a very propitious time.

Eventually as chair of Homiletics at the seminary, he used his teaching position to think about a new formulation for Judaism, one not linked to ideology. "The significance of Jewish milieu and atmosphere, social contact and interaction then began to dawn on me," he would write in *Judaism as a Civilization*," and I realized that unless the synagogue were more than a place for worship its influence was bound to wane..." This thinking led him in 1915 to convince some Jewish friends to establish the Jewish Center, where Kaplan for the first time was able to implement his idea of the synagogue as a center for Jewish living; the synagogue building had excellent athletic and social facilities as well as serving as a place of worship.

In 1920, Kaplan published an important article entitled "A Program for the Reconstruction of Judaism," in the *Menorah Journal* in which he offered a new approach to Judaism.

Rejecting traditional attitudes toward God as a supernatural being from whom salvation comes and repudiating the idea of the Jews as the "chosen people," Kaplan suggested in his writings that God's miracles should not be taken literally because, in his view, they were mostly folklore. God, Kaplan asserted, was the name given to the power in the universe that impels us toward righteousness. Having faith in God means believing that ultimately righteousness will triumph. Kaplan thought that prayer was not an appeal to an undecided God but an act by which worshipers sought the highest potential within themselves.

The more Kaplan observed his students' spiritual struggles, the more he realized how serious was the crisis Jews faced. "In my search for a way to check the devastation of the Jewish spiritual heritage," he wrote,

> I rediscovered Judaism. The eighteenth-century rationalism and nineteenth-century liberalism which progressive Jews so readily assimilated, led them to misconceive the very nature of Judaism. When some interpreted it as nothing more than a revealed religion, and others as nothing more than a religious philosophy, they did so in the hope of fitting it into the framework of a cosmopolitan civilization which they thought was about to be established throughout the world.

The basic fallacy of Jews, he believed, was to reduce Judaism to the status of a religious denomination.

Mordecai Kaplan.

It was no surprise that Mordecai Kaplan had few sympathizers among members of the traditional Jewish denominations. The Orthodox community thought his views were "poisonous." When Kaplan published a series of prayer books that he believed to be better suited to the modern Jew than existing prayer books, the Union of Orthodox Rabbis burned those books during a ceremony in New York in which they also excommunicated him.

In 1922, Kaplan founded the Society for the Advancement of Judaism, in 1935 a biweekly magazine called *The Reconstructionist*, and in 1940 the Jewish Reconstructionist Foundation. The Reconstructionist Foundation listed over three hundred Conservative and Reform rabbis as members, along with two hundred fifty Jewish educators, social workers, and lay people. The Reconstuctionist Rabbinical College opened in Wyncote, Pennsylvania, in 1968. Today there are Reconstructionist congregations throughout the United States.

Kaplan enjoyed a long life. He died in 1983 at the age of one hundred two.

Judith Kaplan Becomes First Bat Mitzvah

1922

Judith Kaplan, eldest daughter of Jewish theologian Mordecai Kaplan, was the first girl to have a Bat Mitzvah, an event that took place in 1922. The ceremony proved revolutionary for it made it possible for countless numbers of Jewish women to play a larger role in Judaism and set in motion a chain of events that enabled Jewish women to become rabbis within the Reform, Conservative, and Reconstructionist movements.

Judith Kaplan had a strong commitment to Judaism. Born on September 10, 1909, she was the oldest of the four daughters of Rabbi Mordecai Kaplan, founder of the Reconstructionist branch of Judaism.

He encouraged free thinking, even when Judith questioned and challenged traditional Jewish views. "When I was eleven I told my father I didn't believe in God," she said in an interview in 1994. She recalled that within her home, "There was a sense of freedom and freedom to change. There was a constant opening up of possibilities and enrichment." Because of her father's strong views about Judaism, "It made my being Jewish a great joy for me rather than a burden."

When she was twelve years old, under her father's guidance at the newly founded Society for the Advancement of Judaism in Manhattan, Judith had the first Bat Mitzvah. Only the day before, her father had thought of the idea. "It came up very casually," she recalled. "Dad said, 'One of these Sabbaths, I'd like you to become Bat Mitzvah,' and I said, 'sure, why not?'" Kaplan suggested that the ceremony take place at his place of worship the very next day. But immediately he ran into opposition from Judith's two grandmoth-

Judith Kaplan at the 70th anniversary of her Bat Mitzvah (in 1992).

ers. "My mother's mother said, 'Talk to your son. Tell him not to do this!'" Grandma Kaplan shot back from her rocking chair: "You know a son doesn't listen to his mother. Get your daughter to stop him from doing this terrible thing." But no one could budge Rabbi Kaplan—or Judith.

That night Judith practiced reading the Torah portion with her father. "I didn't work on it the way kids work on it now, for a half year with lessons every week," she said in 1992, just before her achievement was celebrated on its seventieth anniversary. "All I did was read through with him Friday night and Saturday morning I went into the synagogue and did it." Her father was the rabbi for his daughter's ceremony.

She said of the event: "It all passed very peacefully. No thunder sounded, no lightning struck." That was a slight overstatement. In fact, the Orthodox Jewish press bitterly condemned Judith's act at the time. And there were her grandmothers with whom to contend.

Despite the criticism, Judith Kaplan's bat mitzvah led to other Bat Mitzvahs, all helping to expand the role of women in Judaism, including the eventual ordination as rabbis in the Reform, Reconstructionist, and Conservative movements. Judith's ceremony also has been credited with leading to improvements for Jewish women, including new naming ceremonies for baby girls.

The Bat Mitzvah came to mark a Jewish girl's ceremonial introduction into the life of the synagogue and Judaism in general. The ceremony is held when girls are twelve. Jewish boys celebrate their Bar Mitzvahs at age thirteen.

Reform, Conservative, and Reconstructionist girls are usually called to the Torah during synagogue services, although that practice was not permitted to Judith Kaplan at her ceremony; they sometimes present a sermon as well. Even some Orthodox girls mark the day

by addressing the congregation about the Torah portion of the week, with a party following.

Of greatest significance was that Judith Kaplan's Bat Mitzvah marked the first time a female had stood before the congregation as a leader.

Judith Kaplan went on to earn a bachelor's degree and a master's degree in music from Columbia University. From 1949 to 1954 she taught music education and the history of Jewish music at the Jewish Theological seminary of America. She published a book of children's music called *Gateway to Jewish Song* which was widely used by teachers in Jewish nursery schools.

In 1934, Judith married Ira Eisenstein, who was her father's closest disciple. He had been working as Kaplan's assistant rabbi at the Society for the Advancement of Judaism. She started to write cantatas rooted in Judaism in 1942. She published seven of them, some in conjunction with her husband.

When she was in her fifties, she obtained a doctorate from the Hebrew Union College-Jewish Institute of Religion School of Sacred Music. She taught music there and at the Reconstructionist Rabbinical College (founded by her husband in Pennsylvania in 1968). Her book on the history of Jewish music, *Heritage of Jewish Music*, is still in print. She helped to make Jewish music a respectable discipline, one deserving of serious study.

At age eighty-two, Judith had a second Bat Mitzvah at her home in Woodstock, New York, during which feminist and Jewish leaders paid tribute to her. On that occasion, she expressed her disappointment that the Bat Mitzvah ceremony had, like bar Mitzvahs, become overshadowed by expensive parties. "Bat Mitzvah began not just as a statement of feminism," she said, "but as a statement of dedication to something larger than oneself."

In February 1996 Judith Kaplan Eisenstein died at the age of eighty-six.

Orthodox College Opens Doors in New York

March 29, 1928

Yeshiva College, founded in 1928, was the first college of liberal arts and sciences under Jewish auspices. The school has grown into a multifaceted institution of eighteen undergraduate and graduate schools, with divisions and affiliates at four New York City campuses. The essence of what is now Yeshiva University is expressed in the Hebrew "Torah Umadda" (Torah and Science), which is inscribed at the center of the university's seal. Translated loosely as Jewish learning and worldly knowledge, the term frames a philosophy of education formed by the intersection of Judaism's thirty-five-hundred-year old tradition of learning with Western civilization's approach to science, the humanities, and the professions.

Until the late nineteenth century, Orthodox Jews in America showed little interest in making compromises in order to "adjust" to American culture and life. But Orthodox Jewish leaders eventually realized that they had a growing problem keeping their young people within the Orthodox community. If the generation of Orthodox Jews who had traveled from Europe and Russia to America had remained observant, the next generation was quickly abandoning Orthodox life, leaving their parents' synagogues and heading for Conservative and even Reform ones.

Orthodox educational institutions barely existed in the late 1800s in the United States, and the existing ones were financially troubled. Orthodox rabbis in New York pinned their hopes in part on an Orthodox educational institution known as Yeshiva Eitz Chaim ("tree of life"), which was established on September 15, 1886, and de-

voted to Talmudic learning. With limited financial resources, the yeshiva met in a tiny room on the Lower East Side. After fifteen years filled with uncertainty, the institution seemed about to fold. The Orthodox rabbis also had high hopes for the Rabbi Isaac Elchanan Theological Seminary, which had been organized in 1897 and was named after Europe's leading Orthodox scholar. A yeshiva for the advanced study of Talmud, it prepared older students for rabbinical ordination. Orthodox rabbis were convinced that if an educational format could be developed that would appeal to youngsters who were drifting from Orthodoxy, it might be able to keep them within an Orthodox framework.

The two schools merged in 1915, and the new provisional institution was placed in the hands of Bernard (Dov) Revel, the architect of modern American Orthodoxy. This was the core of the future Yeshiva University. It was Dr. Revel's long held dream to develop an institution that would embody the synthesis of Torah and traditional values with modern science and knowledge.

Revel sympathized with those Jewish students who, in order to acquire a secular education, had to attend classes in the evenings. He wanted to open a school that offered a wide curriculum of Jewish studies but that at the same time would grant the student a Bachelor of Arts. To fulfill that dream, in 1923 Revel launched a five-million-dollar campaign for the new Yeshiva College.

Established on March 29, 1928, Yeshiva College was the first college of liberal arts and sciences under Jewish auspices. By 1929, the first buildings were constructed, which included facilities for both a high school and the college, and finally for the Elchanan Yeshiva.

Reactions were mixed. Yiddish radical newspapers

Yeshiva University in New York City.

graduate institution. Yeshiva College became Yeshiva University.

Four years later the school's board launched a one-hundred-fifty-million-dollar fund-raising campaign for a medical school, a bold departure for Yeshiva University. Still, considering that the Yeshiva leadership was beginning to feel competitive pressure from a new Jewish university looming in Boston (Brandeis University), the decision to build a medical school seemed logical.

Thus, on September 12, 1955, the Albert Einstein College of Medicine, and graduate schools of science, social science, and social work, were founded. The Einstein school opened in the Bronx at Eastchester Road and Morris Park Ave—America's first medical school under Jewish sponsorship. The first class comprised fifty-six students.

complained that the project diverted funds from starving Jews in Eastern Europe. Reform Jews dismissed the very idea of a yeshiva college as parochial. Louis Marshall, the well-known Jewish communal leader, warned that "such a college would be nothing more than a ghetto institution."

Samuel Belkin succeeded Revel as president of the college in 1943. The institution had embarked on the establishment of a graduate school during Revel's last years, and Belkin was determined to build on that academic foundation.

The university's greatest growth came under Belkin, who served as president until 1975. Ordained in Poland, he settled in the United States in 1929 and earned a doctorate in Greek literature and philosophy at Brown University before joining the Yeshiva faculty. In 1945, within two years of assuming the presidency, Belkin won full state accreditation for the school as a

Aware that the medical profession evoked a unique respect among immigrant and second-generation Jews, Belkin and the board of Yeshiva University took a less stringent attitude than might have been expected with regard to the new school's rules and regulations. Orthodox laws that many might have thought would apply to the new school were waived: autopsies were permitted, rounds were conducted and buildings kept open on the Sabbath, and nonkosher food was available for non-Orthodox students. The medical school was a great asset and lent it much stature.

Stern College for Women was established in 1954; it was the first degree-granting liberal arts college for women under Jewish auspices in the United States.

In 1976, a year after Belkin stepped down, the Benjamin N. Cardozo School of Law opened. That same year Dr. Norman Lamm became the third president of

Yeshiva University. He guided the university through trying times, including the payment of a thirty-five-million-dollar debt to avoid foreclosure and a legal battle with the National Labor Relations Board that resulted in a landmark decision by the United States Supreme Court in favor of the university.

Some one-hundred-million dollars was raised to assure that fiscal problems did not recur.

The Sy Syms School of Business was opened on June 30, 1987.

By the 1990s, Yeshiva University had six undergraduate schools and seven graduate and professional schools.

It had an enrollment of seven thousand students (forty-one percent women) and a full-time faculty of over seventeen hundred instructors. Its annual operating budget was two-hundred-eighty-million dollars and supported four centers in Manhattan and the Bronx.

In one century, a small school for boys on Manhattan's Lower East Side grew into a great modern university. The "University of the Jewish People in America," as it is known, Yeshiva University became at once a center of Jewish study and a training ground for scholars in medicine, law, business, human services, education, the rabbinate, government, and community life.

Molly Goldberg Captivates American Audiences

JANUARY 10, 1949

To some, The Goldbergs might seem like any other situation comedy. Yet in its era—the heyday of radio and the birth of television—the program, starring the great comedienne Gertrude Berg, was far more than simply a half hour of comedy: for many viewers, it provided their first opportunity to learn about Jewish-American life. Gertrude Berg was creator, chief writer, producer, and director as well as star of the highly popular show, which was one of the radio's longest-running daytime serials of all time. It aired from 1929 to 1948; from 1949 to 1955, it also was one of television's earliest successes.

The crowning moment of the radio, and later the television, program *The Goldbergs* came when the main character, Molly Goldberg, played by Gertrude Berg, leaned out of her window and tried to get her upstairs neighbor's attention by shouting, "Yoo-hoo, Mrs. Bloom!" That cry became Molly's trademark, known to millions of fans.

Sympathetic, sentimental, plump, humorous, homey, Molly was the focal point of a Jewish immigrant family trying to adjust to life on New York's Upper East Side. Molly managed the household; her husband Jake ran a small clothing business. Molly was both peacemaker and family gossip. Gertrude Berg modeled the character after her own mother and grandmother.

In the aftermath of World War II and the Holocaust, radio and later television programmers were sensitive to the problem of how to portray Jews. If actors playing Jewish roles appeared to be parodying or making fun of the Jews, networks could be charged with fomenting anti-Semitism. That they did not want. Programmers avoided the issue simply by not creating Jewish roles.

The Goldbergs was one of the first exceptions. Clearly, the show's producers felt that Gertrude Berg, in her role as the quintessential Jewish mother, paid tribute to Jews. Indeed to her millions of admirers, Molly Goldberg defined just what a "Jewish mother" was like. Molly became the archetypal Jewish mother, pushing for the "perfect match" for her teenage son or daughter, yearning for her daily dose of gossip, constantly navigating between her Jewish culture and modern American ways.

Yet the show transcended ethnic boundaries and appealed to a wide audience. By the 1940s Gertrude Berg's Molly Goldberg had become one of the fixtures of radio.

Gertrude Edelstein was born in 1899 in New York City. Her father, Jacob Edelstein, ran a resort in the Catskill Mountains of New York. Gertrude wrote and performed skits for the guests. In 1918, she married Lewis Berg, a mechanical engineer. Their son, Cherney, was born in 1922, and their daughter, Harriet, was born in 1926.

When her husband's career started to slip, Gertrude's friends urged her to write for radio. She sold one script entitled "Effie and Laura," a dialogue between two salesgirls, to CBS. Gertrude played one of the characters. The show flopped, however, and was canceled after just one episode.

In 1929, she produced *The Rise of the Goldbergs*, which was a triumph and was broadcast weekly over a national NBC radio network until 1935. Berg earned seventy-five dollars a week for producing the series, from which the salaries of the rest of the cast had to be paid. But as the show became an enormous success, her salary rose to seventy-five hundred dollars a week.

The flavor of the show was distinctly Jewish as this bit of dialogue shows:

JAKE: Molly, your soup is feet for a kink.
MOLLY: You mean a president. Ve're in Amerike, not in Europe.
JAKE: Oy, Molly, Molly, soon ve'll be eating from gold plates.
MOLLY: Jake, d'you tink it'll taste better?
JAKE: Soch a question.

Molly's radio family was incredibly believable, and Americans wrote thousands of fan letters to the characters—not the actors.

Berg wrote, produced, and directed the program. It became one of several successful ethnic comedies during the 1930s and 1940s; others were *Lum and Abner* (Arkansas hillbillies), *Amos and Andy* (blacks in Harlem), and *Life with Luigi* (Italians in Chicago). *The Goldbergs* was radio's longest-running daytime serial, airing from 1929 to 1948.

In 1938, Gertrude Berg branched into the movies, writing the film *Make A Wish*.

When *The Rise of the Goldbergs* finally went off the air in 1948, Gertrude Berg sensed that she might have a chance to get into television, then a budding medium. That year, she wrote and starred in the Broadway production of *Me and Molly*. The play was successful and helped create interest in the television program.

The problem was that NBC didn't think *The Goldbergs* would make a good television show. "Well," said Berg in her book *Molly and Me*: "that was their opinion. I knew different." She told her agent to talk to CBS, which expressed interest and asked Berg to audition. CBS got cold feet, however, and the audition was called off.

Berg was despondent and angry. "If you're turned down by NBC and CBS then you're out of business, and that was something I decided I wasn't. " She stayed up all night thinking about the injustice done to her and the show. The next morning, deciding to bypass the CBS executives who had canceled her audition, she phoned CBS chairman William S. Paley and asked for an appointment. Paley's secretary said he was leaving for a cruise and could only give her fifteen minutes. She said three minutes would be enough.

She told Paley that the television show might be a flop or it might be great, but she had been on radio for twenty years, fourteen of them on CBS, and she felt she deserved an audition. That took the first two minutes. Paley used the third minute to get up from behind his desk, move over to where Berg was sitting, put a hand on her shoulder, and tell her that she would have her audition. By the time she returned home the phone was ringing. The same CBS executives who had spurned her were now apologizing to her and saying that an audition was being arranged. "Believe me," Berg said in her memoirs, "there's nothing like three minutes with the boss."

The television program premiered on January 10, 1949, over the CBS television network with General Foods as a sponsor. The show soon became one of the most popular and lucrative on television. It was CBS's first major television situation comedy.

Even after the shift to television, *The Goldbergs* remained faithful to its successful combination of ethnic humor and everyday family problems. Unlike vaudeville, *The Goldbergs* drew its humor from the complications that arose when its characters confronted working-class situations that hit home to the average viewer.

Phillip Loeb was cast as Jake. He had played that role on radio from 1945 to 1948, then on television from 1949 to 1951. Jake was a strong father who cared deeply for his children; yet if the children misbehaved, he was ready to mete out punishment.

Molly's Uncle David lived with the family and was known for his humorous aphorisms.

The show struck a positive chord with audiences largely because of the interaction between Berg and Loeb. The Girls Club of America honored Gertrude Berg as the Radio and TV Mother of the Year in 1950.

Disaster struck, however, in the spring of 1951. Loeb, suspected of being a Communist, became a target of the McCarthy witchunt. General Foods came under heavy pressure to have Loeb dropped from the show. Finally, the sponsor caved in and told Berg that the company planned to drop its sponsorship of the show unless Loeb was dismissed.

For Gertrude Berg, the choice was agonizing. To rally behind her costar and lose a sponsor seemed foolish, however praiseworthy. To side with the sponsor and drop her costar appeared sensible, but brutal. Certain that Loeb was innocent, she decided to back him, and hoped that the storm would die down. It did not. General Foods withdrew its advertising from the program, contending that it was "dissatisfied with the show's ratings"—a bizarre notion in light of the millions of viewers who continued to tune in.

A scene from The Goldbergs.

AMERICAN JEWISH ARCHIVES, CINCINNATI, OHIO

Responding to the pressure, CBS dropped *The Goldbergs*. NBC immediately picked up the show. No sponsor, however, would lend its support as long as Phillip Loeb was a member of the cast. Gertrude Berg would not budge, sensing all too well, however, that unless *The Goldbergs* returned to TV soon, viewers would switch their allegiances to other shows. Another factor weighed heavily on her: if she retained Loeb, and the show was dropped, she automatically would cause the forty members of the cast to lose work.

Grudgingly, Berg decided in December 1951 to offer Loeb an eighty-five thousand dollar cash settlement if he would quit. But he refused. His only son was a schizophrenic, and the cost of his treatment was extremely expensive.

Loeb continued with his struggle but gained little support. By the time he agreed to a settlement, the offer had dropped to forty thousand dollars. Still, Loeb praised Berg for her behavior throughout the ordeal.

The Goldbergs found a new sponsor, the Vitamin Corporation of America, and the show returned to the air in February 1952 with Harold J. Stone in the role of Jake. (Loeb committed suicide in 1955.)

The Goldbergs became one of television's earliest successes; it aired from 1949 to 1955. For many viewers, it marked the first time that they came into contact with authentic Jewish-American life. In the fall of 1955, with ratings dropping, the Goldberg television family moved to suburbia. But the show's folksy immigrant humor was wearing thin, and that year was its last season.

Leon Uris Popularizes Struggles for Israeli Statehood

July 1, 1958

Leon Uris's novel Exodus, *dealing with the creation of the state of Israel and its defense, proved of enormous importance in explaining the Jewish state to American Jewry. The book glamorized Israelis as heroes and created a positive impression among American Jews of the state of Israel. Until Exodus, the founding of Israel had not been a subject that sold books in the United States, but Uris's novel sold two million copies in its first two years.*

Leon Uris's novel *Exodus*, published in 1958, is a fictionalized account of the struggle for the creation of the modern Jewish state dating back to Zionism's birth in the late nineteenth century and carrying through to the founding of the state in Israel in 1948.

The book had a major impact on American Jewry. It gave American Jews a sense, for the first time, of what this ten-year-old nation was all about; it reinforced the image of the Israeli as superman, as someone who felt morally superior. It made American Jews feel proud to be Jewish, to be connected to the state of Israel.

Stirred by the Sinai Campaign of 1956, Leon Uris was caught up in the fighting while living in Israel. During that period he began research on the novel. The plot of *Exodus* is secondary to its larger theme: the creation of Israel as a refuge for the Jewish people after World War II, especially for those who survived the horrors of the Holocaust.

In the book, Kitty Fremont, a non-Jewish American nurse, works with orphans in the aftermath of World War II in order to forget the deaths of her husband and daughter. She falls in love with Ari Ben-Canaan, a Palestine-born Jew who has played a large role in smuggling Holocaust refugees from Europe to Palestine and in creating an illegal Jewish defense force in the closing days of the British mandate. Various subplots show how European and Russian Jews escaped from Nazi-occupied territory and slowly made their way overland and by sea to the new state of Israel.

The Doubleday book was published in September 1958 and went through thirty printings over the next six years. The Bantam paperback edition was published in October 1959 and, by January 1981, had gone back to press more than fifty times.

Exodus was translated into thirty-five languages and sold over ten million copies. In 1960 a movie based on the novel was made, directed by Otto Preminger and starring Paul Newman and Eva Marie Saint. The movie's great success convinced Hollywood producers that films on Israeli and Jewish themes could do well. In 1971 a Broadway musical based on *Exodus*, called *Ari*, fared less well, closing after only twenty performances.

Uris himself described *Exodus* as the story of the greatest miracle of modern times, an event that had no parallel in the history of mankind, the rebirth of a nation dispersed two thousand years before. *Exodus* recounts the story of the Jews coming back home, as the book jacket notes, "after centuries of abuse, indignities, torture, and murder to carve an oasis in the sand with guts and with blood."

Uris noted candidly:

> All the cliché Jewish characters who have cluttered up our American fiction—the clever busi-

nessman, the brilliant doctor, the sneaky lawyer, the sulking artist . . . all those good folk who spend their chapters hating themselves, the world, and all their aunts and uncles . . . all those steeped in self-pity . . . all those golden riders of the psychoanalysis couch . . . all these have been left where they rightfully belong, on the cutting-room floor.

I have shown the other side of the coin, and written about my people who, against a lethargic world and with little else than courage, conquered unconquerable odds. *Exodus* is about fighting people, people who do not apologize either for being born Jews or the right to live in human dignity. Their story was a revelation to me as I discovered it in the farms and cities of Israel.

Exodus, Uris explained, became a tangible project because of the persistence of his agent Malcolm Stuart. While gathering material for his book, Uris traveled in Israel by train, plane, jeep, and on foot.

Uris saw himself as quite different from other American-Jewish writers, as he once told an interviewer from the *New York Post* : "There is a whole school of American Jewish writers who spend their time damning their fathers, hating their mothers, wringing their hands and wondering why they were born. This isn't art or litera-ture. It's psychiatry."

Leon Marcus Uris—the last name an Anglicization of Yerushalmi— "man of Jerusalem"—was born in Baltimore in 1924 to Anna Blumberg and Wolf William, a Russian paperhanger and storekeeper. Uris was raised in poor Jewish neighborhoods in Baltimore, Norfolk, and Philadelphia.

He enrolled in Baltimore City College in 1941 but never graduated. He served in the United States Marine Corps from 1942 to 1946. Uris's first published article, following many rejections, was "The All-American Razzmatazz," an account of the selection of the All-American football team, which appeared in *Esquire* in January 1951. Once the article appeared, he was encouraged to begin work on a novel. The result was his acclaimed bestseller *Battle Cry* (1953), which documented the psychological and emotional impact of barracks life and the battlefield on a troop of Marines during World War II.

The Angry Hills, a novel set in war-time Greece, was his second book. As a screen-writer and then newspaper correspondent, he became interested in the dramatic events surrounding the rebirth of the state of Israel.

In 1960 Uris published *Exodus Revisited*, a photo-documentary illustrating the places described in the novel. He expanded the account of the Warsaw Ghetto uprising in *Exodus* in *Mila 18*. Uris also authored *Armageddon, Topaz, QB VII, Trinity*, and (with his wife, Jill) *Ireland: A Terrible Beauty*—all bestsellers.

Wiesel's Night *Sensitizes World to Holocaust*

1960

When Elie Wiesel, the Romanian-born writer who would become one of American Jewry's great intellectuals, wrote his autobiographical work Night in 1956, published in the United States in 1960, he became the voice of the six million Jews who perished in the Holocaust. Through his work, Wiesel created tremendous interest in and fresh sympathy for Holocaust victims and survivors.

One morning soon after World War II, a young Jewish newspaperman, Eliezer Wiesel, went to interview the French Catholic philosopher, François Mauriac. The philosopher confided to his young visitor that nothing had affected him during World War II as much as hearing from his wife of the trainloads of Jewish children standing at Austerlitz station. The children had arrived at the station at war's end, without parents, scarred from living through the hell of Hitler's concentration camps.

Wiesel calmly replied that he was one of those children, that he had seen his mother, his little sister, and other relatives—save for his father—led off to the Nazi death furnaces. As for his father, Eliezer was forced to watch him die slowly before his own eyes. Mauriac encouraged the young journalist to write a book about his personal experiences so that everyone would know about the trainloads of Jewish children and what Hitler had done to them and their relatives.

And so it was that in 1956 Elie Wiesel wrote his earthshaking book *Night*, hoping to sear the Nazis' brutal deeds into the memories of all those who otherwise might forget the awful significance of Hitler's Germany.

A portrait of Elie Wiesel.

For nearly two decades after the war, little had been written or spoken publicly about the Holocaust, and many American Jews had little or no understanding of the Nazi atrocities. After the appearance of Wiesel's slim but powerful book in 1956, however, the Holocaust became a legitimate subject for public discussion, among

Christians as well as Jews. Elie Wiesel became an American and Jewish hero, praised for being the conscience of world Jewry, termed by some a "modern Job."

Night is written in simple but forceful sentences, as Wiesel patiently recounts how he and other Jews awaited their fates in the Nazi death camps. Wiesel writes emotionally of what it meant to the inmates to reach the end of another day: "Night. No one prayed so that the night would pass quickly. The stars were only sparks of the fire which devoured us. Should that fire die out one day, there would be nothing left in the sky but dead stars, dead eyes. There was nothing else to do but to get into bed, into the beds of the absent ones; to rest, to gather one's strength."

Wiesel believed that the proper role of the artist was to recreate and remember, not to imagine, since reality was far more shocking than anything that could be imagined.

First published in Buenos Aires in Yiddish, the book was called *Un di velt Hot Gehsvign* (*And the World Has Remained Silent*). Condensed and translated in French as *Le Nuit* in 1958, the 1960 American edition jolted the American Jewish community.

"I wanted to show the end, the finality of the event," Wiesel said. "Everything came to an end—history, literature, religion, God. There was nothing left. And yet we began again with *Night*. Only where do we go from there? Since then, I have explored all kinds of options. To tell you that I have now found a religion, that I believe—no. I am still searching. I am still exploring. I am still protesting."

The publication of *Night* launched Wiesel as a novelist, but it was the publication of the book in the United States that launched his career as a spokesperson for Holocaust victims.

Wiesel was born on September 30, 1928 in Sighet, Romania. He studied Talmud and immersed himself in the Kabbalah with Hasidic rabbis. His father, Shlomo, was a shopkeeper.

In 1944, the Nazis deported the fifteen thousand Jews of Sighet, half of the town's population, to Auschwitz. Elie, his father and mother, and his three sisters, were among the deportees. Elie's mother, Sarah, and his youngest sister died in the gas chambers there. His two older sisters survived.

Elie and Shlomo were transferred from Auschwitz to another concentration camp at Buchenwald, where Elie had to endure the horror of watching his father die a slow death from disease and starvation. It was that memory that led him to write *Night*.

Liberated with other Jewish orphans and shipped to France, in 1946 Elie became a ward of a French Jewish children's agency. From 1948 to 1951, he attended the Sorbonne and studied philosophy. On the side, he taught Hebrew and Bible and served as a choir director.

Between 1948 and 1954, Wiesel worked as a stringer for the French newspaper *L'Arche*, which was the official publication of organized French Jewry. He also was a stringer for the Israeli newspaper *Yediot Aharonot*. In 1956, Wiesel went to New York, where he wrote for the Jewish *Daily Forward*; he continued to write for *L'Arche*.

A significant segment of Wiesel's career was devoted, through his writing and lectures, to bringing the Holocaust to the attention of the public. He achieved notable success, and became one of the leading figures in American Jewry.

He is the author of numerous books including *The Accident* (1962); *The Town Beyond the Wall* (1964); *Twilight* (1988); *The Forgotten* (1992); and his autobiography, *All Rivers Run to the Sea* (1995).

During a visit to Israel in 1991, Wiesel noted that "Whenever I write, I always have in front of me a picture of the house where I was born. We must always ask, 'Where do I come from?' and 'Where are we going?' There must be a sense of history. If I had to sum up my mission in one sentence, it would be: not to make my past your future."

Chagall's Stained-Glass Windows Are Dedicated

FEBRUARY 6, 1962

In 1962 Marc Chagall, one of the most important Jewish artists of the twentieth century, completed a series of twelve stained-glass windows for the Hadassah Hospital in Jerusalem. Each window is dedicated to one of the twelve tribes of Israel. The Hadassah commission allowed Chagall to create a monumental work in Jerusalem based on biblical sources.

Marc Chagall was born into a large, poor, and pious Hasidic family. His father was a herring packer; his grandfather a cantor and kosher butcher. One of his uncles was an amateur violinist. During Marc's youth, he was influenced by a rabbi from Mohiliff, who instructed him in Judaism, and as a result Marc became a more observant Jew. He stopped swimming on Saturdays and studied the Bible.

Marc Chagall's mother was distressed at his interest in becoming a painter; yet in 1906, with the support of an uncle, it was arranged for Marc, then nineteen years old, to study with a Vitebsk artist named Yehuda Pen.

The following year Marc moved to St. Petersburg where he attended a private school named the School of the Imperial Society for the Protection of the Arts. He was forced, however, to live outside the city because he was Jewish. He later studied at the Swanseva School in order to work with the famous Jewish artist Leon Bakst, the designer for the Diaghilev Ballet.

In 1910, Chagall obtained a subsidy from a liberal Jewish attorney and politician named Maxim Vinaver, which permitted Marc to move to Paris, then the artistic capital of the world. In Paris he painted scenes from his native town and of the village of Lyozno where he often visited his grandfather. These paintings depict family, friends, homes, aspects of the life of the Jewish community, landscapes, and skyscapes.

In 1914, Chagall was back in his native Vitebsk. Departing from the Soviet Union for good in 1922, Marc Chagall spent a year in Berlin. There, the Jewish artist Herman Struck taught him printmaking. Chagall then returned to Paris. He made the first of many journeys to Palestine in 1931 for the opening of the Tel Aviv Museum, doing 105 biblical etchings, which have been described as some of the finest masterpieces of the art of etching.

From 1941 to 1948 Chagall lived in the United States, but France always remained his true home.

Chagall's relationship with Judaism was complex. On the one hand, he credited his Russian Jewish cultural background as crucial to his artistic imagination. However ambivalent he was about his religion, he could not avoid drawing upon his Jewish past for artistic material. He once said in the 1920s that "All the little fences, the little cows and sheep, all the Jews, looked to me as original, as ingenuous, and as eternal as the buildings in Giotto's frescoes." But he was not a practicing Jew as an adult and he increasingly tried to suggest that his paintings had more universal messages as he sought to reach out to non-Jewish audiences.

During the 1930s, Chagall often used Christian motifs in his paintings, especially the Crucifixion. He suggested that the Crucifixion was meant to be a metaphor for modern, (including Jewish in his mind,) suffering. He designed many stained-glass windows for Christian churches. His first undertaking was to contribute two windows for the church at Assy, France. Then came an

The synagogue at Hadassah hospital in Jerusalem.

equally challenging commission from the Administration of Historic Monuments, inviting him to design two large windows for the Gothic cathedral of Metz. Much patient preparatory work, including frequent visits to study Chartres cathedral, had to precede Chagall's work, which was completed with two splendid lancets, *Jeremiah* and *Exodus.*

In 1959 plans were made to add a new dimension of beauty to the synagogue on the grounds of Jerusalem's Hadassah Medical Center. Dr. Miriam Freund, then the National President of Hadassah, and Dr. Joseph Neufeld, the architect of the twenty-one structures of the center, decided to ask famed Jewish artist Marc Chagall to create stained-glass windows that would form the lantern of the synagogue. The two stopped in Paris to meet Chagall.

During their two-hour visit Chagall's wife Bella told Dr. Freund and Dr. Neufeld that Chagall had always hoped the Jewish people would call on him for a task such as this. "Now the Jewish people have come to you," Dr. Freund said, speaking to the artist. "This is your opportunity to create something which will live for the ages . . . " Chagall took little coaxing: he agreed to create the windows at no expense to Hadassah other than the actual cost of the materials and of the work of the craftsmen at the Atelier Simon in Reims.

Chagall and his assistant Charles Marq worked on the project for two years. Marq developed a special process of veneering pigment on glass that allowed Chagall to use up to three colors on a single uninterrupted pane, rather than being confined to the customary technique of separating each colored pane by lead strips.

The Hadassah windows represent the twelve sons of the patriarch Jacob, from whom came the twelve tribes of Israel.

The dominant color of the window for Reuben, the oldest of Jacob's twelve sons, is blue; symbolizing fruitfulness. Chagall relied upon the biblical description of

Chagall's windows.

Reuben: " . . . Thou art my firstborn, my might, and the first fruits of my strength . . . unstable as water" (*Genesis* 49:3). In the lower right of the window is a mandrake, the flower brought by Reuben to his mother. In the Song of Deborah (*Judges* 5:15–16) the tribe of Reuben is referred to as a pastoral tribe, and above the mandrake in the window one sees sheep grazing on green slopes. In the sky are positioned the sun and birds. There are eagle claws that may symbolize Reuben's strength.

The priestly Levi has a translucent golden window. The holiness of the Torah guarded by the tribe of Levi (from whom Moses and Aaron are descended) is symbolized by the Ten Commandments. Because human figures could not be used on the windows according to Jewish law, animals are arranged like the priests blessing the Ten Commandments. Throughout the windows, only the eyes and hands of man appear: hands raised in blessing, hands lifting a crown, hands holding the sho-

far. Candles to either side of the tablets of the Ten Commandments symbolize the Temple service. A golden light radiates from the candles and table. A basket of fruit in the upper center evokes the custom of bringing the first fruits to the Temple.

Chagall's windows are populated by floating figures of animals, fish, flowers, and many Jewish symbols. "All the time I was working," Chagall said, "I felt my father and my mother were looking over my shoulder and behind them were Jews, millions of other vanished Jews of yesterday and a thousand years ago."

The Bible provided Chagall's main inspiration, especially *Genesis* 49, in which Jacob blessed his twelve sons, and *Deuteronomy* 33, in which Moses blessed the twelve tribes. The main colors of each window are inspired by three blessings as well as by the description of the breastplate of the high priest in *Exodus* 28:15, which was colored gold, blue, purple, and scarlet and contained twelve gems including emeralds, turquoise, sapphire, jacinth, agate, beryl, lapis lazuli, and jasper.

The floors and interior walls of the Hadassah Medical Center synagogue are made of Jerusalem stone. The synagogue is illuminated by a hanging lantern and by sunlight that streams through the Chagall windows.

Chagall began the project by making about eighty preliminary maquettes or studies in pen and pencil. In later studies he used colored paper to create the patterns of stained glass, over which he made sketchy, calligraphic drawings. Then came a series of gouache paintings in which the final color scheme and symbolic images were established. Fifty sheets of colored glass were blown and rolled at the St. Juste glass works in the Loire Valley. The new technique for staining glass by mixing pigments had been developed there; it is this technique that accounts for the great variety and intensity of color in the windows.

Finally, in the workshop of Jacques Simon in Reims, the glass was cut into patterns following Chagall's earlier studies. Chagall then painted, etched, and scratched on the glass, intensifying some colors and creating new patterns and designs before the glass was fired again. Each window is approximately eleven feet high by eight feet wide.

The windows were first exhibited in Paris in a specially built pavilion at the Louvre and later at the Museum of Modern Art in New York.

Present at the dedication of the windows on February 6, 1962, Chagall said he felt joy in bringing "my modest gift to the Jewish people, who have always dreamt of biblical love, of friendship and peace among all people . . ."

Jean Cassou, in the book *Chagall* (1965) said of the windows:

> We see the motifs of Chagall's personal inner life—his memories, his obsessions, his symbols, all his faithful and dearly-loved friends—being brought to bear on the esoteric world of Hebraic symbolism. All the symbols of his irrepressible fantasy world now obediently and unprotestingly take up their appointed places in the Jerusalem windows, in the celestial light of Jerusalem.
>
> The trees, the plants and the animals—especially the mysterious animals whose exact meaning in Chagall's private mythology escapes us...all here derive their significance from the Scriptures. This significance is manifest in the harmony of the composition, a harmony that is often rich, perfect and luminous.

Those twelve windows, each one dedicated to one of the twelve tribes of Israel, are one of the major tourist attractions in Jerusalem.

Fiddler on the Roof
Opens on Broadway

SEPTEMBER 22, 1964

American Jewish pride grew immeasurably with the arrival on Broadway of the Shalom Aleichem play Fiddler on the Roof *in 1964. If the Holocaust had made American Jews feel uncomfortable, even squeamish about displaying their Jewishness too prominently, cultural events such as the "Fiddler" production on Broadway awakened new and positive feelings among American Jews about their religion. "Fiddler" was based on the stories written by the Yiddish novelist and playwright Shalom Aleichem. In 1972, when "Fiddler" gave its 3,225th performance on Broadway, it became Broadway's longest-running show.*

*F*iddler on the Roof recounts the story of Anatevka, a little town in the middle of nowhere, a bucolic Russian community in which Jewish residents at the turn of the century cling to their religion and their traditions even while their world is on the verge of collapse.

The creator of the characters in *Fiddler on the Roof* was the Yiddish novelist and dramatist Shalom Aleichem. Born in 1859 in the Ukraine, in Pereysalsav, he is considered the most talented writer of Yiddish fiction, particularly humor.

Shalom Aleichem was born Shalom Rabinovitch, but he took the name Shalom Aleichem, the words of the traditional Hebrew greeting, "peace be with you." He was raised in Voronkov, the model for his imaginary *shtetl*, Kaserilevke, (which became Anatevka) "orphaned, dreamy, hypnotized, interested only in itself." Throughout the 1890s Shalom Aleichem wrote sketches about one or the other of his most famous characters, Tevye the Milkman and Menachem Mendel.

Tevye was poor, hard-working, deeply honest and deeply religious, and—deeply troubled because he had seven daughters for whom he had to arrange marriages, but no son. Tevye's life came to exemplify eastern European and Russian Jewish life at a time when Jews could be persecuted without reason at any moment.

Shalom Aleichem's was the authentic voice of his people. But it is the great humor with which he endowed Tevye that makes Tevye such an appealing and sympathetic character.

After the Kiev massacres and the Russian Revolution, both of which occurred in 1905, Shalom Aleichem escaped first to Switzerland, then to London and finally New York, where he hoped to support himself by writing and lecturing. Two of his plays failed and in 1907 he returned to Europe, where he continued to write plays, he also lectured throughout Russia. His readings and recitations became highly popular. He lived in Europe until 1914 where he died two years later at the age of fifty-seven. Nearly every shop and factory on the Lower East Side in New York closed on the day he was buried.

Forty-eight years after Shalom Aleichem's death at the age of fifty seven, Joseph Stein's Broadway version of *Fiddler on the Roof* premiered, September 22, 1964.

The show's opening number, "Tradition," sets the tone. The main question facing Tevye is how far he is prepared to go in abandoning—or reevaluating—the old ways as he tries to cope with the coming revolution in politics and family relations.

Zero Mostel first gave the musical's Tevye extraordinary stage life. In the original 1964 production, and in the 1976 Broadway revival, Mostel transformed a poor,

Zero Mostel as Tevye and Paul Lipson as Lazar Wolf in the New York City production of Fiddler on the Roof.

oppressed, country dairyman into a larger-than-life hero, with wit, humanity, and charm.

Mel Gussow wrote in the *New York Times*: "Both the lyrics and book convey Shalom Aleichem's homespun philosophies. The musical has a seamless fluidity, songs flowing into story into dance. Even the settings seem to dance as Tevye's cottage swirls in time to the music and as, in the song "Sabbath Prayer," the skies are lined with an aurora borealis of families lighting candles."

It seemed only natural that the play would one day be performed in Israel.

In the fall of 1964 a young Israeli actor named Chaim Topol was sent to New York to scout out the new Broadway musical, to see if it was worth optioning for performance in Tel Aviv. He cabled back that it was not. The lead role was that of an older man, one that he did not feel was appropriate for him to play.

Topol also was troubled at seeing the work of a Russian-Jewish author turned into a Broadway play. "To

Americanize Shalom Aleichem seemed a kind of sacrilege," Topol said later. "I was wrong. Thanks to the Americanization of Shalom Aleichem, a man who wrote in a language that hardly a million people in the whole world speak, he is now known to millions all over the world."

Topol starred in the Hebrew adaptation of *Fiddler on the Roof* at Jaffa's Alhambra Theater in June 1965. When the curtain came down, Prime Minister Levi Eshkol rushed backstage. Eshkol toasted the cast and said: "Nu, nu, it's not exactly Shalom Aleichem, but I have never enjoyed an evening in the theater so much in my life." Also in attendance was Foreign Minister Golda Meir.

Israel's most formidable critic, Chaim Gamzu, complained that the musical "is sunk in cauldrons of *schmaltz*." So what else did he expect, bubbled Joseph Stein: "*Schmaltz* is not exactly a Japanese invention, you know."

Chaim Topol played Tevye in the London production of *Fiddler on the Roof* which opened in February 1967, and then won the coveted role of Tevye in the 1971 film. He made his New York stage debut in the revival that opened on November 18, 1990, at the Gershwin Theater.

Topol later laughed at his negative response to *Fiddler* twenty-six years earlier. "Now I know that the play, though it uses Jewish backgrounds, customs and history, for some reason has universal appeal. Wherever I go I do believe that if we are good I can almost guarantee that handkerchiefs will be pulled out in the same place whether we're two hundred yards from Piccadilly Circus, two hundred yards from Times Square, two hundred yards from Dizengoff Square or two hundred yards from the Ginza."

Since its Broadway debut *Fiddler on the Roof* has become a universally loved folk musical. Countless versions have been performed around the world and it has become part of America's musical heritage, just as the Shalom Aleichem stories on which the show was based derived from an earlier European literary heritage.

Spielberg Recreates Schindler's List

1993

Just as the 1961 trial of Adolf Eichmann reminded the world of the true horrors of the Holocaust, Steven Spielberg's film Schindler's List, thirty-two years later, again brought home the awful realities of the Nazi destruction of European Jewry. The film portrayed German businessman Oskar Schindler's courageous effort to save eleven hundred Polish Jews. The film was a commercial triumph and won seven Oscars—one for Spielberg for Best Director; one for Best Picture of the Year.

Steven Spielberg

The movie *Schindler's List* was based on a 1982 book written by Australian journalist Thomas Keneally. The novel told the true story of how German businessman Oskar Schindler had "bought" eleven hundred Polish Jews and employed them in his enamelware factory in Nazi-occupied Poland so that they would be spared Hitler's death chambers. Schindler's motives were not clear—he was known as a womanizer, and he was devoted to lining his own pockets. Yet, he seemed—when it came to his Jewish employees—to care whether they lived or died.

Keneally had been convinced that he should write the book while standing in a leather-goods store in Beverly Hills, while waiting for a credit card authorization from the proprietor, Schindler survivor Leopold Page (born Poldek Pfefferberg).

The idea for the film *Schindler's List* had been floating around Hollywood for years. Leopold Page had been instrumental in selling Schindler's story to MGM in the 1960s. The studio had hired Howard Koch, one of the screenwriters for the film classic *Casablanca*, to put a script together, but the project was dropped and lay dormant for years.

Artur Brauner, a German Jewish filmmaker, wanted to a make a movie about Schindler in the 1970s but could not raise the money. Germans, he said, disapproved of Schindler's woman-chasing and alcoholism.

Steven Spielberg (right) greets Israel President Ezer Weizman at Israeli premiere of Schindler's List *on March 3, 1994.*

When Keneally's book *Schindler's List* was published, Sidney Sheinberg, MCA president, brought the novel to Steven Spielberg's attention. Spielberg was intrigued. After scanning one book review, he told Sheinberg: "It'll make a helluva story. Is it true?"

Upon meeting Spielberg, Page felt certain that Spielberg would do the movie. As for Spielberg, he agreed but planned to start the film years down the road. "Page was heaping on the fact that he was going to die."

Spielberg had passed the project on to director Martin Scorsese. But *"Schindler's List* was on my guilty conscience," Spielberg said; he regretted having given away the project, so the two directors worked out a trade in which Spielberg handed Scorcese a project he had been working on—*Cape Fear*—and took *Schindler's List* back for himself.

Keneally took the first shot at writing the screenplay, turning in a twenty-two-page treatment that seemed more attuned to a miniseries than movie. Hoping to sharpen the focus of the story, Spielberg next hired ex-journalist Kurt Luedtke, who had won an Oscar for *Out of Africa*. Luedtke labored for three and a half years before giving up, never quite convinced that Schindler was a genuine hero. The project landed in the hands of Steven Zaillian (who had written *Awakenings* and *Searching for Bobby Fischer*), who, with much encouragement from Spielberg, saw the screenplay to the finish.

The results were spectacular. The movie proved to be Spielberg's masterpiece. He filmed it almost entirely in black and white. He said he finally decided to do the film because of his increasing Jewish self-awareness.

Although Spielberg is the most commercially successful director in Hollywood history, recognition as a serious director had eluded him until March 1994, when he won the Oscar for directing *Schindler's List*. Spielberg had been nominated for Best Director three times, for *Close Encounters of the Third Kind; Raiders of the Lost Ark*, and *E.T. The Extra-Terrestrial;* and twice as best producer for *E.T.* and *The Color Purple*. His movies *E.T.* and *Jurassic Park* are the two most profitable films ever made. Spielberg's other movies, *Jaws* (1975), and the *Indiana Jones* trilogy were also huge box-office hits.

Spielberg never had the intention of producing a film that would represent a definitive account of the Holocaust. Visiting Israel in March of 1994 he said, "This is just a Holocaust film. It is not the Holocaust film. I don't want *Schindler's List* to ever be known as the Holocaust film, so I am depending on my colleagues to tell other stories of the Holocaust and not let it end with this one . . . The Holocaust was a mural of horror, and *Schindler's List* is a tiny segment of that mural."

Around the world reaction to the film was emotional. Some in Israel found it painful to watch; eating, sleeping, even talking became difficult after seeing the movie. Some Holocaust survivors simply refused to see it, afraid of the memories it would awaken. Others thought the film should be seen by everyone. In Germany, emotions were especially strong. Ordinary Germans watched the scenes of ghettos and concentration camps and openly cried.

A commercial hit, grossing ninety-six-million dollars at the American box office, the movie won seven Oscars altogether.

Lola Ozrech, sixty-eight years old, watched the 1994 Oscar award ceremony with more than one hundred survivors of the Holocaust who had shown up for the reunion at the Simon Wisenthal Museum of Tolerance, including five of the more than twelve hundred Jews whom Schindler saved. Watching the Oscar broadcast, the survivors jumped to their feet and cheered as Steven Spielberg was honored for directing and producing the *Schindler's List*.

"When it comes to *Schindler's List*, I get shivers all over my body," said Ozrech, who wept when the film was announced as best picture. "I'm very overwhelmed. I'm so happy that this has happened. Everything that was inside me has come out." Ozrech, who began working for Schindler when she was sixteen, said the film so accurately portrayed the Holocaust she had nightmares for days after seeing it.

Maurice Markheim, seventy, who was also on Schindler's list, said "I'm thankful really that I can be here. If not for Schindler I most likely wouldn't be here because I wouldn't have survived. God bless him and God bless Steven Spielberg."

Index

negotiations with Israel, 136, 140, 145, 208
peace agreement with Israel, 136
Rabin-Arafat handshake, 140–42
Palestine Liberation Organization, 140–42, 206–208
Popular Front for the Liberation of Palestine (PFLP), 60–62
Paley, William S., 258
Palmach, 38–40, 204–205
Papacy, 55. See also Catholic Church and Vatican.
Benedict XIII (antipope), 168
burning of Talmud, endorsed by, 168
Good Friday prayers, 144
Gregory IX, 168
Gregory X, 166
Innocent II, 166
Innocent IV, 166
John Paul II, 143–45
John XXIII, 144
"Perfidious Jews" reference expunged, 144
Paul VI, 144, 145
Pius X, 144
Pius XII, 144
Urban II, 162
Paris, 264, 267. See also France.
Kristallnacht, 192
Talmud burned, 168
Paris, Matthew, 165–66
Parthians, 156
Parting of Sea of Reeds, 4
Partition agreement (Palestine), 112
Passover
blood libel, 165
home as center of, 16
matzah and, 4
origin of, 4
Patriarchate established, 225–29
political power of, 228
Patriotism, French Sanhedrin and, 182
Paul VI (Pope), 145
Peled, Benny, 210
Pentateuch, 153, 239
Perelman, Eliezer Yitzak. See Ben-Yehuda, Eliezer.
"Perfidious Jews" reference expunged, 144
Peres, Shimon (Prime Minister)
Entebbe hostage rescue, 61–62
Israeli nuclear program and, 53–54
Likud Bloc, election of, 132–33
Rabin assassination, 221
Rabin-Arafat handshake, 142
Perlman, Moshe, 128
Persecution (of Jews), 3. See also Anti-Semitism.
Eastern European pogroms, 105, 188–89, 268
Fiddler on the Roof, depicted in, 268–70
Kishinev pogrom and, 188–89
Kristallnacht, 192–94
Middle Ages, 162ff.
Schindler's List, 271–73
Persian Empire, 79–85, 86, 239
anti-Semitism in, 9
Esther saves Jews, 9–11
Karaites in, 17

growth of religious intolerance in, 229
return to Israel, 79–82
Peter the Hermit, 163
Pharisees, 15
Philadelphia, Pennsylvania., 90–91
Philadelphia Orphan Asylum, 91
Philanthropy, 91, 104–105
immigrants and, 94, 95, 96
Philistines, 4–5, 72, 73
Philo, 7
Phoenicians, 76, 150
Prophecy, 79, 80–81, 82
Physicians, 174, 225
Karaites, forbid physicians, 18
Maimonides, as court physician, 236
Picquart, Colonel Georges, 184–87
Pius X (Pope), 144
Pius XII (Pope), 144
Plehve, Wenzel von, 188, 189
Podolia (Ukraine), 88–89
Pogroms, 105
attempts to prosecute perpetrators, 189
Fiddler on the Roof, depicted in, 268–70
Gomel, Belorussia, 189
immigration to America, 103
Kishinev, 188–89
Poland, 192, 271–73. See also Eastern European Jewish community.
Antifascist Bloc, 33
Beth Jacob Schools, founding of, 26–28
Brother Daniel, 55–56
Cossack invasion, 176
false Messiah and, 176
Hasidic movement, founding of 88–89
ghetto in, 172
Warsaw Ghetto uprising, 32–34
Kabbalism, popularity of, 240
Spanish expulsions, impact on, 240
Political Zionism, 144
Politics (Israel)
election of Likud bloc, 132–33
captured territory, retention of, 133
Israeli right wing and peace process, 218, 219
Labor Party, 132–33
Yisrael B'Aliya party, 139
Natan Sharansky, election of, 139
Pompey, 14
Popular Front for the Liberation of Palestine (PFLP), 60–62
Poran, Ephraim, 63
Poznan, 192
Prayer, 89, 251
Alenu, as martyr's prayer, 165
Ba'al Shem Tov on, 89
daily prayer sequence, 16
as substitute for sacrifice rituals, 16
as offering to God, 16
Prayerbook, 92
Prayer shawls, 92
Preminger, Otto, 260
Prepared Table (Karo), 241–42
Priesand, Sally (Rabbi), 129–31
Principles of the Philosophy of René Descartes (Spinoza), 180
"Program for the Reconstruction of Judaism, A" (Kaplan, M.), 251

Promised Land, 5, 8
Prophecy, 3, 5, 8, 72, 73, 82, 149ff.
prophets as religious guides, 83
social corruption, warning of, 150, 152–54
Protocols of the Elders of Zion, The (Ford), 190
Proverbs, Book of, 245–46
Provisional Committee for General Zionist Affairs in the United States, 24
Psalms, Book of, 74, 85, 243
Pumbedita, academy of, 229, 231
Purim, origin of, 9–11

Queen of Sheba, 75
Qumran, Dead Sea Scrolls, discovery of, 110–11

Rabbenu ha-Kadosh. See ha-Nasi, Judah.
Rabbi Isaac Elchanan Theological Seminary, 254
Rabbi Moses the Maggid ("preacher") of Narbonne, 234
Rabbi Yehiel of Paris, 167–68
Rabbinic Judaism, 86, 87
challenges to, 17–19
founding of, 16
Karaites, influence on, 19
Rabbis. See also False Messiah; French Sanhedrin.
disputations, 167–68
in early Palestine, 228
excommunications, 179, 180, 251
increased importance of, 15–16
ordination, 16
of women, 129–31
Union of Orthodox Rabbis, 251
Rabin, Leah, 220–21
Rabin, Yitzhak (Prime Minister), 128, 132. See also Altalena and Entebbe
assassination of, 218–21
legacy of, 221
political right, opposed by, 218
Rabin-Arafat handshake, 140–42
Rabinovitch, Shalom. See Aleichem, Shalom.
Racism, 215–17. See also Anti-Semitism.
Radio, ethnic comedies (United States), 257–58
Ragoler, Elijah, 243
Rambam. See Maimonides.
Rashi, 27, 233–34
academy of, 233–34
Rashi script, 234
Rath, Ernst vom, (Kristallnacht), 192–94
Rav, 228–29, 239
Rav Ashi, (Babylonian Talmud), 239
Reagan, Ronald (President), 64, 124, 138
Reconstructionist movement, 250–51
Bat Mitzvah, 252–53
women rabbis, 131
Reconstructionist Rabbinical College, 131, 251
Red Sea, confused with Sea of Reeds, 4
Reform Judaism, 93
Bat Mitzvah, 252–53
customary dress, 92